Lecture Notes in Computer Science   7925

Commenced Publication in 1973
Founding and Former Series Editors:
Gerhard Goos, Juris Hartmanis, and Jan van Leeuwen

John Favaro   Maurizio Morisio (Eds.)

Safe and Secure Software Reuse

13th International Conference on Software Reuse, ICSR 2013
Pisa, Italy, June 18-20, 2013
Proceedings

 Springer

Volume Editors

John Favaro
Intecs SpA
Via Umberto Forti 5, 56121, Pisa, Italy
E-mail: john.favaro@intecs.it

Maurizio Morisio
Politecnico di Torino, DAUIN
Corso Duca degli Abruzzi 24, 10129 Torino, Italy
E-mail: maurizio.morisio@polito.it

ISSN 0302-9743   e-ISSN 1611-3349
ISBN 978-3-642-38976-4   e-ISBN 978-3-642-38977-1
DOI 10.1007/978-3-642-38977-1
Springer Heidelberg Dordrecht London New York

Library of Congress Control Number: 2013940198

CR Subject Classification (1998): D.2.13, D.2, D.3, D.1, D.3.3, K.6

LNCS Sublibrary: SL 2 – Programming and Software Engineering

Typesetting: Camera-ready by author, data conversion by Scientific Publishing Services, Chennai, India

Printed on acid-free paper

Springer is part of Springer Science+Business Media (www.springer.com)

Preface

For over two decades the International Conference on Software Reuse (ICSR) has been the premier event in the field of software reuse research and technology. The theme of ICSR 2013 was "Safe and Secure Reuse." Although reuse has been routinely practiced in many domains for several decades, its take-up has been slow in mission-critical domains owing to real and perceived problems in guaranteeing safety and security. However, this is changing as practitioners and researchers in these domains are seeking to reap the economic and quality benefits of systematic reuse.

In the automotive domain, the AUTOSAR architecture promises to deliver wide-scale component reuse, and the recent ISO 26262 standard for the safety of automotive electronic systems defines an explicit scheme for component reuse. In the aeronautics and space domains, standards efforts are seeking approaches for component level certification. Keynote speaker John McDermid of the University of York spoke on the important topic of certification – noting that while code production costs only amount to around 5-10% of the development costs, verification and validation in support of certification is circa 50% of the costs – in his talk on "Safe Reuse: Certification of Software Product Lines in Civil Aerospace."

Builders of mission-critical systems everywhere are looking to COTS to save on costs, but need to ensure the safety and security of those systems. The co-located Third International Workshop on Security and Dependability in Resource Constrained Embedded Systems focused on the combination of model-driven engineering with reusable pattern-based representation of security and dependability solutions, whereas the co-located International Workshop on Critical Software Component Reusability and Certification Across Domains narrowed the focus to the emerging area of compositional certification of component-based systems.

Despite the special focus on mission-critical reuse in this edition of the conference, the foundational issues in software reuse that are the lifeblood of ICSR were fully represented. Keynote speaker Ivar Jacobson, one of the founding fathers of much of software reuse as it is practiced today, recounted his work in the Software Engineering Method and Theory (SEMAT) community – where a kernel of essential software development elements has been distilled that is effectively a reusable methodology base – in his talk on "Creating Your Reuse Method from Reusable Practices and a Method Kernel." The co-located International Workshop on Designing Reusable Components and Measuring Reusability addressed issues that lie at the very core of software reuse practice.

The goal of ICSR is not only to present the most recent advances in the area of software reuse but also to promote an intensive and continuous exchange among researchers and practitioners. The panel discussion led by General Chair Martin Griss on "Software Reuse: Is Research Delivering for Industry?" attested to the vibrancy of the software reuse community today.

June 2013

John Favaro
Maurizio Morisio

Organization

Organizing Committee

General Chair
Martin Griss — Carnegie Mellon University, Silicon Valley Campus, USA

Program Co-chairs
John Favaro — Intecs, Italy
Maurizio Morisio — Politecnico di Torino, Italy

Local Co-chairs
Giuseppe Lami — CNR, Italy
Paolo Panaroni — Intecs, Italy

Workshop Chair
Davide Falessi — Fraunhofer, CESE, USA

Tutorials Chair
Marco Torchiano — Politecnico di Torino, Italy

Demonstration and Tools Chair
Olaf Kath — ikv++, Germany

Doctoral Symposium Chair
Ibrahim Habli — University of York, UK

Industry Chair
Bin Hu — AT&T, China

Panels Chair
George A. Papadopoulos — University of Cyprus, Republic of Cyprus

Publicity Chair
Eduardo Almeida — Federal University of Bahia and Fraunhofer Project Center (FPC) for Software and Systems Engineering, Brazil

Web Chair

Antonio Vetro'   Politecnico di Torino, Italy

Corporate Donations Chair – Europe

Juan Llorens   Universidad Carlos III de Madrid, Spain

Corporate Donations Chair – North America

Okan Yilmaz   SS8 Networks, USA

Corporate Donations Chair – Asia

Kyo Kang   POSTECH, South Korea

Corporate Donations Chair – South America

Vinicius Garcia   Federal University of Pernambuco, Brazil

Program Committee

Anabel Fraga	Carlos III University of Madrid, Spain
Jeffrey Poulin	Lockheed Martin, USA
Claudia Werner	UFRJ, Brazil
Dirk Muthig	Lufthansa Systems, Germany
Marco Torchiano	Politecnico di Torino, Italy
Federico Tomassetti	Politecnico di Torino, Italy
Hassan Gomaa	George Mason University, USA
Jaejoon Lee	Lancaster University, UK
Xin Peng	Fudan University, China
Birgit Geppert	Avaya, USA
Lothar Hotz	HITeC e.V. / University of Hamburg, Germany
Bill Frakes	Virginia Tech, USA
Murali Sitaraman	Clemson University, USA
Reidar Conradi	Norwegian University of Science and Technology (NTNU), Norway
Paris Avgeriou	University of Groningen, The Netherlands
Davide Falessi	Fraunhofer CESE, Maryland (USA)
Rafael Capilla	Universidad Rey Juan Carlos, Madrid, Spain
Maria-Isabel Sanchez-Segura	Carlos III University of Spain
George Papadopoulos	University of Cyprus
Ibrahim Habli	University of York, UK
Wolfgang Pree	Universität Salzburg, Austria
Oliver Hummel	University of Mannheim, Germany
Eduardo Almeida	Federal University of Bahia and Fraunhofer Project Center (FPC) for Software and Systems Engineering, Brazil

Ivica Crnkovic	Mälardalen University, Sweden
Ali Mili	NJIT, USA
Jan Bosch	Chalmers University, Sweden
Leonardo Murta	UFF, Brazil
Stan Jarzabek	National University of Singapore
Michal Smialek	Warsaw University of Technology, Poland
Sven Apel	University of Passau, Germany
Kyo Kang	POSTECH, Korea
Cristina Gacek	City University London, UK
Andreas Winter	Carl von Ossietzky University, Germany
Christa Schwanninger	Siemens AG, Germany
Jason Hallstrom	Clemson University, USA
Uwe Zdun	University of Vienna , Austria
Ted Biggerstaff	Software Generators, LLC, USA
Michael Shin	Texas Tech University, USA
Patricia Rodriguez-Dapena	SoftWcare SL, Spain
Patricia Lago	Vrije Universiteit Amsterdam, The Netherlands
Rainer Koschke	University of Bremen, Germany
Alberto Sillitti	Free University of Bolzano, Italy
Tullio Vardanega	University of Padua, Italy
Markus Voelter	Independent, Germany
Okan Yilmaz	SS8 Networks, USA
Gregory Kulczycki	Battelle Memorial Institute, USA
Hong Mei	Institute of Software, Peking University, China
Christian Bunse	FH Stralsund, Germany
Rick Rabiser	Christian Doppler Laboratory for Automated Software Engineering, Johannes Kepler University, Austria
Helene Waeselynck	LAAS-CNRS, France
Rob Van Ommering	Philips Research, The Netherlands
Sholom Cohen	SEI, USA
Hakan Erdogmus	Kalemun Research Inc., Canada
Klaus Schmid	University of Hildesheim, Germany
Paolo Falcarin	University of East London, UK
Judith Stafford	Tufts University, USA
Ebrahim Bagheri	National Research Council Canada

Sponsors

Table of Contents

Analysis for Reuse

Reuse and Patterns

Short Papers

Emerging Ideas and Trends

Validating Consistency between a Feature Model and Its Implementation

Duc Minh Le[1], Hyesun Lee[1], Kyo Chul Kang[1], and Lee Keun[2]

[1] Division of IT Convergence Engineering, POSTECH, Pohang, Republic of Korea
{lemduc,compial,kck}@postech.ac.kr
[2] Samsung Electronics Co. Ltd., Republic of Korea
gskeun.lee@samsung.com

Abstract. Consistency across different lifecycle artifacts is an important issue in software engineering. In software product line engineering, validating consistency becomes even more complicated because product line assets have embedded variabilities. Commonality and variability (C&V) of a software product line (SPL) are usually captured using a feature model. Then, they are embedded into an implementation (i.e., asset code) using various techniques including preprocessor directives. However, the product line asset code often evolves without properly updating other lifecycle artifacts including the variability model, and verification of the consistency of C&V across different product line assets is a major challenge. In this paper, an approach to validating the consistency between C&V expressed in a feature model and C&V embedded in an implementation is proposed. With this approach, product line engineers can have a method for maintaining consistency of C&V across SPL assets systematically. This method has been applied to the flash memory software product line at Samsung Electronics Co. Ltd. and improvements have been made over the years based on the feedback.

Keywords: Feature model, variability, consistency, preprocessing directive.

1 Introduction

Software product line engineering (SPLE) is an effective paradigm for developing products sharing a large set of common features. In SPLE, engineers create a family of products by identifying commonality and variability (C&V), creating assets with variation points and variants based on C&V, and instantiating and integrating these assets to develop products. Feature modeling [1] is a popular method in SPLE for capturing C&V of the products of a product line because it is an efficient communication medium between customers and developers. A feature model is usually used in the analysis phase to capture features (services, functions, platforms, etc.) that need to be provided by or interfaced with the products of a product line. The information captured by the feature model is then used to define variation points and variants of product line assets including architectures and components.

Several methods are available for embedding features into software product line (SPL) implementations. Annotative methods (also called preprocessor directives)

J. Favaro and M. Morisio (Eds.): ICSR 2013, LNCS 7925, pp. 1–16, 2013.

[2, 3, 4, 5] allow developers to include or remove code segments based on the selection of features. Component-based compositional methods [2, 5], or recently, feature-oriented programming [6] attempts to implement features as cohesive compositional units. The industrial community tends to use simple and proven approaches, hence annotative approaches are more popular in practice. For instance, C/C++ preprocessing directives are widely used in the automotive industry [2].

The annotative approach is easy to learn and allows fine-grained implementation of variation points. However, it tends to make source code complex; thus, SPL assets are difficult to maintain and evolve. In addition, it is very hard to understand complex dependencies between preprocessing directives (i.e., variation points and variants) in asset code. Thus, a systematic method for modeling and understanding complex dependencies between variation points is needed. When a feature model is derived from these variation points, it can be used for analyzing and understanding the dependencies. The asset code (with variation points and variants) can be maintained and evolved along with the feature model which is much easier to understand the dependencies between variation points and is often used for configuration management in SPL.

A feature model is used to model structural/compositional relationships between features such as inclusion, generalization, optionality, and mutual exclusion [1], which must be realized in the asset implementation. While implementing the variability in the code, developers often make mistakes. Table 1 presents two different examples implementing an alternative group of a feature model. The loose structure in Table 1 shows an example of inconsistency between a feature model and its implementation.

Table 1. Implementation of alternative features

Feature Model	Implementation	
	Loose structure	Tight structure
Father / A B	#if A #endif #if B #endif	#if A #elif B #else #error #endif

In the example, features A and B are alternatives; one and only one feature must be selected in the implementation. If a developer uses the loose structure to implement the alternative group, then the alternative group is realized as an Optional variation point. Although the implementation still realizes all the configurations required by the alternative group, the developer has created a variation point that is not consistent with the feature model. The variability expressed in the feature model was not embedded into software correctly as variation points, and both A and B, or neither of these two, can be included in a product.

Maintaining consistency between a feature model and its implementation is one of the most difficult tasks in SPLE. It becomes even more complex when there is constant evolution of a product line, which is a typical case. *In industry, implementation code often evolves ahead of, or independently from, the evolution of the feature model. In order to manage the assets of a product line, synchronizing evolution of the feature model with that of the asset code as well as periodically validating the consistency between the two artifacts are needed.*

There have been several studies on checking consistency of C&V across SPL artifacts. Vierhauser [7] reported their results of applying the DOPLER approach [8] for incrementally checking the consistency between a variability model (a decision model in this case) and its implementation. Based on a decision model, they defined a number of constraints (e.g. attributes of a feature must not be empty), and then validated the consistency between these constraints and SPL implementations. However, in reality implementation often evolves separately from variability models, and the approach did not address this type of scenario. Satyananda [9] provided a formal approach to verifying the consistency between a feature model and a description model of SPL architecture. However, their approach does not include the checking of the consistency between the feature model and its implementations.

To address the above issues, a method for validating the consistency between variability expressed in a feature model and variability embedded in its implementation (as variation points and variants) is proposed in this paper. *This research aims to answer two research questions. The first one is how to extract a feature model from variation points and variants embedded in source code. The second question is how to validate that the extracted feature model is consistent with the original one.* Variability expressed by a feature model needs to be reflected correctly in its implementation.

The assumptions of this research are that: 1) a feature model already exists; and 2) the asset code was implemented based on the feature model, using C preprocessor macros. Note that in the method only service/design features (of a feature model) that are directly mapped to variation points in the implementation are considered; checking consistency between features that are not explicitly mapped to the code (e.g., features for business requirements or quality attributes) and implementation is not in the scope of the paper. Both the feature model and its implementation may evolve, and we like to evolve their variability consistently.

There are SPL support tools (such as Gears [10], pure::variants [11]) available in the market to assist developers to develop and manage SPLs systematically. Our research, however, does not make assumptions about usage of those tools in development/maintenance of SPLs because of the following reasons. First, as detailed technologies used in commercial tools are not open, it is difficult to use their variability management technologies for general research and use. Second, analyzing programs without knowledge of the technologies used is a great impediment to properly managing variability and evolution.

The remainder of this paper is organized as follows. Section 2 provides background knowledge associated with this research. Section 3 provides details on how to recover a feature model from code, and how to compare the recovered feature model with the original one. Related works and discussions of the method are presented in Sections 4.

2   Background

2.1   Features and Feature Models

Since feature modeling was first introduced in FODA [1], there have been many extensions/variants [9, 12, 13]. Our research follows FODA and considers all the model primitives defined in it: features, feature relationships, and feature attributes. Fig. 1 is the feature model of a Memory Management module of MicroC/OS-II [14].

"Features are key distinctive characteristics of a product" [1]. A feature model represents structural/conceptual relationships between features of a family of products as an AND/OR graph. A feature may be decomposed or refined into a set of features, of which some may be mandatory, optional, or alternative. A feature model may also contain additional dependencies. Two common dependency types are *require* and *exclude*. A feature may have attributes whose values may be set for a product. Each attribute has its own name and a value range. (In this paper, attributes of features will not be represented in a feature model, to avoid complexity as was done in FODA.)

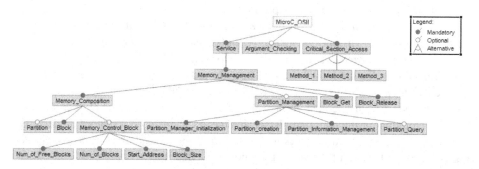

Fig. 1. The feature model of a Memory Management module of MicroC/OS-II

2.2   Embedding Features into Implementation

In this section, we explain the usage of preprocessing directive techniques to embed variability in the source code. Among preprocessing directive techniques, C preprocessor technique is a popular one. In C, the preprocessor handles directives, such as macro variable definition (i.e., #define), conditional inclusion (i.e., #if), and source file inclusion (i.e., #include), and automates the removal of irrelevant parts keeping only relevant parts during the pre-compilation stage.

Conditional inclusion is used to define the inclusion or exclusion of code segments based on the value of "macro variable" or "macro expression". It allows developers to embed variability into source code by creating variation points. The mechanism is used to encapsulate multi-implementations (i.e., variants) or to parameterize variants, and then to select or to instantiate appropriate code segments later following configuration decisions. Typically, a software engineer defines the value of macro variable as 1/0 or TRUE/FALSE to indicate whether or not the associated feature is selected.

The #include directive is used to include the entire text of a file into the position of the directive. Using this directive, developers can implement variants in separate files, and then include them later. This study also considers the #error directive, which is used to stop compilation when the configuration is invalid.

3   The Proposed Method

The proposed method contains two main phases: reverse engineering a feature model from source code and validating it against an analysis feature model.

The purpose of the reverse engineering phase is to address the first research question. This phase focuses on analyzing variation points embedded in source code and recovering a feature model from them semi-automatically (i.e., expert's decisions are required at some points in the recovering process). In addition, the proposed method provides algorithms for recovering the feature model that is "structurally similar" to the original one (i.e., the analysis feature model) as much as possible for cognitive reasons. This is very important, because from one set of variation points, engineers may derive many valid but structurally different feature models [12]. Recovering the feature model that is structurally close to the original one will greatly help maintainers understand differences while a product line evolves.

In the validation phase, the second research question is addressed by comparing the recovered feature model with the original one based on two properties of feature models: "configurability" (i.e., semantic consistency) and "structure" (i.e., syntactic consistency). In [13, 15], the set of feature configurations that a feature model permits is defined as "the semantics of the feature model." However, in our perspective, only semantic consistency is insufficient; Syntactic consistency is also an important property while comparing two feature models. The structure of a feature model is a representation of a domain as perceived by domain experts and engineers like to maintain it throughout the evolution of a product line. Also, the syntactic consistency should be reflected in the implementation to narrow the cognitive gap between a feature model and its implementation. Therefore, even if the semantic consistency is satisfied, engineers still need to be concerned about the syntactic consistency between the original feature model and the recovered one.

3.1   Reverse Engineering Phase

An overview of artifacts and activities of the reverse engineering phase is shown in Fig. 2. Each of the activities is explained in the following subsections.

A. Extracting Variability Information
1) Parsing Code
In this section, rules for extracting the following three types of dependencies are defined.

The first type is dependencies between code segments and macro expressions. The notation "!" is used to denote the negation of an expression, and "&&" and "||" are used to represent the conjunction and disjunction of expressions. The notation "▶" is used to denote a mapping between a variation point *VP* (i.e., a macro expression) and a variant *V* (i.e., a code segment) which is called *VP-V "dependencies"* in short (e.g. $A \blacktriangleright CS1$). This means that the code segment $CS1$ is included in a product if and only if the macro expression A is evaluated to TRUE. VP-V dependencies can be used to extract dependencies between macro expressions, which are explained as follows.

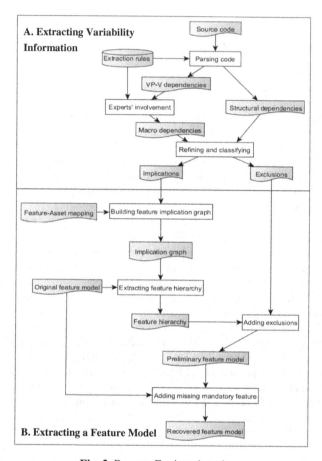

Fig. 2. Reverse Engineering phase

The second type is dependencies between two macro expressions, which are called *macro dependencies*. They are "imply" relationships between macro expressions. The notation "=>" is used to denote "imply", which means that if the expression on the left side is true, then the expression on the right side is also true.

The third type is dependencies between two code segments, which are called *structural dependencies*. They can be represented by "imply" relationships, which means if the code segment on the left side is included, then the code segment on the right side of it is also included.

The rules to extract these dependencies from the code are as follows:

<u>Rule 1:</u> If a code segment (CS) is nested inside conditional inclusion directives, its selection depends on the conjunction (denoted by "&&") of all macro expressions of the directives (as shown in Table 2).

Rule 1 permits transformation of nested directives to semantically equivalent logical expressions, and therefore, the same VP-V mapping can be extracted from different macro structures that are semantically equivalent. For example, "A&&B&&C▶CS" is derived from different macro structures in Table 3.

Table 2. Rule 1 example

Implementation	Obtained VP-V Dependencies
#ifdef (or **#if**) A CS1 **#ifdef** (or **#if**) B CS2 **#endif** **#endif**	A ▶ CS1 A&&B ▶ CS2

Table 3. Semantically equivalent but different macro structures

structure 1	structure 2	structure 3

#if A
  #if B
    #if C
      A code segment
      (CS)
    #endif
  #endif
#endif
	#if A&&B
	  #if C
	    A code segment
	    (CS)
	  #endif
	#endif
		#if A&&B&&C
		  A code segment
		  (CS)
		#endif

Rule 2: Within an if-elif-else structure, a #elif directive can be transformed to the conjunction of its expression and negations of all expressions above the #elif directive, and a #else directive can be transformed to the conjunction of negations of all the expressions above the #else directive (as shown in Table 4).

Table 4. Rule 2 example

Implementation	Obtained VP-V Dependencies
#if A CS1 **#elif** B CS2 **#else** CS3 **#endif**	A ▶ CS1 !A&&B ▶ CS2 !A&&!B ▶ CS3

Rule 3: If there is an #error directive in a conditional inclusion, then the logical expression that makes preprocessor meet the #error directive implies False.

Table 5. Rule 3 example

Implementation	Obtained Expression
#if A&&B **#error** **#endif**	A&&B => False

The #error directive is usually used with conditional inclusion directives to stop the compiler if the condition occurs. Therefore, developers use it to describe an invalid configuration. Table 5 is an example of applying Rule 3. The expression "A&&B => False" can be transformed to "A=>!B" and "B=>!A" (*mutual exclusion dependencies*) which are macro dependencies.

Implicit dependencies between macros can be found following the program structure. Rule 4 is for extracting the program structure.

Rule 4: Call dependencies of methods and inclusion relationships of files (represented by #include directives) are retrieved as "imply" relationships.

A call dependency indicates that a method needs other methods in order to operate correctly, and therefore an "imply" relationship is defined. In the same manner, based on a file inclusion relationship, an "imply" relationship is defined. Methods and files that contain preprocessing directives are only considered in the analysis in order to reduce the computation time. Dependencies extracted using this rule are called *structural dependencies*.

2) Experts' Involvement

According to Rules 1 and 2, logical expressions in VP-V dependencies are conjunctions of macro variables. If there is a disjunction (denoted by "||") in a macro expression, it is treated as one macro variable (i.e., mapped to a feature later). For example, with a VP-V mapping "A&&B&&(C||D) ▶ CS", a new macro variable "X" is introduced and defined as X ≡ (C||D), and then the mapping is converted to "A&&B&&X ▶ CS". In this way, every expression in VP-V dependencies is converted to conjunctive logical expressions.

Although the VP-V dependencies between code segments and macro expressions have been extracted, dependencies between macro variables are not explicit. Due to diverse styles of implementing variability in the code, it is difficult to identify all macro dependencies only from VP-V dependencies; Expert's involvement is required. For example, if "A requires B" was implemented using a macro expression "A&&B", there is no clue to identifying the relationship from the macro. Hence, these types of ambiguous expressions need to be clarified by domain experts. Rule 5 is about this experts' involvement.

Rule 5:

- If the logical expression of a VP-V dependency contains a single macro variable, the code segment is considered as the implementation of the macro variable, and the macro name (which is the name of a feature) is used to represent the code segment.
- If the logical expression of a VP-V dependency is formed by conjunction of macro variables, a domain expert chooses which macro variable(s) is implemented by the code segment. The expert can select more than one macro variable(s). Then, VP of the VP-V dependencies is changed to conjunction of the selected macro variables, and the other macro variable(s) (that is not selected) becomes an "implied macro variable(s)" that are required by the selected macro variables.

For examples, with "A&&B&&C ▶ CS", if the domain expert indicates that CS is the implementation of A, then the mapping is transformed to "A ▶ CS", and two macro dependencies "A => B" and "A => C" (i.e., B and C are implied by A) are identified. If the expert decides that both A and B are implemented by CS, then the mapping is changed to "A&&B ▶ CS" and one macro dependency "A&&B => C" (i.e., A&&B implies C) is derived.

3) Refining and Classifying
If a macro variable has a corresponding feature name of the original feature model, it will be evaluated to 0 (i.e., false, not selected) or 1 (i.e., true, selected) according to the selection of the feature. To reduce the complexity of macro expressions, each comparative expression of macro variables, that is evaluated to a logical value depending on the selection status of the associated features, is simplified to a macro variable. For example, "A > 0" is evaluated to true if A is selected, and false, otherwise; therefore it will be simplified to "A". Finally, after refining all macro dependencies and structural dependencies, these dependencies are classified into two categories: implication (e.g., A=>B) and exclusion (e.g., A=>!B).

B. Extracting a Feature Model.
1) Building an Implication Graph.
An implication graph [12] is built based on extracted implications. Nodes denote macro variables/macro expressions/files/functions and edges are the implication relationships between them. Then, a mapping table between the nodes and corresponding features is used for creating an implication graph of features. Table 7 is an example of such a mapping table.

Table 6. Feature mapping table

Feature	Corresponding node
Partition Management	OS_MEM_EN
Argument Checking	OS_ARG_CHK_EN
Critical Section Access	OS_CRITICAL_METHOD
Partition Creation	OSMemCreate() (function)
Memory Management	os_mem.c (file)

2) Extracting a Feature Hierarchy.
A feature model has the following characteristic: If a feature is selected, so is its parent. With this characteristic, the hierarchy information of a feature model can be derived from an implication graph. However, there can be more than one semantically equivalent but structurally different feature models that can be derived from one implication graph. We would like to derive a feature model that is most structurally close to the original model so the cognitive gap between two models becomes narrow and understanding differences becomes easier than otherwise. To do this, the original feature model is used as the reference to extract an appropriate hierarchical structure from the implication graph.

An implication graph is a weightless directed graph. In our method, each edge is given a weight based on the original feature model and then a spanning tree is extracted from it. An edge connecting two features that are near to each other in the original feature model is given a smaller weight than an edge connecting two features that are further away. Edges that do not appear in the original model are annotated by "U" (means unknown), and given the largest weight. By finding the minimum spanning tree, it is highly likely to get a feature model most close to the original one. Edmonds' algorithm (also called Chu–Liu/Edmonds' algorithm) [16] is used to find the minimum branching in the implication graph.

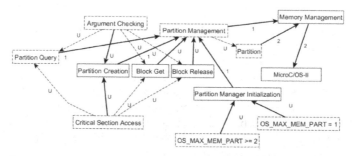

Fig. 3. The recovered feature hierarchy of a Memory Management module

In Fig. 3, solid-line-rectangles represent features derived from files/methods, and dashed-line-rectangles represent features mapped from macro variables/expressions. Weights are given to the edges of the implication graph based on the feature model in Fig. 1. Not all of macro variables have corresponding features because the product line has evolved or because they are implementation of feature attributes. The bold lines in Fig. 3 show a feature model hierarchy that was derived using the Edmond's algorithm. Other edges (i.e., dashed arrows) in the implication graph become *require dependencies* between features.

Annotative approaches provide a mechanism for expressing variability at a fine level of granularity. However, this can also be a disadvantage; with a large project, code segments related to a feature tend to be scattered across asset code, which may create many *require dependencies* between the scattered feature and other features. In this case, the recovered feature model becomes complex because of many *require* dependencies. To address this problem, we can re-organize the recovered feature model using the following guidelines which is based on a previous work by Lee [17]: "*If many features are associated with a common feature through require dependencies, the complexity of a feature model can be reduced by associating the common feature with the nearest common parent of its related features.*" For example, "Critical Section Access" and "Argument Checking" in Fig. 3 can be moved upward as children of "Partition Management".

3) Adding Exclusions.
The recovered feature model so far contains parent-child relationships and *require dependencies*. Based on the exclusion dependencies extracted from macro expressions (in the Refining and Classifying section), alternative groups and/or *exclude dependencies* between features are recovered. If features that have the same parent exclude each other, they form an alternative group. Otherwise, exclusions become *exclude dependencies* in the recovered feature model.

4) Adding Missing Mandatory Features.
Several annotative methods such as ASADAL [18] contain keywords that describe mandatory features. Although C preprocessing directives are effective in embedding variability, they do not provide any mechanism for denoting mandatory features. Hence, some mandatory features, especially abstract container features that are not implemented, are absent from the recovered feature model. Therefore, the recovered feature model does not fully represent the hierarchical structure of the original one.

To make the recovered feature model even more close to the original one, missing mandatory features are added to the recovered feature model based on the original one. The basic idea is to add missing intermediate mandatory features between parent and child features of the recovered feature model. After adding the features, the hierarchy of the recovered feature model becomes closer to that of the original one without changing relative positions between the existing features.

3.2   Validation Phase

In the second phase, consistency between the recovered feature model (RFM) and the original feature model (OFM) is verified. The RFM represents variability embedded in the implementation, and thus, differences between OFM and RFM indicate differences between the analysis feature model and its implementation. This research focuses on two types of consistency: semantic consistency and syntactic consistency.

A. Semantic Consistency
Semantic consistency is evaluated based on configuration comparison that shows the differences between configuration sets expressed by two feature models. In the proposed method, validation of semantic consistency is based on the work done by Thum [19]. Their work has the following advantages. First, it covers all possible cases that can happen in configuration comparison: equivalence, generalization, specialization, and arbitrary cases. In addition, it does not require that two feature models have the same feature set as required by [20]. This is essential property in our research because two feature sets may be different due to the evolution of the product line. Details of se-mantic comparison are in the original paper [20].

Equivalent case is the only case, in which the OFM and the RFM are semantically consistent. Otherwise, the SPL artifacts (feature model and/or implementation) need to be reengineered.

B. Syntactic Consistency
As mentioned in Section 1, using only semantic consistency is insufficient when validating consistency between two feature models. Without structure comparison (i.e., syntactic consistency), it is difficult to determine where to revise the feature model and/or the asset code when semantic inconsistency occurs. Therefore, analysis of the syntactic consistency of two feature models is essential. Syntactic consistency facilitates tracing between the variability model (i.e., feature model OFM) and its

implementation in terms of variation points and variants RFM, thus improving maintainability and evolvability of product line assets. In the reverse engineering phase, an RFM was transformed based on the structure of an OFM, which increases the structural similarity between two feature models and narrows down the cognitive gap.

When syntactic inconsistency happens, we first (1) determine how two models are syntactically different (i.e., syntactic gap, which may cause a cognitive gap between two models) and then (2) determine the most efficient way to transform one model to the other. EMF Compare [21], a generic model comparison tool, is used to perform these activities. Owing to the flexibility of this tool, its match algorithm can be modified as needed. In addition, the comparison result is presented as a model that can be manipulated for our purpose.

It is assumed that feature names of two feature models are consistent and two features of two models are same if and only if their names are same (feature renaming can be addressed easily with a feature mapping table). Based on this, two types of structural changes of feature models are defined: basic and compound edit operations.

1) Basic Edit Operations

The comparison result from EMF is generic; it is described by a differences model [21] that contains basic edit operations such as addition, removal, and modification of model elements, attributes and references. To make the result more meaningful in the context of feature modeling, the generic result from EMF Compare is transformed to detailed edit operations on feature models.

Unlike other works on comparing the hierarchy of feature models [22, 23], which do not fully cover basic edit operations on feature relationships, this research takes into account all the information of feature models (i.e., hierarchical structure, feature dependencies, and feature attributes).

In this research, basic edit operations are categorized into three main types: Add, Remove, and Modify, of three model elements: features, feature dependencies (i.e., require, exclude) and feature attributes. Modify operation on a feature is specialized to Move (i.e., change location of a feature) and Update (i.e., change the type of a feature). Table 8 includes a summary of the basic edit operations.

2) Compound Edit Operations

In previous researches [22, 23], the researchers identified elementary edit operations. However, some of them tend to be executed together to perform a meaningful compound operation. One example of a compound edit operation is breaking an alternative group to *exclude dependencies*. It contains several basic edit operations such as moving features and adding new dependencies. To make feature model editing more efficient, compound edit operations are defined as shown in Table 9. These compound operations are found to be sufficient in the cases we applied our method to. However, other operations can be added as needed.

The first two compound edit operations aim at restructuring a feature model without changing *require* and *exclude* dependencies between features. If a feature is moved across a feature model, its original parent-child relationship is transformed to a *require dependency*. This is defined as a compound edit operation "Composed-of -> Require" which will perform moving a feature to a new location and adding a *require dependency* between the feature and its original parent. The compound edit operation

Table 7. Basic edit operations

	Feature	Feature dependency	Attribute
	Add (f1, f2): Add feature **f1** under feature **f2**	*AddDep(f1, f2, t):* Add a new feature dependency of type **t** (**r**-*require*, **e**- *exclude*) between feature **f1** and feature **f2**	*AddAtt(f, a, vr):* Add new attribute **a** with value range **vr** to feature **f**
Remove	*Remove (f)*: Remove feature **f** from the feature model, and connect the children of it to its parent	*RemoveDep(f1, f2, t):* Remove an existing feature dependency of type t (**r**-*require*, **e**-*exclude*) between feature **f1** and feature **f2**	*RemoveAtt(f, a):* Remove attribute **a** from feature **f**
Modify	*Update (f, t)*: change the type of feature **f** to type **t** (**m**-*mandatory*, **o**-*optional*, **a**-*alternative*)	**None**	*UpdateAttValue (f, a, vr):* Change the value range of attribute **a** to new value range **vr**
	Move (f1, f2): Move existing feature **f1** to under feature **f2**		

Table 8. Compound Edit Operations

Case	AS-IS structure	Edit operations	TO-BE structure	Note
Compose of ↓ *Require*	(f) (p) (g)	*Move(g, p), AddDep(g, f, r), {RemoveDep(g, p, r)}** *: The *RemoveDep* operation inside the brace is executed if there is a *require dependency* between g and p. *"{}" indicates that edit operations inside the brace are optional.*	(f) (p) require (g)	This compound operation aims to change the parent-child relationship to a new *require dependency.*
Alternative ↓ Exclude dependency	(f) (p) (g) (h)	*Move(h, p), AddDep(g, h, e), AddDep(h, f, r), {Update(g, o or m)}*** **: The *Update* operation inside the brace is executed if f has only one child.	(f) (p) require (g) exclude (h)	This compound operation aims to break an Alternative group to exclude dependencies.
Feature ↓ Attribute	(f) (g)	*Remove(g), AddAtt(f, g, v)* → ← *RemoveAtt(g, f), Add(g, f)*	(f) : : Attribute g	This compound operation aims to change a feature to a feature attribute, or vice versa.

"Alternative -> Exclude Dependency" is also related to changing a feature hierarchy. If a child of an alternative group is moved, the alternative group is broken into features with *exclude dependencies* between each pair. The last compound edit operation "Feature <- -> Attribute" is for transforming a feature to an attribute, or vice versa. While an SPL evolves, features may be changed to feature attributes, or vice versa.

4   Discussion

4.1   Related Work

On recovering variability models (i.e., feature models) from implementation, Yang [24] proposed a method for recovering a feature model from multiple legacy applications in the same domain, whereas we extracted a feature model from an SPL implementation with embedded variability and also addressed evolution of this SPL implementation. Czarnecki [12] proposed a method for creating a feature model from a set of propositional formulae not from source code. In their paper, the authors indicated that reverse engineering a feature model from source code is one possible application in the future. She [25, 26] recovered feature models of Linux, eCos kernel, and FreeBSD based mostly on software configuration files. However, there is no discussion on how to extract feature dependencies from the implementation code.

In [27], Kastern et al. proposed a method for parsing C preprocessor code that is very close to our method of extracting macro dependencies. They introduced a tool called TypeChef that supports parsing of C preprocessor code with variability-aware function. We have tried to use this tool with MicroC/OS-II code, but the program did not return parsing result. According to Kastner et al.'s report, they expect that "all features are Boolean and limit presence conditions to propositional formulas". The tool evaluates constraints (i.e., "#if FeatureA > 0") only if "the corresponding macros are defined with #defined within the source, and do not accept numeric constrains over features provided as open command-line parameters". In MicroC-OS II, developers mostly used numerical comparisons in variation points without including #define directives before they use. This is why TypeChef cannot parse the MicroC/OS-II code. Although the authors provided a solution to convert countable parameters with Boolean flags, we decided to develop a parser for our research so that source code does not need to be modified to adapt to the requirements of TypeChef.

Related to the validation of consistency between two feature models, previous works such as Schobbens's [13, 15] considered only semantic consistency between two feature models. Thum [19] presented an algorithm that determines changes of the configuration set while modifying a feature model. We used their work to determine semantic differences between two feature models. Greenwood [28] referred to three aspects when comparing a feature model "designed" by domain experts and a feature model created automatically from requirements documents, which included feature similarity, structural similarity, and relationship similarity. However, they only introduced brief definitions without a concrete method. In [12], Czarnecki et al. also mentioned about semantics of feature model other than configuration semantics, which they call ontological semantics (same as syntactic consistency in this research). They emphasized the importance of analyzing ontological semantics, but did not mention how to do that. Xing and others [22, 23] described feature hierarchy comparison, but they only discussed parent-child relationships. They did not provide a full set of edit operations and did not consider compound edit operations.

4.2   Limitations and Future Research

Experts' involvement in the reverse engineering phase may be a drawback to the scalability of our method. In this manual step, a domain expert needs to inspect every complex VP-V dependencies. This is a time-consuming task, especially while analyzing large-scale systems. If developers follow programming conventions or use specific notations to indicate relationships between features and code segments, additional derivation rules can be defined to minimize domain experts' involvement.

Support tools for the method have been developed and integrated into VULCAN [29]. However, some steps of the method are conducted by external tools (e.g., semantic comparison is conducted using FeatureIDE [19]), and data structures of these external tools are different from that of VULCAN. We will integrate all the functions into VULCAN in a near future.

The proposed method has been demonstrated using MicroC/OS-II. It has also been applied to a subsystem of the flash memory product line at Samsung Electronics Co. Ltd. and improvements have been made over the years based on the feedback we received. (Due to the limitation of space, the result will be reported in a separate paper.) In the future, the method will be applied to the entire flash memory product line at Samsung Electronics Co. Ltd. and the findings will be reported in a separate paper. Furthermore, extending the method to support other variability mechanisms (e.g., aspect-orientation) in addition to the annotative approach is also planned.

4.3   Conclusion

SPLE is a paradigm for achieving high productivity and high quality of software. Currently, there are many proposed methods and support tools for helping software engineers create and manage SPLs efficiently. However, many software engineering problems often occur because engineers do not strictly follow prescribed processes. This research addressed a problem where a feature model and its implementation evolve independently without synchronization, which is typical in industry. A systematic method has been introduced to help software engineers validate the semantic and syntactic consistency between C&V expressed in a feature model and C&V embedded in its implementation based on directives. While product lines evolve, the method will help software engineers maintain product line assets effectively and efficiently. The method has been experimented with various product lines (including MicroC/OS-II and Flash Memory Software product line) and shown promising results.

References

1. Kang, K.C., Cohen, S.G., Hess, J.A., Novak, W.E., Peterson, A.S.: Feature-Oriented Domain Analysis (FODA) Feasibility Study. Technical report, CMU/SEI-90-TR-21 (1990)
2. Kästner, C., Apel, S.: Integrating Compositional and Annotative Approaches for Product Line Engineering. In: McGPLE Workshop, pp. 35–40 (2008)
3. Mengi, C., Fuß, C., Zimmermann, R., Aktas, I.: Model-Driven Support for Source Code Variability in Automotive Software Engineering. In: 1st MAPLE Workshop, pp. 44–50 (2009)
4. Beuche, D., Papajewski, H., Schröder-Preikschatb, W.: Variability management with feature models. Science of Computer Programming - Special Issue: Software Variability Management 53(3), 333–352 (2004)
5. Gacek, C., Anastasopoules, M.: Implementing Product Line Variabilities. ACM SIGSOFT Software Engineering Notes 26(3), 109–117 (2001)
6. Mezini, M., Ostermann, K.: Variability Management with Feature-Oriented Programming and Aspects. In: 12th ACM SIGSOFT International Symposium on Foundations of Software Engineering, pp. 127–136 (2004)
7. Vierhauser, M., Grünbacher, P., Egyed, A., Rabiser, R., Heider, W.: Flexible and Scalable Consistency Checking on Product Line Variability Models. In: 25th International Conference on Automated Software Engineering (ASE), pp. 63–72 (2010)

8. Dungana, D., Rabiser, R., Grünbacher, P., Neumayer, T.: Integrated Tool Support for Software Product Line Engineering. In: ASE 2007, pp. 533–534 (2007)

9. Satyananda, T.K., Lee, D., Kang, S.: Formal Verification of Consistency between Feature Model and Software Architecture in Software Product Line. In: ASE 2007, pp. 63–72 (2007)

10. Gears, http://www.biglever.com/solution/product.html

11. pure::variants, http://www.pure-systems.com

12. Czarnecki, K., Wasowski, A.: Feature Diagrams and Logics: There and Back Again. In: 11th International Software Product Line Conference (SPLC), pp. 23–34 (2007)

13. Schobbens, P.-Y., et al.: Feature Diagrams: A Survey and a Formal Semantics. In: RE 2006 Proc. 14th IEEE International Requirements Engineering Conference, pp. 139–148 (2006)

14. Labrosse, J.J.: MicroC/OS-II, The Real-Time Kernel, 2nd edn., Newnes, UK (2002)

15. Schobbens, P.-Y., Heymans, P., Trigaux, J.-C.: Generic Semantics of Feature Diagrams. Journal: Computer Networks 51(2), 456–479 (2007)

16. Edmonds, J.: Optimum Branchings. J. Res. Nat. Bur. Standards 71B, 233–240 (1967)

17. Lee, K., Kang, K.C., Lee, J.: Concepts and Guidelines of Feature Modeling for Product Line Software Engineering. In: Gacek, C. (ed.) ICSR 2002. LNCS, vol. 2319, pp. 62–77. Springer, Heidelberg (2002)

18. Asadal Case Tool, http://selab.postech.ac.kr/asadal/

19. Thum, T., Batory, D., Kästner, C.: Reasoning about Edits to Feature Models. In: 31st International Conference on Software Engineering (ICSE), pp. 254–264 (2009)

20. Janota, M., Kiniry, J.: Reasoning about Feature Models in Higher-Order Logic. In: SPLC 2007, pp. 13–22 (2007)

21. Brun, C., Pierantonio, A.: Model Differences in the Eclipse Modelling Framework. UPGRADE The European J. for the Informatics Professional 9(2), 29–34 (2008)

22. Xing, Z.: Model Comparison with GenericDiff. In: ASE 2010, pp. 135–138 (2010)

23. Xue, Y., Xing, Z., Jarzabek, S.: Understanding Feature Evolution in a Family of Product Variants. In: 17th Working Conference on Reverse Engineering (WCRE), pp. 109–118 (2010)

24. Yang, Y., Peng, X., Zhao, W.: Domain Feature Model Recovery from Multiple Applications Using Data Access Semantics and Formal Concept Analysis. In: 16th WCRE, pp. 215–224 (2009)

25. She, S., Lotufo, R., Berger, T., Wøsowski, A., Czarnecki, K.: Reverse Engineering Feature Models. In: 33rd ICSE, pp. 109–118 (2011)

26. She, S., Lotufo, R., Berger, T., Wøsowski, A., Czarnecki, K.: The Variability Model of the Linux Kernel. In: 4th VAMOS (2010)

27. Kästner, C., Giarrusso, P.G., Rendel, T., Erdweg, S., Ostermann, K., Berger, T.: Variability-Aware Parsing in the Presence of Lexical Macros and Conditional Compilation. In: 26th OOPSLA, pp. 805–824 (2011)

28. Greenwood, P., Chitchyan, R., Noppen, J., Rashid, A.: Comparing Feature Models: An Initial Impression. In: Workshop on Empirical Evaluation of Software Composition Techniques (2010)

29. Lee, H., Yang, J.-S., Kang, K.C.: VULCAN: Architecture-Model-Based Workbench for Product Line Engineering. In: 16th SPLC, vol. 2, pp. 260–264 (2012)

Mechanisms to Handle Structural Variability in MATLAB/Simulink Models

Andrea Leitner[1], Wolfgang Ebner[1], and Christian Kreiner[2]

[1] Virtual Vehicle Research Center
[2] Graz University of Technology

Abstract. Systematically postponing variability binding is an important design concept in Software Product Line Engineering in order to increase flexibility. One major challenge is the technical implementation of respective binding mechanisms in different tool environments and artifacts.

This work proposes variability and binding mechanisms for model-based development with Matlab/Simulink. The aim is the explicit representation of variability in order to support the development of generic architectures, and the binding of variability in development models before code generation. This means that it should not only be possible to describe variability, but also to derive concrete system models from the generic platform.

We extend the *pure::variants Connector for Simulink* proposed by pure-systems GmbH and Daimler AG, which provides basic variability mechanisms. Based on common variability scenarios identified in industry, 3-layered templates are used to abstract the variability implementation. This abstraction simplifies the platform development process and hides variability mechanisms from the developers. Additionally, we introduce an approach to derive concrete system models by removing variability information and disabled functionality from the model.

Keywords: Software product line engineering, Model configuration binding time, Model-based development.

1 Introduction and Motivation

This work describes experiences and research outcomes from our current project. The overall aim of the HybConS[1] project is the implementation of a generic software architecture for hybrid control units (HCU) of Hybrid Electric Vehicles (HEV) [1]. A hybrid electric vehicle basically consists of at least one electric motor and some other kind of energy source, usually a combustion engine. The main advantages are significant improvements in vehicle performance, energy utilization efficiency, and polluting emissions. Hybrid electric vehicles may vary in different drivetrain configurations (e.g. mild hybrid or full hybrid), different mechanical components (e.g. different types of transmissions), different

---

[1] http://www.iti.tugraz.at/hybcons

J. Favaro and M. Morisio (Eds.): ICSR 2013, LNCS 7925, pp. 17–31, 2013.

software-supported functionalities (e.g. pure electric drive), different supported markets (different legal constraints) and more. Software should support various drivetrain configurations and their respective software functions resulting in a generic control software with commonalities as well as variabilities. Generic in our understanding does not mean to provide all possible solutions, but a defined set of relevant ones. This motivates the use of a software product line (SPL) approach.

The main advantage of software product lines in this context is the possibility to systematically postpone binding and thus, increase flexibility. The binding time indicates when the decision for a specific variant has to be taken at latest [2]. Theoretically, each possible point in time during the product lifecycle can be a potential binding time. Practically this is infeasible, because of the resulting high complexity and due to technical restrictions. Technical restrictions are caused by the unavailability of binding mechanisms for different tools or language implementations, respectively.

Currently, the representation of variability in Simulink models is possible only partly. The *pure::variants Connector for Simulink* provides special blocks, which can be used to describe variability in Simulink. Nevertheless, these blocks are very low level, making their use cumbersome in real world projects, because variability usually does not only occur on statement level. In order to improve the development process, we identified typical variability scenarios and provide variability templates for their representation. What is completely missing with existing means is the possibility to reduce a variant-rich model to a specific system model by removing unnecessary information. Being able to generate specific model instances can be helpful in customer communication in order to not reveal all possible implementations. Another, more technical reason is the independence of code generators. Most code generators are not able to cope with variability information or only to a very limited extent, since they are not part of the original language definition. This is also true for the interoperability with other tools, e.g. architecture analysis. One possibility to handle this problem is the transformation to a model without these language extensions [3].

This work has two main contributions: First, we can improve the representation of variant-rich models by the use of an additional layer of abstraction. This is realized by the concept of variability mechanism templates, which ease the description of typical variability scenarios. The second contribution is the implementation of a binding mechanism for model-based development with Matlab/Simulink, which enables the instantiation of concrete product models from a variant-rich development platform model. This corresponds to the transformation of a variant-rich model into a model without variability. In the following, we refer to this binding time as *ModelConfigurationTime* [4].

The paper is structured as follows: Section 2 discusses related aspects from recent literature. Section 3 gives some basic technical background information on variability representations. Section 4 describes the variability mechanism templates with its 3 layers in detail. Section 5 shows the implementation of model configuration binding. Section 6 describes how these variability mechanism templates can be used in practice. Section 7 gives a small example and Section 8 gives an outlook on possible future work and finally concludes the paper.

2 Related Work

There are many classifications for variability binding times in current literature. The simplest is the classification in compile time, link-time and start-up time [2]. A similar approach is the separation of system configuration into 3 main steps: Compiling, linking, loading. Before, during and after each of these steps variants can be bound. Examples for binding mechanisms before compilation time are code generation, aspect oriented programming and model driven approaches.

For configuration at compile time, precompiler macros and conditional compilation may be distinguished. Precompiler macros are actually evaluated before compilation. In the case of conditional compilation commands are given via parameters. Variant configurations at link time can be implemented e.g. by the use of a Makefile. Depending on the given parameter, certain compilations and linkages are performed. A configuration file can represent all files that have to be loaded together and thus realize different variants at load time. At runtime, components may register their interfaces and access points in a central registry [5].

Krueger [6] gives a good summary and overview of different binding times and their corresponding mechanisms.

Another classification focused on automotive embedded systems has been introduced by Fritsch et al. [7]. The authors distinguish between 4 different binding times: Programming, Integration, Assembly and Run Time.

Czarnecki et al. [8] describe an approach for negative variability. They propose to connect feature models to model templates which are used to instantiate template instances based on a concrete feature selection. The model templates are unions of all possible model elements. We follow a very similar approach.

Haugen et al. [9] describe a separated language approach for specifying variability in domain-specific language models. They propose a Common Variability Language (CVL) and corresponding variability resolution mechanisms embedded in the OMG[2] metamodel stack. This allows for the description of variability in potentially all MOF-based languages, including UML, as well as MOF- and UML profile-based domain-specific languages. Although this represents a general purpose, clean approach for handling variability and providing a single point of control, it is not applicable for the representation of variability in Simulink-based implementations because the Simulink metamodel is proprietary and not publicly available.

Schulze et al. [10] introduce a concept to explicitly separate functionality and variability handling mechanisms in Simulink models. They provide a concept to improve the representation of structural variability (e.g. optional or alternative implementations). Therefore, they introduce so called *variable function modules*.

---

[2] http://www.omg.org/mof/

Several function modules can be connected to a variation point and are selected depending on the variation point value.

Trujillo et al. [11] provide variability mechanisms for SysML[3] in a tool environment consisting of BigLever Gears[4] for variability description and IBM Rational Rhapsody for system modeling. Stereotypes represent the variation points in the system model. Each variable element is annotated with a condition. Product derivation following this concept works as follows: All model elements which are not annotated by a variation point stereotype are included in the final product model. For all other model elements, the condition is evaluated and if it holds, the element will be part of the resulting model.

Since Matlab R2011 there is integrated variant management support[5] in Simulink. With this environment it is possible to represent alternative subsystems and models in Simulink models. The selection of the active alternative is based on conditions which can be defined on *Model Variants* or *Variant Subsystems*, respectively. Conditions consist of variables which are defined in the workspace. Optional behavior can be represented by *Enabled subsystems*. Contrary to our approach it is only possible to use different variants for simulation, but not to reduce the model to a specific variant. Additionally, we use variation points, which can be connected to an external feature model.

3   Background Information and Context

Separation of concerns is an often used approach in order to handle complexity in system development and also for variability representations. A common way of separation is the distinction between a problem and a solution space. They are defined as follows: *"The set of all valid system specifications in a domain (e.g. valid feature combinations) is referred to as the problem space and the set of all concrete systems in the domain is referred as to as the solution space"* [12]. In other words, the problem space contains the explicit description of variability and the solution space corresponds to respective variability mechanisms provided by different system implementations. Figure 1 illustrates this distinction together with configuration links between the two spaces.

Another reason for the use of two spaces is the separation of variability from the system implementation. First, abstraction enables the configuration of products by sales persons without detailed technical knowledge. This requires a variability description consisting of all possible system configurations together with its constraints. Once this knowledge has been encoded in a variability model concrete systems can easily be derived from the family representation. Second, technical realizations are exchangeable. In concrete, a technology independent variability model can be used to configure different technical realizations of the same system. This could be artifacts from different development stages (e.g. requirements, implementation, tests) or implementations for different platforms.

---

[3] www.omgsysml.org/

[4] http://www.biglever.com/

[5] http://www.mathworks.de/help/toolbox/simulink/ug/bskmec9.html

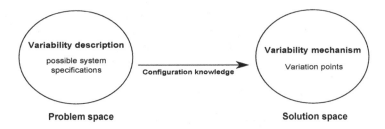

Fig. 1. Distinction between a problem space containing the explicit variability representation and the solution space containing variability mechanisms

3.1   Variability Description

Over the years, several distinct modeling paradigms have emerged in order to solve specific problems. The most important ones are as follows:

Feature-oriented modeling uses features to describe commonalities and variabilities of systems. A feature can be defined as *"a prominent and distinctive user visible characteristic of a system"* [13]. The big advantage of this kind of abstraction is that it can be understood by both, customers and developers [14].

Kang et al. [15] first proposed the use of features to represent the problem domain with the concept of *Feature-Oriented Domain Analysis* (FODA). A feature model consists of a hierarchical representation called feature diagram and composition rules, such as mutual exclusion (excludes) and mutual dependency (requires). Commonality can be described in terms of *mandatory* features and variability in terms of *optional* or *variant* features [16].

Domain-specific modeling uses domain-specific languages for the specification of domain concepts [17]. *"A domain-specific language (DSL) is a programming language or executable specification language that offers, through appropriate notations and abstractions, expressive power focused on, and usually restricted to, a particular problem domain"* [18]. Domain-specific languages provide better solutions for a smaller set of problems. This narrower problem space provides higher expressiveness [19], and can be used to generate products directly from these high level specifications [17].

The main distinction is the use of creative construction for domain-specific languages, and the use of a certain configuration space for feature models [20]. This means that they are applicable to different types of variability.

3.2   Variability Mechanisms

One important part of the variability mechanism is the concept of variation points. Variation points indicate where variation can occur and thus can be regarded as delayed design decisions [21]. They provide several possible variants which can be chosen for a concrete product. At the moment a specific variant is selected, the variation point is said to be bound. The binding time is defined as *"the point in time when the decision upon selection of a variant must be made"* [2]. In many modeling or development environment design decision can be identified and intentionally left open. More precisely, variation points are described explicit.

There are two different strategies to represent variability in the solution space.

- negative variability [22,23,24]: the artifacts contain both, common and variable parts. Parts which are not required in the current selection are removed from the artifact. The main challenge is to ensure correct behavior after removing parts and to avoid unconnected elements.
- positive variability [22]: This strategy starts with a minimal core where optional elements can be added. A common approach here is the modularization in single units (e.g. components). The units are composed to build the concrete system. Main challenges are the definition of common interfaces and cross-cutting features.

The remainder of this paper focuses on negative variability. In the automotive domain, model-based development with Matlab/Simulink is very common. The current work is based on the *pure::variants Connector for Simulink* [25], developed by pure-systems GmbH and Daimler AG. This framework provides basic variability support for our tool environment consisting of two parts: a Simulink part and a pure::variants part. The Simulink part provides a blockset (Simulink library) which is divided into two categories: *Control Blocks* (e.g. VAR_Constant) and *Variability Mechanisms* (e.g. VAR_Switch, VAR_Model). *Variability mechanisms* provide no special functionality in this framework. They only indicate the existence of variability. The actual configuration is only possible with variation points which are assigned to *Control blocks*.

Variation points define and incorporate all possible values for variation. One of these variations can be selected at a time. In order to enable the consistent control of variability, one variation point can be assigned to various *Control blocks*. Variation points are the connection points to pure::variants which are used by the Control Blocks and configured by pure::variants. The pure::variants counterpart uses a variability model, which is based on a pure::variants Family model to represent the variation points. The two parts communicate bidirectionally. The pure::variants import functionality reads the variation points and builds a variability model. Valid selections can be propagated back to the Simulink model by a transformation. Current selections can be used for simulation, but variability information and unused model parts are still part of the model.

3.3   Beyond Existing Technology

Summarized, the *pure::variants Connector for Simulink* provides basic variability representation mechanisms and control blocks. They can be used to represent variability in Simulink and bind variability at code generation time or for simulation.

In order to improve the usability of this existing framework, we propose the use of variability mechanism templates for alternative as well as for optional functionality. These templates use existing technology, but provide an abstraction to hide variability mechanisms from the developer. Additionally, we propose a transformation which removes variability-related information and disabled functionality from the Simulink model.

4 Variability Mechanism Templates

Typical application scenarios present important requirements for an efficient implementation of variability mechanisms. Together with developers we identified two different variability scenarios which are likely to occur in a common industrial development setting. They perfectly fit with *xor* and *optional* constraints from feature-oriented modeling.

Alternative implementation means that one of several subsystem implementations has to be chosen to be part of a concrete product. This is a common scenario, because especially in the automotive domain several aspects of the overall system do have an influence on the software. Changing settings in other parts of the system often cause changes in software as well. Different system settings can be supported by providing alternative implementations.

Optional implementations are part of only some product variants, because functionality is often only possible for some system settings. This case requires a mechanism to enable or disable single parts of the implementation depending on the current system configuration.

The proposed work extends the existing *pure::variants Connector for Simulink* as follows: Additionally to the *Control Block* and *Variability mechanism* blocksets, we provide a blockset called *Variability Template Blocks* including two template blocks inspired by the application scenarios described above. Both template blocks implement the same 3-layered structure as illustrated in Figure 2. The topmost level represents the user-visible block. This block can be used and configured by the system developer for a specific application as will be described later on. We use the existing pure::variants variation point concept in order to control variability mechanisms in the middle layer. The actual varying system implementation is encapsulated on the lowest layer.

This layered structure does not only improve the development of new models. It also supports refactoring of existing models, which is an important aspect in platform development in order to support domain evolution.

4.1 The 3-Layered Structure in Detail

This section describes the implementation, usage, and binding of the two variability templates. In general, each block has only one output signal, either a single signal or a bus signal. A bus signal is a collection of different signals, which graphically appears as one signal in a model.

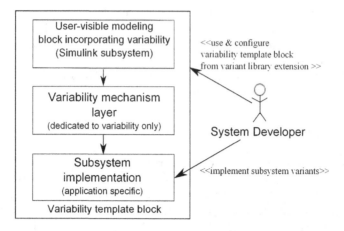

Fig. 2. 3-layered structure of a variability template block

User-Visible Subsystem for Simulink. Variability mechanism blocks on this user-visible layer are not much different from usual Simulink blocks, except their different coloring which indicates variability. The encapsulation of variability reduces complexity for the developer, because not all possible variants are modeled on this layer and thus are hidden from the developer. The developer only has the information that there is variability.

Variability Mechanism Layer. The variability mechanism layer encapsulates the implementation of variability mechanisms for the two templates.

Alternative Implementations. Figure 3 illustrates the variability mechanisms for alternative implementations. For simplicity, we require alternative implementations to have the same interface. The *pure::variants Connector for Simulink* provides a *VAR_Multiport Switch* and a *VAR_Const* block exactly for this scenario. The *VAR_Multiport Switch* consists of a configuration port and several data ports. Depending on the configuration port input, exactly one of the data ports is connected to the outport. The configuration port is connected to the *VAR_Const* block, which in turn is triggered by a variation point.

One advantage of this design is the possibility to simulate variant-rich models, because exactly one signal is connected to the output port and therefore, used in the simulation run. The simulation configuration depends either on the currently selected variation point value or uses the default configuration.

Optional Implementations. Figure 4 illustrates the variability template block for optional behavior. Simulink provides a *Trigger* block for exactly this purpose. This trigger is connected to a *VAR_Const* block with an attached variation point. Depending on the selected variation point variation, the subsystem is either enabled or disabled.

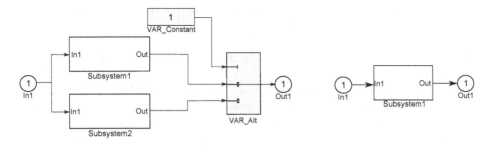

Fig. 3. Middle layer of the variability template for alternative implementations (left), bound for variant 1 (right)

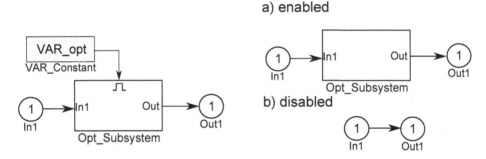

Fig. 4. Middle layer of the variability template for optional implementations (left), result for enabled subsystem (right - a) and disabled subsystem (right - b)

Subsystem Implementation. This layer represents the actual implementation as it would be without variability information.

5 Binding at Model Configuration Time

The *pure::variants Connector for Simulink* supports two binding times for Simulink models: Binding at Simulation and Code Generation Time. Simulation time binding means that the currently selected variation point settings specify the model variant used for the simulation run. If the code generator removes parts of the model based on the current selection, we talk about Code Generation Binding.

In this section, we introduce a third binding time which removes parts of the model before code generation directly in the model. Variability information as well as disabled functionality has to be removed in order to represent a concrete system model. This concept, called binding at Model Configuration Time, is also based on the variability template blocks. Variability template blocks are easily identifiable and have a standardized structure which facilitates the detection and deletion of parts. Of course, elements can not be removed from the original domain model. Therefore, the domain model containing variability is copied first. Further processing steps are then applied on this copy. Processing works as follows:

1. Identification of variability mechanism blocks based on the templates described above.
2. Retrieving the current selection. For an optional implementation, it has to be determined whether or not it is enabled. For alternative implementations, the currently selected implementation has to be determined.
3. Remove variability information. All the variability information can be removed from the model. Since this information is encapsulated in layer 2, this layer can be removed completely.
4. If an implementation (layer 3) should be part of the resulting model, it has to be redirected to layer 1, otherwise it can be deleted as well.

Code generation binding time is supported by additionally using the general *pure::variants Connector for Simulink* variability mechanism blocks.

5.1 Binding Alternative Variability Templates

Alternative implementations require the same interface. Therefore, there is no need to adapt any signals when removing unselected implementations.

5.2 Binding Optional Variability Templates

The main issue in case of optional variability is the handling of signals. Therefore, we require the optional subsystem to support a specific structure. This means that the output port has to be connected to a *BusCreator*. BusCreators are used to collect different signals in a signal bus. If the subsystem is disabled and the signal should be disabled as well, it will be removed from the *BusCreator*. The modeler has to ensure that this signal is not used in the resulting model. More concretely, blocks which use this signal need to be disabled consistently with this block. The input signals are simply deleted for this subsystem. There is either a branch, where the signal is distributed to several blocks or the signal is calculated in the precedent subsystem. In both cases the signal can be deleted until its last usage.

6 Working with Variability Mechanism Templates

Variability mechanism template blocks can either be used to develop models from scratch or to refactor existing models. Development from scratch here means that a template is added before the implementation of optional or alternative functionality. Refactoring refers to the conversion of existing implementations into an optional or alternative subsystem, respectively.

6.1   Using Alternatives Variability Templates

Template blocks need to be configured for the current context first. For alternative variability templates the number of input signals and the number of alternatives has to be adjusted and a variation point has to be connected. The user manually enters the number of input signals. The number of alternatives can automatically be determined by the number of variation point values of the assigned variation point. Using this information, the alternative subsystem templates will be created and the *VAR_MultiPort Switch* will be configured automatically.

Already existing implementations can be marked and converted into an alternative variability template block. In this case, a variation point with equal or more variation point variants than selected alternative subsystem implementations has to be assigned. If the number of alternatives matches exactly, the placeholders in the middle layer are simply substituted by the concrete implementations. In case there are more variation point variants the corresponding number of placeholders has to be added. It is not possible to have more alternatives than variation point variants.

6.2   Using Optionals Variability Templates

The configuration of an optional variability template is similar to alternative templates. First, the number of input signals for the optional implementation has to be selected. The block will be adapted accordingly. In a second step, a variation point has to be assigned and the triggering variation point value has to be selected. This means it has to be decided which variation point value is used to enable the subsystem.

Refactoring a subsystem in order to be optional is simple. In this case a variation point has to be connected and the block simply substitutes the placeholder block in the middle layer of the template with the actual implementation.

7   Sample Application Scenarios

This section describes two application scenarios and how the implementation looks like for one specific subsystem.

1. **Switch between full and mild hybrid setting**
   Full hybrid describes a setting with the ability to drive purely electrical, whereas in a mild hybrid setting the electric motor is used in addition to the combustion engine.

   Purpose of scenario:
   In a platform providing both scenarios it is useful to instantiate a concrete control software and configure the co-simulation framework accordingly.

Variability description:
The control software contains two optional modi which are deactivated in a mild hybrid setting. A full hybrid topology provides e.g. an *EDrive* functionality which simply means to drive purely electrical (without combustion engine). In this example, we completely remove such modi from the Simulink model if they are disabled.

2. **Alternative transmissions (automatic, manual)**
Vehicles may be equipped with different types of transmissions. We consider automatic and manual transmissions here. For manual transmissions, the driver specifies the current gear, whereas for an automatic transmission, the gear is specified by a control unit.

Purpose of scenario:
For automatic transmissions the hybrid control unit specifies the current gear based on the driver request. One goal is the selection of gears in a way that optimizes the drivetrain efficiency. Therefore, the ideal gear together with the ideal split of engine torque and electric motor torque can be specified by the system. In case of manual transmissions, the HCU can only specify the torque splitting between electric motor and engine for the requested gear.

Variability description:
Automatic transmissions require a modus, which calculates and specifies the current gear, the engine torque and the electric motor torque. An alternative implementation of this modus optimizes torque splitting based on the gear requested by the driver. This means, two alternative implementation are required in the Simulink model.

Figure 5 illustrates a sample subsystem with four partly variable subsystems. On the user-visible layer, there is no variability information except the different color of subsystems including variability. Only on variability mechanism layer, variability is implemented. The developer does not need to care about how to implement variability. For optional or alternative variability scenarios the respective template can be selected. This simplifies the implementation. The layered structure hides variability information from the user and thus reduces the complexity of the model.

8   Conclusions, Limitations, and Future Work

This work enhances the variability representation mechanisms in Simulink and enables binding at *Model Configuration Time*. It improves the usability of existing variability mechanisms for Simulink by introducing another layer of abstraction and an additional binding time. The proposed concept has been implemented in the context of the automotive domain, where Matlab/Simulink is a common development environment, but is applicable in other domains as well. The definition of templates and the layered structure could be transfered to other technologies as well.

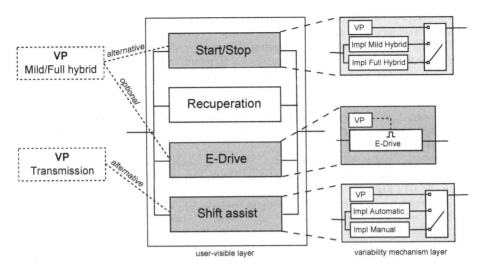

Fig. 5. Implementation of a subsystem including variability using variability mechanism templates

One main drawback is the fact that the user is responsible for ensuring the consistency of the resulting model. In future work an automatic model check could be provided in order to show if an invalid model could be the result of product derivation.

The set of variability mechanism template blocks can be extended with additional application scenarios by including the respective block in the block set and implementing binding mechanisms.

Acknowledgments. The authors would like to acknowledge the financial support of the "COMET K2 - Competence Centres for Excellent Technologies Programme" of the Austrian Federal Ministry for Transport, Innovation and Technology (BMVIT), the Austrian Federal Ministry of Economy, Family and Youth (BMWFJ), the Austrian Research Promotion Agency (FFG), the Province of Styria and the Styrian Business Promotion Agency (SFG).

We would like to express our thanks to our supporting industrial project partner, AVL List GmbH.

Furthermore, we gratefully thank Danilo Beuche and pure-systems GmbH for their support.

References

1. Ehsani, M., Gao, Y., Emadi, A.: Modern Electric, Hybrid Electric, and Fuel Cell Vehicles: Fundamentals, Theory, and Design, 2nd edn. CRC Press (2010)
2. van der Linden, F.J., Schmid, K., Rommes, E.: Software Product Lines in Action: The Best Industrial Practice in Product Line Engineering. Springer, Berlin (2007)

3. Voelter, M.: Language and IDE Modularization, Extension and Composition with MPS. Technical report (2011)
4. Beuche, D., Weiland, J.: Managing Flexibility: Modeling Binding-Times in Simulink. In: Paige, R.F., Hartman, A., Rensink, A. (eds.) ECMDA-FA 2009. LNCS, vol. 5562, pp. 289–300. Springer, Heidelberg (2009)
5. Pohl, K., Böckle, G., van der Linden, F.: Software Product Line Engineering: Foundations, Principles and Techniques. Springer (2005)
6. Krueger, C.W.: Towards a Taxonomy for Software Product Lines. In: van der Linden, F.J. (ed.) PFE 2003. LNCS, vol. 3014, pp. 323–331. Springer, Heidelberg (2004)
7. Fritsch, C., Lehn, A., Strohm, D.T.: Evaluating Variability Implementation Mechanisms. In: Proceedings of International Workshop on Product Line Engineering, pp. 59–64 (2002)
8. Czarnecki, K., Antkiewicz, M.: Mapping Features to Models: A Template Approach Based on Superimposed Variants. In: Glück, R., Lowry, M. (eds.) GPCE 2005. LNCS, vol. 3676, pp. 422–437. Springer, Heidelberg (2005)
9. Haugen, O., Moller-Pedersen, B., Oldevik, J., Olsen, G., Svendsen, A.: Adding Standardized Variability to Domain Specific Languages. In: Proc. of the 12th International Software Product Line Conference, pp. 139–148 (2008)
10. Schulze, M., Weiland, J., Beuche, D.: Automotive model-driven development and the challenge of variability. In: Proceedings of the 16th International Software Product Line Conference, SPLC 2012, vol. 1, pp. 207–214. ACM, New York (2012)
11. Trujillo, S., Garate, J.M., Lopez-Herrejon, R.E., Mendialdua, X., Rosado, A., Egyed, A., Krueger, C.W., de Sosa, J.: Coping with variability in model-based systems engineering: an experience in green energy. In: Kühne, T., Selic, B., Gervais, M.-P., Terrier, F. (eds.) ECMFA 2010. LNCS, vol. 6138, pp. 293–304. Springer, Heidelberg (2010)
12. Czarnecki, K.: Generative Programming: Principles and Techniques of Software Engineering Based on Automated Configuration and Fragment-Based Component Models. PhD thesis, Technical University of Ilmenau (October 1998)
13. Lee, K., Kang, K.C., Lee, J.J.: Concepts and Guidelines of Feature Modeling for Product Line Software Engineering. In: Gacek, C. (ed.) ICSR 2002. LNCS, vol. 2319, pp. 62–77. Springer, Heidelberg (2002)
14. Kang, K.C., Lee, J., Donohoe, P.: Feature-Oriented Project Line Engineering. IEEE Software 19(4), 58–65 (2002)
15. Kang, K.C., Cohen, S.G., Hess, J.A., Novak, W.E., Peterson, A.S.: Feature-Oriented Domain Analysis (FODA) Feasibility Study. Technical report, Carnegie-Mellon University Software Engineering Institute (November 1990)
16. Svahnberg, M., van Gurp, J., Bosch, J.: A taxonomy of variability realization techniques: Research Articles. Softw. Pract. Exper. 35(8), 705–754 (2005)
17. Kelly, S., Tolvanen, J.P.: Domain-Specific Modeling: Enabling Full Code Generation. Wiley-IEEE Computer Society Press (March 2008)
18. van Deursen, A., Klint, P., Visser, J.: Domain-specific languages: an annotated bibliography. SIGPLAN Not. 35(6), 26–36 (2000)
19. Czarnecki, K.: Overview of Generative Software Development. In: Banâtre, J.-P., Fradet, P., Giavitto, J.-L., Michel, O. (eds.) UPP 2004. LNCS, vol. 3566, pp. 326–341. Springer, Heidelberg (2005)
20. Voelter, M., Groher, I.: Product line implementation using aspect-oriented and model-driven software development. In: Proceedings of the 11th International Software Product Line Conference, SPLC 2007, pp. 233–242. IEEE Computer Society, Washington, DC (2007)

21. Bosch, J., Florijn, G., Greefhorst, D., Kuusela, J., Obbink, H., Pohl, K.: Variability Issues in Software Product Lines. In: van der Linden, F.J. (ed.) PFE 2002. LNCS, vol. 2290, pp. 13–21. Springer, Heidelberg (2002)
22. Groher, I., Voelter, M.: Expressing Feature-Based Variability in Structural Models. In: Workshop on Managing Variability for Software Product Lines (2007)
23. Gomaa, H., Olimpiew, E.M.: Managing variability in reusable requirement models for software product lines. In: Mei, H. (ed.) ICSR 2008. LNCS, vol. 5030, pp. 182–185. Springer, Heidelberg (2008)
24. Zhang, H., Jarzabek, S.: XVCL: A mechanism for handling variants in software product lines. Science of Computer Programming, 381–407 (2004)
25. Dziobek, C., Loew, J., Przystas, W., Weiland, J.: Functional Variants Handling in Simulink Models. Technical report, Daimler AG (2008)

An Analysis of Variability Modeling Concepts: Expressiveness vs. Analyzability

Holger Eichelberger, Christian Kröher, and Klaus Schmid

Software Systems Engineering, University of Hildesheim
Marienburger Platz 22, 31141 Hildesheim, Germany
{eichelberger,kroeher,schmid}@sse.uni-hildesheim.de

Abstract. Variability modeling is a core activity of software product line engineering. Over the years, many different approaches to variability modeling have been proposed. Typically, the individual approaches have been designed without a detailed justification on why certain modeling concepts should be used. This yields a rather unfunded selection of modeling approaches in practice, e.g., selecting approaches that provide higher modeling concepts than actually needed, but less analyses capabilities than required. Thus, we propose that the focus of an analysis should not be to determine the best modeling language, but rather to provide a characterization on when to use what kind of approach. In particular, the selection of one approach for a specific situation should be driven from the required modeling concepts (expressiveness) and the required analyzability.

In this paper, we propose a classification of core concepts of variability modeling based on expressiveness and analyzability. We discuss the methodology for and the classification of variability modeling concepts illustrated by a running example. The contribution of this paper is a modeling approach-independent classification of variability modeling concepts and their dependencies to provide a systematic and rationale basis to anyone designing, standardizing, implementing or selecting a specific variability modeling approach.

1 Introduction

Variability management is at the heart of software product line engineering. Over time, many different variability modeling approaches as well as extensions have been proposed. Currently, the dominating family of approaches is Feature Modeling (FM) [8], which was introduced in [26]. Further techniques include Decision Modeling approaches (DM) [42, 39], Orthogonal Variability Modeling (OVM) [34] or the PLUS approach [23]. Today, many variations of these basic approaches exist. For example, Chen et al. list 33 refined approaches for FM, DM, and OVM in [12], Benavides et al. discuss the capabilities of 42 FM approaches in [6] and Schmid et al. compare five different DM approaches in [40]. More recently, some authors argue that Domain-Specific Languages (DSLs) should be combined with FM [44, 46], or that languages themselves should be customizable [28]. Thus, there is still considerable variation in approaches to variability modeling. Nevertheless, attempts exist to standardize variability modeling, e.g., the Common Variability Language (CVL) [32].

J. Favaro and M. Morisio (Eds.): ICSR 2013, LNCS 7925, pp. 32–48, 2013.

Given this diversity of variability modeling concepts, it is difficult for a domain engineer to select the most appropriate concepts for a particular setting, for tool developers to select appropriate concepts for their tools and for standardization bodies to determine the appropriate capabilities of their languages. We recognized the need for such research in a recent project[1], where we aimed to create a sophisticated and customized variability management approach for service-based systems, and noticed the lack of guidance and support for this. Thus, we carried out the analysis described in this paper, which will overcome the above difficulties in terms of answering questions like which concepts should be included and which not in a specific setting.

In order to support the development of variability languages, we will present a classification of variability modeling concepts along two dimensions: *expressiveness* (the range of supported modeling concepts) and *analyzability* (the capability of determining implied properties of a model such as consistency or satisfiability). While this tradeoff is well-known in computer language design, it has not yet been made explicit for variability modeling languages. The contribution of this paper is a systematic classification, which a) categorizes existing variability modeling concepts on a meta-language level, b) describes dependencies among modeling concepts c) covers the range of concepts from basic variability modeling to more advanced variability modeling concepts and d) provides support for selecting the most appropriate modeling concepts by domain engineers, tool developers or standardization organizations.

This paper is organized as follows: in Section 2 we discuss related work. In Section 3, we introduce our categorization for variability modeling concepts. Section 4 describes a running example, which we use as illustration throughout the paper. The main contribution is given in Section 5, where we will describe our classification. Finally, in Section 6 we will conclude and provide an outlook on future work.

2   Related Work

Several analyses on variability modeling have been published. However, they do not provide a comprehensive overview of modeling concepts across all families of modeling approaches to classify expressiveness and analyzability. Existing work can be classified into two classes: *in-depth analysis* within one family and *broad analyses* ranging across multiple families. We will structure this section accordingly.

In-depth analyses are performed for a single family of modeling approaches. Schobbens et al. [41] survey different Feature Diagram (FD) variants to generalize the various syntaxes and to provide a common formal semantics. One aim of that work is *to improve the definition, understanding, comparison and reliable implementation of FD languages* [p. 139, 41]. The contribution of our approach is similar, but as opposed to analyzing a specific family thoroughly, we focus on a comprehensive classification that covers all basic approaches on a meta-level.

Schmid et al. [40] compare multiple aspects of five different DM approaches, ranging from modeling capabilities to product derivation support and analyze their commonalities and variabilities. In contrast, we focus here solely on modeling capabilities and provide an approach-independent discussion of expressiveness and analyzability.

---

[1] EU-funded project INDENICA, http://www.indenica.eu

Benavides et al. [6] review FM languages and operations for automated analysis of 42 different FM approaches. The authors discuss both, FM modeling concepts and analysis operations in isolation, i.e., they neglect the dependencies among modeling concepts, their expressiveness and the analyzability. In our work, these dependencies are a major criterion for structuring and systematically selecting modeling concepts.

Classen et al. [13] compare the definition of the term "feature" in eight different FM approaches. In contrast to our work, the authors do not focus on any aspects regarding modeling capabilities, etc., but develop general definitions to lay down the foundations for a general approach to automated feature interaction detection.

Broad analyses are performed across families of modeling approaches. Berger et al. [8] provide a recent empirical study on the use of variability modeling approaches, tools and perceived problems in industry. However, the authors analyze the used units of variability such as features, but do not detail the underlying modeling concepts. Chen et al. [12] surveyed variability management approaches including FM, DM and OVM to derive a chronological overview of their evolution. The authors derive key drivers for the evolution connecting the approaches to some extent. However, details on these connections are not given in [12]. In contrast, we make these connections explicit in terms of different classes of expressiveness and analyzability.

Czarnecki et al. [15] compare multiple aspects of DM and FM concepts in general, ranging from historical origins to semantic richness and tool support. In contrast, we focus on an approach-independent classification, i.e., not on specific approaches, but on generic concepts and their influence on expressiveness and analyzability.

Istoan et al. [24] classify variability modelling concepts with respect to the support of modelling both variability and assets. While we focus exclusively on the modelling of variability (as opposed to its implementation), we discuss essential aspects of variability modeling such as expressiveness and analyzability in much more detail.

Voelter and Visser [46] point out that (basic) FM lack in concepts such as multiple instances and references among features. The authors suggest using DSLs to overcome these limits by combining FM with DSLs. However, we focus on conservative approaches in this paper. Thus, we will exclude DSLs from our analysis.

In summary, significant work on comparing variability modeling approaches is available. However, to our knowledge this work is the first one, which provides a comprehensive classification that spans across all families of variability modeling approaches. We characterize the considered approaches on an approach-independent meta-language level. The focus of this paper is on the identification of the dependencies among modeling concepts in variability modeling as well as their analyzability.

3   Categorization Approach

In this section we describe our approach to categorize variability modeling concepts. First, we identify the scope of our work, introduce then the applied terminology, and finally derive the construction of our classification schema.

3.1   Scope

The analysis provided in this paper characterizes different classes of variability modeling concepts, their properties and dependencies. As we focus on variability modeling, concepts for realizing variability are out of scope. We exclude modeling concepts which support development in the large as they do not influence the expressiveness of variability modeling per-se. Examples are composition, as in Multi-Software Product Line (MSPL) scenarios [21], modularization, e.g., using interfaces in variability modeling for distributed development [38], or defaults for the support of variability in ecosystems [11]. Further, we focus only on the underlying modeling concepts, i.e., we exclude syntactic sugar, and unify various techniques that can be considered as aliases or can be interpreted as a combination of multiple basic concepts.

While some authors propose DSLs in variability modeling [27, 44, 46], we take a narrow point of view and consider only traditional variability modeling approaches.

3.2   Terminology

We introduce in this section the basic terminology used in the remainder of this paper for discussing variability modeling concepts in an approach-independent way. The terminology we introduce here is not really new. However, we summarize it here for clarity as some terms are sometimes used with a somewhat different meaning.

The *problem space* contains elements describing *what* the systems in a given domain must do. The problem space can be characterized by activities of domain modeling. In contrast, the *solution space* details *how* the elements in the problem space can be realized, e.g., by an architecture model. These definitions follow the "classical" terminology such as in [26]. A variability model defines the *configuration space* of a product line as a particular view on the problem space. Variabilities are implemented as part of the artifacts in the solution space. The configuration space is defined by *configurable elements,* each representing a variability. A specific *configuration* of these elements defines the instantiation of the represented generic software artifacts.

For describing the configuration space, individual approaches provide a set of concepts to model configurable elements in an approach-specific way such as in the different forms of FM or DM approaches [15]. Further, a variability modeling approach usually provides a *constraint language* to restrict valid combinations of configurable elements. This enables a more precise specification of the configuration space. These restrictions guarantee that the configuration of products that can be derived from the variability model yield *valid product configurations*. A product configuration is valid only if the selected element combination does not violate any constraints. A valid configuration is expected to correspond to a valid product in the product line.

Variability modeling concepts can be compared in different ways, as discussed in Section 2. We characterize variability modeling concepts in two dimensions, namely:

- *Expressiveness* - the range of supported modeling concepts for describing configurable elements and constraints.
- *Analyzability* - the capability of determining derived properties by computational methods. An example would be model satisfiability, e.g., to identify whether there exists a valid configuration of the model.

In fact, these two dimensions are neither totally distinct nor orthogonal, but they represent a pragmatic categorization of the knowledge of current approaches in literature. Further, expressiveness and analyzability are two dependent dimensions as an extension of capabilities in one dimension, leads to a reduction on the other dimension. This is a well-known characteristic of logic languages in general. We will focus here on the specific characteristics relevant to variability modeling languages.

3.3   Classification Schema

In this section, we describe the schema we use for classifying variability modeling concepts in an approach-independent way. For this purpose, we describe the two dimensions of our classification in more detail and specify the classes of modeling concepts we will analyze in the remainder of this paper.

It is well-known that variability modeling approaches differ in terms of their expressiveness. More precisely, they differ in terms of *modeling concepts* and the capabilities of defining *constraints*. For defining constraints often a logical language is used, which will provide different ranges of expressiveness, depending on the contained constructs. This implies that the space of variability modeling approaches can be described by specifying its configurable elements (modeling concepts) on the one hand and its constraint language on the other hand.

In principle, the various possible modeling concepts can be constructed and combined in many different ways by arbitrarily selecting a set of configurable elements and a constraint language. However, often there exist dependencies among those concepts. We will use the expressiveness dimension as the primary criterion for structuring our discussion of these dependencies. As the entire expressiveness space cannot be discussed in a comprehensive way in this paper, we will select prominent combinations. For selecting these combinations we carefully reviewed modeling concepts from well-known approaches, which are applied in practice and grouped them into classes. Each class can clearly be distinguished and represents a minimal required set of concepts for specifying configurable elements and constraints. The classes are: 1) Basic (pure Boolean) variability modeling, 2) Cardinality-based variability modeling, 3) Non-Boolean variability modeling, and 4) Configuration references. While the latter can be interpreted as a special case (configuration references can be applied to each of the other classes), we will discuss this concept as an individual class as it provides a true increment in expressiveness (cf. Section 5.4). In fact, some classes may further be decomposed into subclasses representing specific groups of approaches. However, there are already publications which discuss individual subclasses, such as [41] for feature diagrams, a possible subclass of basic variability modeling. In this paper we do not replicate such subclasses but aim at a more general overview.

It is interesting to note that the resulting sequence of combinations follows roughly the historical development of variability modeling languages, especially as it is seen in the area of FM. We will discuss the analyzability dimension for each of the selected combinations in an exemplary way. Further, we will illustrate the modeling concepts of each class using a running example, relate the class to example approaches in literature and discuss when and how to apply the concepts of the individual classes.

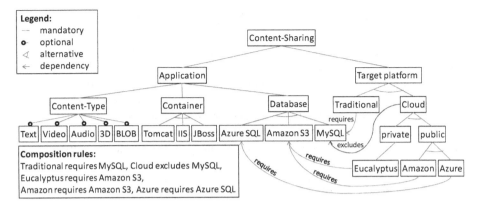

Fig. 1. Running example as a basic variability model

4   Running Example

In this section, we introduce the example, which we will use as a basis for discussing the different classes of variability modeling concepts in Section 5. The example is drawn from the area of service-oriented computing, as our initial motivation for this work originated in this domain. The example centers on modeling the instantiation and deployment of a content-sharing application.

A content-sharing application allows its users to upload, annotate, release and share content of various types. Individual applications differ with respect to:

- The supported `Content-Type` such as text, video, etc.
- The hosting infrastructure, which consists of a web `Container` and an underlying `Database`. A user may choose the desired instances out of several implementations.
- The deployment target, which may either be a private or a public `Cloud` environment or a `Traditional` environment like a hosted server.

Throughout this paper, we will use this running example to illustrate the expressiveness of each class. As we will need slightly different versions of this example to illustrate the different classes, we will describe for each class also some extensions of the basic scenario that particularly require the descriptiveness of this class. The individual extensions will be considered as cumulative.

For illustrating the running example, we will mostly use a graphical notation as known from FM, although FM is only a single family of approaches. We selected the FM notation to support understandability and readability as it is probably the most wide-spread and best-known graphical notation in variability modeling. Fig. 1 shows an example of the notation we will use and also provides a legend.

5   Classification of Variability Modeling Concepts

In this section, we identify several classes of variability modeling concepts and discuss their properties. As introduced in Section 3, we will structure the presentation of the classification by four prominent combinations. Each subsection is structured into a description of the *modeling concept*s, a discussion of the resulting *analyzability*, *example approaches* from literature, a discussion of the *running example* and a *summary*. Finally, we will summarize the results and give an overview of our classification to support the selection of the most appropriate class for a particular setting.

5.1   Basic Variability Modeling

The simplest class of variability modeling concepts, we will discuss, are purely Boolean configurable elements with restricted capabilities in constraining the configuration space. This class corresponds to basic variability modeling approaches such as FDs introduced in the Feature-Oriented Domain Analysis (FODA) approach [26].

Expressiveness - Modeling Concepts. The class of basic variability modeling exclusively provides Boolean configurable elements. These elements basically represent single configuration options that can either be selected or not, i.e., the configuration of a Boolean element either yields *true* (selected) or *false* (not selected).

Expressiveness – Constraints. The definition of constraints allows restricting the configuration space. The capabilities for describing constraints on the level of basic variability modeling may correspond to arbitrary Boolean formula. In approaches like basic FM, these restrictions are represented by relations, such as requires, excludes, alternatives, and options. In such FM approaches, these relations yield decomposition hierarchies of configurable elements and can be represented by a subset of propositional logic ($\wedge$, $\vee$, $\neg$), e.g., as shown in [41].

Analyzability. The analysis operations on purely Boolean variability models, as described in [31], can be roughly categorized into operations for correctness checking, e.g., if the derivation of valid configurations is possible, and configuration support, such as validation of specific configurations. These analysis operations are typically performed using SAT-solvers or BDD-solvers [6]. This requires the translation of a model into propositional formulae, for SAT-solvers even Conjunctive Normal Form (CNF) is required [6]. While satisfiability in general is NP-complete [14], decision problems that include only binary constraints using a subset of propositional logic ($\wedge$, $\vee$, $\neg$) can be analyzed efficiently [31]. Examples of analysis operations, which can be performed using SAT-solvers, include consistency checking in general, the detection of dead or common elements, and the computation of valid configurations.

Example Approaches: Feature diagrams (FDs), introduced in the FODA approach [26][2], are one specific example for this class. All approaches discussed by Schobbens

---

[2] We are aware of a non-Boolean variability in FODA, stated by the constraint *horsepower > 100*. However, this is neither discussed in detail, nor do any other non-Boolean elements or expressions exist in FODA. As a result FODA is treated commonly as a Boolean approach.

et al. in [41] belong to this class. Decision modeling approaches, if their supported data types would be restricted to Boolean, would also fall into this class [20].

Running Example. Fig. 1 depicts the running example that was introduced in Section 4. We selected a FM notation to support understandability and readability as discussed in Section 4. Of course, this is only one specific representation.

The content-sharing application consists of an `Application` part and a `Target Platform` part, which are further decomposed. The `Content-Type` is decomposed into optional features, i.e., each content type as well as arbitrary combinations may be selected. For the web `Container` and the underlying `Database` one may choose exactly one alternative. The `Target Platform` part is either a `Traditional` platform or a `Cloud`, the latter one is decomposed into `Private` and `Public` clouds. The composition rules restrict the set of valid applications, e.g., the `Traditional Platform` requires the `MySQL` database while `MySQL` must not be selected for `Cloud` platforms. Additionally, we visualized the composition rules as graphical dependencies (this is possible in this example as we did not need the full expressiveness of Boolean formulae).

Summary. The class of basic variability modeling concepts corresponds to Boolean logic. Thus, it is possible to model variability in terms of selectable elements each representing exactly one variant. These elements can be further restricted by means of requires, excludes, optional or alternative elements. The analyzability of basic variability modeling concepts includes operations ranging from correctness checking to configuration support [31]. These operations can be performed efficiently on models including only binary constraints. The combination of multiple optional elements may simulate multiple selections to some extent. However, it is not possible to define a specific number of valid simultaneous selections, e.g., in terms of cardinalities. This will be possible in the next class, which we will discuss in the following section.

5.2   Cardinality-Based Variability Modeling

In this section, we discuss the class of cardinality-based variability modeling concepts. Cardinalities enhance basic variability modeling concepts by explicit specifications of the number of configurable elements, which can be selected in a configuration. This corresponds to approaches like cardinality-based FM as described in [17]. However, we need to differentiate bounded and unbounded cardinality. *Bounded cardinality* defines both, lower and upper boundary as specific positive integer values. *Unbounded cardinality* allows unspecified (infinite) boundaries. In the extreme case, the upper boundary may not be concretized by further constraints and, thus, remain unbounded until analysis. Thus, this may lead to infinite configuration spaces, with corresponding consequences for analyzability as we will discuss below.

Expressiveness - Modeling Concepts. This class exclusively provides configurable elements of Boolean type. The expressiveness increases due to the introduction of cardinalities. In literature on cardinality-based FM usually a distinction is made

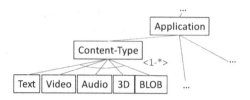

Fig. 2. Example using cardinality-based variability modeling

between feature cardinality and group cardinality [17]. Feature cardinality describes that a feature can be present multiple times, while group cardinality describes that a certain, restricted number of elements can be selected from a group of features. In our work, only the first is considered as a form of cardinality, as the second can be expressed as constraints. In the case of bounded cardinality, the advantage is mostly in the ease of use, e.g., Batory [4] uses a *choose*-operation instead of defining each possible element combination explicitly. In the unbounded case a new class of expressiveness is achieved, which we define as cardinality-based variability modeling.

Expressiveness – Constraints. The capabilities for describing constraints in this class extend the capabilities of basic variability modeling concepts by explicitly defining multiple selections (representing group cardinalities). This type of dependency requires multiple clauses and can be represented in full propositional logic ($\wedge$, $\vee$, $\neg$, $\Rightarrow$, $\Leftrightarrow$) [29]. For the more interesting case of multiple instances, we need to introduce operations such as restrictions on the number of instances [17]. In the bounded case, we can always map this on propositional logic [4]. In the unbounded case, at least basic quantifiers ($\forall$, $\exists$) are required to express constraints over the possibly infinite configuration space [2]. However, as done in most actual work, quantifiers (over final sets) may also be provided in the bounded case as a convenient notation.

Analyzability. The complexity of analyzing cardinality-based variability models with bounded cardinality rises due to multiple clauses in a single constraint and the availability of full propositional logic. Thus, the complexity in this class is NP-complete [14]. However, such models can be translated into Boolean formulas as described in [31] and, thus, can be analyzed, for example, by SAT-solvers or BDD-solvers [6]. In the case of unbounded cardinality we need to take into account the need to express quantification. This goes beyond the capabilities of, for example, SAT-solvers or BDD-solvers in the general case. The analyses on a model including unbounded cardinality are undecidable [35]. However, for specific configurations that define the number of instances, the operation on pure Boolean models can be used.

Example Approaches. Czarnecki et al. introduce a cardinality-based approach to FM [17]. In this approach, cardinalities can be assigned to both solitary features and feature groups. Riebisch et al. extend FDs with UML multiplicity [37]. However, this approach only focuses on group cardinality. The OVM approach [34] also provides cardinalities for the definition of the number of possible variants for a variation point.

Running Example. Fig. 2 shows a fragment of the extended running example using a cardinality-based FM approach. Content-Type is now modeled as a (feature) group and further specified by a cardinality, which restricts the number of selected options for a valid configuration. We use the `<n-m>` notation (n defines the lower bound and m the upper bound) to indicate cardinalities. In Fig. 2 at least one `Content-Type` but at most five types must be selected. If `Content-Type` would not have sub-types, the upper bound (*) would indicate unbounded cardinality.

Summary. This class extends the class of basic variability modeling concepts by supporting the definition of cardinalities for Boolean configurable elements. Thus, it is possible to explicitly define how many instances of a specific element or of a group of elements can be selected in a specific configuration simultaneously. This requires multiple clauses within a single constraint and full propositional logic. Deciding satisfiability for such models that include bounded cardinalities is NP-complete [14], thus, these models can be analyzed [6, 31]. In case of unbounded cardinality, the satisfiability of a model is undecidable, while the satisfiability of a complete configuration remains decidable [35]. However, it is not possible to restrict the cardinality of an element based on the value of another element. This requires relational operators, which leads us directly to the class of non-Boolean variability modeling concepts.

5.3   Non-boolean Variability Modeling

In this section, we introduce the class of non-Boolean variability modeling concepts. This class recently has gained significant interest in the context of FM [6] as it is very relevant to many practical applications [33]. This also corresponds to most approaches based on DM as described in [39]. Variability in this class can also be described in terms of non-Boolean types such as integer, string, etc. The capabilities for describing constraints are extended with respect to the supported types. This extension also enables the definition of constraints among cardinalities. These additional capabilities lead to the need for more sophisticated analysis approaches.

Expressiveness - Modeling Concepts. This class provides Boolean and non-Boolean elements. The set of available non-Boolean types depends on the specific modeling approach. In general, the configuration of non-Boolean elements amounts to the assignment of any type-compliant value. Thus, the definition of non-Boolean elements either requires the specification of a type (which implicitly defines the set of possible values) or the exact (range of) values that the element may assume.

Expressiveness – Constraints. The capabilities for describing constraints in this class go beyond the capabilities of cardinality-based variability modeling. However, the capabilities depend on the non-Boolean types that a specific modeling approach supports. For example, the restriction of integer elements requires relational operators while the restriction of string elements requires string operators such as a substring-operation or regular expressions. Antkiewicz and Czarnecki [2] also provide arithmetic operators for calculating values in constraints.

Analyzability. While the complexity of pure Boolean decision problems (including bounded cardinality) is NP-complete [14], non-Boolean decision problems are

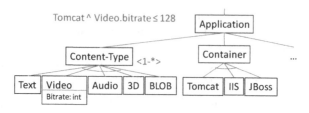

Fig. 3. Example using non-Boolean variability modeling

undecidable [33]. Undecidability of the non-Boolean variability models is due to the possible infinite space of the non-Boolean variabilities. In this context, reasoning is often implemented by translating the problems into Constraint Satisfaction Problems (CSP) and to use CSP solvers [47, 50].

Example Approaches. Non-Boolean elements and expressions are basic modeling elements in most DM approaches [19, 30, 39, 42]. Different FM approaches exist that support similar extensions and the definition of constraints among them [4, 5, 7, 17, 18, 27, 43, 48]. In addition, modeling languages in practical approaches like KConfig [1] and eCos [45] require non-Boolean elements and expressions. Berger et al. [9] show that these modeling constructs can be mapped to modeling concepts in FM.

Running Example. Fig. 3 depicts a fragment of the extended running example with a non-Boolean extension. Here, additional (non-Boolean) attributes can be assigned to a feature like the integer-attribute `Bitrate` of the `Video` feature. A non-Boolean constraint relates `Tomcat` to a maximum video bitrate of 128 kBit/s.

Summary. This class extends the capabilities for defining both, configuration spaces and constraints, by additional types of modeling elements and constraint operators. The types that are actually supported depend on the specific approach. In general, this class enables the definition of fine-grained variability in terms of ranges of values. In addition, these ranges as well as the value combinations can be restricted by constraints. This includes the restriction of cardinalities, which was not possible in the previous class as the necessary operators in the constraint language were not present. However, the analyzability of variability models, which include non-Boolean elements, decreases due to the increasing complexity of possible combinations.

Non-Boolean variability modeling can also be used to introduce restrictions on cardinalities, however, this is often treated independently (i.e., often in non-Boolean approaches no restrictions on cardinalities can be expressed).

5.4   Configuration References

Using the modeling concepts discussed so far, it is not possible to reference individual configurable elements or parts of a variability model. While this may not seem like a big deal, it actually is a powerful tool, depending on the precise semantics of the references. References can be used to define shared configurations or to even configure networks of configurable elements, which is not possible with other concepts

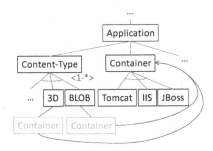

Fig. 4. Example with configuration references

introduced so far. In this section, we will discuss *configuration references* as a class of modeling concepts, which may extend each of the classes discussed before.

Expressiveness - Modeling Concepts. A configuration reference is a link from a configurable element *A* to a configurable element *B*, specifying that *A* becomes a synonym for *B*. Of course, this is most useful, if some hierarchy or grouping as discussed in Section 5.1 is available as then a single reference may denote a number of configurable elements simultaneously.

Expressiveness – Constraints. Configuration references extend the capabilities of underlying variability modeling concepts in a natural way: Constraints defined for a referred configurable element apply when the element is configured from a referring element. In addition, the constraint language can provide an operator for reference equality, i.e., to distinguish between individual and shared referenced objects.

Analyzability. This class does not impact the analyzability of underlying variability modeling concepts as references can be treated as synonyms. However, these synonyms must be resolved before applying the analyses operations discussed above, or specialized tools are required, which support configuration references. For example, the Alloy Constraints Analyzer (Alcoa) [25] provides analysis operations for models of finite space including references [3], such as validation and suggestions on errors.

Example Approaches. Bak et al. provide two different forms of configuration references in their Class Feature Relationships (Clafer) approach [3], namely feature references to (possibly shared) feature instances as well as (exclusive) references to containment features. Further, Clafer provides feature refinement (inheritance) which is of particular benefit in combination with configuration references (polymorphism). At first glance, it seems like inheritance might lead to a further class of expressiveness. We believe that the semantic essence of inheritance in variability modeling can be expressed by alternative selections defining the subtypes as well as *requires*-dependencies, which enforce the propagation of configurable elements along the inheritance hierarchy. However, we are not aware of work, which gives a formal proof of this. In the Compositional Variability Management framework [36], Reiser introduces configuration links between (sub-)feature models to allow the configuration of a feature of a target model depending on the given configuration of a source model. Boucher et al. support custom variability types in their Text-based Variability Language [10], which are linked from features by configuration references.

Table 1. Classification overview

| | Expressiveness | | | | | | | | Analyzability | |
| | Modeling Concepts | | | | Constraints | | | | | |
	Pure Boolean elements	Cardinalities	Typed elements, e.g., integer	Referencing model elements	Propositional logic	Quantifiers	Type-specific operators	Type operators	Model	Configuration
Basic Variability Modeling	x				x				x	x
Cardinality-based Variability Modeling — bounded	x	x			x				x	x
Cardinality-based Variability Modeling — unbounded	x	x			x	x				x
Non-Boolean Variability Modeling	x	x	x		x	x	x			x
Configuration References	*	*	*	x	*	*	*	x	*	x

Running Example. The `Container` of the `Application` represents the configuration of the web container serving the content-sharing application. Let us assume that either the application container or a separate container should be used for individual content-types, e.g., to enable load balancing. In Fig. 4, two configuration references enable either shared or individual configuration of a `Container` for 3D and BLOB. In Fig. 4, we apply an extended FM notation similar to [46], i.e., we denote configuration references as feature attributes in light grey (and highlight them by arrows).

Summary. Configuration references enable arbitrary links among configurable elements, which may be shared or used as individuals and, thus, significantly extend the expressiveness dimension. The analyzability depends on the analyzability of those concepts, to which configuration references are applied. In turn, configuration references do not impact the analyzability. Further, some tools are available, which can deal with references in most situations rather effectively.

5.5 Summary

In Table 1, we summarize the results of our classification. The rows depict the classes discussed above explicitly distinguishing between bounded and unbounded cardinalities. Further, the specific characteristics of configuration references depend on the capabilities of the extended class as indicated by stars (*). The columns represent the two dimensions of our classification, expressiveness and analyzability.

Table 1 illustrates the differences among the different classes, in particular the tradeoff between expressiveness and analyzability. Basic variability modeling provides only Boolean elements and limited concepts to express constraints but enables analysis of the model itself and derived configurations. While adding individual concepts, i.e., increasing the expressiveness dimension, the capabilities to analyze the model may decrease. A clear loss of analysis capabilities happens when unlimited cardinalities and related logical quantors become modeling concepts as this leads to undecidability. However, the validity of configurations can still be determined. Configuration references increase expressiveness but do not impact analyzability.

Practitioners can use Table 1 as a basis for understanding the tradeoffs involved in choosing certain modeling concepts in a particular setting. Based on our results, one may select one of the identified classes, identify the enabled modeling and constraint concepts and derive the resulting restrictions on model analysis. Or one can start with the desired level of analyzability and derive the possible concepts from the expressiveness dimension. Recently, we applied our classification when selecting a variability modeling approach for a project in the logistics domain. The specific setting requires Boolean options (basic variability modeling), multiple selection of workflows (unbounded cardinalities) and specification of rack sizes (non-Boolean), but no configuration references. Using Table 1 we determined for that approach that the analyzability of the models becomes undecidable while configurations can still be validated.

6   Conclusion

Existing work on analyzing and comparing variability modeling approaches either go in depth within one family or provide a broad overview across families of approaches. In contrast, we presented a new comprehensive classification of variability modeling concepts that spans across all basic families of variability modeling approaches.

Our classification characterizes the capabilities of variability modeling in two dimensions, *expressiveness* and *analyzability*. Based on this classification, we discussed four prominent classes ranging from basic variability modeling to the use of references. Thereby, we relied on existing knowledge regarding modeling concepts and analysis methods. However, so far this knowledge was distributed over various publications, which typically focus on certain modeling approach, e.g., FM. The particular contribution of this paper is the consolidation of that knowledge and the systematic organization into classes on a technology-independent meta-language layer.

Our classification enables domain engineers, tool developers or standardization panels to compare concepts and capabilities in variability modeling in an approach-independent way. For each class we discussed the limitations, which arise from the specific expressiveness and analyzability in a systematic manner. In the summary discussion we illustrated how to apply our classification.

In the future, we will investigate the customization of variability modeling languages. We expect that tailored variability modeling languages and related tooling will better fit the needs of domain experts and application engineers than monolithic general-purpose variability modeling languages. We are convinced that our classification is a solid foundation for tailoring and configuring variability modeling languages.

Acknowledgments. This work was partially supported by the INDENICA project, funded by the European Commission grant 257483, area Internet of Services, Software & Virtualisation (ICT-2009.1.2) in the 7th framework programme.

References

1. KConfig Language (2012), http://kernel.org/doc/Documentation/ kbuild/kconfig-language.txt
2. Antkiewicz, M., Czarnecki, K.: Feature Plugin: Feature modeling plug-in for Eclipse. In: Eclipse Technology eXchange Workshop (2004)

3. Bąk, K., Czarnecki, K., Wąsowski, A.: Feature and Meta-models in Clafer: Mixed, Specialized, and Coupled. In: Malloy, B., Staab, S., van den Brand, M. (eds.) SLE 2010. LNCS, vol. 6563, pp. 102–122. Springer, Heidelberg (2011)
4. Batory, D.: Feature Models, Grammars, and Propositional Formulas. In: Obbink, H., Pohl, K. (eds.) SPLC 2005. LNCS, vol. 3714, pp. 7–20. Springer, Heidelberg (2005)
5. Benavides, D., Ruiz-Cortés, A., Trinidad, P.: Automated Reasoning on Feature Models. In: Pastor, Ó., Falcão e Cunha, J. (eds.) CAiSE 2005. LNCS, vol. 3520, pp. 491–503. Springer, Heidelberg (2005)
6. Benavides, D., Segura, S., Ruiz-Cortes, A.: Automated Analysis of Feature Models 20 Years Later: A Literature Review. Information Systems 35, 615–636 (2010)
7. Benavides, D., Trinidad, P., Ruiz-Cortes, A.: Using Constraint Programming to Reason on Feature Models. In: Intl. Conf. Software Engineering and Knowledge Engineering, pp. 677–682 (2005)
8. Berger, T., Rublack, R., Nair, D., Atlee, J., Becker, M., Czarnecki, K., Wasowski, A.: A Survey of Variability Modeling in Industrial Practice. In: Intl. WS on Variability Modelling of Software-intensive Systems, pp. 7:1-7:8 (2012)
9. Berger, T., She, S., Lotufo, R., Wasowski, A., Czarnecki, K.: Variability Modeling in the Real: A Perspective from the Operating Systems Domain. In: Intl. Conference on Automated Software Engineering, pp. 73–82 (2010)
10. Boucher, Q., Classen, A., Faber, P., Heymans, P.: Introducing TVL, a Text-Based Feature Modelling Language. In: Intl. WS on Variability Modelling of Software-intensive Systems, pp. 159–162 (2010)
11. Brummermann, H., Keunecke, M., Schmid, K.: Formalizing distributed evolution of variability in information system ecosystems. In: Intl. WS on Variability Modelling of Software-intensive Systems, pp. 11–19 (2012)
12. Chen, L., Ali Babar, M., Ali, N.: Variability Management in Software Product Lines: A Systematic Review. In: Intl. Conf. Software Product Lines, pp. 81–90 (2009)
13. Classen, A., Heymans, P., Schobbens, P.-Y.: What's in a Feature: a Requirements Engineering Perspective. In: Fiadeiro, J.L., Inverardi, P. (eds.) FASE 2008. LNCS, vol. 4961, pp. 16–30. Springer, Heidelberg (2008)
14. Cook, S.A.: The Complexity of Theorem-Proving Procedures. In: Symp. on the Theory of Computing, pp. 151–158 (1971)
15. Czarnecki, K., Grünbacher, P., Rabiser, R., Schmid, K., Wasowski, A.: Cool Features and Tough Decisions: A Comparison of Variability Modeling Approaches. In: Intl. WS on Variability Modelling of Software-intensive Systems, pp. 173–182 (2012)
16. Czarnecki, K., Helsen, S., Eisenecker, U.: Formalizing Cardinality-Based Feature Models and their Specialization. Softw. Process Improv. Pract. 10, 7–29 (2005)
17. Czarnecki, K., Helsen, S., Eisenecker, U.: Staged Configuration Through Specialization and Multi-Level Configuration of Feature Models. Softw. Process Improv. Pract. 10(2), 143–169 (2005)
18. Czarnecki, K., Kim, P.: Cardinality-Based Feature Modeling and Constraints: A Progress Report. In: Symp. on Object-Oriented Programming Systems, Languages, and Applications, pp. 16–20 (2005)
19. Dhungana, D., Grünbacher, P., Rabiser, R.: The DOPLER Meta-Tool for Decision-Oriented Variability Modeling: A Multiple Case Study. J. Automated Software Engineering 18, 77–114 (2011)
20. El-Sharkawy, S., Dederichs, S., Schmid, K.: From feature models to decision models and back again: An analysis based on formal transformations. In: Intl. Conf. Software Product Lines, vol. 1, pp. 126–135 (2012)

21. El-Sharkawy, S., Kröher, C., Schmid, K.: Supporting heterogeneous compositional multi software product lines. In: Intl. Conf. Software Product Lines, vol. 2, pp. 25:1-25:4 (2011)
22. European Software Institute, IKV++ Technologies.MASTER: Model-driven Architecture inSTrumentation, Enhancement and Refinement, IST-2001-34600, MASTER D1.1 (2002)
23. Gomaa, H.: Designing Software Product Lines with UML: From Use Cases to Pattern-Based Software Architectures. Addison Wesley (2004)
24. Istoan, P., Klein, J., Perouin, G., Jezequel, J.-M.: A Metamodel-based Classification of Variability Modeling Approaches. In: VARiability for You Workshop, pp. 23–32 (2011)
25. Jackson, D., Schechter, I., Shlyahter, H.: Alcoa: The Alloy Constraint Analyzer. In: Intl. Conf. Software Engineering, pp. 730–733 (2000)
26. Kang, K., Cohen, S., Hess, J., Novak, W., Peterson, A.: Feature-Oriented Domain Analysis (FODA) Feasibility Study. Technical Report CMU/SEI-90-TR-21 ESD-90-TR-222 (1990)
27. Kang, K., Kim, S., Lee, J., Kim, K., Shin, E., Huh, M.: FORM: A Feature-Oriented Reuse Method with Domain-Specific Reference Architecture. Ann. Softw. Eng. 5, 143–168 (1998)
28. Liebig, J., Daniel, R., Apel, S.: Feature-oriented language families: A case study. In: Intl. Workshop on Variability Modelling of Software-intensive Systems, pp. 11:1-11:8 (2012)
29. Mannion, M.: Using First-Order Logic for Product Line Model Validation. In: Chastek, G.J. (ed.) SPLC 2002. LNCS, vol. 2379, pp. 176–202. Springer, Heidelberg (2002)
30. Mansell, J.X., Sellier, D.: Decision Model and Flexible Component Definition Based on XML Technology. In: van der Linden, F.J. (ed.) PFE 2003. LNCS, vol. 3014, pp. 466–472. Springer, Heidelberg (2004)
31. Mendonça, M., Wasowski, A., Czarnecki, K.: SAT-based Analysis of Feature Models is Easy. In: Intl. Conf. Software Product Lines, pp. 231–240 (2009)
32. Object Management Group, Inc. (OMG). Common Variability Language (CVL), OMG initial submission. Available on request (2010)
33. Passos, L., Novakovic, M., Xiong, Y., Berger, T., Czarnecki, K., Wasowski, A.: A Study of Non-Boolean Constraints in Variability Models of an Embedded Operating System. In: Intl. WS on Feature-Oriented Software Development (2011)
34. Pohl, K., Böckle, G., van der Linden, F.: Software Product Line Engineering: Foundations, Principles, and Techniques. Springer (2005)
35. Queralt, A., Artale, A., Calvanese, D., Teniente, E.: OCL-Lite: Finite reasoning on UML/OCL conceptual schemas. J. Data Knowledge Engineering 73, 1–22 (2012)
36. Reiser, M.-O.: Core Concepts of the Compositional Variability Management Framework (CVM). Technical Report 2009/16, Technische Universität Berlin (2009)
37. Riebisch, M., Böllert, K., Streitferdt, D., Philippow, I.: Extending Feature Diagrams with UML Multiplicity. In: Conf. on Integrated Design and Process Technology (2002)
38. Schmid, K.: Variability modeling for distributed development - a comparison of established practice. In: Bosch, J., Lee, J. (eds.) SPLC 2010. LNCS, vol. 6287, pp. 151–165. Springer, Heidelberg (2010)
39. Schmid, K., John, I.: A Customizable Approach To Full-Life Cycle Variability Management. Sci. Comput. Program. 53(3), 259–284 (2004)
40. Schmid, K., Rabiser, R., Grünbacher, P.: A Comparison of Decision Modeling Approaches in Product Lines. In: Intl. WS on Variability Modelling of Software-intensive Systems, pp. 119–126 (2011)
41. Schobbens, P.-Y., Heymans, P., Trigaux, J.-C.: Feature Diagrams: A Survey and a Formal Semantics. In: Intl. Conf. Requirements Engineering, pp. 139–148 (2006)
42. Software Productivity Consortium Services Corporation, Technical Report SPC-92019-CMC.Reuse-Driven Software Processes Guidebook, Version 02.00.03 (November 1993)

43. Streitferdt, D., Riebisch, M., Philippow, I.: Details of Formalized Relations in Feature Models Using OCL. In: Intl. Conf. the Engineering of Computer Based Systems, pp. 45–54 (2003)
44. van Deursen, A., Klint, P.: Domain-Specific Language Design Requires Feature Descriptions. JCIT 10, 1–17 (2002)
45. Veer, B., Dallaway, J.: The eCos Component Writer's Guide (2001), http://ecos.sourceware.org/docs-latest/cdl-guide/cdl-guide.html
46. Voelter, M., Visser, E.: Product Line Engineering using Domain-Specific Languages. In: Intl. Conf. Software Product Lines, pp. 70–79 (2011)
47. White, J., Dougherty, B., Schmidt, D.C., Benavides, D.: Automated Reasoning for Multi-step Software Product-line Configuration Problems. In: Intl. Conf. Software Product Lines, pp. 11–20 (2009)
48. White, J., Doughtery, B., Schmidt, D.: Selecting Highly Optimal Architectural Feature Sets with Filtered Cartesian Flattening. J. Systems and Software 82(8), 1268–1284 (2009)
49. White, J., Hill, J., Gray, J., Tambe, S., Gokhale, A., Schmidt, D.: Improving Domain-Specific Language Reuse with Software Product Line Techniques. IEEE Softw. 26, 47–53 (2009)
50. White, J., Schmidt, D.C., Wuchner, E., Nechypurenko, A.: Automating Product-Line Variant Selection for Mobile Devices. In: Intl. Conf. Software Product Lines, pp. 129–140 (2007)

Towards Test Case Reuse: A Study of Redundancies in Android Platform Test Libraries

Suriya Priya R. Asaithambi and Stan Jarzabek

School of Computing,
National University, Singapore
{suriya,stan}@comp.nus.edu.sg

Abstract. Similar software systems have similar test cases. We find much redundancy even within test cases of a single system. In this paper, we describe the results of similarity analysis performed on Android platform framework project's test case libraries. The results confirm our hypothesis that reuse of test cases can boost productivity at least as much as reuse of code. We identified repetition patterns in Android platform framework test case libraries that can be represented in generic form for further reuse using variability techniques adopted from Software Product Line (SPL). By exploiting similarity among test cases, we can design generic test case libraries that are much smaller, easier to develop/evolve than existing test case libraries. In this paper, we present quantitative and qualitative findings from our study of Android platform framework test case libraries. We discuss typical patterns of repetitions and illustrate an example of how they can be treated with variability technique 'XML-based Variant Configuration Language (XVCL)'.

Keywords: Reusability, Android platform framework, Software Product Line Testing, Clone Detection, Unit Test, Integration Test.

1   Introduction

With much development effort spent on testing, approaches for test automation have received much attention in research. Test cases are textually similar codes or scripts with appropriate parametric variations. Additionally, test cases often mirror software under test, thus a similarity in software reflects as similarities among test cases. Test case similarities create an opportunity to reduce the effort to both develop and maintain test libraries: Suppose that for each large enough group of similar test cases we design a 'generic adaptable test case', from which all test case instances in that group can be automatically derived. This would allow us to reduce the size and cognitive complexity of test libraries. Instead of working at the level of individual test cases, we would work with a smaller number of generic test cases – a much simpler task.

In this paper, we explore test case reuse with Android platform framework test libraries as our case study. First, we conducted similarity analysis of Android platform framework test case libraries to assess the degree of redundancies, and investigated the potential benefit of test case reuse. Then, we identified patterns of repetitions

J. Favaro and M. Morisio (Eds.): ICSR 2013, LNCS 7925, pp. 49–64, 2013.

among test cases that are potential candidates for reuse. Finally, we outlined generic representations for such repetition patterns as a practical way to realize the concept of test case reuse. In our study, we used XVCL, a variability technique (explained later in section 5) to manage code reuse developed in SPL research for our reuse proposal.

In our previous work [1], we presented the importance of having a generic adaptable test cases for SPL. In this paper, we present quantitative and qualitative findings from studying Android platform framework test case libraries. We have studied unit test cases and integration test cases of the Android platform framework open source repository. Our study confirms high rates of redundancies that create opportunities to boost testing productivity using reuse-based approaches to build test case libraries. We present a solution that can treat test case redundancies at meta-level, complementing plus extending the power of programming language and testing framework support.

The rest of the paper is organized as follows. Details of the methodical study we conducted are explained in section 2. Section 3 reports test clone analysis from the study. Section 4 is an executive summary of study followed by section 5 explaining a possible XVCL approach for generic adaptable test case design. Related work is presented in section 6. Threats to validity are documented in section 7 and experiences gained from study are presented in Section 8 as conclusion of this paper.

1.1   Background and Motivation

A *test clone* refers to identical or near identical fragments of test case codes. Test clones are often present in test cases related to similar features of a software system under testing. Large granular test clones signify reuse opportunity. The essence of Software Product Line (SPL) [2] approach is to systematically analyze commonalities and differences in a family of software products, and build so-called SPL core assets from which products can be developed and maintained in reuse-based, cost-effective way [3, 4]. Software product line testing (SPLT) [5] refers to approaches that support reuse of test cases such as generic adaptable test case design outlined in the introduction. Test cases forms an important part of SPL core assets. Further, testing of core assets is considered critical because a fault within certain functionality can spread over thousands of products that reuse this functionality. Thus, it is important to prioritize and thoroughly test SPL core assets by taking advantage of reusability. Smith et al [6] describes how open source tools could be specifically tailored for mobile software engineering to avoid duplication.

Android is the first free, open source, and fully customizable mobile platform that includes an operating system (OS), middleware and key mobile applications. Android SDK provides the tools and APIs necessary to develop applications on the Android platform [7],[5]. Android platform spans across different hardware makers (Sony, HTC, Samsung, Google, etc.), applications (i.e., native application, mobile web application) and computing devices (i.e., smart phone, tablet). Android faces variability management challenges in areas of functionalities, memory management, power consumption, screen, display densities, and relevant test automation calls for new reuse based techniques. The exponential growth of the platform poses unique challenges for variability management, reuse at all fronts, efficient quality assurance and quality control procedures, of which testing are an integral part. New software engineering approaches are required for testing Android's device complexity [8]. Android is a massive SPL, in which effective testing strategies play a key role in ensuring the quality of this famous mobile platform.

Let us assume that a particular component of Android platform framework contains 12 variant features that may be different in different Android powered device installations. Then we might have as many as $2^{12} = 4096$ combinations of these variant features in various Android powered device installations. (In practice, only some of those combinations are legal.). The above simple example shows that even a small number of variant features can results in a combinatorial explosion of test cases needed for validation. *Combinatorial explosion of test case libraries* is caused by the need to test individual variant features. This overwhelming number of test cases needed can be reduced if we could exploit the fact that test cases for different product variants are similar, in the same way as respective products are similar.

2   Study Overview

Android was launched in 2003, as a way to advance open standards for mobile devices. Android's architecture naturally promotes component reuse. Platform releases are frequent, introducing new features such as account synchronization, improved media-playing performance, and more geo location support. Complexities in testing and fragmentation concerns are new research challenges. Following the guidelines from 'Software Engineering Research Methodology Guidelines for Case Studies' [9] , our study comprised of five major process steps:

1. *Systematic case study design*: We defined key objectives and execution plan.
2. *Data collection*: We collected data from Android GIT source code repositories. We carefully segregated test cases and analyzed those using Clone Miner and Clone analyzer tools. We studied similarities using various filter criteria.
3. *Analysis*: We collected test clones, grouped them and attempted interpreting the possible causes.
4. *Report*: We organized new found insights and emerging findings in a summary.
5. *Proposal:* We proposed a solution that can treat test clone, complementing and extending the power of programming language and testing framework support.

Objectives. The objective of our study is to identify, understand and classify the nature of redundancy in test case libraries. We hope that this study would guide in designing of generic adaptable test cases, simplifying test case libraries, and enabling test cases reuse and automation.

— *Objective #1: To identify, and analyze, similarities found in the 'Android Platform Framework Test Case Libraries'.*
— *Objective #2: To analyze and classify the findings to come up with insights that would help in design of generic adaptable test cases.*

Tool. We use Clone Miner (CM) and Clone Analyzer (CA) tool [10] for our study. CM/CA finds clones in subject software system(s) and also allows us to filter clones that are of interest in our study. CM/CA, helps us find both simple and large similarities. Simple clones (similar code fragments) are possibly part of a bigger design-level replicated program structures (e.g., files or directories). CM/CA uses token-based techniques to find simple clones and data mining to find higher level structural similarities.

Method. Our case study was carried out in the following steps: (1) Setting up the clone miner and clone analyzer tool (2) Checking out the Android base platform code repositories from GIT server and separating test artifacts directories for further investigation (3) Conducting similarity investigation using clone miner and analyzer tool (4) Analyzing the investigation findings further (5) Reporting the findings, challenges and research findings that will be useful in answering the original research questions defined.

Scope of Test Cases. We studied 'Android platform framework test case libraries', a collection of unit and integration test cases for Android Platform. As our goal is to reuse test cases, we scoped our study to single language; we focused on Java, excluding C++ and C test case libraries.

3   Test Clone Analysis and Discussion

3.1   Data Collection

After initial analysis of Android code repository, we selected platform project and further focused on framework project for the study among four hundred over similar projects from the GIT servers (Shows the focused platform in Fig. 1). It provides common platform services related to kernel interactions.
GIT repository path is:
`https://Android.googlesource.com/platform/frameworks`

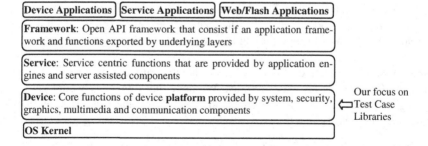

Fig. 1. Android Projects

3.2   Test Case Characteristics

Our study collected all unit and integration test cases, found in the public repository. This would provide insights on 'White Box Testing'.

Android Platform:
Total Android Framework Code Base Size ~17 GB; Total 26767 Files; 9300824 LOC ~9300KLOC
Study focus - Framework:
Framework Codes = 2.23 GB On Disk; Test Files In Framework Project: 1012 *Selected Test Files For Study: 1007 Java Files (Unit /Integration/UI Tests); 12+MB;*

3.3   Types of Test Clones

When writing similar test cases, testers often use copy-paste-modify technique (even though in some situations programming language mechanisms such as inheritance or parameterization might yield a more elegant unified solution). Most test clones we observed seem to result from this approach. In this study, we classified test clones based on clone type as shown in Table 1 below:

Table 1. Classification Based on Token Size and Test Clone Type

TEST CLONES	*SIMPLE*	*PARAMETRIC*	*COMPLEX*
(SIMILAR TOKENS)	Identical Test Clones	Parametric Test Clones	Reordered/Intervened /Gapped Test Clones

Our study assumes the following definitions: *test clones* are fragments of contiguous code having considerable size and significant similarity. *Token* is our unit of measure that refers to test code such as keyword, variable name, constant and operators. In our study we consider clones of minimum token length 30. The *identical test clone* is the simplest type, where the two or more test case portions match exactly, except for the line breaks and white spaces. *Parametric test clones* are test case sections that match except for a one-to-one correspondence between candidates for parameters such as variables, constants, macro names, and structure member names. This apart, there are *reordered test clones* and *intertwined test clones*. In a *reordered test clone*, the exact or parametric matching lines of the test codes are reordered, whereas in an *Intertwined test clone*, these lines are intertwined with each other. In *gapped test clone*, the differences between the matching test case sections cannot be parametric and form gaps of non similarities. Example for parametric test clone is presented in Table 2 below.

Table 2. Parametric Test Clones

```public boolean matches```
`(Object `**`matched`**`) {`
`    if (!(`**`matched`**` instanceof`
`        `**`AccessibilityEvent`**`)) {`
`        return false;      }`
`. . . }`
	```public boolean matches```
	`(Object `**`argument`**`) {`
	`    if (!(`**`argument`**` instanceof `**`Uri`**`)){`
	`        return false;      }`
	`. . .`
	`}`

3.4   Similarity Analysis

First, we grouped test cases based on test clone types. Then, we performed more detailed study on similarities within each group, and attempted to record typical examples. In this section, we illustrate similarity groups with simple examples, and explanation. Although the examples are not equally distributed, each group of test clone indicates few possible causes for redundancies.

GROUP1: Simple and Parametric Test Clones. This group of clones comprises of test cases that are exact copies or parametric copies of each other. A *test method* is a single executable test case that may share a common set-up and tear-down method for *test fixtures* (data). Simple test clones are contiguous segments of exact similar test codes such as test methods, or fragments of test method implementation. Parametric test clone are syntactically identical fragments or test classes or test methods except for variations in parameters, return types, identifiers, literals, types, whitespace, layout and comments. One of the key causes for parametric test clone is the lack of methodical reuse among common '*Test Fixtures*'. Redundancy is also observed to have occurred from lack of appropriate creational test case design patterns.

— *Functional Similarity*: The objective of test cases is to verify specific functional requirements. Many functions are designed symmetrical across the screen. For example hand gestures such as, swipe left or swipe right, pinch zoom in or out. Depending on selected activity, the input data set may be different, but the function calls tested are similar. Thus test methods contain similar method calls for different input sets. This gets reflected as test clones. For example, Table 3 shows a test case checking if a touch gesture used to grab screen works properly. Depending on selected item being hyperlink or UI action, different event activity is being asserted.

Table 3. Simple Clones Based On Functional Similarity

```
public class                        public class
  GridTouchSetSelectionTest           ListSetSelectionTest
    extends  Activity                   extends  Activity
    InstrumentationTestCase             InstrumentationTestCase
    <GridSimple> {                      < ListSimple> {
private GridSimple mActivity;       private ListSimple mActivity;
private GridView mGridView;         private ListView mListView;
...                                 ...
@LargeTest                          @LargeTest
public void testSetSelection()      public void testSetSelection()
  {                                   {
  TouchUtils.                         TouchUtils.
  dragQuarterScreenDown( this);       dragQuarterScreenDown( this);
TouchUtils.                         TouchUtils.
  dragQuarterScreenUp( this);         dragQuarterScreenUp( this);
//... LARGE IDENTICAL CLONE....      //... LARGE IDENTICAL CLONE....
assertTrue( "..." , found);         assertTrue( "..." , found);
  }                                   }
  ...                                 ...
}                                   }
```

— *Collection/Data Structure Management*: Test stubs and drivers are components of reusable test fixtures. Test fixtures manage complex data structures and collections. When the test context is similar, the data structure/collection processing codes are also similar. Processing includes memory management and life-cycle methods such as data setup, data tear-down and verification/assertion causing identical test clones. For example, in Table 4, let us consider test case in media framework targeted for media thumbnails. The unit test class `MediaItemThumbnailTest` comprises of seven identical clones shown in table below that processes, validates and recycles test data. Failing to use best practices, that indetifies similar data structures and organizes related life-cycle methods as reusable components is likely the cause for such test clones.

Table 4. Collection/DataStructure Processing Clones

```
//. . .
for ( int i = 0; i < thumbNailBmp.length; i++) {
        validateThumbnail(thumbNailBmp[i], outWidth, outHeight);
        thumbNailBmp[i] = null;
    }
//. . .
```

— *Exception management:* In situations where test cases make invocation to methods that perform similar functions, similar exceptions are thrown. Thus the test cases have redundant exception managing try-catch block clones. For example, in file `WindowManagerPermissionTests`, every call to the `IWindowManager` interface should throw `SecurityException`. Thus try-catch blocks are redundant inside the test case as shown in Table 5.

Table 5. Redundant clause try – catch- blocks

```
//. . .
try {
        mWm.updateRotation(true, false);
        fail(". . .");
    } catch (SecurityException e) {
        // expected
    } catch (RemoteException e) {
        fail(". . .");
    }
//. . .
```

Test Case Set Up/ Tear Down or Fixture Parameters Test cases are usually run by a test runner class that loads the test case class; set ups needful data or fixtures, runs, and tears down each test. Thus majority of the redundancy in test cases are found in set up and tear down methods. In `RecurrenceProcessorTest` that test recurrence event for the calendar feature, there are fifteen test clone methods with slight variation in test fixture values as shown in Table 6.

Table 6. TestData Redundancy

```
//. . .
@SmallTest
public void testMonthlyXX() throws Exception {
       verifyRecurrence( "20110703T100000" ,
          "FREQ=MONTHLY;BYDAY=SA,SU;BYSETPOS=2,-2" ,
          null /* rdate */ , null /* exrule */, null /* exdate */,
          "20110701T000000" , "20110931T235959",
          new String[]{ "20110703T100000" , "20110730T100000" ,
             "20110807T100000" , "20110827T100000" ,
             "20110904T100000" , "20110924T100000"  } );
    }
    //. . .
```

— *Mock Objects Parameters*: To facilitate dependency injection in testing, Android provides classes that create mock system objects such as `Context` objects, `ContentProvider` objects, `ContentResolver` objects, and `Service` objects. Test cases provide mock `Intent` objects. Testers use these mocks both to isolate tests from the rest of the system and to facilitate dependency injection for testing. These classes are found in the packages `Android.test` and `Android.test.mock`. Mock objects isolate tests from a running system by stubbing out or overriding normal operations. Redundancies found in such mock object life cycle management.

— *Activity / Service Parameters:* `Activity` testing is dependent on the Android instrumentation framework. Activities have a complex lifecycle based on callback methods; these can't be invoked directly except by instrumentation. The activity testing API base class is `InstrumentationTestCase`, which provides instrumentation to the test case subclasses we use for activities. Android provides a testing framework for `Service` objects that can run them in isolation and provides mock objects. The test case class for `Service` objects is `ServiceTestCase`. Since the `Service` class assumes that it is separate from its clients, we can test a `Service` object without using instrumentation. Parametric clones found in such `Activity` and `Service` objects based tests.

— *UI Parameters:* UI testing ensures that the framework returns the correct UI output in response to a sequence of user actions on a device, such as entering keyboard input or pressing toolbars, menus, dialogs, images, and other UI controls. Functional or black-box UI testing does not require testers to know the internal implementation details of the app, only its expected output when a user performs a specific action or enters a specific input. The Android SDK provides tools to support automated, functional UI testing using `UIAutomator` and `TestRunner`.

GROUP 2: Reordered/Intervened/Gapped Test Clones. Contiguous segments of parametric test case clones that have intervened code portions that cannot be parametric. Our study also found similarities spread across files. However no directory level similarities were observed.

— *Device and Configuration:* The study reveals that repetitive test codes belonging to the devices and configuration were found highlighting similarities across files and directories. Closer examination reveals presence of design and architectural similarities. Let us take a simple example of testing permission. There are key permissions to be tested on activities, package managers, windows mangers, service managers, SMS (Short Message Service) managers and vibration services. So there are intervened test clones present. Below Fig. 2 shows the file listing of interest.

Fig. 2. Permission Test Cases

— *Template*: In general test cases had class level and package level templates. Class level structures include set up, tests and tear down. Package level includes groups of test classes as test suites. Owing to the similarity in the domain, similarities are found in the class level and package level templates as shown in Fig. 3.

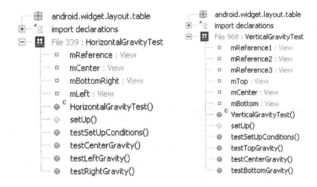

Fig. 3. Template Similarity between two test case files

File Gapped Clones: Using clustering technique based on clone length and coverage metrics CA/CM tool was able to observe file level clones. For example `Download-ManagerBaseTest` shown in Fig. 4, is a file level gapped test clone found in two different directories. They have minor contextual differences. However they are managed as two duplicated gapped clones.

⊿ ⊞ Directory 86 : K:\AndroidPlatformFramework\base\core\tests\hosttests\test-apps\DownloadManager
　　⊞ File 225 : DownloadManagerBaseTest.java
　　⊞ File 229 : DownloadManagerTestApp.java
　　⊞ File 230 : DownloadManagerTestRunner.java
⊿ ⊞ Directory 87 : K:\AndroidPlatformFramework\base\core\tests\coretests\src\android\app
　　⊞ File 226 : DownloadManagerBaseTest.java
　　⊞ File 227 : DownloadManagerFunctionalTest.java
　　⊞ File 228 : DownloadManagerStressTest.java

Fig. 4. File Gapped Clone Occurrences

— *Call Sequence*: Being a component based SPL architecture; Android's complex functionalities get broken down into smaller activities. While testing such complex functionalities, clones emerge in terms of group of assertion statements being called and the sequence in which they are called. An example is shown in Fig. 5.

Fig. 5. Call Sequence Similarity for two different test cases setting up activity

4   Quantitative Analysis

A summary of our study findings is shown in Table 7. Two key observations from our study are: (1) At least 53% of test files contain some form of redundancy. (2) At least 79% of test methods comprised of some form of redundancy.

Table 7. Summary of Clone Analysis

Attribute	Measure
Total Directories Analyzed	224 Directories
Total Test Files (Java Classes) Analyzed	1007 Files
Total Methods Analyzed	9728 methods
% Methods Containing Simple Test Clones	79%
% Files Containing Simple Test Clones	53%
Average Length of Test Clone	53 Tokens
Maximum Length Of Test Clone Found	1290 Tokens
Minimum Length Of Test Clone Found	30 Tokens
Simple Test Clone Class	2407 Files
Simple Test Clone Methods	7731 Methods
Parametric Test Clone Found Within File	779 Instances
Parametric Test Clone Found Across Files	335Instances
Complex Test File Clones Within Directory	12 Files
Complex Test File Clones Across Directories	11 Files

4.1   Similarity Discussion

The following discussion summarizes the study findings against our originally set research objectives.

Objective #1. *To identify, and analyze, similarities found in the 'Android platform framework test case libraries'*. Around 53% of test files have some form of redundancy. Test clones vary in type, complexity, token length, and variations. From the study we observe that there could be various reasons for the cause of test clones. Typical examples such as test smells, lack of design and parametric combinatory of test data need be addressed using appropriate reuse techniques. In our study, Group1 test clone examples such as exception management & UI parameters, along with Group 2 findings confirm absence of reuse techniques to manage test case libraries at the programming language level. For example, exception management test clones are limitations owing to non-runtime exception structure of Java. Thus our study confirms the need to access for a meta-level variant management of test case libraries proposal.

Objective #2. *To analyze and classify the findings to come up with insights that would help in design of generic adaptable test cases*. Removing clones at the language level requires changes to the test case libraries. In existing Android system, test clones are tolerated in spite of their negative effect on maintenance, to avoid the risk of breaking a running test while trying to remove them. Different techniques can be used to realize reuse based evolution of test case libraries. We had discussed the issues of managing test case libraries at programming language level in previous sections. For existing test case redundancy issues, we may still rely on regular maintenance approaches such as test smell identification, refactoring, test case design patterns and library based reuse. However, new methodical reuse approaches are to be explored for managing planned future redundancies.

In the next section, we propose a technique for test clone treatment with mixed-strategy approach. Here test case libraries can be built and maintained with a generative technique, applied on top of exiting test case libraries. The technique is unique, generic, but in adaptable form. The core functionality of test cases still exits as Android Test Cases, but generic test case designs to unify similarities are delegated to XVCL. We hope this technique will aid the tester design better managed generic adaptable test cases that can generate test cases specific to different target Android devices.

5   Towards Generic Test Cases

While designing unit and integration test cases, reuse comes handy by using programming language mechanisms such as inheritance, shared libraries, object composition, and component packaging. One technique that is useful would be meta-generative approach called XVCL. We illustrate generic test case design with XVCL, a variability management technique developed and applied in SPL research. . XVCL [10] is a static meta-programming language and tool, a modern incarnation of Bassett's frames [11]. We introduce the concepts of the solution, using test clones found in the Android test case libraries as an example. Fig. 6 outlines the solution.

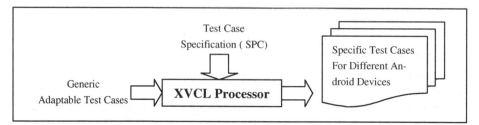

Fig. 6. Generic Adaptable Test Case Design

Similar test structures – test methods, test classes, or test patterns - are represented generically and organized into 'generic adaptable test cases'. Specifics of each test case are described separately in an SPC, as deltas from the generic test case. XVCL Processor generates specific test cases from the generic test case according to SPC. By varying the SPC, we can use the same generic test case as a template to generate required specific test cases. The following example shows how a generic test case, together with the appropriate SPC, is used to generate the multiple test cases. Let us consider the test package for creation views in `com.Android.bidi`. The test involves four possible layouts and two sides for each layout as show in Fig. 7.

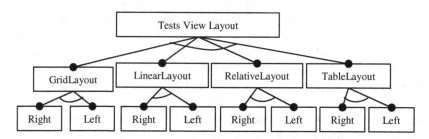

Fig. 7. Feature diagram for view layout test cases

We use two XVCL variables called `layoutName` and `sideName` to represent a class name and layout call constants. The generic test case representation comprises of an SPC and an XVCL component `BiDiTest`, shown in Fig. 8. XVCL variables 'layoutName' and 'sideName' are assigned values in <set> commands, in SPC. XVCL Processor interprets SPC and interprets any XVCL commands found on the way, and emitting Java code accordingly. In our example, test case named `BiDitestGridLayoutRight` is generated. The remaining test cases in this group can be generated from their respective SPCs. The SPC can also contain a generation loop to emit all test cases in a group from a single SPC.

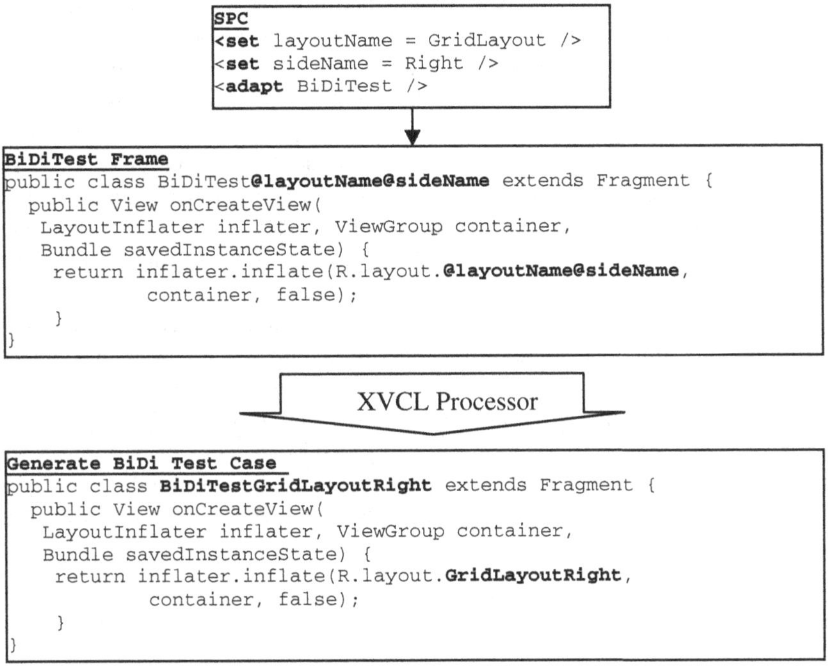

```
SPC
<set layoutName = GridLayout />
<set sideName = Right />
<adapt BiDiTest />
```

```
BiDiTest Frame
public class BiDiTest@layoutName@sideName extends Fragment {
  public View onCreateView(
   LayoutInflater inflater, ViewGroup container,
   Bundle savedInstanceState) {
    return inflater.inflate(R.layout.@layoutName@sideName,
         container, false);
   }
}
```

XVCL Processor

```
Generate BiDi Test Case
public class BiDiTestGridLayoutRight extends Fragment {
  public View onCreateView(
   LayoutInflater inflater, ViewGroup container,
   Bundle savedInstanceState) {
    return inflater.inflate(R.layout.GridLayoutRight,
         container, false);
   }
}
```

Fig. 8. Deriving class of BiDitestGridLayoutRight from a generic BiDiTest

5.1 Discussion

Our example is simple, but the principle of operation is general, meaning that for any group of test cases displaying substantial similarity, we can build a generic adaptable test case in XVCL. In particular, for any type of clones described in our analysis, there is a clear pattern of the corresponding XVCL generic solution possible. The generic test case design described here is language-independent therefore can be seamlessly applied across multiple programming language constructs. Thus Android platform framework comprising of Java, C++ and C test cases can be seamlessly managed by XVCL. Test case generation rules are 100% transparent to a tester, who retains full control over fine-tuning the generated test case code.

6   Related Work

The related work focusing on aspects such SPLT and reuse based testing approaches in mobile context. Software product line testing (SPLT) [5] approaches, support reuse by employing test assets that are commonly maintained as generic core assets and modified as necessary to the tested product dynamically. Smith et al [6] indicates research efforts as to how open source tools could be specifically tailored for mobile software engineering to avoid duplicating early in context of the end to end test assets, automated or otherwise.

Bezerra et al [12] present a systematic review on the existent proposals concerning mobile middleware product lines and their variability management techniques. The proposal suggests use of dynamic-AOP, feature model and ontology combined with intelligent agents. However there is no implementation to substantiate the practical applicability of identified proposals. White et al [13] implemented a constraint solver based on a rule engine tool that takes product line architecture requirements and resource available of a particular mobile device as inputs and outputs optimal variants that could be deployed. The initial experiment of the variant selection tool Scatter seems positive. However, there is a variety of assumption and constraints on how the tool is being utilized.

Many techniques and tools for clone detection, elimination, and removal have been described in the literature, and some of this literature addresses the problem of applying these techniques and tools to software systems written in a variety of languages. NA Kraft et al [14] describe an approach for cross-language clone detection. The work has been implemented in .Net platform and proved to detect clones from C# and VB codes. . While work published so far focuses on SPLT and mobile challenges, Android being a recent platform, has received very less attention from research community.

7   Threats to Validity

This study comprises several steps, combining two research methodologies: the exploratory study and the evaluation based on a tool experiment. There are several threats to validity: the selection of the study repository, the interpretation of test clones as found by the tool, the use of proper metrics and experimental setups for evaluation. Our study does not claim to have generalized all possible test clone occurrences. There could be more causes for the test clones than those being listed in the analysis section. We have attempted to observe and classify as much different groups of test clones possible, based on our past study experiences from other clones using the same tool. We have sought clone expert opinions on the findings where possible to counter the threat. Gapped test clones are human interpreted and recorded and so it is possible that another researcher would have identified a different list of important prioritization factors. However the list proposed in our study is further reviewed, evaluated and thus validated within the scope of our study.

8   Conclusion

In the paper, we described the results of similarity analysis performed on the Android platform framework test case libraries. Our results confirmed the hypothesis that reuse of test cases can boost productivity at least as much as reuse of code: around half of exiting test case files are found to have some form of redundancy. Most redundant test clones we found are either identical or parametric in nature. Our study also uncovered some instances of gapped test clones. We identified repetitive patterns in Android platform framework test cases that could be represented in generic form for reuse with variability techniques used in SPL. The goal of generic adaptable test case design is to identify redundancy, at the test case level and avoid counter-productive test duplications. By exploiting similarity among test cases, we can design generic test case libraries that are much smaller, easier to develop and evolve, than existing test case libraries. We illustrated a simple example on how template unfriendly gapped test clones can be treated using variability technique of XVCL. In this study, we focused on similar test cases found in an Android installation on a single device. We plan to extend our study to explore test case reuse across different Android versions and installations.

8.1   Future Work

Using the observations and findings from studying the Android platform framework test case libraries, we want to construct **"generic adaptable test cases"** to counter test case libraries explosion problem. Our future work will focus on traceability and effort reduction via systematic reuse of generic adaptable test cases by taking advantage of common aspects and predicted variability.

Acknowledgements. We wish to thank Hamid Abdul Basit (School of Science and Engineering, Lahore University of Management Sciences, Pakistan) for providing tool Clone Miner and Clone Analyzer and related support.

References

1. Asaithambi, S.P.R., Jarzabek, S.: Generic adaptable test cases for software product line testing: software product line. In: Proceedings of the 3rd Annual Conference on Systems, Programming, and Applications: Software for Humanity, pp. 33–36. ACM, New York (2012), http://doi.acm.org.libproxy1.nus.edu.sg/10.1145/2384716.2384733, 978-1-4503-1563-0
2. Pohl, K., Böckle, G., Linden, F.V.D.: Software Product Line Engineering: Foundations, Principles, and Techniques. Birkhäuser (2005), 9783540243724
3. McGregor, J.D.: Testing a Software Product Line. Software Engineering Institute (2001), http://repository.cmu.edu/sei/630
4. McGregor, J.D.: Testing a Software Product Line. In: Borba, P., Cavalcanti, A., Sampaio, A., Woodcook, J. (eds.) PSSE 2007. LNCS, vol. 6153, pp. 104–140. Springer, Heidelberg (2010), http://www.springerlink.com.libproxy1.nus.edu.sg/content/63526172267k3311/abstract/
5. Muccini, H., Di Francesco, A., Esposito, P.: Software testing of mobile applications: Challenges and future research directions. In: 2012 7th International Workshop on Automation of Software Test (AST), pp. 29–35 (2012)
6. Smith, L., Laird, C.: Android: open-source scripting for testing and automation. Dr. Dobb's J. 26(3), 99–102 (2001), http://dl.acm.org.libproxy1.nus.edu.sg/citation.cfm?id=544544.544553
7. Burnette, E.: Hello, Android: Introducing Google's Mobile Development Platform, ch. 2. Pragmatic Bookshelf (2009), 1934356492, 9781934356494

8. Hu, C., Neamtiu, I.: Automating GUI testing for Android applications. In: Proceedings of the 6th International Workshop on Automation of Software Test, pp. 77–83. ACM, New York (2011), http://doi.acm.org.libproxy1.nus.edu.sg/10.1145/1982595.1982612, 978-1-4503-0592-1

9. Runeson, P., Höst, M.: Guidelines for conducting and reporting case study research in software engineering. Empirical Software Engineering 14(2), 131–164 (2009), http://link.springer.com.libproxy1.nus.edu.sg/article/10.1007/s10664-008-9102-8

10. Basit, H.A., Jarzabek, S.: A Data Mining Approach for Detecting Higher-Level Clones in Software. IEEE Transactions on Software Engineering 35(4), 497–514 (2009)

11. Jarzabek, S., et al.: XVCL: XML-based variant configuration language. In: Proceedings of the 25th International Conference on Software Engineering, pp. 810–811 (2003)

12. Bezerra, Y.M., Pereira, T.A.B., da Silveira, G.E.: A Systematic Review of Software Product Lines Applied to Mobile Middleware. In: Sixth International Conference on Information Technology: New Generations, ITNG 2009, pp. 1024–1029 (2009)

13. White, J., et al.: Automating Product-Line Variant Selection for Mobile Devices. In: 11th International Software Product Line Conference, SPLC 2007., pp. 129–140 (2007)

14. Kraft, N., Bonds, B., Smith, R.: Cross-language clone detection. In: Proceedings of the 20th International Conference on Software Engineering and Knowledge Engineering, SEKE (2008)

An Assessment of Test-Driven Reuse: Promises and Pitfalls

Mehrdad Nurolahzade, Robert J. Walker, and Frank Maurer

Department of Computer Science
University of Calgary
Calgary, Alberta, Canada
{mnurolah,walker,frank.maurer}@ucalgary.ca

Abstract. Test-driven reuse (TDR) proposes to find reusable source code through the provision of test cases describing the functionality of interest to a developer. Proponents claim that their TDR approaches work well. This paper presents the results of an experiment to evaluate the ability of state-of-the-art TDR tools to locate reusable source code for realistic tasks. We find that non-trivial functionality, like that needed in the daily tasks of developers, can largely *not* be retrieved by these approaches. We provide an analysis of the shortcomings and underlying problems in the existing approaches, and a discussion of potential solutions.

1 Introduction

Recent research considers locating and reusing source code by leveraging test cases [5, 13, 8]. Such *test-driven reuse* (TDR) is a reasonable proposition in development practices where test cases are written prior to implementing the functionality under test—called *test-driven development* (TDD)—such as in several agile development methodologies [e.g., 1]. While the TDR literature reports good results, it is not clear how the approaches compare, nor whether the results generalize to realistic TDD scenarios.

In TDR, the developer starts from test cases to indicate what they seek. The test cases are typically interpreted by automated TDR approaches as precise specifications to be satisfied by the located source code. And therein lies the crux of the potential problem: in test-driven development, the developer may have at best a fuzzy notion (initially) of the functionality she wants—TDD is inherently iterative. If a TDR approach places too much weight on the details of the test cases written (such as the particular names of types and methods), it is unlikely to find appropriate source code nor source code that can be trivially transformed to become a perfect match for those test cases.

The evaluation of TDR tools to-date [5, 13, 8] has been performed using a collection of classic tasks commonly used in the software reuse literature. Most of these tasks involve common data structures and functions, for which the developer can be expected to use the standard domain-specific vocabulary. We claim that these tasks are not representative of the daily requirements of developers performing TDD, where a developer cannot be expected to know of a standard domain-specific vocabulary.

To evaluate the existing test-driven reuse tools, we conducted an experiment with a set of trial tasks discovered from the daily development activities of developers.

J. Favaro and M. Morisio (Eds.): ICSR 2013, LNCS 7925, pp. 65–80, 2013.

We found that known solutions for such tasks are largely not retrieved by the existing TDR approaches, but instead, these approaches tend to recommend irrelevant source code. We analyze the published descriptions of the approaches and details of the returned solutions to identify the problems underlying this failure.

The rest of this paper is organized as follows. An overview of related work in TDR is provided in Section 2. We describe our experiment in Section 3. Results from the experiment and additional discussion are presented in Section 4.

2   Related Work

The reuse of source code through copying and modifying has a long history. While this approach of *pragmatic* software reuse can be abused, a growing body of evidence exists that it is a standard industrial practice, that it can be performed in a disciplined and principled manner, and that the use of pragmatic reuse and pre-planned reuse techniques could be coordinated to complement each other [for an overview, see 2].

A number of techniques have been used for indicating desired functionality for reuse, including signature matching [10], and specification matching [6]. Signature matching and specification matching both place a high burden on the developer to provide precise input; both approaches either will fail to retrieve pertinent source code if exact but inappropriate details are provided, or will retrieve an excessive number of results, demanding laborious examination by the developer. We note that both approaches mention the possibility of more approximate matching strategies.

Podgurski and Pierce [12] proposed behaviour sampling, an approach to retrieve reusable components using searcher-supplied samples of input/output for desired operations. As a pre-filtering step, behaviour sampling uses signature matching to limit the components to be tested, resulting in the same potential drawbacks. Podgurski and Pierce proposed two extensions to the classic form of behaviour sampling to overcome its limitations. Test-driven reuse realizes one of these extensions that permits the searcher to provide the retrieval criteria through a programmed acceptance test.

Three approaches to test-driven reuse have appeared in the literature: Code Conjurer [4, 5], CodeGenie [8], and S6 [13]. The prototype tool for each approach operates on source code written in the Java programming language.

Code Conjurer and CodeGenie are JUnit[1]-based implementations of test-driven reuse. The plug-in to the integrated development environment (IDE) provided by each of the tools automatically extracts operation signatures from the searcher-supplied JUnit test code. Search is then performed via a source code search engine and results are presented to the searcher for inspection in the IDE. The Merobase and Sourcerer [9] code search engines power Code Conjurer and CodeGenie searches respectively. CodeGenie further assists the searcher in slicing the source code to be reused; however, unlike Code Conjurer, the current implementation of CodeGenie can only be used to search for a single missing method, and not an entire class [8].

S6 complements the use of behaviour sampling with other forms of semantic specifications. It implements the abstract data type extension proposed by Podgurski and Pierce to handle object-oriented programming. Unlike Code Conjurer and CodeGenie,

---

[1] JUnit is an automated testing framework for Java code.

S6 does not utilize JUnit test code as a query language, but requires that the searcher provide the interactions of a class's methods through its web user interface. S6 attempts a small set of limited transformations on candidate source code, in an attempt at relaxing the constraints imposed by literal interpretation of the input query. S6 can use a local repository or remote code search engine like Google Code Search as the codebase searched through for candidate source code. Similar to Code Conjurer and CodeGenie, S6 depends on being able to find an appropriate initial result set.

All three approaches initially filter the repository on the basis of lexical or syntactic similarity with the supplied test case/query specification. All three claim to then execute the test case on each of the filtered results to assess semantic similarity as well; this acts solely to further constrain the set of potential matches.

3   Experiment

Our research question is "Do existing TDR tools recommend relevant source code for which minimal effort should be needed to integrate with an existing project?" In particular, we consider whether each tool is able to recommend known source code that solves a task, given modified forms of the existing test cases—taken from the same codebase—that exercise that source code. Section 3.1 describes how we selected tasks. Section 3.2 describes our experimental method. To improve the construct validity of our measurements, we had other developers assess a sample of our suitability assessments, and compared them with our own; we detail our and the external assessments of suitability in Section 3.3.

3.1   Task Selection

We located the 10 programming tasks in Table 1 for this experiment. We explain below our methodology for obtaining these.

Sources of Tasks. As the existing TDR tools all operate on Java source code, we focused on Java-oriented sources of information. We first examined material designed for developer education, including Oracle's Java Tutorial (http://docs.oracle.com/javase/tutorial). Such tutorials are usually developed by experienced developers to teach other developers what they should know about a language or technology because they are likely to come across tasks that would require that knowledge. In a similar fashion, we looked in source code example catalogues including java2s (http://www.java2s.com), which features thousands of code snippets demonstrating common programming tasks and usage of popular application programming interfaces (APIs). These two sources represent material designed for consumption by developers. To find what kinds of problems developers seek help to solve, we also looked at popular developer forums: Oracle Discussion Forums (https://forums.oracle.com/forums/category.jspa?categoryID=285) and JavaRanch (http://www.javaranch.com).

Locating Known Solutions and Their Test Cases. After locating descriptions of pertinent tasks, we sought existing implementations relevant to those tasks on the internet

Table 1. Brief task descriptions

Task	Description
1	A Base64 coder/decoder that can Base64 encode/decode simple text (String type) and binary data (**byte** array); should ignore invalid characters in the input; should return **null** when it is given invalid binary data.
2	A date utility method that computes the number of days between two dates.
3	A HTML to text converter that receives the HTML code as a String object and returns the extracted text in another String object.
4	A credit card number validator that can handle major credit card types (e.g., Visa and Amex); determines if the given credit card number and type is a valid combination.
5	A bag data structure for storing items of type String; it should provide the five major operations: add, remove, size, count, and toString.
6	An XML comparison class that compares two XML strings and verifies if they are similar (contain the same elements and attributes) or identical (contain the same elements and attributes in the same order).
7	An IP address filter that verifies if an IP address is allowed by a set of inclusion and exclusion filters; subnet masks (like 127.0.1.0/24, 127.0.1/24, 172.16.25.* or 127.*.*.*) can be used to define ranges; it determines if an IP is allowed by the filters or not.
8	A SQL injection filter that identifies and removes possible malicious injections to simple SELECT statements; it returns the sanitized version of the supplied SQL statement; removes database comments (e.g., − −, #, and *) and patterns like INSERT, DROP, and ALTER.
9	A text analyzer that generates a map of unique words in a piece of text along with their frequency of appearance; allows for case-sensitive processing; it returns a Map object that maps type String to Integer where the key is the unique word and the value is the frequency of the word appearance.
10	A command line parser with short (e.g., −v) and long (e.g. −−verbose) options support; it allows for options with values (e.g. −d 2, −−debug 2, −−debug=2); data types (e.g. Boolean, Integer, String, etc.) can be explicitly defined for options; it allows for locale-specific commands.

through code search engines, discarding search results that did not also come with JUnit test cases. After locating pertinent candidates we checked that both the solution and the test cases that exercised the solution existed in the repositories of the tools. Dissimilarity of the tools' underlying repositories made it difficult to select targets that simultaneously existed in all three repositories. Therefore, we settled for targets that exist in at least two of the three investigated repositories. Task selection and experimentation was performed incrementally over a period of three months; we found this process to be slow and laborious and thus we limited the investigated tasks to ten.

Coverage of Multiple Units. JUnit tests can cover more than one unit (despite the apparent connection between its name and "unit testing"). For example, an integration test can cover multiple classes collaborating in a single test case. Ideally, a test-driven reuse tool should be able to recommend suitable candidates for each missing piece referred to in a test scenario. Instead, current TDR prototypes have been designed around the idea that tests drive a single unit of functionality (i.e., a single method or class) at a time. We aimed our trial test cases to those targeting a single unit of functionality.[2]

3.2   Experimental Method

The experiment involved, for each identified task, (a) modifying the associated test case to anonymize the location of the known solution, (b) feeding the modified test case to the interface of each TDR tool, and (c) examining the resulting recommendations from each tool in order to assess their suitability to address the task (discussed in Section 3.3).

For simplicity of the study design, we assume that iterative assessment of recommendations and revision of the input test cases can be ignored. We further assume that a searcher would scan the ranked list of recommendations in order from the first to the last; however, we only consider the first 10 results, as there is evidence that developers do not look beyond this point in search results [7].

Anonymization. We wished to minimize experimenter bias by using (modified versions of) the existing test cases of the solutions. The query for each task then consisted of the modified JUnit test cases—thereby defining the desired interfaces, vocabulary, and testing scenarios of the trial tasks.

The test code used in the experiment was anonymized by a four step process: (1) any **package** statement is removed; (2) any **import** statements for types in the same project are removed (by commenting them out); (3) the set of test methods is minimized, by ensuring that all required methods for the sought functionality are exercised no less than once, while removing the rest; and (4) the statements within each test method are minimized, for cases where multiple conditions are tried, by retaining the first condition and removing the rest. This process was intended to reduce the test cases to the point that would resemble the minimal test scenarios developed in a TDD setting.[3]

Tool-Specific Adjustments. Minor adjustments were made to some test cases in the end to make them compatible with individual tools. For instance, Code Conjurer does not fire a search when no object instantiation takes place in the test code, preventing Code Conjurer from triggering a search when the target feature is implemented through **static** methods. To get around this problem, we revised test cases for Tasks 1, 2, and 4 and replaced **static** method calls with instance method calls preceded by instantiation of the unit under test. The example in Figure 1 demonstrates some of the changes made to the query test class Base64UtilTest used in Task 1 for replacing **static** method calls with instance method calls.

Unlike Code Conjurer and Code Genie, S6 comes with a web-based search interface; a class-level search through the Google or Sourcerer search provider was selected for all

---

[2] In one case, this constraint was not strictly met: the known solution for Task 4 relies on a set of **static** properties defined in a helper class CreditCardType.

[3] The complete set of known solutions and test cases, and their transformed versions used as inputs, can be retrieved from: http://tinyurl.com/icsr13.

```
@ Test public void testEncodeString() {
  final String text = "This is a test";
// String base64 = Base64Util.encodeString(text);
// String restore = Base64Util.decodeString(base64);
  Base64Util util = new Base64Util();
  String base64 = util.encodeString(text);
  String restore = util.decodeString(base64);
  assertEquals(text, restore);
}
```

Fig. 1. A sample test query illustrating the replacement of **static** calls

the searches performed through the S6 web interface. As S6 cannot process test code directly, a conversion process was followed to transform individual test cases into a form acceptable by the S6 interface (as a "call set"). Minor changes were made in some transformations due to the limitations imposed by the interface. In the case of Task 1, we could not provide the three test cases to S6 all at the same time; tests were therefore provided to the S6 search interface one at a time but S6 did not return results for any of them. For Task 9, we were not able to exactly reproduce the test case using an S6 call set. More specifically, we were not able to manipulate the returned java.util.Map object from the getWordFrequency() call; neither removing the assertions on the returned java.util.Map object nor using the "user code" feature produced any results. Task 10 involves the inner class CmdLineParser.Option that made S6 complain about an unknown type; we replaced the inner class with the type Object in order for the search to be launched.

3.3   Suitability Assessment

Many factors can make unplanned reuse difficult [2]. Two pieces of code of similar quality might satisfy the same feature set; however, developers are inclined to reuse the one that requires less adaptation and accommodation—after all, major motivations for reuse are to save time and effort and to reduce the likelihood of bugs. Therefore, it is important to present the developer with choices that they are likely to consider as relevant to their task, suitable for integration in their code, and whose adaptation would result in a net cost savings. To assess the quality of retrieved results, we thus recorded two subjective, qualitative measurements: relevance and effort.

Relevance and Effort. Relevance is a measure traditionally used in evaluation of information retrieval (IR) systems, to indicate how well a retrieved resource meets the information needs of the user. In the context of this study, relevance measures how many of the features expected by a trial task are covered by a search result. For TDR, good relevance is necessary but not sufficient.

Effort is a measure of the work involved to adapt the retrieved source code. Effort is a compound measurement of size and complexity of the source code to be integrated, external objects it refers to, and the amount of mismatch it has with the existing development context; for our study, the "existing development context" comprised the test suite used as input to the search.

Two recommendations with the same relevance level may have completely different effort levels. For example, one recommendation can be considerably larger, more complex, or have more external dependencies than an equally relevant one. However, relevance and effort are not orthogonal. As the relevance starts to decline, the effort tends to increase; for example, additional effort might be required to add missing features. Ultimately the developer will avoid reusing located source code if the adaptation effort is (apparently) comparable to that of reimplementation.

To account for partial suitability, we adopted 5-point scales of relevance and of effort, as shown in Tables 2 and 3 respectively. For rating relevance, 1 stands for no/minimal relevance and 5 stands for complete relevance. For rating efforts, 1 stands for little/no effort while 5 stands for excessive effort.

Assessments of Suitability. After running the 10 trial tasks against the three test-driven reuse tools we collected 109 individual recommendation results (out of 300 possible results), as the number of results was less than our cut-off of 10 for some task/tool combinations.

There are 25 potential combinations of relevance and effort scores; however, only some of those combinations are expected to be observed, due to the relationship between relevance and effort discussed above. Table 4 indicates our classification of each possible combination, as good (a solution), ok (a near-solution), bad (a non-viable recommendation), or impossible (left as blank). We deem combinations of fairly low relevance and low effort to be contradictory and hence impossible, since lack of relevance

Table 2. Guidelines for classifying relevance

Level	Description
1	There is no meaningful connection between the given task and the recommended code. I would not reuse this code to finish this task.
2–4	There is a noticeable overlap between the given task and the recommended code. However, some of the required features of the described functionality are missing or implemented in a different way (the smaller the mismatch, the higher the relevance).
5	The recommended code exactly or closely matches the functionality described in the task.

Table 3. Guidelines for classifying effort

Level	Description
1	This code can be reused to develop the entire functionality described in the task. I may only need to do one or two very simple adjustments.
2–4	I may or may not choose to reuse the recommended code or its design ideas. However, to reuse it I would have to refactor it, make modifications to its design, or write new code for missing features (the fewer the adjustments, the lower the effort).
5	I would not reuse this code to develop the functionality described in the task. It would require too much effort to build upon this code.

implies high effort would be needed. In the absence of a good solution, a developer might consider a near-solution, which is a relevant result that still requires non-trivial effort to use for the task.

Relevance and effort ratings were assigned to the results following a manual inspection of the retrieved source code. An attempt was made to integrate the query test cases with the retrieved code, if possible. To make the tests run, external dependencies of the source code were resolved and refactorings were performed, if necessary. Ratings were given based on the effort spent to make the tests run and an estimate of the extent of the missing features in each case.

External Validation. As relevance and effort are subjective measures, different developers can disagree on the reuse suitability of a piece of code in a certain context. To improve construct validity of the experiment, we compared our relevance and effort ratings with those from five experienced Java developers. Participants consisted of two graduate students and three industrial developers, all with 3–5 years of industrial experience in developing Java software. All participants reported that being familiar with the JUnit framework, having developed unit tests, and having conducted code reviews in the past. A short training example was used at the start of the session to familiarize participants with the procedures. A random sample of results (12 out of 109 recommendations) were selected, and provided to each participant for evaluation; each participant was asked to evaluate the same sample. In a short post-study questionnaire, all participants indicated that they have developed code for tasks similar to the ones they were given in the experiment, confirming that these are realistic tasks.

Participants were given a guide that described the purpose of this experiment and the rationale behind the relevance and effort scores, along with—for the results in the sample to be validated—a short description of each task, the test cases, and the source code retrieved by a tool. Participants were asked to rate each result's relevance and effort according to our 5-point scales. Participants were asked to justify their choice through additional comments, which we used to check that their reasoning conformed to their numerical ratings. Spearman's rank correlation coefficient (ρ) was used to measure the inter-rater reliability of the rankings made by the first author and each participant; Spearman's ρ can measure pairwise correlation among raters who use a scale that is ordered. Table 5 displays the ρ values computed for participants P1 to P5. In all five cases, there is strong positive correlation between relevance and effort ratings of the first author and those of the external validators.

Table 4. Quality classes

| | | \multicolumn{5}{c}{Relevance} | | | | |
		1	2	3	4	5
Effort	1					good
	2				ok	good
	3			bad	ok	ok
	4		bad	bad	bad	bad
	5	bad	bad	bad	bad	bad

Table 5. Inter-rater reliability scores

	P1	P2	P3	P4	P5
Relevance	0.86	0.89	0.93	0.84	0.81
Effort	0.72	0.75	0.82	0.74	0.72

4   Results and Discussion

Table 6 summarizes the results of the experiment for each tool/task pairing, indicating: the number of recommendations returned; how many of these were duplicates; the ranking by the respective tool of the recommendation that we deemed the best, within the first 10 results (or fewer if fewer were recommended); and the quality of the best solution. To be clear, in some cases, the recommendation by a tool that we deemed best amongst its results, we still assessed as badly suited; the tools' rankings and our assessment of quality often did not correlate.

We can see that each of the tools did a poor job at recommending solutions. Code Conjurer provided a good solution for only one task, and near-solutions for two others; for five of the remaining tasks only bad recommendations were provided. CodeGenie provided a good solution for only one task, and a near-solution for one other; no recommendations were provided for seven out of eight of the remaining tasks, so false positives were relatively low. S6 only provided a good solution for one task, and no near-solutions; again, no recommendations were provided for seven out of eight of the remaining tasks, so false positives were relatively low. For Task 8, none of the tools provided a recommendation. For Tasks 4–7 & 9, each tool either provided no recommendations or only bad recommendations. In fairness, for task/tool combinations in which we were unable to verify the presence of the known solution (marked with asterisks), the associated repository may not have contained a viable alternative but this only affects four of the tasks for CodeGenie and none for the other two tools.

Table 7 summarizes our classifications of all recommendations produced by the tools for the 10 tasks. Code Conjurer has a much larger number of false positive (i.e., bad)

Table 6. Results of the experiment for each tool/task combination. The columns for each tool indicate: the number of recommendations produced (rec); the number of these that are duplicates of other recommendations (dup); the ranking by the tool of the recommendation that we deemed the best within the results (best); and the quality of that best recommendation (qual). In cases marked with an asterisk, we were not able to verify the presence or absence of the known solution within the tool's repository.

Task	Code Conjurer				CodeGenie				S6			
	rec (#)	dup (#)	best (rank)	qual	rec (#)	dup (#)	best (rank)	qual	rec (#)	dup (#)	best (rank)	qual
1	8	(1)	8	ok	*8	(3)	3	good	0			
2	9	(1)	1	bad	*10		2	ok	10	(6)	1	good
3	10	(1)	3	ok	*0				0			
4	0				*0				10	(6)	1	bad
5	2	(1)	1	bad	*0				0			
6	10	(2)	1	bad	2		1	bad	0			
7	10	(5)	2	bad	0				0			
8	0				*0				0			
9	*10	(4)	1	bad	0				0			
10	10	(3)	3	good	0				0			

Table 7. Summary of quality classifications for all recommendations. The number of duplicate recommendations included is shown in parentheses.

Quality	Code Conjurer	CodeGenie	S6
good	4 (3)	3 (2)	10 (6)
ok	3	11 (2)	—
bad	62 (15)	6	10 (6)
Total	69 (18)	20 (3)	20 (12)

recommendations than the other two, but all three tools produce many bad recommendations, when they produce any recommendations at all.

The results of our experiment indicate that there is a serious problem at work with the existing TDR approaches. Could the problem simply be due to implementation weaknesses, or is there a more fundamental shortcoming with the underlying ideas? To address this question, we first examined similarities between the input test cases and the results, described below.

4.1   Lexical and Syntactic Matching

From the published literature on the TDR approaches, we recognized the importance that each places on lexical and (to a lesser extent) syntactic similarity between potential hits in the repository and the input test case. Specifically, Code Conjurer and CodeGenie both utilize similarity of type and method names plus similarity of method signatures; S6 utilizes similarity between user-supplied keywords and potential hits plus similarity of method signatures. We manually examined each recommendation returned by the tools to determine if lexical or syntactic similarities existed with the input test case for each task. We empirically discerned four kinds of matching criteria: type name, method name, signature, and other keywords.

Table 8 presents the results of our similarity examination. We can see that Code Conjurer places great emphasis on type name similarity while S6 ignores it. But ultimately, every recommendation could be traced to a mostly lexical similarity.

This heavy reliance on lexical/syntactic similarity to the supplied test case, in making recommendations, yields many false positive results—especially when simple functionality is sought. For example, the utility program sought in Task 2 consists of a single function with two parameters of type java.util.Date and a return value of type **int**. Code Conjurer retrieved 9 results all of which match this signature but none of which match the desired functionality.

Each approach had the greatest success when multiple kinds of similarity occurred simultaneously; again, this is not surprising since the likelihood that similarities in multiple dimensions are spurious seems much lower than in few dimensions. Unfortunately, it appears from the results that simply demanding multiple kinds of lexical/syntactic similarity simultaneously would lead to limited applicability of these tools. Others have noted the tradeoff limitations to lexical/syntactic similarity in code search [3].

Table 8. Classification of matches between recommendations and input test cases

Match kind	Code Conjurer		CodeGenie		S6	
	High similarity	Partial similarity	High similarity	Partial similarity	High similarity	Partial similarity
Type name	62		15			
Method name	5	8	1	8		6
Signature	15	8	10	8	20	
Other keyword	21		2		20	

4.2   Issues with the Approaches

We see several issues that arise not from weaknesses in tool implementation, but more fundamentally from the ideas behind the TDR approaches.

Signature Matching. The existing test-driven reuse approaches make signature matching a necessary condition to the relevance and matching criteria: a component is considered only if it offers operations with sufficiently similar signatures to the test conditions specified in the original test case. However, semantic similarity neither implies nor is implied by structural similarity. This limits the applicability of the test-driven reuse to situations in which the design of the feature sought is very simple or known in advance. A more flexible approach to signature matching could improve recall. For example, operation argument and return value types, order, or count could be ignored. Unfortunately, this would in turn make the execution of test cases for validating candidate results difficult. Automated tests can only be run if a match can be established between missing elements in the tests and those in the retrieved source code. Code Conjurer retrieved testable results (source code that has sufficiently close signatures for at least some of the operations) for Tasks 1, 3, and 10, while CodeGenie could achieve the same goal only for Tasks 1 and 2. S6 tries to take advantage of simple transformations to generate possible candidates that can pass the tests; however, a candidate is considered for applying the transformations only if structural dissimilarities are minor. Consequently, S6 ended up retrieving results for only two of the tasks (Tasks 2 and 4) because candidates retrieved for other tasks did not meet the input criteria of the transformations.

Filtering By Lexical Relevance. Filtering candidate results based on their lexical relevance before other relevance criteria are considered leaves out all potential solutions that do not match the searcher's choice of program vocabulary. For example, the date utility function in Task 2 is named getNumberOfDaysBetweenTwoDates() and is defined in a class named DateUtils. Tokenizing these two names, as is performed by Code Conjurer and CodeGenie, would give a list of generic words that can be matched with almost any date utility class. All the 9 classes retrieved by Code Conjurer are named DateUtils and each has at least one method matching the signature of the method sought after; however, none of them is a method that computes the distance between two dates. CodeGenie manages to find an instance of the function for Task 2 that is given the same name and is defined in a class with the same name. Other results are false positives arising from lexical and signature similarities.

Code Conjurer and CodeGenie use terms in the signature of methods as a key component of relevance. While S6 uses a supplied keyword list to shrink the candidate space in which signature matching and transformations are to be performed, the use of keywords in the search has been limited to lexical matching that in turn results in tool performance being limited by the searcher's choice of vocabulary [13, 8]. We designed our experiment to favour the evaluated tools: we used test code taken from the same project in order to retrieve the feature under test. Changing the original program vocabulary instead—which would be reasonable in modelling situations where the developer does not know the needed vocabulary—would have limited lexical relevance, resulting in even worse performance of the tools.

Automatically Compiling and Running Source Code. The existing test-driven approaches all attempt to execute the supplied test case on potential matches in the repository. This has the advantage that additional semantic constraints implied by the supplied test case can be checked, eliminating false positive matches. Given the large number of false positives that we obtained from the approaches, it is clear that this idea is not working as intended; in fact, for Code Conjurer in particular, we believe that test case execution remains an unimplemented idea, judging from the very large number of false positives.

The retrieved source code has to be runnable in order to execute test cases, but automatically compiling and running arbitrary source code accumulated in a repository is no easy task, often because of dependencies on external source code. A number of heuristics have been proposed by the research community to resolve external dependencies without developer intervention [11]. In the context of our trial, only Task 4 has an external dependency on the org.apache.commons.lang project, while Tasks 6, 7, and 8 have dependencies to other source code in the same project, and the rest of the tasks can be compiled using a standard JDK by itself.

Even if source code can be compiled, there is still no guarantee that it can also be run, as programs can rely on specific runtime environments or resources. For example a web or mobile component relies on a specific container to run. A database or network application requires those external resources to offer its services. To the benefit of the evaluated tools, none of our tasks required an external environment or resources to run.

In a similar fashion, the TDR query test cases may also rely on resources external to the JUnit program. For example, the original version of the XML utility for Task 6 relied on XML strings loaded from the file system. For the sake of our experiment, we modified the test[4] (Figure 2) to utilize XML strings embedded in the source code, but there is no a priori reason to expect that the developer will not wish to rely on external resources in this fashion.

Contextual Facts. Test cases are in fact simple examples demonstrating the use of the system-under-test. They show helper types that may interact with the system-under-test in typical scenarios. The existing TDR approaches disregard the elements of this interaction like participating types and the data/control flow between them. They merely

---

[4] We repeated this experiment with the original version of the test case. Code Conjurer and CodeGenie produced the same result. S6 does not allow using external resources.

```
import static org.junit.Assert.*;
import org.junit.Test;
import org.xml.sax.SAXException;

public class TestXmlDiff {
    String xml1 = "<?xml version=\"1.0\" encoding=\"ISO−8859−1\"?><a><b>text1
        </b><c>text2</c></a>";
    String xml2 = "<?xml version=\"1.0\" encoding=\"ISO−8859−1\"?><!−− copy
        −−><a><c>text2</c><b>text1</b></a>";

    /* @Test public void testDiff() throws XmlException, IOException, SAXException {
        DomainsDocument dd1 = DomainsDocument.Factory.parse(new File("src/test/
            resources/instances/test1.xml"));
        DomainsDocument dd2 = DomainsDocument.Factory.parse(new File("src/test/
            resources/instances/test2.xml"));
        Diff myDiff = new Diff(dd1.toString(), dd2.toString());
    } */

    @Test public void testDiff() throws IOException, SAXException {
        Diff myDiff = new Diff(xml1, xml2);
        assertTrue(myDiff.similar());
        assertFalse(myDiff.identical());
    }
}
```

Fig. 2. Test case for validating equality and similarity of XML strings (Task 6)

extract lexical and syntactic features of missing elements from the tests while the context in which those elements appear might also help to understand their semantics.

For example, by solely relying on names and signatures, Code Conjurer did not retrieve anything related to XML processing for Task 6. Only one of the results out of the 10 retrieved happened to contain the keyword "xml" that was a statement importing the class org.allcolor.xml.parser.CStringTokenizer. The exception type org.xml.sax.SAXException thrown by the test method testDiff is part of a well-known API for processing XML documents. SAXException is not thrown by any of the resolvable methods in the test scenario; therefore, the functionality being sought should throw that exception. Incorporating this additional semantic fact could have helped to improve the relevance of retrieved results.

Searching for a Specific Implementation. Code Conjurer and CodeGenie managed to retrieve relevant results for Task 1 in which a Base64 encoder/decoder is sought. The class name, base64 is the name of a well-known algorithm. The method names encode and decode are common choices for a utility class offering such services. However, the Base64 encoder/decoder described in the tests extends the common variation of this algorithm and adds a few constraints. When decoding Base64 character sequences, it should detect and ignore invalid sequences and simply return NULL. Therefore, our

Task 1 is slightly different from most of the Base64 encoder/decoders available on the internet. None of the recommendations by Code Conjurer and CodeGenie offers the special behaviour expected. S6 fails to retrieve any results for the very same task. We speculate that it has retrieved various implementations of the Base64 algorithm through its initial keyword search, but not exactly the variation described in the tests; as none of them could pass the tests, they were all discarded in the end.

Most of the tasks reported by proponents of test-driven reuse approaches seek common variations of well-known algorithms and data structures. Using lexical and signature relevance criteria would yield multiple instances of such programs that can possibly pass the tests. However, similar to the example given above, if a variant were sought, relying on common terms and operation signatures would not suffice.

4.3   Threats to Validity

The primary question regarding generalizability of our study is the representativeness of the tasks. We took task ideas from the discussions in the Java developer community websites, and from code example catalogues commonly used as a reference by Java developers. Developers evidently find these features worthwhile to discuss and learn from, and not so easy to develop or to find. In addition, our five external evaluators consisting of three industrial developers and two graduate students found the tasks familiar in the sense that they had previously developed similar functionality. The number of trial tasks is another limiting factor of our study. However, it is comparable to the average number of tasks used in the evaluations in the TDR literature [5, 8, 13].

The modifications we made to the trial test cases in our study also threatens the validity of our study. Anonymization was performed to ensure that the facts in the test cases, other than the identity of the target project, could still contribute to identification of the solution. Test case refinement was done to remove test cases that exercised features beyond the scope of the study tasks. Neither anonymization nor refinement should negatively affect the retrieval capacity of the tools. To find the best strategy to overcome the tools' limitations, we experimented with different alternatives and compared results in each case. The alternative that yielded better results was chosen over others.

Test-driven reuse is a repetitive process. Searchers might reformulate their queries based on the current results in a way that may result in finding better results. This brings up the question of whether having a static query set is the right way to evaluate a code search tool. We deliberately ignored this issue by giving the tools the best possible queries by providing them with the test cases developed for the same code. We considered different existing variations of the features, and chose the ones that came with a reasonable test suite. This should have biased the results in favour of the tools.

Code relevance and effort categorization are subjective, and thus may differ from one developer to the next. It is often easy to say that one source code recommendation is more suitable than another, but the quantification of this difference is somewhat arbitrary. While our categorization of the relevance and effort of each recommendation represents our best judgment, a random subset of our categorizations was independently evaluated by experienced Java developers. The strong positive correlation between raters suggests our categorization of the results is reasonable.

Considering only the top 10 results for evaluating a retrieval algorithm might be overly restrictive, despite evidence that developers generally do not investigate more than the first 10 results [7]. However, in our experiment, the tools provided fewer than 10 recommendations in 22 out of the 30 cases. Therefore, we have considered all the results collected by the tools in more than 70% of the cases.

4.4 Precision versus Accuracy

The measures we used in our evaluation are qualitative and imprecise. Nevertheless, the results suffice to demonstrate that the approaches work poorly for these examples, and point to the need to address their underlying designs. Thus the results do provide *accuracy*: our criteria for rating the results are sufficiently well defined that our participants' ratings agreed to a degree that is quantitatively demonstrable.

The greater precision that would be obtained by using quantitative measures is not warranted—measuring degrees of "poor performance" would not provide us with a deeper understanding of the cause of the failure of these approaches. Only with an acceptable level of performance is it worthwhile to invest in precise measurements.

5 Conclusion

As test-driven development has gained in industrial popularity, the prospect of utilizing test cases as the basis for software reuse has become tantalizing: test cases can express a rich variety of structure and semantics that automated reuse tools can potentially utilize. However, the practice of test-driven development implies that the test cases that are written cannot be too heavily depended on as the absolute truth regarding the functionality that is sought.

We have performed an experiment on the three state-of-the-art tools for test-driven reuse, in which we found realistic, non-trivial tasks in developer forums, and for which a known solution existed in the tools' repositories. We used existing test cases that exercised the known solution as the basis of the input to the tools. All the tools failed in most cases to locate relevant source code that would be simple to reuse, and often recommended irrelevant source code.

One may posit that it is unrealistic to expect any TDR approach to *not* depend on the presence of specific names. If one works in a context where domain vocabulary is well-established (within a specific organization, or while utilizing a specific application programming interface [3]), this dependency could even be reasonable. However, we have illustrated that these approaches still do not suffice to find uncommon variations of functionality in the presence of a common vocabulary. Furthermore, we believe that demanding this limitation is defeatist: the desire to find useful functionality in the absence of known vocabulary is industrially reasonable and should not be dismissed.

We remain convinced of the value of the idea of TDR. To overcome the problems we have identified, alternative approaches need to be more flexible in recommending solutions, recognizing the inability of the developer to know exact vocabulary and that such vocabulary will often fail to suffice in locating a desired variation on common functionality. Other aspects of the rich information available in test cases could be leveraged to reduce the dependency on specific names, which would allow TDR to become a more general purpose and hence more generally useful approach. We are currently investigating alternative solutions to achieve this.

Acknowledgments. We thank Steven Reiss, Oliver Hummel, Werner Janjic, and Sushil Barjracharya for assisting us with their tools, and Brad Cossette, Rylan Cottrell, Soha Makady, and Valeh Hosseinzadeh Nasser for helpful suggestions in editing this paper. This work was supported by scholarships and grants from NSERC and IBM.

References

[1] Beck, K., Andres, C.: Extreme Programming Explained: Embrace Change, 2nd edn. Addison-Wesley Professional (2004)

[2] Holmes, R., Walker, R.: Systematizing pragmatic software reuse. ACM Trans. Softw. Eng. Methodol. 21(4), 20/1–20/44 (2012)

[3] Holmes, R., et al.: Approximate structural context matching: An approach to recommend relevant examples. IEEE Trans. Softw. Eng. 32(12), 952–970 (2006)

[4] Hummel, O., Atkinson, C.: Supporting agile reuse through extreme harvesting. In: Concas, G., Damiani, E., Scotto, M., Succi, G. (eds.) XP 2007. LNCS, vol. 4536, pp. 28–37. Springer, Heidelberg (2007)

[5] Hummel, O., et al.: Code Conjurer: Pulling reusable software out of thin air. IEEE Softw. 25(5), 45–52 (2008)

[6] Jeng, J.-J., Cheng, B.: Specification matching for software reuse: A foundation. In: Proc. ACM Symp. Softw. Reusabil., pp. 97–105 (1995)

[7] Joachims, T., et al.: Accurately interpreting clickthrough data as implicit feedback. In: Proc. ACM SIGIR Int. Conf. Info. Retrieval, pp. 154–161 (2005)

[8] Lemos, O., et al.: A test-driven approach to code search and its application to the reuse of auxiliary functionality. Info. Softw. Technol. 53(4), 294–306 (2011)

[9] Linstead, E., et al.: Sourcerer: Mining and searching internet-scale software repositories. Data Min. Knowl. Discov. 18(2), 300–336 (2009)

[10] Zaremski, A., Wing, J.: Signature matching: A key to reuse. In: Proc. ACM Int. Symp. Foundations Softw. Eng., pp. 182–190 (1993)

[11] Ossher, J., et al.: Automated dependency resolution for open source software. In: Proc. Working Conf. Min. Softw. Repos., pp. 130–140 (2010)

[12] Podgurski, A., Pierce, L.: Behavior sampling: A technique for automated retrieval of reusable components. In: Proc. Int. Conf. Softw. Eng., pp. 349–361 (1992)

[13] Reiss, S.: Semantics-based code search. In: Proc. Int. Conf. Softw. Eng., pp. 243–253 (2009)

Improving the Runtime-Processing of Test Cases for Component Adaptation

Dominic Seiffert[1] and Oliver Hummel[2]

[1] University of Mannheim, Germany
seiffert@informatik.uni-mannheim.de
http://score.informatik.uni-mannheim.de
[2] Karlsruhe Institute of Technology, Germany
hummel@kit.edu
http://sdq.ipd.kit.edu/

Abstract. Reusing existing code instead of reinventing it is considered a good development practice. However, current software search engines often deliver merely somewhat similar results that usually need to be adapted when they should be integrated into an existing system. Since adaptation is a tedious and error-prone activity it has been the target of automation approaches for numerous years, but only recently the use of test-driven adaptation, based on ordinary JUnit test cases, was able to provide a working prototype for this purpose. Unfortunately, the adapter creation lacks acceptable runtime behavior because it is based on a brute force algorithm, which significantly hinders the usability of test-driven adaptation in a test-driven reuse context where numerous, potentially complex candidates need to be adapted. Hence, in this paper, we present an optimized algorithm for this purpose that works in a branch-and-bound manner and demonstrate its capability by an "in-vitro" evaluation.

Keywords: signature matching, object adaptation, automated adapter generation, tool support.

1 Introduction

1.1 Reuse

In the 1960s McIlroy [22] proposed his vision of a market place for buying reusable software artifacts that could be simply plugged together to form complex applications. Ever since the composition of systems from reusable components or services has been a hallmark of a more engineering-like approach to software development. Beyond the use of common libraries and frameworks, however, reuse remains still complicated since syntactically not matching building blocks, i.e. components or services, are rather the rule than the exception. In order to overcome these mismatches, the ability to create adapters for mismatching building blocks has a high importance. However, since adaptation is an error-prone and tedious task it has been the target of numerous automation

J. Favaro and M. Morisio (Eds.): ICSR 2013, LNCS 7925, pp. 81–96, 2013.

attempts in recent years as we will discuss in the section on previous work later. Most of these previous approaches were based on formal description techniques and never produced a practically working tool, most likely due to fundamental problems caused by the halting problem and the complex description techniques required. Only recently, the idea of using test cases [15] for checking the feasibility of automatically created adapters paved the way towards a practically usable solution for this challenge. As of today this solution is unfortunately still based on a brute force approach that needs to check all theoretically possible adaptations against the test case to eventually identify a working mapping of operations and parameters in the adapter.

This paper contributes and evaluates an accelerated version of this fully automated adapter generation approach that is able to decrease runtime considerably. This is clearly the basis for better scalability and usability, e.g. for recent test-driven software reuse approaches [17]. Its remainder is structured as follows: First we will give a short introduction to test-driven development and its extension test-driven reuse. Then follows an introduction and motivation to adaptation and an overview of previous work from other authors. Then, the naive adaptation approach is introduced briefly in section no. 3 followed a comparison with the new approach by an "in-vitro" evaluation in section 4. Finally, we summarize the results and give an outlook on future work in section no. 5.

1.2   Test-Driven Reuse

The basic development cycle of test-driven development [3] is based on a maxim that originates from Extreme Programming [4]: "Design a little, test a little, program a little", i.e. writing the test case happens before (re)writing the code for the unit under test. Test-driven reuse [17] [16] goes one step further, as the interface of the unit under test is extracted automatically from the test case and used as input for a software search. The received syntactic information can then be used with a recent component search engine like Merobase [13] or Sourcerer [2] to find potential reuse candidates that can then also be tested automatically in a subsequent step.

Unfortunately, test cases can get quite large and therefore provide a lot of syntactic information for the desired component. In such a case, or when simply no exact match is available, even modern software search engines often deliver only similar results that usually do not fully match syntactically. Such a syntactic mismatch, however, does not necessarily imply a semantic mismatch as well. Nevertheless, in order to overcome such syntactic mismatches, usually the need for adaptation arises as we will discuss in the next section.

1.3   Adaptation

According to Becker et al. [5] "Software Component Adaptation is the sequence of the steps required to bridge a component mismatch." Thereby a component mismatch can occur on different levels, as technical or signature mismatches, for instance. In this paper we focus on signature mismatches and thereby aim to adapt Java objects on primitive type level. In the context of adaptation, objects are an even bigger challenge than components as they include state, identity and inheritance [7] which are usually immaterial for components or services.

Adaptation itself clearly has a long tradition (not only) in object oriented programming. In 1994, the Gang of Four recognized it as so important that the basic approach made its way into the well-known GoF design pattern catalog as the Adapter Pattern [12]. As this pattern still holds great importance in the context of object oriented programming and reuse today, we will summarize it briefly in the following. The pattern comes in two forms, namely a static and a dynamic variant. As we focus on adapting Java objects we will neglect the static variant since it is based on multiple inheritance which is not supported by Java. Figure 1 illustrates the adaptation problem where a *Client* relies on some *Target* interface. However, the *Client* would like to use the functionality provided by the *Adaptee* behind a different interface. Thus, an interposed adapter object is necessary that provides the interface required by the client and also translates the messaging between *Client* and *Adaptee*. In the best case the *Client* should not recognize that he is communicating with the *Adaptee* only indirectly, or in other words, the adapter is supposed to be fully transparent.

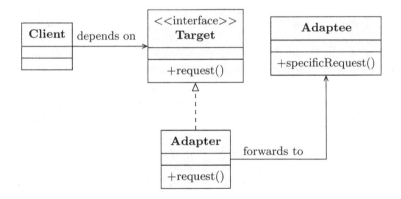

Fig. 1. Gang of Four Adapter Pattern

Let us assume that the *request* method of the *Target* interface is a method that encapsulates the exact same functionality as the *specificRequest* method by the *Adaptee*. We further assume that both methods expect 4 integer parameters, but we do not know the order in which the *specificRequest* method expects them. Thus, it would be a task of the assigned developer to check the factorial of 4 possible parameter mappings and to wire them into the adapter.

This simple example already shows that adaptation can easily become a very time consuming and error-prone task. That automatic adaptation is something developers have an actual need for, can for example be underlined by a query *adapter** on the Merobase component search engine, that delivers 91,926 results.

Other motivating examples on the interoperability in Java based computer algebra software can be found, for instance, in [20]. Furthermore, Kell [18] provides a comprehensive overview on numerous adaptation techniques that have been developed in recent years. Thus, we can conclude that there is obviously a practical need for highly automated tool support in adapter creation.

Our goal is hence to provide a fully automated adapter generation solution for Java objects improving previous work [15] in terms of runtime and memory usage. Thereby, although different mismatch types exist, as further explained by [5, page 197], in this work we focus on mismatches caused by deviating method names and parameter ordering. Our ongoing research [27] is concerned with the solution of the other mismatch types, which shall get integrated later. We will explain previous works in automating software adaptation and the test-driven adaptation approach that is the basis for this work in the following sections.

2   Previous Work

To our knowledge there have been numerous attempts to automate software adaptation, however, there has no fully automated approach been published in literature until very recently. Those approaches that actually have been existing for a longer time, usually only partially automate the adaptation creation or require some (semi-)formal adapter description to be able to establish an adapter at all. This obviously forms an additional overhead for the users of the approach compared to using simple test cases. For instance, Bracciali et al. [8] present a methodology that enriches component interfaces with behavioral descriptions and uses a high-level notation for expressing adapter specifications to automatically generate concrete adapters. These high-level notations are more complex to write than simple test cases and therefore already create an additional overhead in the context of adaptation and reuse. The same applies for Autili et al.ś approach [1] where a high level behavioral description for each component plus a specification of the component interactions is required as manually defined input for automatically deriving a composition code for a component-based system. This specification and high level description are an overhead compared to test cases. Canal et al. [9] provide an approach that takes behavioral interfaces of components to be adapted and an adaptation contract as input for a tool that automatically generates adapter protocols only. Again, the adaptation contract is based on a formal language and thus an additional overhead to master. Martin et al. [21] propose the automatic generation of adaptation contracts from the behavioral description of services. Future work should generate adapters from these contracts, but so far their approach takes more time for adapter contract generation the bigger the incompatibilies between the services get, which means a possible long waiting period. Bertolino et al. [6] present with Strawberry an interesting method, concerning orchestration in the context of web services that automatically derives an automaton from a web-service signature that models its behavior protocol with a combination of synthesis and testing techniques. Unfortunately, as a case study shows, testing takes long time and is therefore more usable for offline-analysis. Nita et al. [24] propose a tool called Twinning that allows programmers to maintain differences from an existing base program in terms of code level mappings. The prototype uses an iterative approach where type errors thrown during compilation should help to identify the next piece of code to address in the mapping of the adapter. Only recently, Kell [19] introduced Cake, a rule based language for describing relations between the interfaces of binary components that also allows adapting complex object structures. However, it is still neccessary to learn a language for manually defining the rules and the approach heavily depends on the knowledge of the programmer, as the programmer should understand the interface he is coding against, whereby debug informations is intended to help gaining that understanding.

As we see, there is no fully automated adaptation approach existing yet and relatively complex formal description languages are widely used for specifying the internal wiring of the adapter manually. Merely the approach developed in our group in recent years is able to work fully autonomously, based on simple unit tests that enable the testing environment to figure out the internal adapter wiring automatically.

3   Automating Adaptation

In this section we start with a simple adaptation challenge for a component performing arithmetic operations. The required interface extracted of the client (the test case) is shown on the left-hand side and the one provided by the adaptee SimpleMath on the right-hand side. The naming of the methods indicates the solution for the method mappings already, as shown by the arrows. At a first glance the equal method names indicate that a direct mapping is possible. But it is not, as SimpleAdaptee expects the parameters x and y in inverse order for each method to deliver the results as expected.

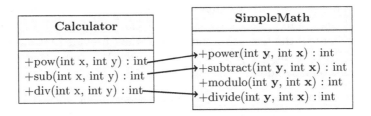

Fig. 2. An exemplary adaptation challenge

Starting with the first step of test-driven reuse resp. development, the test case for the Calculator is provided in listing 1.1. There, in line no. 11, a new *Calculator* object is declared and initialized. Lines 12 to 14 check for the semantic fitness the Calculator expects.

Listing 1.1. JUnit testcase example

```
1
2    package  testcases;
3
4    import junit.framework.TestCase;
5
6    import adapter.Calculator;
7
8    public class SimpleTest extends junit.framework.TestCase {
9
10     public void testMethod(){
11       Calculator calculator = new Calculator();
12       assertEquals(2, calculator.pow(2, 1));
13       assertEquals(2, calculator.sub(4, 2));
14       assertEquals(5, calculator.div(10,2));
15     }
16   }
```

The attempt to compile this code will obviously yield an error, since the *Calculator* object does not exist yet. This problem is solved by an internal parser of the adaptation tool which is part of a so called *TestCoordinator* that parses the interface to test out of the testcase file and creates a temporary adapter file *adapter.Calculator*, as specified in the import in line 6.

The concrete adapter file for each test run is only temporary since the method and parameter mappings for the adaptee change during for each test run so that it would be a significant overhead to create a new adapter each time the mappings change. Thus, the wirings are managed by a so called *Permutator* instance which stands between the adapter and the adaptee. This instance is able to change its wirings dynamically on request. When the processing has come to a successful end, the result is automatically hardwired into the final adapter which has the correct wirings fixed then. More information on this idea can be found in [14].

3.1 Naive Approach

In this section we briefly explain the processing of the naive approach [15] which is based on a brute force assessment. In the first step all possible adapters are created. This step can be further subdivided: First, as illustrated by the algorithm in listing 1.2, signature matches are established for each method of the interface extracted out of the test case, and each method provided by the adaptee. Thereby signatures do match, if the return type and the number and respective types of parameters are equal.

Listing 1.2. Discovering feasible method mappings

```
for each method in the adapter
  initialize empty List listₘ of method mappings
  for each method in the candidate
    if signatures do match
      add method mapping to listₘ
    endif
  endfor
endfor
```

After the algorithm in listing 1.2 has been executed, $list_m$ contains the following entries, whereby the right arrow is used to indicate a "is forwarded to" relation:

```
pow -> power + subtract + divide + modulo
sub -> power + subtract + divide + modulo
div -> power + subtract + divide + modulo
```

After these mappings have been established, they are combined according to the next algorithm in listing no. 1.3. For the sake of practicality, no method of the candidate may appear twice in an adapter combination.

Listing 1.3. Combine Mappings

```
initialize empty List list₁ of combinations
for each method in the adapter
 initialize empty List list₂ of combinations
 for each mapping in the listₘ
  for each entry in list1 or once if empty
   if candidate method not used in list2 so far
  add method mapping to list2
  endfor
 endfor
 list1 = list2
endfor
```

Three of six feasible combinations (one per line) as obtained from the algorithm above are for instance:

```
1. div -> divide, sub -> subtract, pow -> power
2. div -> subtract, sub -> power, pow -> divide
3. div -> power, pow -> divide, pow -> subtract
```

Next, we consider parameter mappings for each method. That is, the mappings above have to be combined with the feasible parameter permutations which can be derived in the next two stages of the permutation creation process. In the first stage, each method needs to identify which of its parameter can be matched on which parameter in the candidate method, as demonstrated by the div $\to$ div mapping:

```
div(int x, int y) ->
    divide(int y, int x)

This yields to:

x -> y (int -> int)
x -> x (int -> int)
y -> x (int -> int)
y -> y (int -> int)
```

This list is combined under the constraint that no parameter is used twice per method adaptation.

Finally, in the last step, all possible combinations are created, i.e. method adaptations are combined with their appropriate parameter permutations. Thereby the notation (1) as the first and (2) as the second permutation step is used. One possible adapter combination (out of the set of all possible adapter combinations) is (pow $\to$ power (2), sub $\to$ subtract (2), div$\to$ modulo (1)) for instance.

Obviously, the set of adapter combinations can get quite large for many possible method and parameter mappings.

In the last step each combination is tested for its semantic fitness in a brute force manner one after the other.

3.2 Optimized Approach

The main novel ideas of the new approach are, first, to avoid calculating large permutation tables for the parameter permutations. This is realized by adapting an algorithm from Rosen [26] that allows us to calculate the next permutation step with the knowledge of the former step and some other spare info. Therefore a wrapper instance is assigned for each method of the extracted interface, and the wrapper instance holds a reference to the currently assigned adaptee method match. This wrapper instance controls the permutation processing for that match. We use a tree representation as provided in figure 3 to illustrate the approach in the following. The three levels of the tree represent method mappings, the nodes permutation steps. The dashed node connections remind us that these paths i.e. combinations will be calculated on demand only. For illustration reasons we assume that (pow → power, sub → subtract, div → modulo) are the first method mappings to start with, each initialized with the first permutation step, which leads to combination (pow → power (1), sub → subtract (1), div → modulo (1))

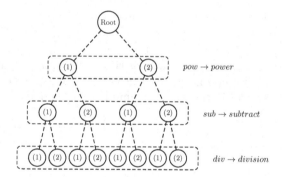

Fig. 3. Initialization of the new approach

The second idea is, that we use the semantics delivered by the test file, i.e. the expected results for each call, to approach the expected solution(s) of the test file in a branch-and-bound manner. For instance, as the testing process starts with (pow → power (1), sub → subtract (1), div→ modulo (1)) in our example, the test run already fails for the first position as shown by figure 4 on page 90. Thus, combinations that have the failing mapping set on the first position can be neglected (branched) as shown by figures 5 to 8, and combination (pow → power (2), sub → subtract (1), div → modulo (1)) is chosen next. The brute force approach would have continued with any arbitrary combination according to its storage structure instead.

The processing continues as shown by figures 9 to 10 and reaches the adapter combination (pow → power (2), sub → subtract (2), div→ modulo (1)) in figure 11. The first two mappings are tested successfully in the test run, but the third mapping div → mod (1) fails. Therefore the two successful mappings specify a bound as they are remembered for the next test run, i.e. their current permutation steps are kept fixed whereas the mapping on third position div → mod (1) is incremented from permutation step 1 to 2. That is, the combination (pow → power (2), sub → subtract (2), div→ modulo (2)) in figure 13 is tested next. Since the third mapping fails again, but no more permutation step is available, this mapping needs to find another method match which is available by div → div. After changing the method match the processing continues as illustrated by figures 14 to 17.

In the given example the third mapping was able to change its method mapping as illustrated by figure 14 and 15. But if a situation occurs where this is not possible, backtracking to an earlier position needs to happen. For instance, given a combination (a → b (1), c → d(2), e → f(2)) where the first two positions are tested successfully but the third mapping is wrong for a test run, and e cannot find another match, backtracking happens back to the second position. Thereby the permutation step for the second mapping would be incremented and the next combination to search for is (a → b (1), c → d(3), e ≠ f). If we assume that no third permutation step is available for the second position, backtracking happens to the first position. This means (a → b (1), c ≠ d, e ≠ f) would be the combination to search for.

4   Evaluation

In this section we present a comparison between the naive algorithm and the new approach by the following two criteria, and also discuss the question if the current approach has the potential to adapt components than we can find in the "wild":

1. method invocations
2. time

The first criterion `method invocations` states the frequency of how often an actual adaptee method is invoked during the whole testing process. This is an important criterion since a method invocation eats up sifnificant time during processing. The second criterion,`execution time`, was measured on an Intel(R) Core(TM) i5 CPU M480 2.67GHZ machine with 4 GB RAM.

For a detailed listing of all JUnit test and adaptee files, we briefly present in the following, please see our homepage[1] again for details.

For the sake of completeness we provide the correct adapter-adaptee method mappings for the test files in table 1 on page 93. The first column states the test case and its extracted methods to test. The third column shows possible

---

[1] `http://oliverhummel.com/adaptation/tool.zip`

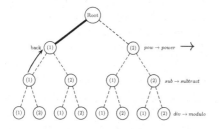

Fig. 4. Combination no. 1

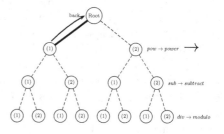

Fig. 5. Backtracking

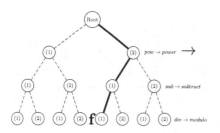

Fig. 6. Skipping comb. no. 2

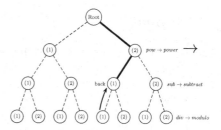

Fig. 7. Skipping comb. no. 3 and 4

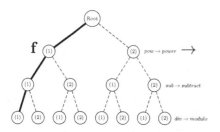

Fig. 8. Testing comb. no. 5

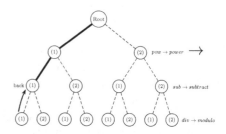

Fig. 9. Backtracking

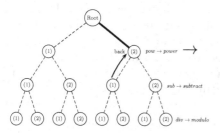

Fig. 10. Skipping comb. no. 6

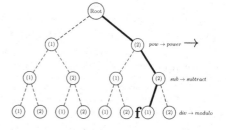

Fig. 11. Testing comb. no. 7

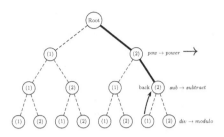

Fig. 12. Backtracking

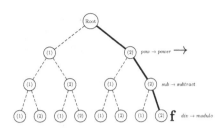

Fig. 13. Testing comb. no. 8

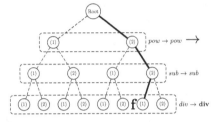

Fig. 14. Changing method and testing config no. 15

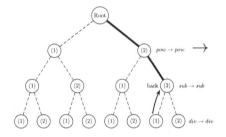

Fig. 15. Backtracking

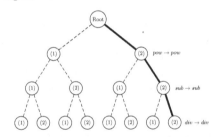

Fig. 16. Success with config no. 16

mappings on the adaptee's methods. The fourth column states the number of possible permutation steps for each mapping, that is, a method with three parameters provides 3! possible permutation steps. This corresponds exactly with the number of possible method invocations. The last row shows the worst case for all mappings, i.e. the limit of possible steps (method invocations) to run through in order to find the correct mappings. For instance, the MatrixTest, in the upper part of table table 1, has a limit of 48 possible permutation steps (method invocations) to run through. Thereby, *MatrixTest* sets some values on three matrix objects and does a matrix multiplication then. The method `multiply(Matrix):Matrix` provides and delivers a self-referencing type. The former implementation and the new implementation can handle such a situation automatically, i.e. adaptation for self-referencing types is supported by our tool, through maintaining references to instances, as further explained in [14]. This idea is similar to the "Identity Map" pattern suggested by Fowler [11] for keeping track of object instances loaded from a database.

The *CalculatorTest*, in the middle part in table 1, searches for calculation and parameter changing methods.

The test files *Test5 ... Test8*, in the lower part, are especially interesting for runtime reasons because they provide a lot of possible permutations steps and therefore a lot of possible method invocations to run through. To be more precise, the test methods in *Test5 ... Test8* expect numbers (as Strings) to be returned by the adaptee in an ascending order, whereas the adaptee, played by *SimpleAdaptee*, returns them unordered if the adaptee's method is invoked with the parameter ordering by the test case. Thus, the naive algorithm has to run through a lot of combinations to find the correct wirings.

4.1   Results

The results are presented in table 2 where the first column of each table contains the JUnit test files. The second column shows the results of the new approach in comparison with the naive approach shown in the third column. The fourth column shows what is saved by the new approach compared to the naive approach. No results are available for Test7 and Test8 when using the naive approach, since execution time simply takes too long.

Obviously, the new approach is much faster than the naive approach [15], as for instance, the brute force approach takes more than 155,500 method invocations for Test6, which leads to a waiting period of approximately 48 minutes on our system, whereas the new approach takes only 810 method invocations, what takes less than a second. The difference for the CalculatorTest is much smaller with about 49 seconds (6,609 method invocations) for the naive approach and about 1 second (341 method invocations) for the new approach. For the MatrixTest the difference concerning execution time is negligible because both approaches take less than a second, with 129 respectively 55 method invocations.

4.2   Discussion

Our current approach shows acceptable runtime behavior and thus a promising scalability. Currently the adaptation processing is possible if primitive or self-referencing types are provided by the adaptee's methods. Furthermore, methods with different names and different parameter names and parameter orders can be adapted. Thus, there are still some more complex adaptation challenges open, which are currently under research [27], and whose solutions should be integrated later. These challenges are identified by the following signature mismatch types [5, page 197] that we briefly want to list:

1. Naming of Exceptions.
2. Typing of Methods, Parameters and Exceptions.

Table 1. Mappings overview

MatrixTest	→	MatrixAdaptee	Possible permutation steps
set	→	set	$3! = 6$
get	→	get	$2! = 2$
multiply	→	add + sub + mult + mulitply	$1! + 1! + 1! + 1! = 4$
Limit of possible steps			$6*2*4 = 48$

Calculator	→	CalculatorAdaptee	Possible permutation steps
sub	→	doNothing5 + sub	$3! + 3! = 12$
add	→	doNothing4 + add	$2! + 2! = 4$
checkIt	→	checkStorage + crash + getStorage + test	$0 + 0 + 0 + 0 = 0$
getVariable	→	checkStorage + crash + getStorage +test	$0 + 0 + 0 + 0 = 0$
testThis	→	testIt + doNothing2	$1! + 1! = 2$
noParam	→	checkStorage + crash + getStorage + test	$0 + 0 + 0 + 0 = 0$
getAnotherCalculator →		getAnother + doNothing1	$1! + 1! = 2$
changeVariable	→	changeStorage + doNothing3	$4! + 4! = 48$
Limit of possible steps			$12 * 4 * 2 * 48 = 4{,}608$

Test5	→	SimpleAdaptee	Possible permutation steps
permutate5	→	fiveParams	$5! = 120$
permutate6	→	sixParams	$6! = 720$
Limit of possible steps			$5! * 6! = 86{,}400$

Test6	→	SimpleAdaptee	Possible permutation steps
permutate3	→	threeParams	$3! = 6$
permutate5	→	fiveParams	$5! = 120$
permutate6	→	sixParams	$6! = 720$
Limit of possible steps			$3! * 5! * 6! = 518{,}400$

Test7	→	SimpleAdaptee	Possible permutation steps
permutate4	→	fourParams	$4! = 24$
permutate5	→	fiveParams	$5! = 120$
permutate6	→	sixParams	$6! = 720$
Limit of possible steps			$4! * 5! * 6! = 2{,}073{,}600$

Test8	→	SimpleAdaptee	Possible permutation steps
permutate3	→	threeParams	$3! = 6$
permutate4	→	fourParams	$4! = 24$
permutate5	→	fiveParams	$5! = 120$
permutate6	→	sixParams	$6! = 720$
Limit of possible steps			$3! * 4! * 5! * 6! = 12{,}441{,}600$

3. Structuring of Complex Types.
4. Numbering of parameters.

If we compare our approach with the techniques and approaches presented in the previous work on page 84 we see that we have presented the basis for an automated adaptation approach that involves the least overhead for human developers so far, as the semantic descriptions used for adapter creation in our case are ordinary test cases that are usually created during software development

Table 2. Evaluation Results

Number of method invocations			
Testcase	brute force approach	new approach	saving (%)
MatrixTest	129 invocations	55 invocations	57.4
CalculatorTest	6,609 invocations	341 invocations	94.5
Test5	42,591 invocations	176 invocations	99.6
Test6	155,500 invocations	810 invocations	99.5
Test7	-	846 invocations	-
Test8	-	889 invocations	-

Time			
Testcase	brute force approach	new approach	saving (%)
MatrixTest	312 ms	92 ms	70.5
CalculatorTest	$\approx$ 49 sec	1,119 ms	97.7
Test5	15 min	398 ms	99.9
Test6	48 min	892 ms	99.9
Test7	-	1,125 ms	-
Test8	-	1,203 ms	-

anyway. Clearly, the evaluation in its current form is only a proof of concept and thus a first step as it only deals with rather artificial examples. However, it is currently only intended to demonstrate the improvements concerning speed, which it does. Especially the examples Test5 and Test6 require a large number of possible method invocations on an adaptee instance.

5   Outlook and Future Work

Although we are able to adapt Java objects on a subset of signatures mismatching types [5, page 197] (which are the ordering of parameters and the naming of methods and parameters), there are still open research challenges beyond supporting these missing mismatch types: Currently, we are considering other research areas such as schema [25] or ontology mapping [10], in order to further improve the mapping performance of our approach based on heuristics from natural language processing. Another question is whether numerous partially matched candidates can also be addressed by one adapter, that is, we are attempting to call more than one adaptee from one adapter (which than becomes rather a facade [12]) or even try to adapt an ensemble of classes at once. Important future work thus includes covering some additional adaptation challenges, a comprehensive evaluation with numerous arbitrary "real-world" adaptation challenges, e.g. retrieved from common open-source repositories and last but not least an integration of our tool into a common development environment such as Eclipse or into a tool like Code-Conjurer [16] so that speed and applicability of test-driven reuse can be further improved.

6   Conclusion

In this paper we have presented an approach that speeds up the automatic adaptation of Java objects based on ordinary (JUnit) test cases. Our solution integrates seamlessly and without additional overhead into common test-driven software development processes where test cases are supposed to be created before production code is written and thus simplifies so-called test-driven reuse [17] in this context. For this purpose, we have explained how the partial semantic description of desired functionality contained in test cases can be used as a starting point for adapter creation. Furthermore, we have presented an efficient algorithm that can be used for implementing the "matchmaking" between an interface specified by a test case and a reuse candidate at hand (i.e. the adaptee), and made available a tool that demonstrates the approach in practice. We believe that it nicely complements recent research efforts for improving software reuse through powerful software search engines for source code, components and services and in fact, we intend towards further improving the adaptation capabilities for this context.

References

1. Autili, M., Inverardi, P., Navarra, A., Tivoli, M.: Synthesis: A tool for automatically assembling correct and distributed component-based systems. In: Proceedings of the 29th International Conference on Software Engineering, pp. 784–787 (2007)
2. Bajracharya, S., Ossher, J., Lopes, C.: Sourcerer: An internet-scale software repository. In: Workshop on Search-Driven Development-Users, Infrastructure, Tools and Evaluation. SUITE 2009, pp. 1–4. ICSE (2009)
3. Beck, K.: Test-Driven Development by Example. Addison-Wesley (2003)
4. Beck, K., Andres, C.: Extreme Programming Explained: Embrace Change, 2nd edn. Addison-Wesley Professional (2004)
5. Becker, S., Brogi, A., Gorton, I., Overhage, S., Romanovsky, A., Tivoli, M.: Towards an engineering approach to component adaption. In: Reussner, R., Stafford, J.A., Ren, X.-M. (eds.) Architecting Systems with Trustworthy Components. LNCS, vol. 3938, pp. 193–215. Springer, Heidelberg (2006)
6. Bertolino, A., Inverardi, P., Pelliccione, P., Tivoli, M.: Automatic synthesis of behavior protocols for composable web-services. In: ESEC/SIGSOFTFSE, pp. 141–150 (2009)
7. Booch, G.: Object-oriented development. IEEE Transactions on Software Engineering 12(2), 211–221 (1986)
8. Bracciali, A., Brogi, A., Canal, C.: A formal approach to component adaptation. Journal of Systems and Software 74, 45–54 (2005)
9. Canal, C., Poizat, P., Salauen, G.: Model-based adaptation of behavioral mismatching components. IEEE Transactions on Software Engineering 34, 546–563 (2008)
10. Euzenat, J., Shvaiko, P.: Ontology Matching, 1st edn. Springer Publishing Company, Incorporated (2010)
11. Fowler, M.: Patterns of Enterprise Application Architecture. Addison-Wesley (2003)
12. Gamma, E., Helm, R., Johnson, R.E., Vlissides, J.: Design Patterns: Elements of Reusable Object-Oriented Software. Addison-Wesley (1995)

13. Hummel, O.: Semantic Component Retrival in Software Engineering. Phd thesis, Fakueltaet fuer Mathematik und Informatik, Universitaet Mannheim (2008)
14. Hummel, O., Atkinson, C.: The managed adapter pattern: Facilitating glue code generation for component reuse. In: Edwards, S.H., Kulczycki, G. (eds.) ICSR 2009. LNCS, vol. 5791, pp. 211–224. Springer, Heidelberg (2009)
15. Hummel, O., Atkinson, C.: Automated creation and assessment of component adapters with test cases. In: Grunske, L., Reussner, R., Plasil, F. (eds.) CBSE 2010. LNCS, vol. 6092, pp. 166–181. Springer, Heidelberg (2010)
16. Hummel, O., Janjic, W., Atkinson, C.: Code conjurer: Pulling reusable software out of thin air. IEEE Computer 25, 45–52 (2008)
17. Hummel, O., Janjic, W.: Test-driven reuse: Key to improving precision of search engines for software reuse. In: Sim, S.E., Gallardo-Valencia, R.E. (eds.) Finding Code on the Web for Remix and Reuse, vol. 1. Springer (2013)
18. Kell, S.: A survey of practical software adaptation techniques. Journal of Universal Computer Science 14, 2110–2157 (2008)
19. Kell, S.: Component adaptation and assembly using interface relations. In: Proceedings of the ACM International Conference on Object Oriented Programming Systems Languages and Applications, OOPSLA 2010, pp. 322–340. ACM, New York (2010) ISBN 978-1-4503-0203-6
20. Kredel, H.: Fostering the interoperability in java-based computer alegra systems. In: International Conference on Advanced Information Networking and Applications Workshops, vol. 26, pp. 443–447 (2012)
21. Martin, J.A., Pimentel, E.: Automatic generation of adaptation contracts. In: Proceedings of the 7th International Workshop on the FOCLASA 2008. Electronic Notes in Theoretical Computer Science, pp. 115–131 (2009)
22. McIlroy, M.D.: In software-engineering: Report of a conference sponsored by the nato science commitee, germisch, germany. In: Mass-Produced Software Components (1968)
23. Meyer, B.: Applying design by contract. IEEE Computer Society Press 25, 40–51 (1992)
24. Nita, M., Notkin, D.: Using twinning to adapt programs to alternative apis. In: 2010 ACM/IEEE 32nd International Conference on Software Engineering, vol. 1, pp. 205–214 (May 2010)
25. Rahm, E., Bernstein, P.A.: A survey of approaches to automatic schema matching. The VLDB Journal 10, 334–350 (2001) ISSN 1066-8888
26. Rosen, K.H.: Discrete Mathematics and Its Applications, 2nd edn. McGraw-Hill (1991)
27. Seiffert, D.: Automating the wrapping of software building blocks with test cases. In: Proceedings of the 17th International Doctoral Symposium on Components and Architecture, pp. 19–24 (2012)

REARM: A Reuse-Based Economic Model for Software Reference Architectures

Silverio Martínez-Fernández[1], Claudia P. Ayala[1], Xavier Franch[1],
and Helena Martins Marques[2]

[1] GESSI Research Group, Universitat Politècnica de Catalunya, Barcelona, Spain
{smartinez,cayala,franch}@essi.upc.edu
[2] *everis*, Barcelona, Spain
hmartinm@everis.com

Abstract. To remain competitive, organizations are challenged to make informed and feasible value-driven design decisions in order to ensure the quality of their software systems. However, there is a lack of support for evaluating the economic impact of these decisions with regard to software reference architectures. This damages the communication among architects and management, which can result in poor decisions. This paper aims at ameliorating this problem by presenting a pragmatic preliminary economic model to perform cost-benefit analysis on the adoption of software reference architectures as a key asset for optimizing architectural decision-making. The model is based on existing value-based metrics and economics-driven models used in other areas. A preliminary validation based on a retrospective study showed the ability of the model to support a cost-benefit analysis presented to the management of an IT consulting company. This validation involved a cost-benefit analysis related to reuse and maintenance; other qualities will be integrated as our research progresses.

Keywords: Software architecture, reference architecture, economic model, architecture evaluation, cost-benefit analysis, quality attributes.

1 Introduction and Motivation

Nowadays, the size and complexity of software systems, together with critical time-to-market needs, demand new software engineering approaches to software development. One of these approaches is the use of software reference architectures (RA), which are becoming widely studied and adopted in research and practice [3][19].

As defined by Bass et al. [5], an RA is "a reference model mapped onto software elements (that cooperatively implement the functionality defined in the reference model) and the data flows between them". An RA encompasses the knowledge about how to design concrete software architectures (SA) of systems of a given domain; it must address the business rules, architectural styles, best practices of software development, and the software elements that support development of systems [28].

The motivations behind RAs are: to systematically reuse knowledge and software elements when developing concrete SA for new systems and thereby harvest potential

J. Favaro and M. Morisio (Eds.): ICSR 2013, LNCS 7925, pp. 97–112, 2013.

savings through reduced cycle times, cost, risk and increased quality [11]; to help with the evolution of a set of systems that stem from the same RA [18]; and to ensure standardization and interoperability [3].

However, although the adoption of an RA might have plenty of benefits for an organization, it also implies several challenges, among them the need for an initial investment [18]. Hence, in order to use RAs, organizations face a fundamental question: "Is it worth to invest on the adoption of an RA?"

Thus, organizations need to ensure the feasibility of adopting an RA by assessing their goals, the resources they can invest and the expected benefits. In spite of this need, there is a lack of research methods for economics-driven RA evaluation [29]. Besides, there is a shortage of economic models to "precisely evaluate the benefit of 'architecture projects' - those that aim to improve one or more quality attributes of a system" [8]. Thus, the adoption of RAs is usually made without evaluating their economic impact. To make informed decisions, it becomes necessary to make a business case in order to know how many instantiations (i.e., applications) are necessary before savings pay off for the up-front investment in building an RA.

The goal of this paper is to present a pragmatic preliminary economic model to perform cost-benefit analysis on the adoption of RAs as a key asset for optimizing architectural decision-making (referred to as REARM, REference ARchitecture Model). This goal is of interest for researchers for the need of formulating accurate models and practitioners for the opportunity of making more informed decision-making about whether to implement the strategic move to RA adoption. Due to the aforementioned lack of research in this specific area, we have aimed at adopting and adapting existing results in related areas, from classical software reuse to product line engineering.

It is worth mentioning that the paper has its origin in an ongoing action-research [36] initiative among our research group and *everis*, a multinational consulting company based in Spain. The architecture group of *everis* experienced the inability to calculate the return on investment (ROI) derived from RAs that they create for organizations. The model stemming from this collaboration is currently under formative evaluation [36], but results so far are already triggering change in some development processes in the organization (e.g., bug reporting). As part of the collaboration, we had the chance to provide an initial validation of the economic model. It comprises a retrospective evaluation of an RA created by *everis* for the IT department of a public administration center in Spain.

2   Background and Related Work

Current research on RA evaluation consists of analysis methods [2][17][21] that involve the analysis of risks, non-risks, benefits and trade-offs. Although they facilitate the analysis of those aspects based on the most important and critical scenarios, they have little support to analyze the cost and benefits of RAs based on economics.

Introducing an RA into an organization involves making a decision of a greater degree than only considering the aforementioned aspects, since it should not only include quality, but it should also include productivity issues. Whereas architectural quality is usually estimated in relation to eliciting implicit and explicit requirements of the different stakeholders affected by the development of the system, productivity is actually measured in terms of effort, cost, and economic benefits. Nevertheless, both views are necessary to achieve a comprehensive analysis of the system.

Up to our knowledge, there is no specific economic model for estimating whether it is worth or not to invest in an RA for an organization. Due to the lack of research in this specific area, we have aimed at adopting and adapting existing results in related areas: economic models for software product lines (SPL), cost-benefit analysis methods for SAs, and more generic metrics about cost savings.

Economic Models for Software Product Lines and Software Reuse. The terms RA and product line architecture (PLA) are sometimes used indistinctly inside the SPL engineering context, in which the term RA is used to refer to "a core architecture that captures the high-level design for the applications of the SPL" [33, p. 124] or "just one asset, albeit an important one, in the SPL's asset base" [9, p. 12].

However, out of the SPL context, RA and PLA are considered different types of artifacts [3][12][19][28]. In Fig. 1 we show the main similarities and differences:

- PLAs are RAs whereas not all RAs are PLAs [3], i.e. PLAs are one type of RAs [19]. PLAs are just one asset of SPL [9, p. 12].
- RAs are more generic and abstract than PLAs that are more complete architectures [3][19]. Hence, "RAs can be designed with an intended scope of a single organization or multiple organizations that share a certain property" [3] whereas PLAs are produced for a single organization [19].
- RAs provide standardized solutions for a broader domain (i.e., "spectrum of systems in a technology or application domain" [19]) whereas PLAs provide standardized solutions for a smaller subset of the software systems of a domain [28] (i.e., "group of systems that are part of a product line" [19]). Therefore, PLAs give a coherent and more congruent view of the products in a project (i.e., possible to track the status of) [12] whereas by means of RAs it is more difficult to obtain congruence [3], since they can only provide guidelines for applications' development.
- PLAs specifically address points of variability and more formal specification in order to ensure clear and precise behavior specifications at well-specified extension points [3]. In contrast, RAs have less focus on capturing variation points [3][12][28]. Although variability is not typically addressed by RAs in a systematic manner, it is also a key fact for RAs [18], and it can be treated as a quality attribute, rather than explicitly as 'features' and 'decisions' [18].
- RAs include "the reuse of knowledge about software development in a given domain, in particular with regard to architectural design" [28] and dictate the patterns and principles to implement, i.e. "what the design should be" [12]. Conversely, PLAs specifically indicate deviations, i.e. "what the design is" [12].
- RAs include architectural knowledge and the instantiation of this architectural knowledge (i.e., reference model) into software elements [5]. In this sense, both RAs and PLAs are "a superset, a tool box, with every possible architecture element described, which can be used in the design of a product architecture" [12].

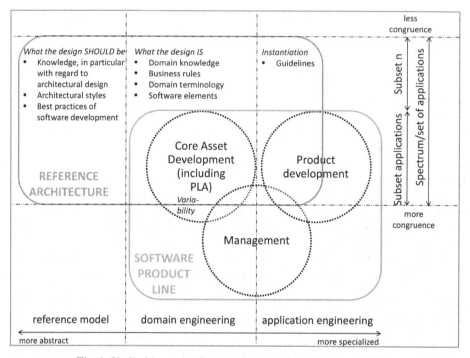

Fig. 1. Similarities and differences between RAs, PLAs, and SPLs

Although we also consider that RA and PLA are different, some perceived benefits of RA (e.g., cost saving from reusing software elements) and cost-benefit factors (e.g., common software costs, unique development costs) are applicable to both, since both have reuse as their core strategy. For this reason, we studied the applicability of some economic models originally conceived for SPL to RAs. Below, we summarize our results with respect to cost and benefit factors. To see more models, the reader is referred to [1], in which Ali et al. surveyed twelve economic models for SPL, and to [16][27] in which the authors surveyed economic models for software reuse.

Cost and Benefit Factors of Economic Models. SIMPLE [10], Poulin's model [34], and COPLIMO [7] are some of the most widespread economic models for SPLs.
    SIMPLE [10] comprises a set of seven cost factors:

- C_{org}, upfront investments to establish a SPL infrastructure.
- C_{cab}, the cost to build reusable assets of the SPL.
- C_{unique}, the cost to develop unique parts of products in a SPL.
- C_{reuse}, the cost of reusing reusable assets in a product inside the SPL.
- C_{cabu}, the cost to evolve the core asset in a SPL.
- C_{prod}, the cost to build a product in a stand-alone fashion.
- C_{evo}, the cost to evolve a product in a stand-alone fashion.

These cost factors and benefit functions can be used to construct equations that can answer a number of questions such as whether the SPL approach is the best option for development and what is the ROI for this approach. Ganesan et al. extended SIMPLE by considering infrastructure degeneration over time [20].

On the other hand, Poulin [34] and Boehm et al. [7] base their reuse-based models in two parameters: RCR and RCWR.

- RCR (Relative Cost of Reuse). Assuming that the cost to develop a reusable asset equals one unit of effort, RCR is the portion of this effort that it takes to reuse a reusable asset without modification (black-box reuse).
- RCWR (Relative Cost of Writing for Reuse). Assuming that the cost to develop a new asset for one-time use equals one unit of effort, RCWR is the portion of this effort that it takes to write a similar "reusable" asset.

For those cases in which there are difficulties to obtain historical data of building and evolving products in a stand-alone fashion (C_{prod}, C_{evo}), we consider more adequate the use of RCR and RCWR (see Section 4.1, step 2).

Finally, we must note two models (Schmid [37], InCoME [30]) that integrate cost and investment models in different layers, which make them more comprehensive.

Value of Software Architecture Design Decisions. There exist a few economics-based SA analysis methods that drive the decision-making process during SA review and design. In this direction, CBAM [22] is a useful method for prioritizing architectural decisions that bring higher value. In addition, Ozkaya et al. proposed an economic valuation of architectural patterns [32].

These approaches help to find the optimal set of decisions that maximizes the ROI [15]. They pursue to solve the same problem of this paper, but their scope is broader and general for any kind of SA decision and do not reflect fundamental characteristics of adopting an RA. Therefore, their applicability for studying the ROI of RA adoption would require more effort, since specific cost-benefit factors for architecture-centric reuse are not considered. Hence, they are not the most convenient approaches for making the business case of adopting an RA and calculating its payback time.

Generic Software Metrics. There exist several approaches that propose metrics for estimating cost savings in software development and maintenance. Metrics as dependency structure matrices (DSM) have been applied to assist architecture-level analysis, such as value of modular designs, and they have proven to be particularly insightful for validating the future value of architecting modular systems [8]. MacCormack et al. extracted coupling metrics from an architecture DSM view for inferring the likelihood of change propagation and, hence, future maintenance costs [25]. Baldwin et al. presented a generic expression for evaluating the option to redesign a module also based on DSMs [4].

In addition, the concept of technical debt (either architecture-focused [31] or code-based [24]) is a way to measure unexpected rework costs due to expediting the delivery of stakeholder value in short.

Summary. Although there is a lack of research in evaluating the economic viability of RA adoption, there is a strong base of research in related areas. The most important related area is economic models that identify cost and benefit factors for PLA adoption. Although there is a significant amount of research is this direction, it falls short in:

- Validation in industry. "Very few [economic models for SPL] actually have been used as a basis for further development or adopted in industry" [23]. Thus, "there is a clear need for many more empirical studies to validate existing models" [1].
- Easy adoption of models in industry by identifying realistic metrics to collect and report. "It is difficult for the practitioners to evaluate the usability and usefulness of a proposed solution [economic model for SPL] for application in industry" [23]. Not guidelines exist to fully operationalize the models in practice [37].

Economics-driven SA analysis methods do not specifically aim at making an investment analysis of the adoption of an architecture-centric program. RA adoption is a subarea inside their generic decision-making context.

At a lower level, more simple metrics like DSM, could also be adequate for calculation the cost and benefit factors of RA adoption and make more complete models.

This state of the art drove us to the formulation of an economic model for RAs, which is currently on its formative stage. The formulation of the model aims to:

- Adapt cost and benefit factors from SPL models that are easy-to-apply by industry. The goal is to provide guidelines to fully operationalize the model in practice.
- Fill the gap of RA economics inside the SA decision-making context.
- Look for generic software metrics that can quantify new cost and benefit factors.

3   Industrial Context

The architecture group of *everis* is an initiative to manage architectural knowledge, best practices and lessons learned from previous experiences; and to provide efficient solutions to a better cost, flexibility and agility to the demands of client organizations.

This architecture group offers solutions for big businesses (e.g., banks, insurance companies, public administration and service, and industrial organizations) that offer a wide spectrum of services to their clients. Often, already existing commercial packages are not completely aligned with the business needs of these organizations, thereby requiring custom development and maintenance of applications. In this scenario, *everis* foster the use RAs for managing a wide spectrum of applications.

The architecture group of *everis* experienced the inability to calculate the ROI derived from RAs that they create for organizations. The purpose of our research is to create a method for extracting costs and benefits of RAs based on data that they were already collected.

4   An Economic Model for Reference Architectures

4.1   Method for Formulating the Economic Model

An RA cost-benefit analysis should be based on giving an economic value to its activities. We designed our economic model through the three following steps:

1. **Identify the costs and benefits stemming from the use of an RA.** Although cost modeling is already a mature field within software engineering, benefits have traditionally been far more elusive to quantify [8]. For this reason, it is necessary to identify the RA quality attributes that bring more benefit to the development and maintenance of applications, and the costs of constructing these applications [22]. These attributes may vary depending on the architecturally-significant requirements coming from the applications based on the RA. It is crucial to involve relevant stakeholders to ensure the trustworthiness of the collected information [38].

   The outputs of this step are, therefore, the costs factors of adopting an RA and the list of quality attributes in which the RA brings more benefit.

2. **Adopt metrics that quantify the costs and benefits identified in the first step in order to convert them into a monetary value.** The metrics to quantify them may vary depending on the data available in the organization involved.

   The output of this step is providing guidelines for collecting simple metrics that make possible to calculate the cost and benefits factors in practice.

3. **Make the business case for the adoption of the RA.** Add the costs and benefits calculated in the second step to the formula for calculating the ROI (proposed by Boehm [6]), where the benefits are the improvements of applications quality attributes, and the costs are the expenses in constructing the systems and the RA.

   The output of this step is a business case that captures the reasoning for adopting an RA. The RA business case analysis involves determining the relative financial costs, benefits, and ROI across its life-cycle.

$$ROI = \frac{Benefits - Costs}{Costs} \tag{1}$$

4.2   Execution of the Method for Formulating the Economic Model

The action-research collaboration with *everis* provided us the opportunity of implementing this general-purpose method in a particular case.

Step 1. We conducted a survey involving project managers, architects and developers of 9 organizations in Europe (7 from Spain) [26]. The survey pointed out that the main perceived economic benefits on the use of RAs were: (1) an increased value from the improvement of quality attributes, since their reused architectural knowledge is incrementally improved with previous successful experiences from its application domain; (2) cost savings in the development and maintenance of systems due to the reuse of software elements and the adoption of best practices of software development that increase the productivity of developers. Therefore, RAs bring most of the benefit because of the improvement of reusability and maintainability quality attributes. One of the reasons why RAs were adopted in these organizations is that the most important architecturally-significant requirement was reusability. Thus, we decided to focus our cost-benefit analysis over reusability and maintainability.

We found that some of the potential metrics to be used were not as pragmatic as the organization needed. In other words, the organization should have been invested extra time which was not an option. Furthermore, we faced the problem that some of the required data to apply the proposed metrics was not previously registered by the organization. Thus, we stressed the emphasis on formulating a practical model that incrementally deals with diverse cost-benefit aspects.

We identified six cost-benefit factors for RA adoption. We started the formulation of factors by adopting Poulin's method for measuring code reuse [34][35]. We adapted Poulin's model because it has been applied in industry, offers parameters to operationalize it, and we could feed it with available data in *everis* (see Step 2 below). We adopted its benefit factors (DCA, SCA) published in [35]. Conversely, we consider more appropriate for RAs to adopt the cost factors defined for SPL (CSW_{dev_costs}, $CSW_{service\_costs}$) in [35], instead of the additional development costs [34].

To complete the model we add the unique development costs of applications. Also, with the help of the propagation cost metric [25], we also consider necessary changes to reusable elements (which are not considered by Poulin's method) and, therefore, evolution. These two new factors include parameters to operationalize them.

The former three factors are for development and the latter ones for maintenance:

- DCA (Development Cost Avoidance). It is the *benefit* from reusing RA's software modules in applications compared to building the applications independently.
- UDC (Unique Development Costs). It is the *cost* to develop the unique parts of an application that are not already implemented in the modules of the RA. UDC is equivalent to $C_{reuse}+C_{unique}$.
- CSWD (Common Software Development costs). It is the *cost* of the initial investment, i.e., developing an RA. CSWD is equivalent to $C_{org}+C_{cab}$.
- SCA (Service Cost Avoidance). It is the *benefit* of modifying reused code once.
- CSWS (Common Software Service costs). It is the *cost* of fixing bugs in the (reusable) RA modules. CSWS calculates the cost of changes due to bugs in C_{cabu}.
- CSWE (Common Software Evolution costs). It is the *cost* of changing or adding functionalities to the RA modules. CSWE calculates the cost of evolutions in C_{cabu}. Therefore, CSWS+CSWE are equivalent to C_{cabu}.

Putting everything together, given a number n of applications built in top of the RA, and a number m of RA modules changed as it evolves, the benefits and costs of adopting an RA are defined as:

$$\text{Benefits}=\sum_{i=1}^{n}(DCA_i+SCA_i) \tag{2}$$

$$\text{Costs}=CSWD+CSWS+\sum_{i=1}^{n}UDC_i+\sum_{j=1}^{m}CSWE_j \tag{3}$$

Step 2. We divide the second step in two activities: checking the data available in practice and guide the information extraction from this data.

Data commonly available in practice that should be collected. The data that typically is available in order to calculate the aforementioned costs and benefits are effort and software metrics [26]. It allows converting cost-benefit factors into a monetary value.

On the one hand, the invested effort from the tracked activities allows the calculation of costs. We distinguish between three types of activities: training, development and maintenance. JIRA[1] and Redmine[2] are tools that support keeping track of activities and their invested time. Keeping track of activities is common in practice for project management and auditing. Activity tracking is also known as tickets [8].

On the other hand, software metrics help to analyze the benefits that can be found in the source code. For example, since the cost of applications' development is lower because of the reuse of RA, we estimate the cost avoidance of reusing its LOC. Sonar[3] offers tool support for obtaining general software metrics such as LOC, dependencies between modules, technical debt [24], and percentages of tests and rules compliance.

Software development is a naturally low-validity environment and reliable expert intuition can only be acquired in a high-validity environment. As stated by Erdogmus and Favaro [14], the adoption of practices like time tracking and tools to collect data is the basis for moving software development from its usual low-validity environment, to a high-validity environment.

Table 1. Basic parameters in order to feed the factors of Table 2

	Description of the parameters (adapted for the RA context)
RCR	Relative Cost of Reuse: effort that it takes to reuse a component without modification versus writing it new one-at-a-time [34]
RCWR	Relative Cost of Writing for Reuse: effort that it takes to write a reusable component versus writing it for one-time use only [34]
ER	Error Rate: the historical error rate in new software developed by your organization, in errors per thousand lines of code [34]
EC	Error Cost: your organization's historical cost to fix errors after releasing new software to the customer, in euros per error [34]
NMSI	New Module Source Instruction: the LOC that the changed or new module has, which can be the average of previous ones
PC	Propagation Cost: the percentage of code affected in the RA when performing evolutions (i.e., changing modules) [25]
CPKL	Cost per KLOC: the historical cost to develop a KLOC of new software in your organization [34]
USI	Unique Source Instructions: the amount of unique software (i.e., not reused) that was written or modified for an application
RSI	Reused Source Instructions: it is the total LOC of the RA's modules that are reused in an application. It supports variability. In other words, reuse of RA might not be complete but partial, since different applications can reused different RA's modules. Therefore RSI depend on each application [34].
TSI	Total Source Instructions: it is the total LOC of the RA that can be reused [34].

---

[1] JIRA, http://www.atlassian.com/es/software/jira/overview
[2] Redmine, http://www.redmine.org/
[3] Sonar, http://www.sonarsource.org/

Table 2. Cost-benefit factors to calculate the ROI of adopting an RA in an organization

Description of the cost-benefit factors (adapted for the RA context)	
DCA	Development Cost Avoidance: the benefits from reusing RA's modules [34] DCA = RSI * (1-RCR) * CPKL
CSWD	Common Software Development costs: the costs to develop the RA [35] CSWD = RCWR * TSI * CPKL
UDC	Unique Development Costs: the costs to develop the unique part of an application UDC = USI*CPKL
SCA	Service Cost Avoidance: benefits from maintaining only once RA's modules [34] SCA = RSI * ER * EC
CSWS	Common Software Maintenance costs: cost of fixing bugs in reusable modules [35] CSWS = TSI * ER * EC
CSWE	Common Software Evolution costs: the costs of changing or adding a new functionality and maintaining it to the RA CSWE = evolution development + evolution maintenance + propagation = (NMSI*RCWR*CPKL)+(NMSI*ER*EC)+(TSI*CPKL*PC)

We experienced difficulties collecting historical data (as in [20]), especially for the "before" state of adopting an RA. We noted that C_{prod} and C_{evo} were seldom available since the "before" state did not exist. For this reason, we use RCR and RCWR.

Using commonly available data in practice to quantify the costs and benefits. In Table 1, we present ten basic parameters that are required for calculating the six cost-benefit factors of the Step 1. Table 2 shows the formulas to calculate this six cost-benefit factors as well as parameters that are needed for these calculations.

Step 3. As final step, we can use calculated factors in order to calculate the ROI:

$$\text{ROI} = \frac{[\sum_{i=1}^{n}(DCA_i + SCA_i)] - [CSWD + CSWS + \sum_{i=1}^{n} UDC_i + \sum_{j=1}^{m} CSWE_j]}{CSWD + CSWS + \sum_{i=1}^{n} UDC_i + \sum_{j=1}^{m} CSWE_j} \quad (4)$$

We also suggest using these cost-benefit factors to make a business case for calculating the ROI of building an RA vs. building the applications independently. Table 3 shows an example of business case and how to calculate the cost and benefits for three years since the RA adoption. The parameters n_1, n_2, n_3 indicate the number of applications developed per year respectively, and m the number of evolved modules.

Table 3. Example of design of a business case with the cost-benefit factors of the model

	Year 1	Year 2	Year 3
Total benefit	n_1*(DCA+SCA)	n_2*(DCA+SCA)	n_3*(DCA+SCA)
Total cost	CSWD+ n_1*UDC+CSWS*$^1/_5$	n_2*UDC+ CSWS*$^2/_5$+m*CSWE	n_3*UDC+ CSWS*$^2/_5$+m*CSWE

As Boehm points out [6], two additional factors may be important in business case analysis: unquantifiable benefits, and uncertainties and risk.

First, the economic model that we propose promotes benefits in reusability and maintainability. However, other quality attributes, such as security, could be as relevant as those for this analysis, even when they may be difficult to quantify. This other benefits should also been taken into account when adopting and RA. Unquantifiable benefits are also considered as "flexibility" in TEI[4], the economic model of Forrester.

Second, to adjust cost and benefits to risk, they can be multiplied by percentages that generally increase the costs and reduce the benefits (assuming the worst case). For instance, TEI propose to multiple costs by values that range from 98% to 150% and benefits by values between 50% and 110%.

5   Preliminary Validation

To assess the feasibility of the economic model, we conducted a retrospective analysis of a particular case. We calculated the costs and benefits (and hence the ROI) of an RA adoption driven by *everis* in the IT department of a public organization.

By the time we performed the validation, the public organization had already: (1) adopted an RA, (2) created an application using the RA –which we consider "exemplar" application–, and (3) fixed errors discovered in the RA software elements that were reused by the application.

The validation consisted of 4 parts. First, a post-mortem analysis in which our challenge was to extract the parameters of Table 1 from already collected data. The values that we got are shown in Table 4.

Table 4. Values of the basic parameters in the study

RCR	RCWR	ER	EC	NMSI	PC	CPKL	USI	RSI	TSI
0,064	1,243	2,879 err./kLOC	7,02 hours/err.	1.526 LOC/module	9,7 %	75,22 hours/kLOC	2.885 LOC	8.364 LOC	41.189 LOC[*]

[*] In TSI, 9.231 LOC were refactored from previous project. So, 31.958 were new.

Recommended values for RCR range from 0,03 and 0,25, and for RCWR from 1 to 2,2 [34]. Therefore, with the values that we got in the study, we can see that both RCR and RCWR are low for RAs. A low RCR could show the trend of moving the complexity to the architecture in order to simplify the development of applications. We can also see this trend comparing the code of the RA software elements with the code of applications. RA code present higher values for complexity metrics such as coupling and cohesion. A reason why RCWR is low could be that RA architectural knowledge speeds up the development.

Second, with the data of Table 4, we had real data to calculate (see Table 5):

- CSWD, the RA initial investment, which lasted 6 months.
- DCA, the benefit of reusing RA code in the exemplar application development.
- SCA, the cost from fixing the errors of the reused code in the exemplar application.
- UDC, the cost of developing the application.

---

[4] Total Economic Impact, http://www.forrester.com/marketing/product/consulting/tei.html

The above costs were accurately computed because *everis* keeps track of activities with their invested time. Third, it was necessary to estimate the rest of factors:

- CSWS, the cost of fixing all bugs in RA code. Since we knew the SCA for the exemplar application and the percentage of reuse, we calculated the error rate and error cost, which we used to estimate CSWS.
- CSWE, the cost of: (1) changing or developing a module with new functionality, (2) fixing its bugs, (3) making changes in the rest of the RA to integrate it.

Table 5. Values of the cost-benefit factors in the study[*]

DCA	CSWD	UDC	SCA	CSWS	CSWE
589 hours	**2.988 hours**	**217 hours**	**169 hours**	*832 hours*	*474 hours*

[*] Values in **bold** are real data. Values in *italic* are estimated.

Fourth, we made the business case analysis with two different scenarios:

Scenario 1. *Is it worth to invest on the adoption of an RA?* We constructed a business case for 3 years starting when the organization decided to adopt the RA, in order to calculate the ROI. For the first 8 months of those 3 years, we have real data about the RA development and the exemplar RA-based application. To estimate the costs and benefits for the rest of these 3 years, we conducted some additional interviews to the involved stakeholders. Stakeholders were carefully selected according to their knowledge and experience to increase the degree of confidence on the data gathered. After these interviews, we made the following assumptions:

- Future applications will have similar characteristics and complexity as the exemplar one.
- The public organization will develop 8 applications per year. Since the RA creation lasted 6 months, the first year they will develop just 4 applications.
- The totality of CSWS is computed proportionally starting the seventh month.
- A module is evolved (with new functionality) or added to the RA every year since the second year.

Under these assumptions, the costs and benefits in hours for the future can be calculated as shown in Table 3. They can be converted into a monetary value by multiplying them by an hourly rate. Assuming a rate of 30' per hour for an application developer (which affects to DCA, SCA, UDC) and a rate of 40€ per hour for a developer and maintainer of the architecture (which affects to CSWD, CSWM, CSWE), Fig. 2 summarizes financial results for first three years of the RA. This organization will realize a ROI within 2 years through gains in systematic reuse.

Scenario 2. *How many instantiations (i.e., applications) are necessary before savings pay off for the up-front investment in building an RA?* In this scenario we calculated how many applications need to be build based on the RA to have a positive ROI. Fig. 3 shows the ROI due to developing and maintaining applications based on an RA rather than in a stand-alone fashion.

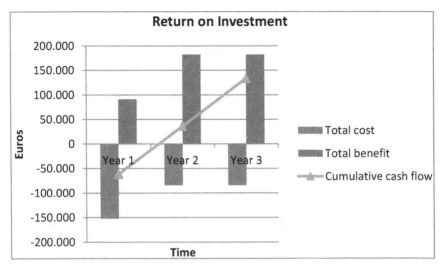

Fig. 2. Summary financial results

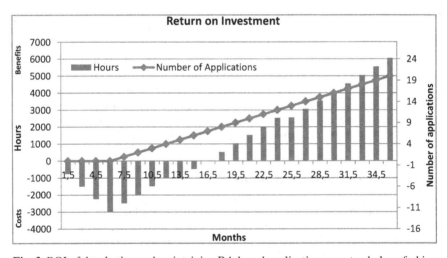

Fig. 3. ROI of developing and maintaining RA-based applications vs. stand-alone fashion

As Fig. 3 shows, after building 7 applications, savings pay off for the up-front investment in the RA. It must be noted that the exemplar application is small and only 20% of the RA is being reused (RSI/TSI). On the other hand, the application has a high reuse percentage of 74% (RSI/USI+RSI). The higher these percentages are (likely in medium to large applications), the greater the benefit from the RA is.

Moreover, applications are introduced into the market earlier from the seventh month on. This is due to the effort avoidance of 589 hours (DCA) of reusing the RA.

To sum up, this study illustrates the potential way in which an organization can evaluate the value of RA adoption. We calculated a three-year ROI of 42% with a payback period of 16,5 months and 7 applications.

6   Discussion

Once we applied the economic model and calculated the ROI, a last question remains: How accurate are these calculations and the obtained quantitative data? If the economic model is applied with existing data (as we have done in Section 5), the calculation of the ROI reaches a high degree of correctness, since the data that feeds the model is trustworthy. The metrics coming from code analysis (e.g., size in LOC) do not reflect any error. Also, we saw that time tracking is reliable. During data collection we found invested time in activities in two different sources: JIRA, which is optionally used by the project team and keeps the invested time of the project's activities; and a mandatory corporate financial tool, which is used by the financial department. This data differ in 8,75%, being lower internally time tracking of the project. The reason could be that JIRA does not include other activities out of the scope of the project like traveling. To adjust the calculations to this risk, we have always considered the worst case (i.e., greater costs).

Contrary, when the economic model is used to predict the ROI of a completely new RA adoption in an organization, there is not real data since it does not exist yet. In this case, the accuracy totally depends on expert intuition and historical data. Historical data can be scarce in small and medium organizations; especially considering that reuse of architectures is still a research area in progress. In addition, historical data must be continuously updated, since some values of effort-related parameters (such as RCR) are expected to decrease each time a developer instantiates the RA.

As a final remark, the construction of an economic model from the data available in software companies is yet-another-instance of research question which needs to balance soundness with applicability. The awareness of this problem by the software engineering community is increasing and even dedicated events are being organized (See CESI 2013 @ ICSE, http://www.essi.upc.edu/~franch/cesi2013/).

7   Conclusions and Next Steps

Architecture improvements are extremely difficult to evaluate in an analytic and quantitative way, contrary to business efficacy (sales, marketing, and manufacturing) [8]. Methods and models for changing this state of the practice are demanded.

This paper has opened the path on the area of using economic models for RA assessment. We think that this area has a significant impact not just for researchers but also for practitioners in software development and organization's executives. We presented REARM, an economic model to translate measured or estimated data (i.e., metrics) into monetary terms (i.e., cost-benefit analysis). Then, we use them as the basis for analyzing the economic value of an RA (i.e., valuation) that is adapted by an organization in the pursuit of its business strategies. Thus, our work aligns with Erdogmus et al. vision on economic activities in software industry, that fall into 4 levels: metrics, cost-benefit analysis, valuation and business strategy [13].

We have conducted a preliminary validation to calculate the ROI of adopting an RA in a real organization. This organization will realize a return on their investment within two years through gains in systematic reuse and applications maintainability. The method presented is generic enough to be used when other quality attributes are prioritized by relevant stakeholders. The presented economic model allows quantifying the value that an RA of Type 2 or 4 (those designed with an intended scope of a single organization) [3] brings to an organization. Its strongest points are:

- It translates RA costs and benefits into monetary values, which can be considered an innovative approach in RA research and practice.
- The integration of different metrics from existing models that complement each other evaluating several RA-relevant aspects.
- It provides guidelines for easily collecting and reporting data for practitioners, and for using it to make a business case.
- The model has been applied in a public organization and validated with real data.

On the other hand, potential weaknesses of this approach are:

- It does not consider RA's software elements degeneration over time [20].
- The risk increases when neither real nor historical data are available.

As future work, we plan to enrich the economic model by: (1) adding more metrics (such as technical debt [24], degeneration over time [20], risk metrics, homogeneity metrics [10]), and (2) validating it for bigger applications and in more organizations.

Acknowledgements. This work has been supported by "Cátedra *everis*" and the Spanish project TIN2010-19130-C02-00. We would also like to thank all participants of the data collection process for their kindly cooperation.

References

1. Ali, M., Babar, M., Schmid, K.: A comparative survey of economic models for software product lines. In: Software Engineering and Advanced Applications, pp. 275–278 (2009)
2. Angelov, S., Trienekens, J.J.M., Grefen, P.: Towards a method for the evaluation of reference architectures: Experiences from a case. In: Morrison, R., Balasubramaniam, D., Falkner, K. (eds.) ECSA 2008. LNCS, vol. 5292, pp. 225–240. Springer, Heidelberg (2008)
3. Angelov, S., Grefen, P., Greefhorst, D.: A framework for analysis and design of software reference architectures. Information and Software Technology 54(4), 417–431 (2012)
4. Baldwin, C.Y., Clark, K.B.: Design Rules: The Power of Modularity. MIT Press (1999)
5. Bass, L., Clements, P., Kazman, R.: Software Architecture in Practice. Addison-W (2003)
6. Biffl, S., Aurum, A., Boehm, B., Erdogmus, H., Grünbacher, P.: Value-Based Software Engineering. Springer (2005)
7. Boehm, B., Brown, A., Madachy, R., Yang, Y.: A software product line life cycle cost estimation model. In: Empirical Software Engineering, pp. 156–164 (2004)
8. Carriere, J., Kazman, R., Ozkaya, I.: A cost-benefit framework for making architectural decisions in a business context. In: ICSE, vol. 2, pp. 149–157 (2010)
9. Clements, P., Northrop, L.: Software Product Lines. Addison-Wesley (2002)
10. Clements, P., McGregor, J., Cohen, S.: The structured intuitive model for product line economics (SIMPLE). Tech. rep., DTIC Document (2005)
11. Cloutier, R., Muller, G., Verma, D., Nilchiani, R., Hole, E., Bone, M.: The concept of reference architectures. Systems Engineering 13(1), 14–27 (2010)
12. Eklund, U., Jonsson, N., Bosch, J., Eriksson, A.: A reference architecture template for software-intensive embedded systems. In: WICSA/ECSA (2012)

13. Erdogmus, H., Favaro, J., Strigel, W.: Return on investment. IEEE Software 21(3) (2004)
14. Erdogmus, H., Favaro, J.: The Value Proposition for Agility–A Dual Perspective (2012), http://www.infoq.com/presentations/Agility-Value
15. Falessi, D., Kruchten, P., Cantone, G.: Issues in applying empirical software engineering to software architecture. In: Oquendo, F. (ed.) ECSA 2007. LNCS, vol. 4758, pp. 257–262. Springer, Heidelberg (2007)
16. Frakes, W., Terry, C.: Software reuse: metrics and models. Comput. Surv. 28(2) (1996)
17. Gallagher, B.P.: Using the architecture tradeoff analysis method to evaluate a reference architecture: A case study. Technical Report CMU/SEI (2000)
18. Galster, M., Avgeriou, P.: Empirically-grounded reference architectures: a proposal. In: Proceedings of the Joint ACM SIGSOFT Conference QoSA/ISARCS (2011)
19. Galster, M., Avgeriou, P., Tofan, D.: Constraints for the design of variability intensive service-oriented reference architectures an industrial case study. IST 55(2), 428–441 (2013)
20. Ganesan, D., Muthig, D., Yoshimura, K.: Predicting return-on-investment for product line generations. In: SPLC, pp. 13–24 (2006)
21. Graaf, B., van Dijk, H., van Deursen, A.: Evaluating an embedded software reference architecture. In: CSMR, pp. 354–363 (2005)
22. Kazman, R., Asundi, J., Klien, M.: Making architecture design decisions: An economic approach. Tech. rep., DTIC Document (2002)
23. Khurum, M., Gorschek, T., Petersson, K.: Systematic review of solutions proposed for product line economics. In: Decision Support Software Intensive Product Management (2008)
24. Letouzey, J.: The sqale method for evaluating technical debt. In: MTD@ICSE (2012)
25. MacCormack, A., Rusnak, J., Baldwin, C.: Exploring the duality between product and organizational architectures. Harvard Business School Research Paper (08-039) (2011)
26. Martínez-Fernández, S., Ayala, C., Franch, X., Ameller, D.: A Framework for Software Reference Architecture Analysis and Review. In: ESELAW@CIbSE (in press, 2013)
27. Mili, A., Chmiel, S., Gottumukkala, R., Zhang, L.: An integrated cost model for software reuse. In: ICSE, pp. 157–166 (2000)
28. Nakagawa, E.Y., Oliveira Antonino, P., Becker, M.: Reference architecture and product line architecture: A subtle but critical difference. In: Crnkovic, I., Gruhn, V., Book, M. (eds.) ECSA 2011. LNCS, vol. 6903, pp. 207–211. Springer, Heidelberg (2011)
29. Nakagawa, E.: Reference architectures and variability: current status and future perspectives. In: Proceedings of the WICSA/ECSA, pp. 159–162 (2012)
30. Nóbrega, J., Almeida, E., Meira, S.: Income: Integrated cost model for product line engineering. In: SEAA, pp. 27–34 (2008)
31. Nord, R., Ozkaya, I., Kruchten, P., Gonzalez-Rojas, M.: In search of a metric for managing architectural technical debt. In: WICSA/ECSA, pp. 91–100 (2012)
32. Ozkaya, I., Kazman, R., Klein, M.: Quality-attribute based economic valuation of architectural patterns. In: ESC (2007)
33. Pohl, K., Bockle, G., Van Der Linden, F.: Software product line engineering, vol. 10 (2005)
34. Poulin, J.: Measuring Software Reuse. Addison-Wesley, Reading (1997)
35. Poulin, J.: The economics of product line development. International Journal of Applied Software Technology 3, 15–28 (1997)
36. Robson, C.: Real world research, vol. 2. Blackwell Oxford (2002)
37. Schmid, K.: An initial model of product line economics. In: van der Linden, F.J. (ed.) PFE-4 2001. LNCS, vol. 2290, pp. 38–50. Springer, Heidelberg (2002)
38. van Solingen, R.: Measuring the ROI of software process improvement. IEEE Software 21(3), 32–38 (2004)

Cross-Domain Reuse:
Lessons Learned in a Multi-project Trajectory

Silvia Mazzini[1], John Favaro[1], and Tullio Vardanega[2]

[1] Intecs S.p.A.
via Umberto Forti 5, 56121 Pisa, Italy
{silvia.mazzini,john.favaro}@intecs.it
[2] University of Padova
Department of Mathematics
via Trieste 63, 35121 Padova, Italy
tullio.vardanega@math.unipd.it

Abstract. Systematic reuse has been traditionally associated with a single domain, in which domain analysis leads to a single domain terminology, domain architecture, and intra-domain reuse. The product line movement is an example of that trend. Although reuse of small artifacts has always worked across domains, systematic reuse of more substantial artifacts across domains has not been much explored. In recent years, there has been an interest especially in large European industrial research cooperation programs, to facilitate reuse across disparate domains, to derive the known economic and technological benefits. Progress is being made, but significant challenges remain. Lessons learned in the definition and elaboration of a cross-domain reference architecture over the trajectory of three large projects are described.

1 Introduction

The promise of systematic reuse has been fulfilled in many respects, with a flourishing product line community adopting a domain engineering approach to software development, in domains ranging from consumer products such as television sets to large infrastructure such as telecommunications systems. In Europe in particular, however, in the large co-financed industrial research programs, especially ARTEMIS [19], there has been a significant push toward seeking systematic cross-domain reuse, to pursue both technological and economic benefits. This is in keeping with the European Union's desire to have its financed R&D activities deliver the maximum impact across the largest possible segment of its industrial sectors.

However, this new ambition creates significant challenges. The reuse of low-level components is inherently cross-domain in the sense that it is naturally domain-independent by virtue of being far removed from the end application needs. But the kind of high-level reuse implied by cross-domain systematic reuse is different: what worked in a single domain may not work across domains.

This paper reports on lessons learned in pursuing a cross-domain reuse vision in a large and encompassing research program that progressed along two parallel and

J. Favaro and M. Morisio (Eds.): ICSR 2013, LNCS 7925, pp. 113–126, 2013.

complementary lines and over three large projects. One line of research took place as part of an initiative launched by the European Space Agency (ESA) intended to guide the development of on-board software for satellites across all of its software supply chain, using the component-based approach described in [16]. The other line of research occurred within an ARTEMIS project for the realization of a model-based, component-oriented approach to the development of embedded real time software systems across the domains of telecommunications, space, and railways [15].

2   Phase 1: Single-Domain Basis in COrDeT-1

COrDeT-1 was a preliminary study launched by ESA in the context of an initiative for space avionics standardization. The overall goal of the project was to facilitate the achievement of systematic reuse over space applications. The rationale behind that effort was the observation that satellite missions often share significant characteristics with high reuse potential. COrDeT-1 was determinant in the experience discussed in this paper because fundamental decisions about the approach taken to achieve systematic reuse were taken in it. ESA decided to adopt domain engineering techniques to achieve a design architecture for future reuse in preference to building a library of potential reusable code, a more frequent choice in other, similar initiatives.

Our first proposal was to adopt an approach that is closely associated the domain engineering process: *generative reuse* [8]. Generative reuse is achieved by encoding domain knowledge and relevant system building knowledge into a domain specific specification language [1]. New systems are created by writing specifications using modeling languages according to an approach where an automated engine translates the specification into code for the new system in a target language.

We were particularly attracted to the generative approach because the Object Management Group (OMG) has developed its own initiative for a generative, *model-based* approach called Model-Driven Architecture (MDA) [2]. The MDA concept allows developers to produce models of the application and business logic and generate code for a target platform by means of transformations. Instead of writing platform-specific code in some high-level language, developers focus on developing models that are specific to the application domain but independent of the platform. In this way, MDA raises the level of abstraction in software development.

Historically, however, generative reuse had been considered to be a mutually exclusive alternative to a *component based* approach, the other major paradigm in reuse [5]. In our experience, architectural decisions had a strong impact on reusability in general, and especially on the non-functional properties of high integrity software as found in space applications; we therefore strongly felt that it was important to define a *reference architecture* [3] for our application domains.

A reference architecture is essentially an agreed basis and a kind of template solution for the domain, and embodies the lessons learned in that domain in the form of patterns, principles, best practices, functional elements, and interfaces. (An important defining characteristic of a reference architecture is that *conformance* to that architecture can be ascertained.) But as mentioned earlier, a reference architecture carries with it a strong flavour of component orientation. Thus, one important goal of the study was to successfully combine the generative, model-based approach with the elements of a component-based approach implied by a generic reference architecture.

The principles of a reference architecture and component based approach implied one last basic principle: to make reuse practical and effective, many of the components in the reference architecture need to offer some degree of *variability*. Jacobson *et al.* [6] described seven variability mechanisms for providing variation points in a product line: inheritance, uses, extension points, parameterization, configuration of alternative components, template instantiation and generation. Bosch [7] described five variability mechanisms: inheritance, extensions, configuration, template instantiation and generation. Our own work on variability in the COrDeT-1 project culminated instead in the definition of a system-level feature oriented domain analysis methodology [9].

The four main principles of model-based, component-based, generic reference architecture, and variability modeling were elaborated into the scheme shown in Fig. 1, in which the model-based orientation is represented by its generative capability in the "Generate" arrow.

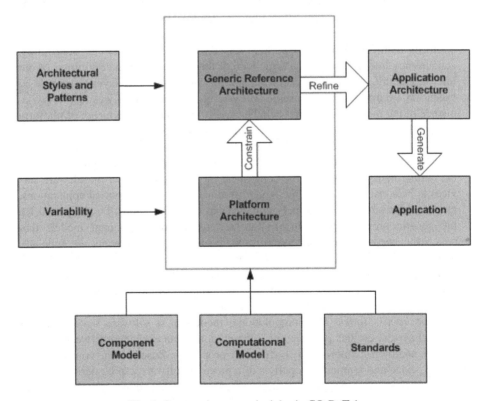

Fig. 1. Systematic reuse principles in COrDeT-1

Further concepts than the cited principles appear in the scheme outlined above. This is so because of lessons we learned from previous experience in the ASSERT project (Automated proof-based System and Software Engineering for Real-Time systems) from the Sixth Framework Program of the European Commission [14]. We came to realize that these other concepts proceed from the four main principles enumerated above, that is:

- *Architectural Styles and Patterns.* An important aspect of a reference architecture is the ability to capture different architectural perspectives and partitioning strategies. Different kinds of problems lend themselves to different styles, idioms or paradigms of design, analysis and implementation. An architectural style captures common computation and communication paradigms used to address a particular class of programming problems. For example, we found the layered system to be a central architectural style in the space domain. At a lower level of abstraction than style, architectural patterns include N-tier client-server architectures, agent-based architectures, and service oriented architectures.
- *Platform Architectures.* Platform architectures are middleware software layers on which the application and components for implementation of an application can be developed. Middleware typically provides standardized communication between components. In particular it facilitates distribution of applications and services. A platform architecture provides various services such as transactions, scheduling, concurrency, messaging and naming. One of the key goals of the definition of our reference architecture was to define an appropriate middleware layer to provide an execution environment for reusable software components. This was also a consequence of the model-based approach, because it introduced the concept of platform independent models (PIM) and platform specific models (PSM).
- *Component Model.* The component approach necessitated the adoption of a component model. The definition and scoping of a reference architecture determines the requirements imposed on the component model and the set of middleware services to be considered. Given the large differences between supported applications, ranging from simple to extremely complex, an assessment must be performed for the generic architecture to incorporate state-of-the-art component models that match the needs of intended systems. State-of-the-art components are typically deployed into a so-called *container* which manages their lifecycle and provides various services for them. Our particular interpretation and use of the container concept for managing high integrity non-functional characteristics turned out to be a major contribution of our approach to the state of the art.
- *Computational Model.* The computational model for a software system defines abstract system entities representing computations, data exchange between computations, and their temporal and concurrency properties. Based on the computational model, space and temporal properties of a piece of software can be derived, which is essential in our high-integrity environment. In order to reuse software components across different systems, the computational models of these systems must be the same or at least compatible – an interesting challenge in its own right.

- *Standards*. The last key concept in our schema was not strictly related to the four fundamental principles, but acquired an outsized and unexpected importance later in the cross-domain context. First, *design to interfaces* is an emerging reuse practice [12], whereby all external dependencies must be defined using widely accepted interface standards as much as possible. Secondly, we stipulated that the design itself be defined using widely accepted standards as much as possible, in order to be compatible with existing real world solutions, tools and techniques, and to make models reusable assets. In this respect UML and the related OMG standards, such as MOF and XMI, represent the most mature, widespread used and tool supported candidates for the specification of the reference modeling language. Finally, we required that the reference architecture also try to incorporate and reflect software engineering standards such as those of IEEE.

All the concepts described above became the basis for the domain engineering approach in the space domain, as well as for exploring cross-domain engineering in the next project. It proved to be remarkably resilient.

3   Phase 2: Cross-Domain Realization in the CHESS Project

This section describes the experience acquired with the CHESS (Composition with Guarantees for High-integrity Embedded Software Components Assembly) ARTEMIS JU Call 2008 project [24]. The project aimed at promoting the adoption of component-based development and Model Driven Engineering to support the development of real-time embedded systems across several domains of interest, namely telecom, space and railways. Thus, the project provided an opportunity to implement and to extend into multiple domains the basic principles that had been identified in COrDeT-1. However, building on the experience gained in the ASSERT project [15], CHESS added two more distinct pillars:

- *separation of concerns* between functional and non-functional properties of software components;
- *correct-by-construction* automated derivation of platform independent user models into platform-specific implementations with high-integrity runtime guarantees.

CHESS involved a significant elaboration of the component model hypothesized but not defined in detail in COrDeT-1. The CHESS Component Model extends traditional component models by explicitly separating functional from non-functional aspects. Components are modelled in a dedicated view, in which the designer describes only their functional aspects. A distinct design view permits to annotate the component description with the declaration of the desired non-functional attributes. This has the advantage that for certain types of non-functional properties (e.g. real time), the separation of concerns makes it possible to reuse the same functional specification with different non-functional annotations. This capability turned out to have extremely positive implications for functional reuse, consequently with large potential for cross-domain application.

Non-functional properties are analyzed and verified for individual components in isolation and are retained after the component is assembled with other components and deployed to the target system, thereby assuring the *composability* of non-functional properties of components. Properties of components can be used to derive the properties of the overall system, therefore contributing to the *compositionality* of non-functional properties of components. In this way the system can be built as an assembly of reused components, where both functional and non-functional concerns can be adequately taken into consideration at design time.

The declarative specification of non-functional attributes of components (for instance the real time activation pattern of a given provided operation) is used in CHESS for the *automated generation* of the *container*, to be regarded as a component wrapper responsible for the realization of the non-functional attributes declared for the component to be wrapped. As a consequence, in the CHESS approach components at design level encompass functional concerns only; in particular, they are devoid of any constructs pertaining to tasking and specific computational model concerns.

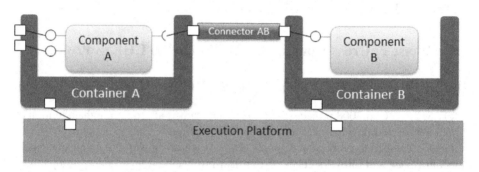

Fig. 2. Components, containers, and connectors in the CHESS Component Model [20]

Components (and containers) in CHESS are independent of communication concerns, which are handled by the dedicated *connector*. The existence of specific properties about the binding between two components in the design model (for instance regarding safety protocols to be adopted in the communication) is used to generate the connector, which manages the interaction between the components – which is actually a mediated communication between their containers. The use of connectors ensures that components and containers do not require any adaptation under different binding requirements and deployment specifications (see Fig. 2).

The CHESS component specification, as defined at user level in terms of functional behaviour and non-functional property specification, is therefore completely platform-independent (hence it represents the Platform Independent Model or PIM). However the definition of containers and connectors is platform specific (it resides in the Platform Specific Model or PSM); in particular it is bound to:

- the semantic constraints of the specific computational model supported by the target platform;
- the adoption of a specific programming model;
- the specific run-time services offered by the execution platform.

A synthesis of the essential elements of the CHESS approach is depicted in Fig. 3. It is worth noting that the CHESS approach has large potential for cross-domain reuse in so far as the principal dependence on domain-specific needs rests with the Execution Platform and all that must strictly conform to it (which may include middleware libraries as well as connector and container bindings to them).

Separation of concerns is supported in CHESS both at specification (PIM) and implementation (PSM) level: the former, by way of user design views to address distinct design concerns; the latter by the platform-specific implementations which are derived by transformation engines as a correct-by-construction product.

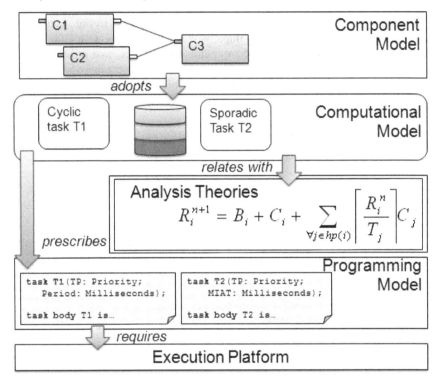

Fig. 3. CHESS approach [23]

Operationally it is the CHESS toolchain that guarantees the implementation of the correct by construction paradigm by supporting:

- analysis and verification of non-functional properties (e.g. upon the target computational model);
- propagation of the results back to the model;
- consistent and property-preserving automated generation of code and deployment on the target execution platform.

Here *property preservation* means that the non-functional properties statically assumed in the PIM and PSM models, and verified by the analysis, are preserved in the generated code and monitored at run-time. The monitoring at run-time allows the notification of any events that violate the guarantees proved at model level and their treatment in accord with the applicable system level policies.

As a result, the development process investigated in the CHESS project supports the definition of reusable functional components that may be decorated with different non-functional property specifications so as to target different implementations and different platform-specific middleware across multiple domains.

The specificity of the different implementations on different targets can be easily accommodated by advanced use of model based generative techniques. Interestingly, this claim held true in the experiments that were performed within all the industrial domains covered in CHESS.

The final, overall cross-domain CHESS vision is illustrated in Fig. 4: the generative techniques were successfully implemented for different middleware and platforms in the three domains of telecommunications, space, and railways. The automotive domain was "monitored" over the course of the project by experts within the domain from within the consortium, although implementation resources were only employed in the first three domains.

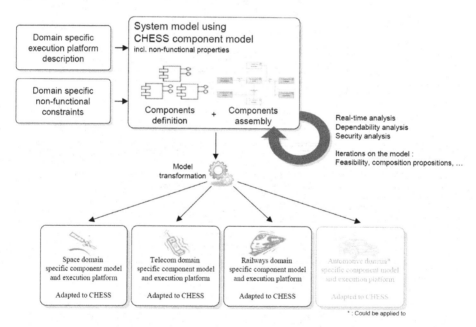

Fig. 4. Overall cross-domain CHESS approach

A comparative evaluation with respect to the main principles elaborated in the original single-domain COrDeT-1 vision yielded the following observations when cross-domain aspects were considered in CHESS:

- The CHESS Component Model turned out to be useful across all domains. In fact, the contents of a single component (that is, its functional implementation) appeared to be much less reusable across domains than the container and connector model itself, which worked well in all domains. That made it possible to share component assembly solutions across domains, where the respective contents had to change according to the applications within the domains. It was a great challenge to identify non-functional properties that had a single-domain utility, but which could also be usefully generalized across domains.

• The computational model turned out to be extremely useful. The Ravenscar Computational Model (RCM) is a language-agnostic conceptual concurrency model inspired by the Ravenscar Profile of the Ada programming language [21]. The rationale for the Ravenscar Profile is to provide a restricted tasking model suited for the development of high-integrity real-time systems. The model was successfully adopted across all the CHESS domains.

• The middleware concept to support the platform architecture turned out to be fundamental in all domains considered, but there was much more of a problem of finding a solution at the proper level of abstraction, because in the different domains the middleware solutions adopted vary considerably, or even for some large companies (e.g. Thales) proprietary solutions exist.

• The heavy use of standards postulated in COrDeT-1 turned out to be very useful in a cross-domain context. The modeling language adopted by CHESS is a profile of the OMG UML, MARTE and SysML, providing a standard common design language that is appropriate across domains. Tool support from the Eclipse EMF turned out to be the *de facto* standard framework for development of the CHESS tool chain.

4   Phase 3: Consolidation in the COrDeT-2 Project

The experience gained in the COrDeT-1 and CHESS projects came to its culmination in the COrDeT-2 project [17] of the European Space Agency.

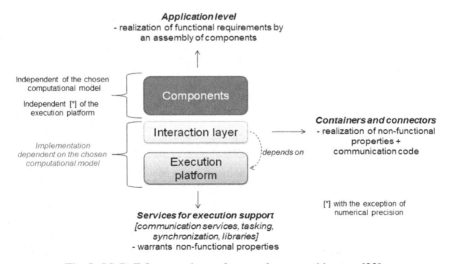

Fig. 5. COrDeT-2 approach to software reference architecture [22]

In the context of the initiative for space avionics standardization mentioned in previous section, which was the origin of COrDeT-1, ESA organized then the SAVOIR-FAIRE working group, with representative participation from across all the European Space Industry [25]. Building on COrDeT-1, SAVOIR-FAIRE elaborated the concepts of the On-Board Software Reference Architecture (OBSW-RA), later consolidated by other studies, of which the most recent was the COrDeT-2 project.

There was a strong overlap in the technological research teams of this project and CHESS, making it possible for the reference architecture vision of COrDeT-2 and CHESS to be brought to fruition. The COrDeT-2 approach to a reference architecture is depicted in Fig. 5.

The main result of COrDeT-2 was the incorporation of the salient elements of its precursor work into a reference architecture that consolidated the main ideas into a conceptually simple, straightforward, and elegant form. A major effect of this simplicity was that it made it very clear where cross-domain aspects reside and, in contrast, where domain-specific variability resides. The OBSW-RA defined by COrDeT-2 is shown in Fig. 6.

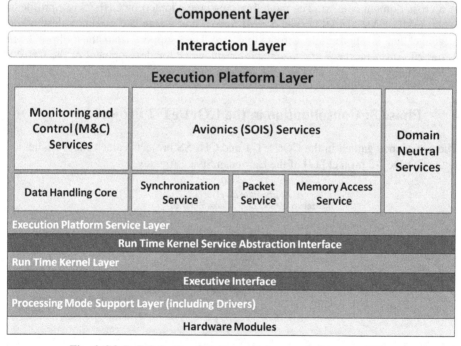

Fig. 6. COrDeT-2 On Board Software Reference Architecture [22]

The OBSW-RA has three layers. At the top is the component layer, which hosts the component model. The essential elements of this layer are *entirely domain independent*. Furthermore, all components developed within this layer are free from non-functional concerns. Within the intended context of space software development, it is suitable for reuse across different project participants; but it is also suitable for the development of applications that can be reused across domains. This top layer of the OBSW-RA precisely corresponds to the CHESS PIM.

The bottom layer (called the "execution platform layer" in COrDeT-2) is where all of the domain specific concerns are addressed. This is done in the form of "provided services". The platform layer is able to expand to accommodate whatever domain-specific services are desired, while the upper layers can remain thin. The figure provides an illustrative example, with three major groups of services that are essential to space missions: Monitoring and Control (M&C), Avionics Spacecraft Onboard Interface Services (SOIS), and hardware-specific mission-neutral services (which are often termed Basic Software).

- M&C services are specific to the satellite domain and, for example, may implement a standard such as the Packet Utilisation Standard [17];
- Avionics (SOIS) services are specific to the avionics domain and operate within the context of the standardized SOIS service architecture;
- Hardware-specific mission-neutral services are those which are common to any embedded software domain (e.g. tasking, I/O management).

The ability to concentrate most domain-specific concerns in the platform layer was an important result of the work.

The middle layer (called the "interaction layer" in COrDeT-2) is where the containers and connectors (which transparently encapsulate components) operate. They keep the components free of the relevant concerns and bind them to the platform services (often domain-dependent) that are needed to ensure the resources' needed for their execution.

- *Containers* (as conceived in CHESS) are domain-independent artifacts in COrDeT-2, which however are specific to families of computational models.
- *Connectors* (likewise introduced in CHESS) are also domain-independent artifacts, which however rely on a platform-specific middleware that they can use to provide distribution transparency to component binding.

5   Discussion and Conclusions

An important result of COrDeT-2 was that the principal large industrial participants – Astrium and Thales Alenia Space, along with the European Space Agency itself – came to fully embrace the approach represented by the first three principles of the original COrDeT-1 project and carried through CHESS – that is, a reference architecture that is both model-based and component-based. (The fourth principle of variability modeling likewise received thorough attention but was treated in a more technical and pragmatic than theoretical fashion). This is remarkable given the understandable reluctance of large entities to adopt potentially disruptive approaches.

The merits of this approach to reference architecture have been confirmed elsewhere. The AUTOSAR initiative [4] in particular has developed a reference architecture that shares very similar characteristics.

In AUTOSAR there is a component layer, which hosts components that are free from concerns about the underlying platform.

The bottom layer in AUTOSAR is known as the Basic Software, and encapsulates specific services in much the same way as the very bottom layer of the COrDeT-2 reference architecture does, captured by the "Run Time Kernel layer" box in Fig. 6, offering basic communication, memory access, and operating system kernel services.

The interaction layer is where there is some similarity but also divergences between COrDeT-2 and AUTOSAR. The Virtual Functional Bus of AUTOSAR corresponds to some degree to the component/connector paradigm of COrDeT-2. The middleware is represented in the Runtime Environment. But there is no concept of container in AUTOSAR for separating out non-functional concerns. This has the ramification that the AUTOSAR software component designer must specify non-functional concerns such as timing *within* the software components, for example in the specification of so-called *runnables* (which may have periodic or sporadic characteristics): this carries obviously negative consequences on functional reusability as the reuse of AUTOSAR components can only happen for *identical* non-functional conditions since any change in them may require algorithmic modifications.

Other non-functional concerns such as resources required (e.g. non-volatile memory) are likewise requested within the specification of the software components. Therefore, although it can be fairly said that the software components in AUTOSAR are to a great extent platform-independent, they do not separate non-functional concerns as cleanly as the COrDeT-2 *container* approach. Indeed, this has proven to be a complicating factor as a number of initiatives [11] have been undertaken to improve the handling of non-functional aspects, and tended to tie the software components of AUTOSAR to automotive domain-specific non-functional characteristics.

Despite the above difficulties and on the spin of its positive potential, the AUTOSAR community has also begun to realize that the adopted approach to a reference architecture is potentially usable across domains, and has launched an initiative called Derived Applications [13] to expand AUTOSAR into other domains. We can take this notion to be yet another confirmation that the approach that was conceived in COrDeT-1, elaborated in CHESS, and consolidated in COrDeT-2 – which we consider to encompass the AUTOSAR intent – is a powerful facilitator of systematic cross-domain reuse. Interestingly, the CONCERTO ("Guaranteed Component Assembly with Round Trip Analysis for Energy Efficient High-integrity Multi-core Systems") project has been recently selected by the ARTEMIS JU program office[1] to continue this promising line of investigation, carrying it toward further industrial domains.

Acknowledgements. The authors acknowledge the foundational work carried out by Marco Panunzio as part of his PhD and post-doc activities as an essential enabling factor to the achievements of the CHESS and COrDeT-2 projects. Stefano Puri contributed valuable clarifications to a number of issues addressed in the text. Special thanks to the consortia and funding authorities of the COrDeT-1 (ESA), CHESS (ARTEMIS JTI), and COrDeT-2 (ESA) projects, as well as the SAVOIR-FARE working group participants, whose successful collaboration produced the results described in this paper.

---

[1] http://www.artemis-ia.eu/programcall/index/view/?programcall=5

References

1. Frakes, W., Kang, K.: Software Reuse Research: Status and Future Directions. IEEE Transactions on Software Engineering 31(7) (July 2005)
2. Object Management Group, Model Driven Architecture, http://www.omg.org/mda/
3. Clements, P., Bachmann, F., Bass, L., Garlan, D., Ivers, J., Little, R., Merson, P., Nord, R., Stafford, J.: Documenting Software Architectures: Views and Beyond, 2nd edn. Addison-Wesley, Boston (2010) ISBN 0-321-55268-7
4. AUTOSAR: Automotive Open System Architecture, http://www.autosar.org/
5. Szyperski, C., Gruntz, D., Murer, S.: Component Software- Beyond Object-Oriented programming, 2nd edn. Addison-Wesley/ACM Press (2002)
6. Jacobson, I., Griss, M., Jonsson, P.: Software Reuse: Architecture, Process and Organization for Business Success. Addison-Wesley-Longman (May 1997)
7. Bosch, J.: Design & Use of Software Architectures: Adopting and Evolving a Product Line Approach. Addison-Wesley (2000)
8. Czarnecki, K., Eisenecker, U.: Generative Programming: Methods, Tools, and Applications. Addison-Wesley (2000)
9. Favaro, J., Mazzini, S.: Extending FeauRSEB with Cocepts from Systems Engienering. In: Edwards, S.H., Kulczycki, G. (eds.) ICSR 2009. LNCS, vol. 5791, pp. 41–50. Springer, Heidelberg (2009)
10. Angelov, S., Grefen, P., Greefhorst, D.: A Classification of Software Reference Architectures: Analyzing Their Success and Effectiveness. In: Joint Working IEEE/IFIP Conference on Software Architecture and European Conference on Software Architecture, WICSA/ECSA (2009)
11. TIMMO-2-Use, http://www.timmo-2-use.org/
12. Gamma, E., et al.: Design Patterns: Elements of Reusable Object-Oriented Software. Addison-Wesley (1994)
13. AUTOSAR Consortium, Development Partnership AUTOSAR to extend scope of applications to non-automotive areas (November 16, 2011), http://www.autosar.org
14. Mazzini, S., Puri, S., Vardanega, T.: An MDE Methodology for the Development of High Integrity Systems. In: Proc. of the Design, Automation & Test in Europe (DATE) Conference (2009)
15. Vardanega, T.: Property Preservation and Composition with Guarantees: From ASSERT to CHESS. In: Proc. of the 12th IEEE International Symposium on Object/Component/Service-Oriented Real-Time Distributed Computing, pp. 125–132 (2009)
16. Panunzio, M., Vardanega, T.: A Component Model Fit for Embedded Real-Time Systems. Submitted to: ACM Transactions in Embedded Computing Systems: Special Issue on Rigorous Embedded Systems Design
17. CorDeT2, ESA/ESTEC Contract No. 4000100991, Report 6, On-Board Software Reference Architecture Specification (December 2012)
18. Telemetry and Telecommand packet utilization standard (PUS), ECSS-E-70-41A
19. ARTEMIS Joint Undertaking for R&D in Embedded Systems, http://www.artemis-ju.eu
20. CHESS Consortium, CHESS Modeling Language and Editor V1.0.2, Project Deliverable, (March 31, 2010)

21. Burns, A., Dobbing, B., Romanski, G.: The Ravenscar Tasking Profile for High Integrity Real-Time Programs. In: Asplund, L. (ed.) Ada-Europe 1998. LNCS, vol. 1411, pp. 263–275. Springer, Heidelberg (1998)
22. Rodriguez, A., Alaña, E., Ferrero, F., et al.: COrDeT-2 R6 – On-Board Software Reference Architecture Specification, GMVAD 20566/12 Issue v2.1 (December 11, 2012)
23. CHESS Consortium, Technology-neutral specification of property-preserving run-time environment, V1.0, Project Deliverable, (January 31, 2011)
24. CHESS Project Web Site, http://www.chess-project.org
25. SAVOIR-FAIRE Working Group: Space on-board software reference architecture. Proceedings of DASIA Conference, Budapest (May 2010)

Automatic Analysis of Software Architectures with Variability*

Gustavo G. Pascual, Mónica Pinto, and Lidia Fuentes

Departamento de Lenguajes y Ciencias de la Computación
University of Málaga, Spain, CAOSD group
{gustavo,pinto,lff}@lcc.uma.es
http://caosd.lcc.uma.es

Abstract. Software Product Line Engineering is successfully applied in the development of families of related products. Basically, it allows reusing the software artifacts that are common to all the products, and adding/removing the variable ones. There are two alternatives to manage variability, one that models the commonalities and variabilities separately from the software product line architecture (SPLA), using, for instance, feature models (FM), and another one that models the variability as part of the SPLA. These two alternatives have both benefits and limitations. Our approach picks the best of both alternatives and, on the one hand, models variability as part of the SPLA (as in the second alternative), but, on the other hand, maps the SPLA with variability into an FM, generating an Architectural FM. By doing this our approach takes advantage of the FM tools and formal reasoning (as in the first alternative) to provide the automatic support that it is not available in other SPLA with variability approaches to: (i) check the consistency of architectural variability specifications, (ii) generate valid architectural configurations, and (iii) reason about variability at the architectural level.

1 Introduction

Software Product Line Engineering (SPLE) is being successfully applied in the specification and implementation of families of related products. There are two distinguishable phase in SPLE, the domain engineering and the application engineering phases[1]. In the domain engineering phase, the SPL architect defines domain specific commonalities and variabilities, as well as the software architecture of the family of products (SPLA - Software Product-Line Architecture). In the application engineering phase, the customer specifies a list of characteristics that are required for a given product, and an SPLE process generates custom-made software architecture configurations that meet the input requirements. So, how to specify variabilities and commonalities, and how to describe the SPLA in order to facilitate future generation of software products are the central activities of SPLE.

* Work supported by Projects TIN2008-01942, P09-TIC-5231 and INTER-TRUST FP7-317731.

J. Favaro and M. Morisio (Eds.): ICSR 2013, LNCS 7925, pp. 127–143, 2013.

One alternative to manage variability in an SPL is to specify the variabilities and commonalities separately from the SPLA, by using a variability language or formalism. Different variability languages can be used, such as Feature Models (FM) and Orthogonal Variability Management (OVM) [2]. Among the existing proposals that take this approach, we find that the majority of them use FMs [3], which model variability by means of high-level features that are close to the requirements specification. As another alternative, there is plenty of work that propose defining variability as part of the software architectural model, focusing on the reuse of those software artifacts that are common to all the architectural configurations, and on the addition and/or removal of the variable architectural elements. These works primarily use UML profiles or extensions of architecture description languages [3]. They can be considered architecture-centric approaches, where the SPLA models both the base structure of the family member products and the conditions under which their software artifacts can vary (i.e. the architectural variation points). These two alternatives have both benefits and limitations and, as shown in [3], they are equally popular. In this recent study, 97 papers reporting variability management approaches were surveyed, where 33% of them propose specifying variability as part of the SPLA, and another 33% propose the use of FMs (the main representative of the first alternative).

One of the main benefits of specifying variability separately from the SPLA, using, for example FMs, is that existing approaches are generally well-supported by tools that make it possible to formally reason about variability and to manage the product generation phase easily and with the guarantee of a formal basis. The main drawback is that an additional process is required to derive architectural configurations that meet an FM configuration. In this sense, the VML language in [4], VSpecs links in CVL [5], just to name a few, are mechanisms that connect the variability specification to the SPLA. Regarding the second alternative, one important benefit of using UML profiles is that UML is well known by all SPL practitioners, including those in the industry, which makes the adoption of an SPLE process easier. Another benefit is that architecture variability is directly managed using the architectural artifacts, i.e., components/connectors. However, the drawback is that the tool support that is needed for consistently managing architectural variability is a long way from being mature enough to be equivalent to the support already provided by existing FM tools[1] (i.e., first alternative). This makes the management of architecture variability in architecture-centric SPLE processes error prone and difficult to employ in large SPLs.

Specifically, we have identified several challenges that an SPLA with variability approach must address in order to help the Software Architect (SArch): (C1) analysis of the correctness and consistency of the SPLA with variability; (C2) derivation of correct and minimal architectural configurations, and (C3) reasoning about the variability degree of the SPLA by helping the SArch to answer questions like: "What is the impact of adding/deleting a component in

---

[1] Hydra (http://caosd.lcc.uma.es/spl/hydra/), FaMa (http://www.isa.us.es/fama), S.P.L.O.T. (http://www.splot-research.org), and FeatureIDE (http://wwwiti.cs.uni-magdeburg.de/iti_db/research/featureide/)

product configurations?"; "How can an architectural constraint affect product configurations?", or "How many configurations fulfill a given subset of input constraints?". As shown in the following sections, these tasks are not properly supported by tools in the current SPLA with variability approaches.

In this paper we propose to address the aforementioned limitations of SPLA with variability approaches, picking the best of both alternatives. Thus, in our approach, the SArch first models the SPLA with variability using a UML profile (ADOM [6]). This means that the common components and connections to be reused for all product configurations, the architectural variation points, and the constraints that determine how the family of products can vary, are all specified at the architectural level. Then, in order to reason about the consistency and other properties of the SPLA architecture with variability, and about product configurations, we use FMs. Specifically, we propose mapping the SPLA with variability into an FM, defining an Architectural Feature Model (AFM). In this way, our approach takes advantage of the FM tools but, instead of high-level features, our FM tree contains architectural artifacts (i.e. components and connectors). It is important to highlight here that the SArch does not have to manipulate the AFM at all. Instead, he/she only has to interpret the results of the FM tool, which will be provided in terms of architectural artifacts. The utility of an AFM has already been explored in [7,8], as part of a refactoring process that specifies the variability of a list of related products that had been previously developed by the authors without using an SPL approach. Also, in [9] authors generate an FM from a design model with variability, the considered features being the package, class and operation, although this cannot be considered a pure AFM as it is closer to a design feature model.

Following this introduction, the paper is organised as follows. Section 2 compares related work with our approach, while Section 3 focuses on the motivation for our work. The modelling of SAs with variability is described in Section 4 using a running example, and the mapping from an SA to an AFM is detailed in Section 5. Section 6 shows the advantages of using the AFMs to check the consistency of architectural models with variability. In Section 7 we evaluate our approach and, finally, Section 8 presents the conclusions and on-going work.

2   Related Work

In this section, we focus on SPLE approaches that are comparable to our work. We have analysed several proposals focusing on the three challenges (labeled as C1-C3 in Table 1) that we have identified in the introduction as important to be addressed by SPLA with variability approaches. We have organised the different approaches into several groups. The first group is shown in the first rows of Table 1 ([10,11,12,13,14]) and just focus on the variability modelling. They do not address any of the challenges we have identified and, thus, their applicability is mainly descriptive, being only appropriate for SPL architecture description [16].

A second group of approaches are those that provide support for product derivation (C2) but do not provide any kind of support for variability

Table 1. Related Work Classification

Approach	Variability Modelling	C1. Consistency analysis	C2. Product derivation Support	C3. Variability reasoning
Razavian [10], Gomaa [11], Clauss [12]	UML Stereotypes	No	No	No
Δ-MontiArc [13]	ADL extension	No	No	No
PL-AspectualACME [14]	ADL extension	No	No	No
Jézéquel [9]	Ecore models weaving	No	Yes (FM)	Manual
Oliveira Junior [15]	Tables, use cases, class models	No	Yes (Variability Implementation Model)	Manual
Acher [7]	Refactored Feature Model	Yes (Manual FM Comparison by Software Architect)	Yes (FM)	Manual (compare two FMs)
Ziadi [16]	UML Profile	Yes (OCL constraints)	Yes (UML Model Transformation)	Manual (Decision model)
Parra [8]	Aspect and Feature metamodels	Yes (FM constraints + Aspect dependencies)	Yes (Weaving)	Manual at metamodel level
Our approach	**UML Stereotypes**	**Yes (FM constraints)**	**Yes (FM)**	**Automatic**

reasoning (C1). Moreover, the feature selection criteria to reason about variability (C3) is manual. In [9] authors propose to add variability to an Ecore/EMOF metamodel using aspect-oriented modelling techniques, but no checking about architectural consistency is performed. They also propose a product derivation mechanism that uses transformation techniques to generate a design FM (being the package, class and operation the considered features) from the metamodel with variability (fulfill C2). Regarding C3, the SArch could reason about the variability of the design FM, but since the features considered are package, class and method, the connection with the source metamodel is lost. In the second work of this group, the variability is modeled using a set of variability models (tables, use cases and class models) [15]. The product derivation is led by a manually defined table that includes fields such as the affected class/component, variability implementation mechanisms and strategy. The applicability of these approaches is clearly different from ours since: (1) there are no automatic mechanisms for reasoning about architectural variability (not C1); (2) the selection of a FM configuration is performed manually by the domain engineer (not C3), and (3) these approaches are only suitable for detailed design-time.

The rest of approaches in Table 1 provide some kind of support for both variability reasoning (C1) and for product derivation (C2). As in previous ones, the feature selection criteria (C3) is manual. In [7] FMs are used to reverse engineer the variability of an existing system by recovering an FM from the actual architecture. There are important differences between this work and our work. The first of them is that variability is not explicitly represented in their SAs, and thus their main motivation is to define a process to be able to "capture" and model the variability of existing related products by means of FMs. In order to do that, and similarly to the work in [17], an architectural FM is automatically extracted by means of the legacy code exploration. Also, the SArch must manually specify another FM, which need to be manually reconciled with the automated FM to obtain an AFM compatible with both the SA view and the actual architecture. In our approach, the SArch must specify the SA with variability and then the rest of the process, including the generation of the AFM, is completely automatic. We guarantee that our mapping is consistent meaning that all the variability expressed in the SA is consistently propagated to the generated AFM. In [16], the variability is modelled using a UML profile and, then, a *decision model* is manually specified which guides the derivation process based on transformation of UML models. However, in this approach, the support for variability reasoning is very limited (only 2 OCL restrictions to avoid basic inconsistencies) and the product derivation is performed manually. Finally, [8] defines variability with a feature metamodel, which governs the composition between aspects and software components. They make a combined analysis of the inter-feature constraints of the feature metamodel and the dependencies between the corresponding aspect models, in order to generate correct assembled products by means of model weaving implemented as model transformations. So, none of the presented approaches (nor similar ones [3]) address adequately the challenges C1-C3 posed in this paper, and, thus, their applicability is limited.

3   Our Approach - Challenges

Figure 1 shows an overview of our SPLE process. The first step is the specification of the SPLA with variability (box (1)) using UML stereotypes. Since there is no standard profile for modelling variability in UML, we have chosen the ADOM profile that provides all the elements identified in the literature as being necessary to model variability at the architectural level. We would like to stress that the validity of our approach does not depend on the use of a particular UML Profile, so any other profiles for modelling variability at the architectural level could have been used. This SPLA with variability is the input for our mapping algorithm (box (2)) that generates an AFM, which is one of the main contributions of our approach (Section 5). An AFM is a feature tree with mandatory and optional features representing components and connectors, and a set of *cross-tree constraints* expressing dependencies between features, which in our case are architectural artifacts. Using the generated AFM and the existing tool support for FM our approach addresses the identified challenges:

C1. Automatic Analysis of the Consistency of an SPLA with Variability. In SPLE architecture-centric approaches, the SArch manually defines the architectural variability and some constraints between architectural artifacts, so it is possible that he/she may introduce some inconsistencies. The challenge is to provide the SArch with tool support to make the automatic checking of architectural variability inconsistencies possible. In our process, we detect and solve some of these inconsistencies during the mapping process. Also, by using FM tools (box (3)) it is possible to detect some anomalies in the AFM, which could mean that the variability has not been defined well at the architectural level (Section 6). The SArch can then check the generated configurations from an architectural point of view, refining them if they are not correct (box (4)).

C2. Automatic Derivation of Correct Architectural Configurations. In order to generate a product configuration, the SArch specifies the optional elements (product requirements) that must be present in the derived product.

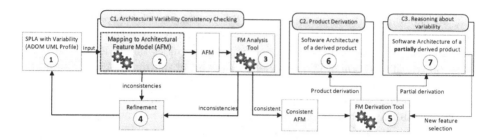

Fig. 1. Overview of our approach

Thus, it is necessary to provide tool support to generate valid and minimal configurations that fulfill the product requirements. One of the interesting applicabilities of our approach is that it allows the automatic derivation of valid architectural configurations using existing FM tools, without any model transformation. SArchs can use standard tools to specify the SPLA, such as UML editors, but with the important advantage of having the possibility to generate correct configurations by using existing FM product derivation tools (box (5)). Furthermore, FM tools guarantee that the generated configuration is minimal in terms of the number of features, components and connectors in our case.

C3. Support for Reasoning about an SPLA with Variability. The challenge here is to provide the SArch with tool support to explore the variability possibilities. Most FM tools provide the possibility of generating "partially" derived products by instantiating only a subset of the variation points. Our approach takes advantage of this characteristic of FM tools in order to reason about the software architecture (SA) with variability, by allowing the SArch to partially instantiate the AFM (box (7)). For instance, by selecting or un-selecting a component the SArch can analyse the impact of having that component in the final configuration. Moreover, it makes it easier to analyse how the software product line changes when a new architectural constraint is incorporated into the design. Another example may be to obtain information about how many configurations fulfill a given subset of input constraints. The benefit of our approach is that this reasoning about the SA can be automatically performed by combining the use of existing FM tools with the AFM generated by our algorithm.

4   Modelling the Software Architecture with Variability

As discussed in previous section, the first step in our approach is modelling the SPLA with variability. In order to do that, we use UML 2.0 and the ADOM UML Profile (see Table 2). Any approach that includes these concepts can be the source model of our mapping process, and can then benefit from our work.

Figure 2 shows the SA with variability of our case study, a *RemoteAssistant* application, which aims at providing technical support to remote clients, which communicate with the technician using different communication mechanisms. Variability is modelled by (a) providing different component realizations

Table 2. ADOM Architectural Modelling Stereotypes

Stereotypes	Description
Variation point	Indicates that a component can be realized by different variants. Its cardinality defines the minimum/maximum number of variants that can be simultaneously selected.
Variant	Each one of the alternative realizations of a variation point.
Optional single	Applied to a component, connector, variation point or attribute, indicates that the architectural element is optional. In case it is selected, it can be included only once.
Requires	When an architectural element A requires an architectural element B, it means that in case A is selected in the configuration, B should be selected too.
Excludes	When an architectural element A excludes an architectural element B, it means that in case A is selected in the configuration, B should not be selected.

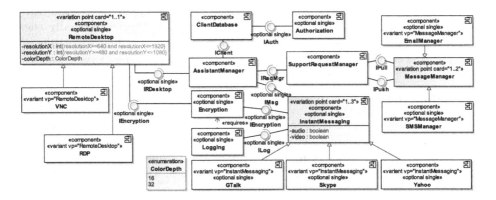

Fig. 2. Architectural Model of a "RemoteAssistant" application with variability

using *variation point* and *variant* stereotypes; (b) defining optional architectural elements; (c) adding attributes to the components (*parameterization*) and (d) introducing constraints among architectural elements. Connectors have been modelled using the *ball-and-socket* notation for legibility reasons.

Component attributes can be boolean, integer, real or enumerate values, among others. We support the definition of OCL constraints in the component attributes to limit the minimum and maximum values for that attribute and take advantage of the extended FMs' support for specifying allowed ranges of values. For instance, remote desktop variants have (resolutionX, resolutionY and colorDepth) attributes . The first ones are integers in the [640, 1920] and [480, 1080] ranges respectively, and the last one can take the values 16 and 32 (ColorDepth enumeration). Similarly, instant messaging variants contain two boolean attributes (audio and video), which enable/disable voice/video chat.

Constraints among architectural elements are specified using the requires and excludes stereotypes. For instance, as shown in the figure, including the Logging component implies including also the Encryption component. Moreover, in order to generate consistent architectures, a connector has be removed if the components it connects are not selected. To this end, a requires constraint is specified from the connector to the optional components that communicate through it. On the other hand, if we want to avoid certain components from getting disconnected from the rest of components of the architecture, a similar cross-tree constraint can be added in the opposite way (from the component to the connector). For legibility reasons, these constraints are omitted from Figure 2.

5   Mapping the Software Architecture to the AFM

In this section we describe the mapping algorithm that we have defined to automatically transform the variability of our SA into an AFM. The mapping has been split into several steps. First, the components of the architecture are introduced in the AFM calling Algorithm 1 (the output is Figure 3). Second, the connectors are mapped calling Algorithm 2 (the output is Figure 4). Finally, the constraints defined by the SA are also added to the AFM calling Algorithm 3 (Figure 5). These algorithms are detailed in the following subsections.

5.1   Mapping the Components of the Architecture

All the information about the components of the SA is added to the AFM by Algorithm 1, under a feature called Components (line 1), which is a child of the root feature (line 3). Mandatory components are always included in every valid configuration of the architecture, unlike the optional ones, which have the *optional* stereotype. Therefore, mandatory components are added as mandatory features in the AFM while the optional components are added as optional features (lines 6-10). For instance, in Figure 3, we can see some mandatory features such as AssistantManager or ComplaintManager that represent the mandatory components, while other features (RemoteControl, Logging, etc.) are optional.

Next, the attributes of the component are mapped. In attributed FMs, attributes are added to the FM adding annotations to the features. Therefore, we add annotations to the features which model the parameterized components. First, we distinguish whether the attribute is of an enumerated type. In that case, an annotation containing the list of values of the enumerated type is created. If the attribute is not of an enumerated type (e.g. integer, double...) then the lower and upper bounds are extracted from the OCL constraints related to the attribute, creating then the appropriate annotation. Figure 3 shows examples of both kinds of annotations. Concretely, an annotation for the enumerated attribute colorDepth and the integer attributes resolutionX and resolutionY are shown.

On the other hand, we have to take into account whether the component is a variation point, which is distinguished with the *variation point* stereotype. If true, we evaluate its cardinality. Attributed FMs support two kinds of groups: (1) *alternative groups*, in which only one feature of the group can be selected and (2) *or groups*, in which one or more features (up to all the features of the group) can be selected. Thus, due to the limitation of the attributed FMs, we can only support the cases where minimum cardinality is 1 and maximum cardinality is either 1 or equals to the number of variants that can realize the variation point. Then, once the group is created, all the variants, together with their attributes, are added to the group as children of their variation point. In Figure 3 we can see that the RemoteDesktop feature, which represents the RemoteDesktop component,

Algorithm 1. *MapComponents*: Maps the components to the AFM.

Input: The architecture (*Architecture*) and the architectural feature model (F_{model}).
Output: The architectural feature model populated with components features (F_{model})
1: $f_{components} \leftarrow CreateFeature("Components")$
2: $f_{root} \leftarrow GetRoot(F_{model})$
3: $F_{model} \leftarrow AddMandatoryFeature(F_{model}, f_{root}, f_{components})$
4: **for all** c **in** *Components* / *variant* $\notin Stereotypes(c)$ **do**
5:    $f_c \leftarrow CreateFeature(c)$
6:    **if** *optional* $\in Stereotypes(c)$ **then**
7:       $F_{model} \leftarrow AddOptionalFeature(F_{model}, f_{components}, f_c)$
8:    **else**
9:       $F_{model} \leftarrow AddMandatoryFeature(F_{model}, f_{components}, f_c)$
10:   **end if**
11:   $f_c \leftarrow MapAttributes(f_c, c)$
12:   **if** variation point $\in Stereotypes(c)$ **then**
13:      $vp \leftarrow VariationPoint(c)$
14:      **if** $MaximumCardinality(vp) = 1$ **then**
15:         $f_g \leftarrow CreateAlternativeGroup()$
16:      **else**
17:         $f_g \leftarrow CreateORGroup()$
18:      **end if**
19:      **for all** $v \in Variants(vp)$ **do**
20:         $f_v \leftarrow CreateFeature(v)$
21:         $f_v \leftarrow MapAttributes(f_v, v)$
22:         $f_g \leftarrow AddFeatureToGroup(f_g, f_v)$
23:      **end for**
24:      $F_{model} \leftarrow AddGroup(F_{model}, f_c, f_g)$
25:   **end if**
26:   $F_{model} \leftarrow AddFeature(F_{model}, f_{components}, f_c)$
27: **end for**

has a alternative group as child with two different members, which represent the two variants specified in the SA for the component, while the InstantMessaging feature has an OR group as child because the variants of the InstantMessaging component are not mutually exclusive.

5.2 Mapping the Connectors of the Architecture

The next step in our algorithm is mapping the connectors. This process is performed by Algorithm 2, and an excerpt of the part of the AFM containing this information can be seen in Figure 4. All the features are children of the

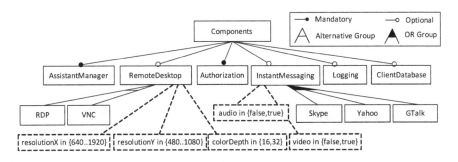

Fig. 3. Excerpt of the Components part of the AFM

Algorithm 2. *MapConnectors*: Maps the connectors to the AFM

Input: The architecture (*Architecture*) and the architectural feature model (F_{model}).
Output: The architectural feature model with the connectors mapped (F_{model})
1: $f_{connectors} \leftarrow CreateFeature("Connectors")$
2: $f_{root} \leftarrow GetRoot(F_{model})$
3: $F_{model} \leftarrow AddMandatoryFeature(F_{model}, f_{root}, f_{connectors})$
4: **for all** cc in $Connectors(Architecture)$ **do**
5:    $f_{cc} \leftarrow CreateFeature(cc)$
6:    **if** $optional \in Stereotypes(cc)$ **then**
7:      $F_{model} \leftarrow AddOptionalFeature(F_{model}, f_{connectors}, f_{cc})$
8:    **else**
9:      $F_{model} \leftarrow AddMandatoryFeature(F_{model}, f_{connectors}, f_{cc})$
10:   **end if**
11:   $[p_s, p_t] \leftarrow GetPorts(cc)$
12:   $[c_s, c_t] \leftarrow GetPortsComponents(p_s, p_t)$
13:   **if** $optional \in (Stereotypes(c_s) \cup Stereotypes(c_t))$ and $optional \notin Stereotypes(cc)$ **then**
14:     $NotifyOptionalityInconsistency(cc)$
15:   **end if**
16:   $constraints \leftarrow GetConstraints(Architecture)$
17:   **if** $optional \in (Stereotypes(c_s))$ and $requires(cc, c_s) \notin constraints$ **then**
18:     $NotifyConstraintInconsistency(cc, c_s)$
19:   **end if**
20:   **if** $optional \in (Stereotypes(c_t))$ and $requires(cc, c_t) \notin constraints$ **then**
21:     $NotifyConstraintInconsistency(cc, c_t)$
22:   **end if**
23: **end for**

Connectors feature, added as a child of the root feature. A new feature is created for each connector of the architecture. Connectors with the *optional* stereotype are added as optional features, while the rest are added as mandatory features. Next, stereotypes are checked in order to detect inconsistencies in the specification of the variability. For instance, an inconsistent architectural configuration would exist if a mandatory connector is specified between two components where one or both of them are optional. Then, a configuration with the unwired connector selected would be valid according to the specifications, but not consistent. Concretely, lines 13-14 check this inconsistency, notifying it to the SA in case the *optional* stereotype is missing from the connector's variability specifications. Actually, the selection of a connector should imply adding both source and target components to the configuration. Therefore, for each optional component that is connected through a connector, a *requires* association should be added to the variability specifications. This is checked in our algorithm in lines 16-22.

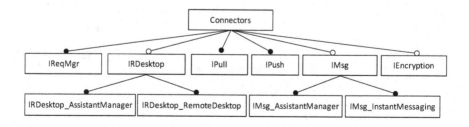

Fig. 4. Excerpt of the Connectors part of the AFM

5.3   Mapping the Constraints among Architectural Elements

The last step is mapping the constraints specified among architectural elements, specified by defining associations stereotyped as *requires* or *excludes*. For instance, a connector that connects optional components will *require* the selection of those optional components. Algorithm 3 shows how these constraints are mapped to cross-tree constraints in the AFM. For each architectural constraint, the features related to the source and target architectural elements are extracted from the feature model. Then, a cross-tree constraint equivalent to the architectural constraint is added to the AFM. Some of the cross-tree constraints specified for the case study are shown in Figure 5. The cross-tree constraint 1 is the result of mapping the architectural constraint between components which has been specified in the architectural model. On the other hand, constraints 2-5 model associations between connectors and their related components.

Algorithm 3. *MapConstraints*: Maps the architectural constraints

---

Input: The architectural constraints (*Constraints*) and the architectural feature model (F_{model}).
Output: The architectural feature model with the mapped constraints (F_{model})
1: **for all** $c \in Constraints$ **do**
2:    $[s_c, s_t] \leftarrow GetConstraintElements(c)$
3:    $f_s \leftarrow GetFeature(F_{model}, s_c)$
4:    $f_t \leftarrow GetFeature(F_{model}, s_t)$
5:    **if** $Stereotype(c) = requires$ **then**
6:        $F_{model} \leftarrow AddRequiresConstraint(f_s, f_t)$
7:    **else**
8:        $F_{model} \leftarrow AddExcludesConstraint(f_s, f_t)$
9:    **end if**
10: **end for**

| 1 | Logging REQUIRES Encryption | 2 | IRDesktop REQUIRES RemoteDesktop | 3 | IEncryption REQUIRES Encryption |
| 4 | IEncryption REQUIRES RemoteDesktop | 5 | ILog REQUIRES Logging | | |

Fig. 5. Excerpt of the cross-tree constraints of the RemoteAssistant AFM

6   Reasoning about the Architectural Model Variability

6.1   Checking Consistency

The mapping algorithm ensures that the AFM does not allow the generation of products that comply with the variability specifications but are inconsistent from an architectural point of view. Specifically, as shown in Section 5.2, the algorithm that maps the connectors prevents the system from reaching configurations where connectors are selected but not the components whose ports are connected using them. However, there are other mistakes in the variability specification that, although do not lead to inconsistent configurations, can be a symptom of variability anomalies. We propose to detect them using FM tools applied to our AFM. For this, we extend previous results [18] that identify FM anomalies, and adapt them to the architectural viewpoint, mainly by relating the AFM anomalies with the possible mistakes introduced by the SArch. Once these mistakes has been detected, the SArch is notified in order to refine the architectural model (box 4 of Figure 1).

Dead Features. Dead features are features that, due to cross-tree constraints, cannot appear in any valid configuration of the FM. These features can be detected easily using FM tools such as S.P.L.O.T.. In our approach, a dead feature can appear due to a variability constraint defined by the SArch. For instance, assuming that the SArch would have defined the constraint AssistantManager excludes InstantMessaging in the architectural model of Figure 2, since the Assistant-Manager component is mandatory, InstantMessaging would never be selected in a valid configuration, resulting in a dead feature.

False Optional Features. A false optional feature is a feature that, despite being optional, is included in every valid configuration of the FM. As it happened with the dead features, this anomaly can only be introduced due to cross-tree constraints. When we translate this FM anomaly to an architectural level, we can conclude that false optional features are related to components or connectors with the optional stereotype which should be, in fact, mandatory, because it is impossible to get a valid architectural configuration in which that component or connector is not present. For instance, a mandatory connector that connects an optional component would lead to a false optional feature because a cross-tree constraint where the connector, which is mandatory, requires the component, would be introduced, resulting in the component being mandatory despite it has been modelled as *optional*.

Wrong Group Cardinality. The cardinality of a group is the range (minimum and maximum number) of features that can be selected from a group simultaneously. The cardinality is wrong if there are constraints that make the features of the group mutually exclusive. For instance, if there is an OR-group $G = \{FeatureA, FeatureB, FeatureC\}$ and a cross-tree constraint such as *FeatureA excludes FeatureC*, the real cardinality of the group is *1..2* instead of *1..3*. It is not possible to get this kind of anomaly unless variability restrictions leading to it are introduced manually by the SArch. Theses mistakes are notified to the SArch because they reduce the degree of variability in a way that probably contradict the behaviour expected by the SArch.

Redundancy. Redundancy is introduced in a FM when the same information is specified in different ways. Redundancy itself does not necessarily represent a problem. Although it can decrease the maintainability of the FM, this is not relevant in our approach because the AFM is not intended to be managed by the SArch. However, redundancy is notified because removing them it is possible to simplify the architectural variability specifications.

6.2   Derivation of Minimal Architectural Configuration

One of the main benefits of FMs is the availability of tools for automatically derive valid configurations. One of these tools is Hydra, which allows generating minimal configurations of an FM, where the minimal configuration can be defined as the configuration which includes the least feature count. This configuration represents, on the other hand, the configuration with the lowest amount of architectural elements. Applying Hydra to the FM of our case study, the results shown that the minimal configuration consists of 11 features, which represents an architectural configuration with 4 components (AssistantManager, ClientDatabase, SupportRequestManager and either EmailManager or SMSManager) and 3 connectors (IReqMgr, IPull and IPush). When architectural configurations are derived either manually, or by model transformations is not so easy to assure they indeed generate minimal architectural configurations, and that they are correct.

6.3   Reasoning about the Variability Degree

One of the most important points when designing systems with variability is evaluating the degree of variability because it allows the SArch to determine if the variability specifications result as expected. However, current tools for modelling architectural variability lack this support. For instance, there are no tools for calculating the number of valid architectural configurations when variability is added to the architecture. However, it is very straightforward to calculate the number of valid configurations of a FM using any of the existing FM tools. In our approach, the architectural variability is totally mapped into the AFM and, therefore, we can take advantage of the FM tools in order to exactly know the number of valid architectural configurations [19] [20], by executing the following operations over the AFMs:

Number of Products. It allows the SArch to know the flexibility of the architecture that he/she is specifying, reducing or increasing it as necessary.

Filtering Products. The SArch can apply filters to the variability specification, forcing the presence (or absence) of certain components or connectors. Therefore, it is possible to answer questions such as *"'Is it possible to generate a valid product with instant messaging and encryption simultaneously?"'*, *"'How many configurations allow having VNC and Gtalk enabled at the same time?"'* or *"'How many/which valid configurations are added or removed if a concrete component/connector/stereotype is added or removed?"'*.

List of Products. It is possible to get all the solutions of the AFM, which are all the valid and consistent configurations of the SA. Moreover, this operation can be combined with filtering, allowing the SArch to get the list of configurations that meet his/her concrete requirements.

Commonality. The SArch can assess what is the percentage of architectural configurations in which a concrete component or connector appears.

Product Is Valid?. The SArch can check if a manually constructed architectural configuration satisfies the architectural variability specifications.

7   Evaluation

In this section we evaluate our approach by: (1) showing the correctness of the mapping algorithm, the central part of our proposal; (2) evaluate if the mapping algorithm scales well when the number of components and connectors increases, and (3) discuss the potential of the analysis of the variability degree performed with FM tools. The rest of the proposal is based on the capabilities of the FM tools, whose results have been proven by third.

7.1   Mapping Algorithm Correctness

Ensuring that the mapping algorithm is correct is necessary to provide validity to the reasoning mechanisms that can be applied to the AFM. The architectural variability represented by the AFM is correct if:

1. The variability of the architectural elements has not been modified. Therefore (a) each mandatory architectural element should be mapped to a feature or set of features that are common to every AFM valid configuration; (b) each optional architectural element should not be mapped as a core feature/set of features; (c) the cardinality of the variation points should not be affected by the mapping process and (d) the constraints between architectural elements should be mapped as equivalent constraints between AFM features.
2. Every valid AFM configuration represent a consistent architectural configuration. In other words, it implies that all valid but inconsistent configurations that can be obtained taking into account the architectural model variability specifications have been removed (and, consequently, the variability specifications have been refined) during the mapping process.

The first condition is accomplished because, in our mapping algorithm, (a) each mandatory architectural element is mapped to a mandatory feature; (b) optional architectural elements are mapped to optional features; (c) variants are linked to variation points as a child group of features where the cardinality matches the one defined in the architectural model and (d) this 1-to-1 mapping between architectural elements and features allow us to directly translate the variability constraints of the architectural model to similar cross-tree constraints between the related AFM features. The second condition is satisfied because Algorithm 2 ensures that it is not possible to generate valid AFMs configurations which lead to loose connectors. Although the refinement process continues after the mapping process has been completed, the anomalies detected in this stage are not related to consistency but to possible mistakes that unintentionally modify the expected variability of the SA.

7.2   Scalability

On the one hand, the complexity of the mapping algorithm increases linearly with the number of architectural elements and constraints among them, because it mainly traverses these lists of elements. Therefore, the algorithm is highly scalable, especially taking into account that it is applied at design stage of the software development life cycle.

7.3   Variability Degree

We have applied our mapping algorithm to the case study presented in this paper, as well as to the *CongressAssistant* case study, which is available in [21], and to the case study presented by Razavian in [10]. We have calculated the number of features, configurations and constraints of the generated AFMs. The results, which have been obtained using the Hydra tool, are shown in Table 3. Note that the number of configurations shown in the table does not take into account the different values for the component attributes, but the addition/deletion of architectural elements. This information cannot be obtained using the approaches presented in Section 3, since they do not provide any kind of support for assessing the degree of variability. Once the SArch knows the number of valid configurations, it is possible for him/her to evaluate if there is less or more variability than expected, and also to get a list of the valid configurations, checking if any configuration should be removed. In case that a configuration has to be removed, it could be done modifying the variability stereotypes or specifying additional architectural constraints. The idea is not that the SArch explores each one of the possible configuration (normally thousands of them), but that he reasons about a subset of them, that fulfill concrete product requirements.

Table 3. Evaluation of Variability

Case Study	Features	Constraints	Configurations
This paper	29	13	1062
CongressAssistant	41	20	2496
Ravazian case study	34	0	32

8   Conclusion and Future Work

In this paper we have presented an approach to model and reason about variability at the architectural level. The contributions of our approach are twofold. First, we define a mapping process that automatically transforms a SA with variability into an AFM. This allows the use of the existing tool support for FM to reason about the variability of architectural elements – i.e. components, connectors and attributes. Second, due to the formal semantics of FM and its tool support, we have defined an inconsistencies checking process that allows identifying and correcting variability inconsistencies at the architectural level. As part of our on-going work we are using the generated AFMs in different applicability scenarios, such as runtime reconfiguration of mobile applications.

References

1. Klaus Pohl, G.B., van der Linden, F.: Software Product Line Engineering. Springer, Heidelberg (2005)
2. Czarnecki, K., et al.: Cool features and tough decisions: a comparison of variability modeling approaches. In: Proceedings of VaMoS 2012, pp. 173–182. ACM (2012)
3. Chen, L., Babar, M.A.: A systematic review of evaluation of variability management approaches in software product lines. Information and Software Technology 53(4), 344–362 (2011)
4. Loughran, N., Sánchez, P., Garcia, A., Fuentes, L.: Language support for managing variability in architectural models. In: Pautasso, C., Tanter, É. (eds.) SC 2008. LNCS, vol. 4954, pp. 36–51. Springer, Heidelberg (2008)
5. Common Variability Language (CVL),
   http://www.omgwiki.org/variability/doku.php
6. Reinhartz-Berger, I., Sturm, A.: Comprehensibility of uml-based software product line specifications. Empirical Software Engineering, 1–36 (2012)
7. Acher, M., Cleve, A., Collet, P., Merle, P., Duchien, L., Lahire, P.: Reverse engineering architectural feature models. In: Crnkovic, I., Gruhn, V., Book, M. (eds.) ECSA 2011. LNCS, vol. 6903, pp. 220–235. Springer, Heidelberg (2011)
8. Parra, C., Cleve, A., Blanc, X., Duchien, L.: Feature-based composition of software architectures. Software Architecture, 230–245 (2010)
9. Morin, B., Perrouin, G., Lahire, P., Barais, O., Vanwormhoudt, G., Jézéquel, J.-M.: Weaving variability into domain metamodels. In: Schürr, A., Selic, B. (eds.) MODELS 2009. LNCS, vol. 5795, pp. 690–705. Springer, Heidelberg (2009)
10. Razavian, M., Khosravi, R.: Modeling variability in the component and connector view of architecture using uml. In: IEEE/ACS International Conference on Computer Systems and Applications, AICCSA 2008, pp. 801–809 (April 2008)
11. Gomaa, H.: Designing software product lines with uml 2.0: From use cases to pattern-based software architectures. Reuse of Off-the-Shelf Components, 440 (2006)
12. Clauss, M.: Generic Modeling using UML extensions for variability. In: Proceedings of OOPSLA Workshop on Domain-specific Visual Languages, Tampa, FL, USA, pp. 11–18 (2001)
13. Haber, A., et al.: Delta-oriented architectural variability using monticore. In: Proceedings of the 5th European Conference on Software Architecture: Companion Volume, pp. 6:1–6:10. ACM, New York (2011)
14. Adachi Barbosa, E., Batista, T., Garcia, A., Silva, E.: PL-AspectualACME: an aspect-oriented adl for software product lines. In: Crnkovic, I., Gruhn, V., Book, M. (eds.) ECSA 2011. LNCS, vol. 6903, pp. 139–146. Springer, Heidelberg (2011)
15. Junior, E.A.O., et al.: Systematic management of variability in uml-based software product lines. Journal of Universal Computer Science 16(17), 2374–2393 (2010)
16. Ziadi, T., Jézéquel, J.M.: Product Line Engineering with the UML: Deriving Products. In: Pohl, K. (ed.) Software Product Lines, pp. 557–586. Springer (2006)
17. Pashov, I., Riebisch, M.: Using feature modeling for program comprehension and software architecture recovery. In: 11th IEEE International Conference on the Engineering of Computer-Based Systems, pp. 406–417 (May 2004)
18. Benavides, D., Segura, S., Ruiz-Cortés, A.: Automated analysis of feature models 20 years later: A literature review. Information Systems 35(6), 615–636 (2010)
19. Benavides, D., Trinidad, P., Ruiz-Cortés, A.: Automated reasoning on feature models. In: Pastor, Ó., Falcão e Cunha, J. (eds.) CAiSE 2005. LNCS, vol. 3520, pp. 491–503. Springer, Heidelberg (2005)

20. Segura, S., et al.: Betty: benchmarking and testing on the automated analysis of feature models. In: Proceedings of VAMOS 2012, pp. 63–71. ACM (2012)
21. Pascual, G.G., Pinto, M., Fuentes, L.: Run-time adaptation of mobile applications using genetic algorithms (submitted, 2013)

A   Appendix: Summary of Algorithms Functions

The functions that are used in the algorithms presented along the paper have names that are self-descriptive. Anyway, in order to improve the understanding of the algorithms, we include this appendix where the behaviour of those functions is briefly described.

Table 4. Summary of functions used in the algorithms

Function	Description
IsEnumerated	Returns true if the type of an attribute is enumerated.
CreateEnumeratedAnnotation	Creates an enumeration for an enumerated attribute (e.g. $MEMORY\_SIZE$ in $\{256, 512, 1024, 2048\}$)
CreateBoundedAnnotation	Creates an enumeration for a non-enumerated attribute with lower and upper bounds (e.g. $PRIORITY$ in $\{1, 10\}$)
GetBounds	Extracts the values of the OCL constraints expressing the lower and upper bound for the value of an attribute (eg. $GetBounds("BATTERY >= 60\ AND\ BATTERY <= 90") = [60, 90]$)
GetPorts	Returns the source and target ports of a component.
GetPortComponents	Returns the components which owns the specified ports.
GetConstraints	Returns the constraints among architectural elements, which are modelled as associations stereotypes with *requires* or *excludes*.
NotifyConstraintInconsistency	Notifies to the software architect that a *requires* association between two architectural elements is missing.
NotifyOptionalityInconsistency	Notifies to the software architect that a mandatory architectural element should be optional in order to prevent the system from reaching inconsistent architectural configurations.
GetConstraintElements	Returns the source and target architectural elements of an architectural constraint (e.g. $GetConstraintElements("A\ requires\ B") = "[A, B]"$)
AddRequiresConstraint	Add a cross-tree constraint to the AFM with the syntax $FeatureA$ $REQUIRES$ $FeatureB$
AddExcludesConstraint	Add a cross-tree constraint to the AFM with the syntax $FeatureA$ $EXCLUDES$ $FeatureB$

On Software Reference Architectures and Their Application to the Space Domain

Marco Panunzio* and Tullio Vardanega

University of Padova
Department of Mathematics
via Trieste 63, 35121 Padova, Italy
{panunzio,tullio.vardanega}@math.unipd.it

Abstract. In high-integrity systems a rising portion of software assets and development activities address quality and conformance issues in several non-functional dimensions. For those systems the software architecture acquires a prominent role: it does in fact express the framework that hosts the required functionalities, while the principles and guarantees that underpin its definition assure the desired non-functional quality on the software product. A software reference architecture holds for a set of systems and prescribes the form that concrete software architectures have to have for those systems. The software reference architecture can thus be seen as a generic software architecture, whose assets are recognized by domain stakeholders as befitting the construction of a given class of systems, for which they have been proven to meet the applicable industrial needs and technical requirements. This paper discusses the rationale for the understanding and definition of a software reference architecture and present its use in an initiative promoted by the European Space Agency for its future satellite systems.

1 Introduction

High-integrity systems must fulfil stringent requirements in a number of *non-functional* dimensions, such as timing predictability, dependability, and, more recently, security [16]. For those systems, the *software architecture* becomes the cornerstone for realizing a software product that provides all the required functionality while fulfilling all the non-functional requirements.

A software reference architecture may be regarded as a software architecture that applies to the realization of a certain class of software systems. It is fixed after a thorough domain analysis and becomes a solution recognized by the domain stakeholders for the fulfillment of the industrial needs of interest in that domain.

The work presented in this paper was prompted by an initiative undertaken by the European Space Agency (ESA), to promote the establishment of a software reference architecture for use among its industrial suppliers in the development of the on-board software of their future satellite systems. This paper discusses why the concepts of software architecture and the software reference architecture were central to that effort and

---

* This author is now with Thales Alenia Space - France.

J. Favaro and M. Morisio (Eds.): ICSR 2013, LNCS 7925, pp. 144–159, 2013.

formed a solid basis on which the industrial needs of interest to the domain stakeholders could demonstrably be met. It provides a comprehensive articulation of the principles that guided that initiative, narrated by authors who were directly involved in it from its outset, with the full concurrence of all the relevant industrial actors.

The remainder of the paper is organized as follows: section 2 discusses the role of software architecture in high-integrity software development, and argues why it is crucial to the satisfaction of the governance of the industrial domain; section 3 illustrates the consequences ensuing from elevating a software architecture in an industrial domain to the status of reference architecture for that domain; section 4 outlines the context of the European space market, discusses the industrial needs placed on future missions of ESA, and relates them to the definition of a software reference architecture for that context; section 5 presents the cornerstones on which the ESA software reference architecture was built; and finally, section 6 draws some conclusions.

2   The Role of the Software Architecture

One disconcerting situation in the software engineering practice is the exceedingly informal and liberal interpretation of the concept of *software architecture*. A brilliant exercise carried out by the Software Engineering Institute [22] testifies this confusion, which is patently at odds with the centrality of that concept for the discipline.

The main misconception is that software architecture is often liberally used as a synonym of *software design*. Software design instead is just one of the concerns addressed by the software architecture, whose overarching role is to govern the software and the process by which it will be built and operated. More importantly, the software architecture deals with the *principles* guiding the design and evolution of a software system. This aspect is central and *precedes in importance* software design.

The definition of architecture given in the IEEE 1471 standard, later adopted and approved by ISO/IEC as ISO 42010 [12], was singled out as the reference for this work, as the best and most authoritative one: *"The fundamental organization of a system embodied in its components, their relationships to each other, and to the environment, and the principles guiding its design and evolution"*.

This definition helps singling out the concerns that are addressed by the software architecture [17], which figure 1 captures diagrammatically with a numbering that we will use later for tracing the proposed solution to the corresponding concerns:

- *Software decomposition*: the organization of the software in terms of parts, so that every individual part has its own architectural cohesiveness and the interactions between parts are minimized so as to reduce coupling;
- *Externally visible attributes of software "components"*: the attributes of those software parts ("components" in our case) that are externally visible. They represent features or needs specific to the component that can influence other parts of the software or its overall properties. The other internal attributes shall remain invisible to the outside with no influence on the software architecture;
- *Relationship between software "components"*: how components relate to one another to provide services and fulfil needs;

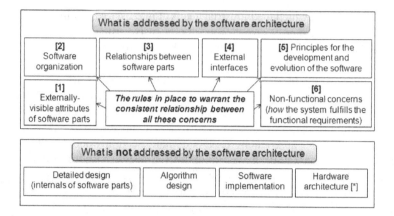

Fig. 1. The concerns addressed by the software architecture and those outside its perimeter

- *Non-functional concerns*: the abstraction level where most non-functional concerns are best addressed;
- *External interfaces*: the way the software interacts with the external environment (e.g. by commanding sensors or actuators, or serving external interrupts);
- *Principles for the development and evolution of the software*: the software design process fixes the rules for its development and provides means to perform software maintenance and evolution and dictates the supported form of reuse;
- *The rules in place to warrant the consistent relationship between all the above concerns*: every software system descends (at least implicitly) from some software architecture [12] ; however, to establish a software architecture that truly supports the given goals, a methodology must be defined that underpins the development approach and warrants consistency for all the aspects mentioned above.

Interestingly, the following aspects are not of pertinence to a software architecture:

- *Detailed design*, which is the refinement of the software decomposition performed at architectural level by providing the internal organization of components;
- *Algorithm design*, which is the design of the algorithmic behaviour of the software to fulfill the functional requirements;
- *Software implementation*, which is the activity for the implementation of software;
- *Hardware architecture*, which is addressed completely outside of the the software architecture concerns and yet needs to present a description of its essential characteristics, constraints and limitations to the latter, especially for those hardware aspects that concern communication and feasibility analysis.

3   The Concept of Reference Architecture

Much like for "software architecture", also the concept of *reference architecture* misses a single agreed definition. The gloss that makes the most hits is probably that provided by the "Rational Unified Process" (RUP) [13]: *"a predefined architectural pattern, or set of patterns, possibly partially or completely instantiated, designed, and proven for use in particular business and technical contexts, together with supporting artefact to enable their use. Often, these artefacts are harvested from previous projects."* Though generic, the cited definition includes interesting aspects, which deserve discussion.

First, we should clarify the difference between a software architecture and a software reference architecture. The software reference architecture prescribes the form of the concrete software architectures for a set of systems for which it was developed. Arguably, the reference architecture is a form of "generic" software architecture, which prescribes the founding principles, the underlying methodology and the architectural practices that were recognized by the domain stakeholders as the best solution to the construction of a certain class of software systems. The architecture of one target software system can then be considered as an "instantiation" to the specific system needs of the software reference architecture.

The other interesting element in the citation is that a reference architecture is "proven for use in particular business and technical contexts". This observation underlines:

1. the importance of the elicitation of the industrial needs and technical requirements from which the reference architecture emanate;
2. the need for *validation in use* as well as for some quantifiable *evaluation* of the reference architecture. Validation demonstrates empirically that software architectures resulting from application of the software reference architecture to concrete systems satisfactorily fulfill all the industrial needs that originated it. Evaluation ascertains the goodness of the reference architecture by analysing to what extent it satisfies the industrial needs, and can be facilitated by appropriate methodological support, for example the Architecture Tradeoff Analysis Method [11] (though it would require some adaptation to apply to the level of reference architecture [2]).

There exist multiple kinds of reference architectures. Angelov et al. [1] propose a characterisation in terms of *context*, *goal* and *design*. The context dimension discriminates: *where* the reference architecture will be used (i.e., within a single organization or multiple organizations), *who* defines it (i.e., user organizations, software organizations, research centres, standardization bodies), *when* is it defined (a *preliminary* reference architecture is defined before an implementation of it exists, or *classical* when experience on the application on the target class of systems has already been acquired). The goal dimension describes the main usage of the reference architecture: it may be a *standardization* of existing software architectures, or a *facilitation* for the design of concrete architectures (by providing guidelines, methodologies and patterns of the software architecture). The design dimension describes the main design choices of the reference architecture: *what* is described (components, interfaces, protocols, guidelines, etc.), the *abstraction level* of the description (concrete, semi-concrete, or abstract; corresponding to decreasing levels of dependence with technological and implementation decisions) and the level of formality of the description (*informal, semi-formal, formal*).

4   An Application Case

European space industry has entered an economic climate in which the funding availed to future missions is tightly capped. To win the day, proponents are therefore compelled to take on increasingly more ambitious scientific challenges. The resulting growth in complexity is thus plainly at odds with capped budgets.

One of the major consequences of this situation is that the activities that contribute the most to the value added of the mission, i.e., mission analysis and system engineering, will play an even bigger role in the overall economy of the project, with a proportional increase of the time and cost invested on them.

This situation calls for a rise in the *cost-effectiveness* of software development, to increase the "value" of the software product delivered with a given budget. The best way to succeed in this challenge is to increase the efficiency of software development by singling out the recurring costs and abating them as much as possible.

It is therefore necessary to first understand where this can be done, i.e., to identify which factors can be intervened on and with what degree of freedom; and subsequently, to investigate the definition of a solution.

The European Space Agency (ESA) has recently decided to cope with this emerging scenario with the definition, realization and adoption of a software reference architecture for the development of on-board software for satellites.

4.1   Domain Analysis

A typical satellite system includes two main constituent parts: the payload and the service module (also known as bus, or platform) [10]. The payload part comprises the instruments necessary for the scientific mission (telescopes, spectrometers, detectors, etc..). The service module is used to govern the satellite position, orientation and manoeuvres, communicate with ground, and ensure that the thermal and power needs are satisfied; for this reason the service module is equipped with various sensors (gyroscopes, Earth sensors, magnetometers, thermistors, etc...), actuators (reaction wheels, thrusters, heaters, etc..) and other equipment (e.g., solar arrays, batteries).

The satellite payload is mission-specific: hence, it will differ in form and instruments from one mission to another. Conversely, the service module may present a recurrent structure (i.e., shape and decomposition in subsystems) in several missions.

The on-board software of a satellite conceptually mirrors the same (physical) separation of the satellite structures. Accordingly, the on-board software can be conceptually split in two parts: the payload software and the platform software. Also in this case, the payload software is vastly – if not completely – different from one mission to the other; the platform software may instead assume a recurrent organization, which in software engineering parlance, is the *software architecture*.

The platform software comprises a set of traditional *functional contents*: the Attitude and Orbit Control System (AOCS) or a Guidance, Navigation and Control (GNC) system [15] of a deep-space mission; the Data Handling System (DHS); the thermal management; the power management; etc.. Additionally it may require the inclusion of more advanced functions that realize the functional requirements of future missions, such as advanced autonomy and planning or formation flying.

On-board software for satellites can be classified as high-integrity software; its realization is therefore subject to stringent requirements at both process and product level in dimensions such as: time and space predictability, safety, dependability, security. As a consequence, the output of the various stages of the development process are strictly regulated by domain-specific standards (such as ECSS-E-ST-40C [8] on software development and ECSS-Q-ST-80C [9] on software product quality). Moreover, the software product is subject to extensive verification and validation campaigns to to determine that it performs as expected while fulfilling all *non-functional* requirements.

The software architecture can come of use especially under cost-reduction constraints, as it (i) expresses the architectural framework that can best host the required functional contents, and (ii) enforces conformance to architectural properties and methodological principles that most contribute to the attainment of the required product quality.

The European space domain is strongly influenced by the historical structure of the industrial market, which used to be dominated by Astrium and Thales Alenia Space. For various reasons those two competitors adopted different concepts, methodologies and technologies for on-board software development, resulting in distant production styles and strategies: at the present state, a software supplier can competitively bid as a subcontractor only in a single supply chain, with adverse effects on the market economy. Whereas new and smaller prime contractors have lately made their way into the European space market, their role is less relevant to this discussion, as they operate within business conditions that currently favor opportunistic solutions over consolidation.

The ESA software reference architecture is also expected to respond to this rupture. Furthermore, the novel approach shall be able to accommodate and control the *incremental* and *iterative* development models that are inherent to the space domain. The on-board software is not simply a product to be released at the end of the development: incremental releases of it are needed to perform additive hardware/software integration and validation activities, in strict schedule coordination with other satellite development teams. Iterations are determined by the rectification, improvement and eventual finalization of system and software requirements experienced by every project, with carried risk of destructive backtracks of design and implementation decisions.

4.2   Industrial Needs

The ESA initiative for the definition of a software reference architecture is a harmonization of methodologies and technologies around the Agency charter, seeking to earn relevant benefits for all involved stakeholders: ESA as the procurement agency, software prime contractors and software suppliers. Not surprisingly, a very similar strategy was taken by NASA [6], which recommended investing on software architecture in general and software reference architectures in particular to cope with their needs for future missions. Under ESA sponsorship, one of the authors of this work devoted his entire PhD project [17] to all the essential challenges of this initiative. Much of the theoretical, methodological and technological results of that effort were first spun-in by ESA after clearance by a working group comprised of experts from ESA, software primes and suppliers, and then consolidated in the ESA-funded COrDeT-2 study project[1].

---

[1] http://cordet.gmv.com

The first input to the definition of the reference architecture consisted in gathering all the industrial needs that ESA or other stakeholders set as strategic goals.

Table 1 outlines the industrial needs. Some of those needs are common to all software domains; a few others are in common or similar to the needs of other high-integrity domains; a sizeable subset of them are instead specific to the European space domain.

Table 1. The main industrial needs of the European space domain. Type C denotes a need common to all software domains; type HI a need similar or common to other high-integrity domains; for type DS the need is domain specific.

ID	Industrial need	Type
IN-01	*Reduced software development schedule*	C
IN-02	*Higher cost-effectiveness of software development*	C
IN-03	*Support for incremental and parallel software development*	C
IN-04	*Multi-team development and product policy*	HI/DS
IN-05	*Quality of the software product*	HI
IN-06	*Lower effort intensiveness of Verification and Validation*	HI
IN-07	*Role of software suppliers*	DS
IN-08	*Mitigation of the impact of late requirement definition or change*	HI
IN-09	*Simplification and harmonization of Fault Detection Isolation and Recovery*	DS
IN-10	*Lower effort for flight maintenance*	DS
IN-11	*Future needs*	HI/DS

IN-01: Reduced Software Development Schedule. Future projects require software to be developed in a shorter schedule. The definition and finalization of software requirements occur later in the project schedule than in the past as the mission definition and system engineering phases take longer because of their greater economic incidence to the final value added. As the release of the product is usually tied to astronomical events which determine the launch window or other external factors (for example, the procurement of the launcher vehicle), the implementation activities, including software development, are compressed within the residual time toward the tail-end of development.

Moreover, staggered incremental releases of the on-board software are required so that electrical integration and HW/SW integration tests can be performed incrementally and the relevant workmanship is more efficiently deployed.

For all these reasons, although the software itself only accounts for a modest fraction of the total cost of the satellite, delayed software releases may have inordinately costly impact on the overall project schedule.

Even though the reasons that generate this industrial need are specific to the space domain, the call for reduced development schedule and shorter time-to-market is common to all software domains.

IN-02: Higher Cost-Effectiveness of Software Development. Not only will the software development budget not rise in the foreseeable future but it may instead decline in favour of other cost elements. Yet, the performance and complexity of core functions of the satellite platform may grow in response to end-user demands, while new complex functions may also be required (i.e., formation flying, advanced autonomy, etc.).

This need is common to all software domains; the means to fulfill it shall be specific to the space domain and in accord with all the other industrial needs.

IN-03: Support for Incremental and Parallel Software Development. The novel approach shall accommodate different system and software development practices and also support common, established needs.

The on-board software is built incrementally (cf. [14]), gradually adding more functionalities to an early initial release that enable electrical and avionic integration tests. On-board software is also built in *parallel development*, whereby distinct teams, possibly under different organizations, develop parts of the software system. The novel development approach shall not get in the way of the desired development model and instead help facilitate cross-team and cross-organization dialogue.

This industrial need may also apply to other high-integrity domains.

IN-04: Multi-team Development and Product Policy. Easy and clear-cut decomposition of the software product to facilitate subcontracting is crucial to the geopolitical economy of the European space domain. This need originates from the *geographical return* policy sanctioned in the ESA charter, which requires to "ensure that all Member States participate in an equitable manner, having regard to their financial contribution, in implementing the European space programme". Multiple demands descend from this need: (1) enforcement of subcontracting schemes to software primes or software suppliers only; (2) subcontracting of distinct processing units to different companies (also part of IN-03), including the responsibility for the deployed software; (3) subcontracting from software primes to software suppliers by enabling the maximum flexibility in the choice of the subcontractor, in order to maximize the adherence of the bid to the contingent needs originated by the geographical return policy.

This industrial need is specific to the space domain in Europe.

IN-05: Quality of the Software Product. The quality of the on-board software (in both functional and non-functional terms) shall be no less than attained with current practices. The novel development approach shall therefore center on a well-defined development process and qualified methodologies and technologies.

This industrial need is common to all other high-integrity domains.

IN-06: Lower Effort Intensiveness of Verification and Validation. In the space domain, no different from other embedded systems industry where correctness of operation is paramount and depends to a large extent on correct hardware-software interaction, Verification and Validation (V&V) activities are by far the largest and most labour-intensive contributor to the software development cost. The new development approach shall therefore strive to contain the labour intensiveness of V&V.

This industrial need is common to all high-integrity domains.

IN-07: Role of Software Suppliers. The market structure of space industry in Europe promoted a diversification of concepts, methodologies and technologies for software the development to the extent that a software supplier can only competitively bid in a single supply chain. ESA wish to allow suppliers to extend their competitiveness, without the need to adapt the software they produce to the specific development policies of each prime. However, since the amount of ESA satellite projects is limited, the market is not big enough to sustain the presence of several software suppliers. Therefore, a significant change in the market players cannot be realistically expected, but rather a change in the focus of their business activities.

This is a space-specific need that stems from the limitations of the European market.

IN-08: Mitigation of the Impact of Late Requirement Definition or Change. New software requirements or changes to them may occur during development. In the space business the most typical causes of this instability include: late finalization of system design; modifications in the operational strategy; late clarification of system-level contingency or mission management needs. Software modification may also be required to compensate for hardware problems found during system integration. The compression of the software development schedule (as in IN-01) is expected to exacerbate this risk.

Unstable software requirements can disrupt the software development schedule by causing longer time-to-release and occurring when fundamental decisions on software architecture and software design have already been fixed. The novel approach shall be able to mitigate the effects of those hazards.

This industrial need may also hold in other high-integrity domains.

IN-09: Simplification and Harmonization of Fault Detection Isolation and Recovery. Fault Detection, Isolation and Recovery (FDIR) is a system function that handles contingencies that threaten system integrity or its operational objectives. A simplification and hopefully harmonization of the FDIR approach is highly desired as all too often it is tackled in ad-hoc manners that cause massive integration and verification difficulties.

FDIR is problematic in two principal respects: (i) the software element of the FDIR often is attributed to the system team and therefore escapes the visibility, the understanding and the control of the software development team; (ii) FDIR is the software part whose design and finalization occurs later in the development, so that the pressure to integrate it in the software system may cause costly retrofits. These difficulties threaten the attainment of a sound separation of concerns in software development. FDIR is present in all missions and is one of the most important contributors to the complexity of the overall on-board software.

The novel approach should aim at providing a clean separation between the FDIR strategy (that is the policy to be realized to fulfil the applicable system and software requirements) and the mechanisms to realize it. Such a separation is also expected to mitigate the effects of late definition of FDIR requirements (which are part of IN-08).

This industrial need is space specific.

IN-10: Lower Effort for Flight Maintenance. Software flight maintenance is part of the specificity of the space domain. In contrast to similar domains (like civil avionics, or automotive) where it is always possible to physically access the system to perform maintenance operations, after satellite launch, all software maintenance operations have to be performed remotely. Remote software maintenance may be required to adjust configuration parameters, to upload a software patch to mitigate the consequences of faulty hardware, or to correct software bugs. The need to replace in-flight parts of the on-board software is thus inherent to the domain.

Flight maintenance contributes to the operational costs of the satellite (hence to operation budget as opposed to development costs). Reduction of the effort for maintenance operations, as well as a harmonization of the maintenance strategy will decrease the operational cost of maintenance.

In-flight maintenance operations often require a reboot of the on-board software after the upload of a new software image. Reboot constitutes a hazard for the spacecraft, as in that time span it cannot process ground commands. Problems occurring during bootstrap may thus compromise the spacecraft mission or leave the operational team with crippled means to communicate and operate the spacecraft for further troubleshooting. It is therefore highly desirable to minimize the risk of in-flight maintenance operations by updating parts of the software without having to reboot the processor unit.

Another interesting maintenance scenario occurs when managing a constellation of satellites. In general every satellite of a constellation is initially launched with the same on-board software. During operation however, different patches may be applied to distinct satellites, so that their on-board software evolves separately and starts to diverge. Easy recording of the evolution, annotation of the justification for the modification and tracing of the modifications to each version of the on-board software would decrease the maintenance effort through the whole software life cycle.

IN-11: Future Needs. As the novel development approach is targeting future ESA missions, it shall also accommodate support for future software needs. This need is necessarily loose and open ended and follows from the long-ranging goal of the ESA initiative. The most important needs that were identified include: (a) ensuring that the proposed approach shall not be undermined by the shift in hardware technology that may result from, e.g., the advent of multicore processors; (b) allowing the execution of software of different levels of safety in the same processor board.

5   A Software Reference Architecture for Space Applications

It is now in order to summarize the central concepts on which the proposed definition of software reference architecture is based.

The starting point was the derivation of high-level technical requirements from the industrial needs discussed in section 4.2: those were retained as the technical objectives to be achieved by the software reference architecture. Two overarching goals were added to the founding principles of the proposed software reference architecture:

- *composability*, that is achieved when the properties (in the form of assume/guarantee tuples) of individual components are preserved on component composition and deployment on the target system;
- *compositionality*, that is achieved when the properties of the system as a whole can be derived (economically and conclusively) as a function of the properties of its constituting components.

This work seeks to attain those two properties in the form of *composition with guarantees* [24], whereby they can be (1) assured by static analysis, (2) guaranteed throughout implementation, and (3) actively preserved at run time.

The proposed approach was centred on four primary constituents [18]:

1. a *component model* [4], to design the software as a composition of individually verifiable and reusable software units;

2. a *computational model* [23], to relate the design entities of the component model, their execution needs and their non-functional properties for concurrency, time and space, to a framework of analysis techniques which ensures that the architectural description is statically analyzable in the dimensions of interest;

3. a *programming model*, which consists in a tailored subset of a programming language and a set of code archetypes, and is used to ensure that the implementation of the design entities conforms with the semantics, the assumptions and the constraints of the computational model;

4. a *conforming execution platform*, which is in charge of preserving at run time the system and software properties asserted by static analysis and it is able to notify and react to possible violations of them.

In order to increase the industrial applicability of the approach, and as a response to industrial needs of the space domain, the formulation of the approach further included: (a) a development process centred on Model-Driven Engineering (MDE) [21]; (b) the provisions for domain-specific aspects, which complement the approach, yet are consistent to all its underlying principles.

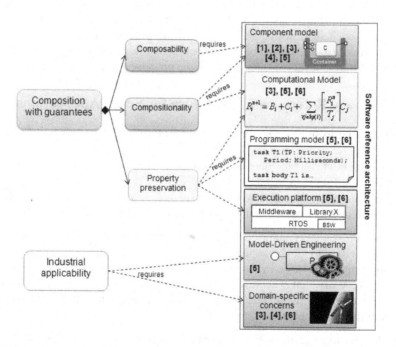

Fig. 2. The goals set for this work and the constituents of the software reference architecture that facilitates their achievement. Square brackets capture the concerns of the software architecture addressed by each individual constituent with the nomenclature shown in figure 1.

Figure 2 recapitulates the goals of our approach and the constituents that needed for their achievements. They collectively form the authors' interpretation of software reference architecture, as originally formulated in [17] and subsequently adopted by the ESA initiative. The same figure depicts which concerns of the software architecture are addressed by each constituent (cf. fig. 1).

Compositionality is earned at the level of the *computational model* and *component model*, as it depends on the adopted body of analysis theories as well as how the architectural entities in use relate to them. Composability is earned at the level of the *component model*. Composability and compositionality, augmented with *property preservation* [24] (i.e., preservation of the analyzed properties at run time), together lead to the achievement of composition with guarantees.

It is thus interesting to observe that, our choice of essential constituents carries an original interpretation of a software reference architecture that achieves properties of vital interest to space stakeholders, and it does so by construction.

5.1   Realization and Validation

As mentioned in section 4.2, ESA funded the COrDeT-2 study project to finalize the definition and prototype realization of the software reference architecture. The component model developed in [19] was adopted as the first constituent of it, together with an implementation built on top of a domain-specific metamodel (short-named "SCM" for "Space Component Model"), equipped with a specialised graphical editor based on the Obeo Designer framework[2].

In a true example of separation of concerns, the designer specifies the on-board software as a set of collaborating components which comprise functional concerns only. It later annotates those components with non-functional requirements, which are then only declaratively specified. Those non-functional requirements are implemented by *containers*, and *connectors*: the former are wrappers taking care of the tasking and synchronization needs of the component; the latter take care of interaction and communication needs (mainly logical and physical distribution of components, data encoding). Containers and connectors are collectively termed "Interaction Layer" in COrDeT-2. Their form depends on the chosen computational model and the associated programming model. In COrDeT-2, in line with preceding studies, the Ravenscar Computational Model [3] was adopted. Thanks to this choice, containers and connectors can be automatically generated following defined property-preserving code patterns [20].

The execution platform of the approach conforms to the description given in section 5. It comprises space-specific services, such as those specified in the "Packet Utilization Standard" [7], which are used for *commandability* and *observability* of the on-board software from ground. The component model offers domain-specific extensions so as to allow the configuration of those space-specific concerns, without breaking the principles or the methodology of the domain-neutral part of the component model.

COrDeT-2 validated the definition and implementation of the reference architecture against an ESA Earth Observation mission reference case[3].

---

[2] http://www.obeodesigner.com
[3] http://cordet.gmv.com/activity3.htm

In parallel to COrDeT-2, ESA launched the OSRAc study ("On-board software reference architecture consolidation"[4]) with focus on domain engineering, to gather recurrent solutions and architectural best practices for the functional contents of platform on-board software. OSRAc was to define how to develop reusable software for them using the software reference architecture. The software primes are involved in that study too, to assess the proceedings against a sizeable set of reference missions of interest to ESA and to the French national space agency (CNES).

5.2   Apportionment of Industrial Needs

It is now in order to examine how the software reference architecture as a whole fulfils the industrial needs presented in section 4.2. Table 2 recalls the industrial needs and relates to each of them the architectural constituent, discussed earlier in section 5, that specifically addresses it. Industrial need IN-11 is excluded from the list, as it fell outside of the scope of that phase of the investigation. Another ESA-funded study project (SISTORA[5]) separately addressed those issues; its results will be taken into account in subsequent iterations on the software reference architecture definition.

Table 2. The industrial needs and the constituent of the software reference architecture addressing them. Legend: [CM: Component model; CPM: Computational Model; PM: Programming model; EP: Execution platform; MDE: Model-driven engineering]

ID	Industrial need	Addressed by
IN-01	*Reduced software development schedule*	CM, MDE
IN-02	*Higher cost-effectiveness of software development*	CM, PM, MDE
IN-03	*Support for incremental and parallel software development*	CM, MDE
IN-04	*Multi-team development and product policy*	CM
IN-05	*Quality of the software product*	CM, CPM, PM
IN-06	*Lower effort intensiveness of Verification and Validation*	CPM, PM, MDE
IN-07	*Role of software suppliers*	CM
IN-08	*Mitigation of the impact of late requirement definition or change*	CM, MDE
IN-09	*Simplification and harmonization of FDIR*	CM, EP, MDE
IN-10	*Lower effort for flight maintenance*	CM, PM, EP

The adoption of our component model tailored with domain-specific aspects, and the automation capabilities of MDE (for code generation) serve the purpose of coping with the reduced development schedule for future projects (IN-01). Those same constituents, together with the programming model, are used to increase cost-effectiveness of the development. Our component model supports the specification of non-functional concerns related to tasking, synchronization and communication, separately from the functional concerns and their realization is entirely delegated to code generation [20].

---

[4] http://www.congrex.nl/11c22/docs/11C22_ADCSS/
    10--implementation-stragy--the-sw-perspective.pdf
[5] http://congrexprojects.com/docs/
    12c25_2310/sa1025_jung.pdf?sfvrsn=2

The proposed component model [19] facilitates incremental development (part of IN-03) and the mitigation of the impact of late requirement changes (IN-08). In doing so, it requires the use of a set of progressively more defined entities: *component types*, for the relationship of individual components to the rest of the software system; *component implementations*, for the concrete realization of components amenable to reuse; *component instances*, to relate to other components for the fulfilment of functional needs and for the declaration of non-functional properties and deployment directives. The ensuing design flow, together with the capability of supporting iterations provided by early model-based analysis, help mitigate the need and impact of late modifications.

As regards parallel development (from IN-03) and decomposition of software to fulfil contingent needs imposed by the the geographical return policy (IN-04), the proposed component model supports parallel development by requiring the definition of well-defined interfaces as part of software decomposition. *Component implementations* are the subcontracting units of the approach. Implementation constraints (in terms of resource consumption bounds) can be set on component implementations prior to outsourcing their realization to suppliers. In that manner the software integrator can better master complex supply chains.

Quality of the software product (IN-05) is achieved by adopting the component model, which informs the design by imposing the design methodology that underpins it; adopting a computational model and a conforming programming model provides for static analyzability of the software product, with the confidence of consistency between analysis and implementation.

The V&V effort is lowered by the use of model-based analysis and code generation. The former permits to converge faster to a system behaviour that fulfills the required non-functional requirements. The latter permits – thanks to the adoption of the programming model – the production of the complete code for tasking, synchronization, communication and interfaces between components. Another important advantage consists in the automated generation of all the test cases needed to confirm the correctness of the generated code, delivering the software engineers from the burden of writing this error-prone part of the software and its associated test suites.

The realization of a component implementation in our component model can be delegated to a software supplier, which can focus on the implementation of functional contents only (as non-functional concerns are dealt only by the software integrator) without needing to adapt the component to the practices of the different software integrator (as required by IN-07); the software integrator can then easily integrate the implemented component in the software system.

A set of mechanisms for the realization of Fault Detection Isolation and Recovery (FDIR) policies are provided by the execution platform. A set of patterns for their use is provided in the domain-specific part of the component model and the code to use them can be automatically generated. The code that implements FDIR concerns is then kept separated from functional code, thus also increasing the reuse potential of components. This contributes to the fulfilment of IN-09.

Finally, the effort for flight maintenance (IN-10) is potentially reduced in our approach by reasoning in terms of components or their constituents instead of memory regions, which earns us better control on the abstraction and granularity of the software to uplink. Moreover, with support from the execution platform, it will be possible to reload and re-start individual components at run time, without needing to reboot the whole software from an updated software image (which is the current state of practice).

6 Conclusions

This paper reported on the motivation and proceedings of an initiative undertaken by the European Space Agency for the development of a software reference architecture for the on-board software of their future satellite systems. This paper is intended an as enunciation of guiding principles that propose a specific understanding of the concept of software reference architecture and trace its constituents to the industrial needs captured by the relevant domain stakeholders. The reference architecture is being extensively validated in a number of ESA-funded studies with promising results; however only medium-term efforts, much longer than the horizon covered by this work can gather conclusive evidence for or against the proposed approach.

While the reference architecture was a response to needs of the space domain, its stipulation is centred on core domain-neutral concepts and accommodates room for domain-specific extensions or specialization, making it attractive for domains other than space. As an evident confirmation of it, the 4-constituent reference architecture was also successfully adopted by the CHESS project[6], which targeted the industrial needs of telecommunication and railway domains in addition to those of space industry. Each domain covered in CHESS used the same shared component model [19] (extended with domain-specific concerns), and were able to adopt a programming model and execution platform that fit their domain-specific needs. Some of the CHESS results are summarised in [5].

Acknowledgements. The views presented in this paper are the authors' only and do not necessarily engage those of the European Space Agency. This work was supported by the Networking/Partnering Initiative of ESA/ESTEC and by the CHESS project, ARTEMIS JU grant nr. 216682.

References

1. Angelov, S., Grefen, P., Greefhorst, D.: A Classification of Software Reference Architectures: Analyzing Their Success and Effectiveness. In: IEEE/IFIP Conference on Software Architecture and European Conference on Software Architecture, WICSA/ECSA (2009)
2. Barbacci, M., Clements, P., Lattanze, A., Northrop, L., Wood, W.: Using the Architecture Tradeoff Analysis Method (ATAM) to Evaluate the Software Architecture for a Product Line of Avionics Systems: A Case Study. Tech. rep., SEI, Carnegie Mellon University (2003)
3. Burns, A., Dobbing, B., Vardanega, T.: Guide for the Use of the Ada Ravenscar Profile in High Integrity Systems. Technical Report YCS-2003-348, University of York (2003)
4. Chaudron, M., Crnkovic, I.: Component-based software engineering. In: van Vliet, H. (ed.) Software Engineering: Principles and Practice, ch. 18, Wiley (2008)

---

[6] http://www.chess-project.org/

5. Cicchetti, A., Ciccozzi, F., Mazzini, S., Panunzio, M., Puri, S., Vardanega, T., Zovi, A.: CHESS: A Model-Driven Engineering Tool Environment for Aiding the Development of Complex Industrial Systems. In: 27th Int'l Conference on Automated Software Engineering (ASE 2012), pp. 362–365. IEEE/ACM (September 2012) ISBN: 978-1-4503-1204-2

6. Dvorak, D. (ed.): NASA Study on Flight Software Complexity. Tech. rep., Commissioned by the NASA Office of Chief Engineer (2009)

7. European Cooperation for Space Standardization: Space Engineering - Ground systems and operations - Telemetry and telecommand packet utilization, ECSS-E-70-41A (2003)

8. European Cooperation for Space Standardization: Space engineering - Software, ECSS-E-ST-40C (2009)

9. European Cooperation for Space Standardization: Space product assurance - Software product assurance, ECSS-Q-ST-80C (2009)

10. Fortescue, P., Swinerd, G., Stark, J. (eds.): Spacecraft Systems Engineering, 4th edn. Wiley (2011) ISBN: 978-0470750124

11. Gallagher, B.: Using the Architecture Tradeoff Analysis Method to Evaluate a Reference Architecture: A Case Study. Tech. rep., SEI, Carnegie Mellon University (2000)

12. ISO/IEC/(IEEE): Systems and Software engineering - Recomended practice for architectural description of software-intensive systems. ISO/IEC 42010 (IEEE Std) 1471-2000 (2007)

13. Kruchten, P.: The Rational Unified Process: An Introduction, 2nd edn. Addison-Wesley (2000)

14. Larman, C., Basili, V.R.: Iterative and incremental development: A brief history. Computer 36, 47–56 (2003)

15. Lin, C.F.: Modern Navigation, Guidance, And Control Processing. Prentice Hall (1991) ISBN: 978-0135962305

16. Malan, R., Bredemeyer, D.: Defining Non-Functional Requirements. Tech. rep., Bredemeyer Consulting (2001),
    http://www.bredemeyer.com/pdf_files/NonFunctReq.PDF

17. Panunzio, M.: Definition, realization and evaluation of software reference architecture for use in space application. Ph.D. thesis, University of Bologna, Italy (July 2011),
    http://www.informatica.unibo.it/ricerca/
    technical-report/2011/UBLCS-2011-07

18. Panunzio, M., Vardanega, T.: On Component-Based Development and High-Integrity Real-Time Systems. In: Proc. of the 15th International Conference on Embedded and Real-Time Computing Systems and Applications (2009)

19. Panunzio, M., Vardanega, T.: A Component Model for On-board Software Applications. In: Proc. of the 36th Euromicro Conference on Software Engineering and Advanced Applications, pp. 57–64. IEEE (2010)

20. Panunzio, M., Vardanega, T.: Ada Ravenscar Code Archetypes for Component-Based Development. In: Brorsson, M., Pinho, L.M. (eds.) Ada-Europe 2012. LNCS, vol. 7308, pp. 1–17. Springer, Heidelberg (2012)

21. Schmidt, D.C.: Model-Driven Engineering. IEEE Computer 39(2), 25–31 (2006)

22. Software Engineering Institute (editor): Defining Software Architecture - Modern, Classic, and Bibliographic Definitions, SEI - Carnegie Mellon (2010),
    http://www.sei.cmu.edu/architecture/start/definitions.cfm

23. Vardanega, T.: Development of On-Board Embedded Real-Time Systems: An Engineering Approach. Tech. Rep. ESA STR-260, European Space Agency (1999)

24. Vardanega, T.: Property Preservation and Composition with Guarantees: From ASSERT to CHESS. In: Proc. of the 12th IEEE International Symposium on Object/Component/Service-Oriented Real-Time Distributed Computing, pp. 125–132 (2009)

Automated Analysis in Feature Modelling and Product Configuration

David Benavides[1], Alexander Felfernig[2], José A. Galindo[1], and Florian Reinfrank[2]

[1] University of Seville
Av. de la Reina Mercedes S/N, 41012 Seville, Spain
{benavides,jagalindo}@us.es
[2] Institute for Software Technology
Graz University of Technology
Inffeldgasse 16b/II
Graz, Austria
{afelfern,freinfra}@tugraz.at

Abstract. The automated analysis of feature models is one of the thriving topics of research in the software product line and variability management communities that has attracted more attention in the last years. A recent literature review reported that more than 30 analysis operations have been identified and different analysis mechanisms have been proposed. Product configuration is a well established research field with more than 30 years of successful applications in different industrial domains. Our hypothesis, that is not really new, is that these two independent areas of research have interesting synergies that have not been fully explored. To try to explore the potential synergies systematically, in this paper we provide a rapid review to bring together these previously disparate streams of work. We define a set of research questions and give a preliminary answer to some of them. We conclude that there are many research opportunities in the synergy of these independent areas.

Keywords: Software Product Lines, Feature Models, Product Configuration, Rapid Review, Knowledge-based Systems.

1 Introduction

Variability modelling and management is a key issue in software product line engineering. Feature models are one of the most used mechanisms to model the variability within a software product line. A feature model consists of a set of features and a set of relationships that connect features. It is arranged in a tree–like structure with additional cross-tree constraints. There are different feature model dialects identified in the literature [53] which include basic feature models, cardinality based feature models and extended feature models using feature attributes.

J. Favaro and M. Morisio (Eds.): ICSR 2013, LNCS 7925, pp. 160–175, 2013.

Figure 1 shows an example feature model using the most well known modelling elements[1]. The model illustrates how features are connected to specify a software product line in the *mobile phone* domain. We assume that the software loaded in the phone is determined by the features that it supports. According to the model, all phones must include features supporting *calls*, and displaying information in either *basic, colour* or *high resolution* screens. Furthermore, it is possible to optionally include support for *GPS* and multimedia elements such as *camera, MP3* player or both of them.

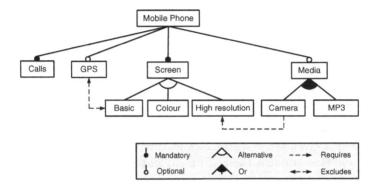

Fig. 1. A sample feature model

The automated analysis of feature models is one of the areas of research that have attracted more attention in the last two decades [8]. It can be defined as the computer–aided extraction of information from feature models. The analysis is performed by means of *analysis operations* which take several inputs and provide an output. As input we have a feature model with optionally some additional information such as a set of features to be selected or deselected. As output it is possible to find numbers, set of features and others depending on the kind of analysis operation. An example of a feature model analysis operation would be counting the number of possible products represented by the feature model. In the example of Figure 1 the number of products is 14. 30 different analysis operations have been surveyed [8] including operations for model consistency, error detection, explanations, and feature model configuration capabilities. The general analysis process is shown in Figure 2 where a feature model is translated to a logical representation and using some technique (e.g. logical solvers or specific algorithms) the analysis operations are performed.

The configuration of feature models can be defined as the process of selecting and deselecting features in a feature model until reaching a full configuration, i.e. a configuration where no additional decision on the feature model needs to be made to have all the information to configure a given software product of the software product line. The configuration of feature models is no more than

---

[1] This Figure has been taken from [8].

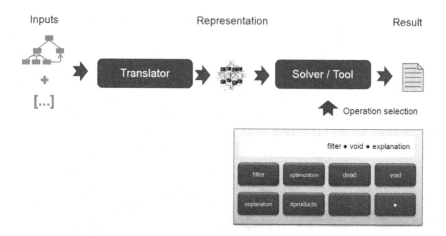

Fig. 2. Process for the automated analysis of feature models taken from [8]

an analysis operation where the input is a feature model with a set of decisions on the state of a given set of features (a feature can be selected, deselected or undecided) and the output is the feature model together with the new states of the features.

Product configuration is an independent area of research from software product line engineering that has a long history as an application of Artificial Intelligence technologies [43,23,52]. The first paper on product configuration was published back in 1978 [36]. Similar to feature model based configuration, product configuration can be interpreted as the process of partially or completely instantiating component types and related attributes with concrete components and attribute values [52] in a way that preserves the consistency with a predefined set of constraints (restrictions). Configuration technologies are typically applied in complex product domains such as telecommunication [23], automotive [34], and digital equipment [7,19].

Although product configuration is a well established area of research with numerous industrial applications, the synergies between feature model configuration and product configuration have been rarely explored. Our hypothesis, that can be easily formulated from the previous descriptions, is that feature model and product configuration have a lot of potential synergies that can be explored and exploited. In this paper, we show first steps to explore those synergies towards a more systematic literature review to fully gather the spread knowledge from the different areas to start a cross fertilization process to benefit both communities from the independent results.

This hypothesis of existing synergy potentials is not really new. In the past, there have been already some attempts to connect these two areas [6,39] and the importance of such a connection has been explored in the last years within the software product line community. As an example, there have been 2 invited keynotes in recent workshops of the software product line conference by well known researchers from the configuration area (see [16,47]). Also, a recent contribution to a workshop in the product configuration area proposes a research roadmap to try to connect these two areas and revealed the importance of surveying the literature to find synergies [31]. In this paper, in difference with respect to previous work, we give a first step forward to complete a systematic literature review to bring together these previously disparate streams of work and we provide first answers to some research questions. Thus, we define a set of research questions and give a preliminary answer to some of them which start opening research opportunities.

Although in a systematic literature review a well established method is required [10], we do not present such a systematic method in this paper. We rather use a rapid review approach which is also a very common method in evidence-based research in areas such as medicine [27]. A rapid review is a method to provide an assessment of what is already known in a given research field. In contrast to literature reviews, it does not need a tedious and time–consuming method trying to be "quick but not dirty" [27]. In this sense, it can serve as a first step towards a more systematic literature review. It is fair to recognize that this rapid literature review has an important bias due to the fact that there is a good amount of the surveyed references that are works done by the authors. However, we still think it is valuable to show these results since the authors have been working independently in the surveyed areas namely, automated analysis of feature models and product configuration. In any case, this bias is also addressed adding a good amount of references to other existing work.

In the following section we discuss research questions related to the further development of both research fields. Thereafter – in Section 3 – we try to provide first answers to the posed questions.

2   Research Questions

The goal of this review is to provide first answers to the following research questions (RQ 1–4). Some of them have been already answered in a recent literature review about the automated analysis of feature models [8]. The main goal here is to investigate how these questions have been addressed in the product configuration field and see the similarities, differences and discover research opportunities. We will try to answer these questions always comparing how different activities are performed in the feature modelling field and how they are addressed in the product configuration field. Although there are also other potential research questions to be addressed we selected these 4 mainly because they cover important parts of the engineering process such as modelling (RQ1), implementation and design (RQ2-3), quality assurance (RQ4).

RQ1: How are the different modelling approaches related? There are different dialects of feature models as described in [53]. In contrast, how are configuration problems modelled? Can a feature model configuration problem be represented as a configuration problem? Are there modelling elements in product configuration that are not used in feature models? And the opposite? Are there approaches to standardize configuration knowledge representations and how can these representations be exploited in the context of feature model development?

RQ2: Which are the automated mechanisms proposed? There are mainly three basic reasoning approaches used when automatically analysing feature models [8]: propositional logic based analysis, constraint programming based analysis and description logic based analysis. Are those paradigms also used in product configuration? Are there any special techniques developed in that field that could be used in feature model configuration?

RQ3: Are there similar operations? In feature models, 30 different analysis operations have been recently reported [8]. How similar are the operations in configuration problems? In product configuration it is well known that one of the main important tasks is the user support which includes providing explanations when a erroneous configuration step is reached. Are there special mechanisms developed in the product configuration community that could be used in feature model configurations?

RQ4: Which are the functional and performance mechanisms used? In feature models, there are some proposals to perform functional and performance testing of analysis tools [56,54,55,57]. The challenge is how to assess the quality of feature model analysis tools in terms of functionality (is the analysis tool doing what is supposed to do?) and performance (is the analysis tool performing well?). Are there also functional and performance testing mechanisms described in the product configuration literature? How are the different mechanisms related?

3   Preliminary Results

To provide a preliminary answer to the research questions of Section 2 we searched papers in academic databases guided from our previous experience in the field. In this section we give a first answer to some of the research questions by quoting and explaining some of the papers studied to show the potential synergy between the two areas.

3.1   RQ1: How Are the Different Modelling Approaches Related?

From our rapid review we have detected that the existing research on product configuration does not have a well established or standard language to define configuration problems. There have been attempts to use domain-specific languages for product configuration, for example, on the basis of the Unified Modeling Language (UML) [15]. Furthermore, ontology based configuration knowledge representations [60] and description logics based representations have been developed [18,40]. These representations are either not supporting the needed expressivity (for an in-depth analysis of description logic based knowledge representations see [18]) or are not based on a formal semantics (UML is based on a semi-formal definition, the same holds for the ontology specified in [60]). In other cases, configuration problems are formally defined on the basis of logic-based approaches which are often not accessible for domain experts and even developers. In this sense, it is easy to find configuration problems described in description logic, constraints or propositional logic (see Section 3.2) but there is still a need for a standardized representation with a clear underlying formal semantics. There have been some general standardization efforts in constraint representations [45] but not specifically in the product configuration domain. Also, there have been some efforts to clearly define configuration tasks [43].

In contrast, configuration problems in software product lines are mainly modelled using any of the following families of notations: decision-based modelling notations or feature model–based notations [12]. There are also other notations such as OVM [49] or COVAMOF [59] but these are less common in the literature. There is even a current effort to define a common variability modeling language (CVL) [24] which could also serve as a basis for the definition of configuration problems. There exist different dialects of feature models as described in [53] and also some textual syntax of feature models like TVL [11]. In addition, formal semantics of feature model dialects have been reported [13,53].

We will now try to answer the following sub question: *can a feature model configuration problem be represented as a configuration problem?* To do so, we provide the following definitions adapted from the discussions in Section 1 and from any general definition of a configuration problem that can be found in the literature. Note that this definition can be exploited for the representation of basic configuration problems which do not include complex connection structures and component hierarchies [23,38]. However, it is a good basis for having a common representation for both, basic configuration problems and feature model configuration problems.

Definition 1 (Feature Model Configuration Problem). A feature model configuration problem is defined by the tuple (F,D,C) where $F = \{f_1, f_2, ..., f_n\}$ is a set of features f_i. Furthermore, $D = \{\text{dom}(f_1), \text{dom}(f_2), ..., \text{dom}(f_n)\}$ is the set of corresponding feature domains where $\text{dom}(f_i) = \{\text{true, false}\}$. Finally, C = CR ∪ CF is a set of constraints restricting the possible configurations which can be derived from the feature model. In this context, CR = $\{c_1, c_2, ..., c_k\}$ represents a set of user requirements (e.g. selection or deselection of features) and CF = $\{c_{k+1}, c_{k+2}, ..., c_m\}$ represents a set of feature model constraints.

The hypotheses here is that any relationship defined in a feature model dialect can be translated to a constraint in a Constraint Satisfaction Problem (CSP)(see [5] for an introduction on CSP).

Definition 2 (Feature Model Configuration). A feature model configuration for a given feature model configuration problem is a complete assignment of the variables $f_i \in F$. Such a configuration is consistent if the constraints $c_i \in C$ are consistent with the given variable assignment. Furthermore, a feature model configuration is valid, if it is consistent and complete, i.e. it does not violate any constraint defined in the feature configuration problem and all the variables have an assigned value.

Results. We conjecture that a feature model configuration problem in particular and any software product line configuration problem in general could be seen as a special case of a product configuration problem.

In configuration problems not only boolean constraints are used as in most of the cases of feature model configuration problems. In product configuration problems there is no standard language to describe configuration problems while in software product lines there is de facto standard which are feature models and an effort to a standardized notation such as CVL. These more established notations in software product line engineering could inspire product configuration researchers to identify ways to share, disseminate, and model configuration problems. On the other hand there are also challenges with respect to product domains (e.g., telecommunication switches [23]) where complex connection structures and related (aggregation) constraints have to be specified (see, e.g., [18]). We want to emphasize that a detailed analysis of needed extensions of existing feature model representations is a major challenge for future research if feature models want to be adopted as a sort of standard language in the product configuration field.

3.2   RQ2: Which Are the Automated Mechanisms Proposed?

There are mainly three categories of mechanisms used for the automated analysis of feature models [8]: propositional logic based analysis, constraint programming based analysis, and description logic based analysis. In a survey on product configuration in 1998[2], Sabin et al. [52] divided the existing paradigms on product configuration as the following: *rule-based reasoning* and *model-based* approaches. In the former, rules of the form *if condition then action* are used to represent configuration knowledge. According to [52], this kind of configuration systems have maintenance problems. In model-based configuration systems, the assumption is that the configuration knowledge is expressed in an explicit language in terms of a *model*. Among the approaches in model–based configuration problems, description logics and constraint–based approaches are presented [52].

Results. Among constraint based approaches there are some based on so–called *conditional constraint satisfaction problems* (CCSP) [26], *dynamic constraint satisfaction problems*(DCSP) [42], and *generative constraint satisfaction problems* (GCSP) [23,38]. There are also some proposals to combine description logics and constraint satisfaction problems [35]. Furthermore, we have found papers in the product configuration literature that use *binary decisions diagrams* (BDD) to represent and solve configuration problems [9,4,28] and also proposals which combine CSPs with BDD techniques to obtain better product configurators [61].

A product configuration problem is *interactive* if the configuration process is performed interactively, i.e. the user makes selections and the system has to provide feedback to the user as soon as possible. In such scenarios the response time of the systems is crucial. It is desirable to guarantee a given response time. In this sense, there is a branch of research on product configuration that deals with the *off-line compilation* of configuration problems for a later *on-line* configuration process. An off–line compilation of a configuration problem is a

---

[2] It is interesting to note that we have not found any more recent review on product configuration.

process where the configuration problem is translated to a given representation that ensures a good response time. In the best case, the compilation will deliver a backtrack-free configurator. Once the compilation is performed, the system can be used for an on-line configuration process. There are several proposals in the literature of product configuration using compilation techniques, some are based on translation the configuration process into a BDD representation [33,29] and others are based on transforming a configuration problem into an automata [14,50].

Although there have been some efforts to use efficient techniques for feature model analysis [41], in general, these techniques have been rarely studied in the feature model analysis literature and there is significant work to be done to include those techniques in the feature model analysis field.

3.3   RQ3: Are There Similar Analysis Operations?

An analysis operations over a feature model, as stated in Section 1, is an operation that takes a feature model as input and returns a result as output. An analysis operation over a configuration model would be the same but taking as input a configuration model. In feature models, 30 different analysis operations have been recently reported [8] and it is common to find more and more papers describing some new operations or a sort of redefinition of them (e.g. [44]).

Results. In the product configuration field, it is not common to find new operations besides the basic ones like propagate a configuration decision, provide feedback to the user in terms of explanations or maintain the consistency of the configuration knowledge base. This could be the case because in software product line models such as feature models, a very important aspect is the connection of the variability model with other software artefacts like code, software components, test cases or UML diagrams among others. It would be necessary to have a catalogue of operations in product configuration similar to the one found in feature model analysis [8] to explore if there are operations in one side or the other that could be used as well as existing techniques to automate them.

A special case of analysis operations are the so-called *explanations*. In the feature model analysis field an explanation is defined as an operation of analysis that not only provides a result but also an explanation of *why* or *why not* a given result is provided [64]. There are some proposals to explain why a feature model is inconsistent, why a feature is *dead* or why a feature is *false optional* [63]. Also, there are some proposals to explain why a given configuration is erroneous with respect to a given feature model [66,65]. Most of these approaches are based on Reiter's theory of diagnosis [51] which means that the method is complete and provides an explanation which is minimal. A minimal explanation is the one that explain a given analysis result with the minimum number of elements. For instance, given a flawed configuration with a set of selected features and a set of deselected features, an explanation could be used to determine the changes to be made in the configuration to repair it [65]. It would be possible to say that all the selections or deselections have to be changed, but usually the interesting information is to know the minimum changes required to repair the flawed configuration.

In product configuration it is well known that the methods based on Reiter's theory of diagnosis are computationally hard to solve. To face this problem, there are several proposals in the product configuration literature to provide faster explanations that either preserve minimality (in terms of the number of needed repair actions) [17,32,48] or focus on the determination of personalized repairs which are also minimal but are not necessarily minimal cardinality repairs [46,20,22].

From this discussion it seems clear that explanation mechanisms for feature model analysis have to be synchronized with respect to existing product configuration mechanisms.

3.4   RQ4: Which Are the Functional an Performance Mechanisms Used?

Developing and maintaining feature model analysis tools is difficult and costly as any other software system due to its complexity and changeability [56]. As any other software tool, a feature model analysis tool has to use functional testing mechanisms to detect bugs in the development and evolution process. In product configuration, tools for providing configuration capabilities are known as *configurators*. Configurators suffer from the same problems that feature model analysis tools, i.e. they are difficult to develop and maintain and most of the configuration operations are computationally hard to tract.

Results. In the feature model analysis literature we have found specific functional testing mechanisms to detect bugs in analysis tools [56,54]. The basic idea is to have an automated test data generator that can generate a feature model together with its represented set of products by means of so-called *metamorphic relations*. Once we have a feature model and its set of products, this test input can serve as an *oracle* to see if the expected output of an analysis tool is correct with respect to the test data. The conceptual underpinning of this idea is that most of the analysis operations could be calculated once the set of products represented by the feature model is available. This is a black box testing technique that has been shown to be useful in detecting bugs in some feature model analysis tool like FaMa[3] and SPLOT [4] [56].

Besides functional testing mechanisms for feature model analysis tools, performance is also an additional problem to be taken into account when assuring the quality of this kind of tools. Most of the feature model analysis operations are known to be computationally complex to perform [53] and this is especially important when analysis operations are used for feature model interactive configuration. Most of the times, feature model analysis tools have been tested for performance evaluation using random inputs [8], i.e. a set of random feature models are generated to stress the analysis tools to see how they perform when

---

[3] www.isa.us.es/fama

[4] www.splot-research.org/

increasing the size of the models or the percentage of modelling elements like cross-tree constraints. Although this mechanisms are useful to be used to get averages (e.g. in terms of time or memory consumption) there are some proposals to provide mechanisms to build hard feature models in pessimistic situations [55,57]. The idea is to define the problem of looking for hard feature models as an optimization problem. A tool is build to generate hard feature models using metaheuristic algorithms like evolutionary search to explore the space and try to guide the tool to find hard feature model instances for a given tool for a given operation. For instance, the tool can be used to find feature models with between 100 and 200 features with 10% of cross-tree constraints that take more than 5 minutes in detecting the set of dead features which could be considered as an non affordable time constraint.

There are some similar approaches in the product configuration literature to what has been done in feature model analysis. For instance, a configurator can be performance tested by using real configuration models (a.k.a configuration benchmarks [1]) or by using randomly generated configuration models [62]. On the other hand, we found a work providing a technique for white-box testing of configuration systems [21]. However, we have not found any approach to systematically perform functional testing of configurators using metamorphic relations as we found for feature model analysis tools. Similarly, we have not found techniques to systematically search for difficult configuration problems as proposed for hard feature models.

3.5   Summary of Findings

Figure 3 provides a first overview[5] of existing related research in the fields of variability models (putting special attention to feature model related results) and product configuration and how they can be used in the other area. Next, we explain the results from our literature review detecting opportunities for cross–fertilization either from feature model analysis to product configuration or backwards.

Feature model analysis can contribute to product configuration in:
- Defining a standard configuration language similar to some of the existing variability languages in the software product line community like any variant of feature models [53], CVL [24] or TVL [11] and providing formal syntax and semantics to the standard configuration language as it has been done in feature models [13,53].
- Providing a historical catalogue of configuration operations similar to what has been reported in the feature model analysis literature [8]. In the feature model literature more than 30 analysis operations exists. Finding a similar catalogue in the product configuration field remains as a challenge. Having such a catalogue can help to summarize the results in the product

---

[5] Due to the fact that we are reporting first results of our ongoing research, we do not claim for completeness with regard to this overview.

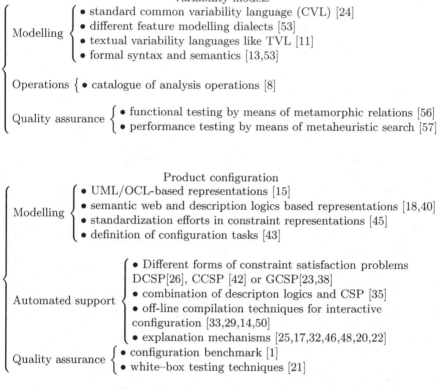

Fig. 3. Summary of potential synergies

configuration field and ease the adoption of the results by the feature model community.

– Providing more elaborated mechanisms for functional and performance testing of configurators like the ones reported for feature model analysis tools either for functional testing using an automated test data generator [56] or using metaheuristic techniques for finding difficult configuration instances for a given configurator [55,57].

Product configuration can contribute to feature model analysis in:

– Exploring similar automated mechanisms to perform analysis operations using existing approaches like DCSP [26], CCSP [42] or GCSP [23,38]. Also combinations of different paradigms depending on the kind of the operation like description logics and CSP [35].
– Adapting off-line compilation techniques for interactive configuration remains as a challenge in feature model configuration tools in order to provide back–track free feature model configurators [33,29,14,50].
– Reusing explanations mechanisms [25,17,32,46,48,20,22] since the known feature model explanation mechanisms mostly rely on Reiter's theory of diagnosis.

4   Conclusions and Future Work

Feature model analysis and product configuration has a lot more in common than what has been reported until now. We think that the cross–fertilization of these two independent areas is a mandatory step for the next years at least in the software product line and variability management communities. In this paper, we have reported a rapid literature review that put this fact in evidence and give concrete research opportunities.

To better explore the results of one and other communities a more exhaustive literature review specially in the field of product configuration seems to be desirable and this paper is a first step forward.

Other research questions remained can be related to other engineering task such as maintenance or requirement analysis. In this sense, we have found in the recent variability management related venues papers about reverse engineering of variability models [2,3,30,37,58,67]. Exploring if similar problems haven been addressed in the configuration literature remains as part of our future work.

Acknowledgements. We would like to thank Sergio Segura for giving some comments on a previous version of this paper. This work was supported, in part, by the European Commission (FEDER), the Spanish Government under project SETI (TIN2009-07366) – by the Andalusian Government under project THEOS (TIC-5906), and the Austrian Research Promotion Agency under the project ICONE (827587).

References

1. Configuration Benchmarks Library,
   http://www.itu.dk/research/cla/externals/clib
2. Acher, M., Baudry, B., Heymans, P., Cleve, A., Hainaut, J.: Support for reverse engineering and maintaining feature models. In: Proceedings of the Seventh International Workshop on Variability Modelling of Software-intensive Systems, p. 20. ACM (2013)
3. Acher, M., Cleve, A., Perrouin, G., Heymans, P., Vanbeneden, C., Collet, P., Lahire, P.: On extracting feature models from product descriptions. In: Proceedings of the Sixth International Workshop on Variability Modeling of Software-Intensive Systems, VaMoS 2012, pp. 45–54. ACM, New York (2012)
4. Andersen, H.R., Hadzic, T., Pisinger, D.: Interactive cost configuration over decision diagrams. J. Artif. Intell. Res (JAIR) 37, 99–139 (2010)
5. Apt, K.R.: Principles of Constraint Programming. Cambridge University Press, Cambridge (2003)
6. Asikainen, T., Männistö, T., Soininen, T.: Kumbang: A domain ontology for modelling variability in software product families. Advanced Engineering Informatics 21(1), 23–40 (2007)
7. Barker, V., OConnor, D., Bachant, J., Soloway, E.: Expert systems for configuration at digital: Xcon and beyond. Communications of the ACM 32(3), 298–318 (1989)

8. Benavides, D., Segura, S., Ruiz-Cortés, A.: Automated analysis of feature models 20 years later: a literature review. Information Systems 35(6), 615–636 (2010)
9. Bouquet, F., Jegou, P.: Using obdds to handle dynamic constraints. Information Processing Letters 62(3), 111–120 (1997)
10. Brereton, P., Kitchenham, B., Budgen, D., Turner, M., Khalil, M.: Lessons from applying the systematic literature review process within the software engineering domain. Journal of Systems and Software 80(4), 571–583 (2007)
11. Classen, A., Boucher, Q., Heymans, P.: A text-based approach to feature modelling: Syntax and semantics of tvl. Sci. Comput. Program. 76(12), 1130–1143 (2011)
12. Czarnecki, K., Grünbacher, P., Rabiser, R., Schmid, K., Wasowski, A.: Cool features and tough decisions: a comparison of variability modeling approaches. In: VaMoS, pp. 173–182 (2012)
13. Durán, A., Benavides, D., Segura, S., Trinidad, P., Ruiz-Cortés, A.: Flame: Fama formal framework (v 1.0). Technical Report ISA–12–TR–02, Seville, Spain (March 2012)
14. Fargier, H., Vilarem, M.-C.: Compiling csps into tree-driven automata for interactive solving. Constraints 9, 263–287 (2004)
15. Felfernig, A.: Standardized configuration knowledge representations as technological foundation for mass customization. IEEE Transactions on Engineering Management 54(1), 41–56 (2007)
16. Felfernig, A.: Intelligent techniques for software product line engineering. In: Proccedings of the 2nd International Workshop on Formal Methods and Analysis in Software Product Line Engineering, FMSPLE at SPLC (2011), www.iese.fraunhofer.de/en/events/fmsple2012.html
17. Felfernig, A., Friedrich, G., Jannach, D., Stumptner, M.: Consistency-based Diagnosis of configuration knowledge bases. Artificial Intelligence 152(2), 213–234 (2004)
18. Felfernig, A., Friedrich, G., Jannach, D., Stumptner, M., Zanker, M.: Configuration Knowledge Representations for Semantic Web Applications. Artificial Intelligence in Engineering, Design, Analysis and Manufacturing (AIEDAM) 17(2), 31–50 (2003)
19. Felfernig, A., Friedrich, G., Jannach, D., Zanker, M.: Web-based configuration of virtual private networks with multiple suppliers. In: Proceedings of 7th International Conference on Artificial Intelligence in Design (AID 2002), Cambridge, UK, pp. 41–62 (2002)
20. Felfernig, A., Friedrich, G., Schubert, M., Mandl, M., Mairitsch, M., Teppan, E.: Plausible repairs for inconsistent requirements. In: IJCAI, pp. 791–796 (2009)
21. Felfernig, A., Isak, K., Kruggel, T.: Testing knowledge-based recommender systems. OEGAI Journal 4, 12–18 (2005)
22. Felfernig, A., Schubert, M., Zehentner, C.: An Efficient Diagnosis Algorithm for Inconsistent Constraint Sets. Artificial Intelligence for Engineering Design, Analysis, and Manufacturing (AIEDAM) 25(2), 175–184 (2011)
23. Fleischanderl, G., Friedrich, G., Haselboeck, A., Schreiner, H., Stumptner, M.: Configuring large systems using generative constraint satisfaction. IEEE Intelligent Systems 13(4), 59–68 (1998)
24. Fleurey, F., Haugen, Ø., Møller-Pedersen, B., Olsen, G.K., Svendsen, A., Zhang, X.: A generic language and tool for variability modeling. Technical Report A13505, SINTEF, Oslo, Norway (2009)
25. Gedikli, F., Ge, M., Jannach, D.: Explaining online recommendations using personalized tag clouds. I-com 10(1), 3–10 (2011)

26. Gelle, E., Faltings, B.: Solving mixed and conditional constraint satisfaction problems. Constraints 8, 107–141 (2003)
27. Grant, M.J., Booth, A.: A typology of reviews: an analysis of 14 review types and associated methodologies. Health Information and Libraries Journal 26(2), 91–108 (2009)
28. Hadzic, T., Andersen, H.R.: A bdd-based polytime algorithm for cost-bounded interactive configuration. In: Proceedings of the 21st National Conference on Artificial Intelligence, AAAI 2006, vol. 1, pp. 62–67. AAAI Press (2006)
29. Hadzic, T., Subbarayan, S., Jensen, R.M., Andersen, H.R., Møller, J., Hulgaard, H.: Fast backtrack-free product configuration using a precompiled solution space representation. In: Proceedings of the International Conference on Economic, Technical and Organisational Aspects of Product Configuration Systems, pp. 131–138 (2004)
30. Haslinger, E., Lopez-Herrejon, R., Egyed, A.: Reverse engineering feature models from programs' feature sets. In: 18th Working Conference on Reverse Engineering, WCRE 2011, Limerick, Ireland, October 17-20, pp. 308–312 (2011)
31. Hubaux, A., Jannach, D., Drescher, C., Murta, F., Männistö, T., Czarnecki, K., Heymans, P., Nguyen, N., Zanker, M.: Unifying software and product configuration: A research roadmap. In: Proceedings of the Configuration Workshop at ECAI (2012)
32. Jannach, D., Liegl, J.: Conflict-directed relaxation of constraints in content-based recommender systems. In: Ali, M., Dapoigny, R. (eds.) IEA/AIE 2006. LNCS (LNAI), vol. 4031, pp. 819–829. Springer, Heidelberg (2006)
33. Jensen, R.M.: Clab: A c++ library for fast backtrack-free interactive product configuration. In: Wallace, M. (ed.) CP 2004. LNCS, vol. 3258, p. 816. Springer, Heidelberg (2004)
34. Juengst, E., Heinrich, M.: Using resource balancing to configure modular systems. IEEE Intelligent Systems 13(4), 50–58 (1998)
35. Junker, U., Mailharro, D.: The logic of ilog (j)configurator: Combining constraint programming with a description logic. In: Proceedings of the IJCAI-2003 Configuration Workshop, pp. 13–20 (2003)
36. Liguori, F., Schreiber, F.: The software configurator: an aid to the industrial production of software. In: Proceedings of the IEEE Second International Computer Software and Applications Conference (COMPSAC), pp. 487–492 (1978)
37. Lopez-Herrejon, R.E., Galindo, J.A., Benavides, D., Segura, S., Egyed, A.: Reverse engineering feature models with evolutionary algorithms: An exploratory study. In: Fraser, G., Teixeira de Souza, J. (eds.) SSBSE 2012. LNCS, vol. 7515, pp. 168–182. Springer, Heidelberg (2012)
38. Mailharro, D.: A classification and constraint-based framework for configuration. Artificial Intelligence for Engineering, Design, Analysis and Manufacturing (AIEDAM) 12(4), 383–397 (1998)
39. Männistö, T., Soininen, T., Sulonen, R.: Product configuration view to software product families. In: Software Configuration Management Workshop, SCM-2010 (2001)
40. McGuiness, D., Wright, J.: An industrial strength description logics-based configurator platform. IEEE Intelligent Systems 13(4), 69–77 (1998)
41. Mendonça, M., Wasowski, A., Czarnecki, K., Cowan, D.: Efficient compilation techniques for large scale feature models. In: Proceedings of the 7th International Conference on Generative Programming and Component Engineering, GPCE, pp. 13–22 (2008)

42. Mittal, S., Falkenhainer, B.: Dynamic constraint satisfaction problems. In: AAAI, pp. 25–32 (1990)
43. Mittal, S., Frayman, F.: Towards a generic model of configuration tasks. In: Proceedings of 11th International Joint Conference on Artificial Intelligence (IJCAI 1989), Detroit, MI,USA, pp. 1395–1401 (1989)
44. Mohalik, S., Ramesh, S., Millo, J.-V., Krishna, S.N., Narwane, G.K.: Tracing spls precisely and efficiently. In: Proceedings of the Software Product Line Conference, SPLC(1), pp. 186–195. ACM (2012)
45. Nethercote, N., Stuckey, P.J., Becket, R., Brand, S., Duck, G.J., Tack, G.: Minizinc: Towards a standard CP modelling language. In: Bessière, C. (ed.) CP 2007. LNCS, vol. 4741, pp. 529–543. Springer, Heidelberg (2007)
46. O'Callaghan, B., O'Sullivan, B., Freuder, E.C.: Generating corrective explanations for interactive constraint satisfaction. In: van Beek, P. (ed.) CP 2005. LNCS, vol. 3709, pp. 445–459. Springer, Heidelberg (2005)
47. O'Sullivan, B.: Tutorial on product configuration. In: ASPL 2008, First Workshop on Analyses of Software Product Lines at SPLC (2008), www.isa.us.es/aspl08/
48. O'Sullivan, B., Papadopoulos, A., Faltings, B., Pu, P.: Representative explanations for over-constrained problems. In: AAAI, pp. 323–328 (2007)
49. Pohl, K., Böckle, G., van der Linden, F.J.: Software Product Line Engineering: Foundations, Principles and Techniques. Springer, Heidelberg (2005)
50. Rao, V.N.: Solving constraint satisfaction problems using finite state automata. In: Proceedings of the Tenth National Conference on Artificial Intelligence, AAAI 1992, pp. 453–458. AAAI Press (1992)
51. Reiter, R.: A theory of diagnosis from first principles. Artificial Intelligence 32(1), 57–95 (1987)
52. Sabin, D., Weigel, R.: Product configuration frameworks - a survey. IEEE Intelligent Systems 13(4), 42–49 (1998)
53. Schobbens, P., Heymans, J.T.P., Bontemps, Y.: Generic semantics of feature diagrams. Computer Networks 51(2), 456–479 (2007)
54. Segura, S., Benavides, D., Ruiz-Cortés, A.: Functional testing of feature model analysis tools: a test suite. IET Software 5(1), 70–82 (2011)
55. Segura, S., Galindo, J., Benavides, D., Parejo, J.A., Ruiz-Cortés, A.: Betty: benchmarking and testing on the automated analysis of feature models. In: VaMoS, pp. 63–71 (2012)
56. Segura, S., Hierons, R.M., Benavides, D., Ruiz-Cortés, A.: Automated metamorphic testing on the analyses of feature models. Information & Software Technology 53(3), 245–258 (2011)
57. Segura, S., Parejo, J.A., Hierons, R.M., Benavides, D., Ruiz-Cortés, A.: Ethom: An evolutionary algorithm for optimized feature models generation (v. 1.1). Technical Report ISA-2012-TR-01, ETSII. Avda. de la Reina Mercedes s/n, 2 (2012)
58. She, S., Lotufo, R., Berger, T., Wasowski, A., Czarnecki, K.: Reverse engineering feature models. In: ICSE, pp. 461–470 (2011)
59. Sinnema, M., Deelstra, S., Nijhuis, J., Bosch, J.: COVAMOF: A framework for modeling variability in software product families. In: Nord, R.L. (ed.) SPLC 2004. LNCS, vol. 3154, pp. 197–213. Springer, Heidelberg (2004)
60. Soininen, T., Tiihonen, J., Männistö, T., Sulonen, R.: Towards a general ontology of configuration. Artificial Intelligence in Engineering Design Analysis and Manufacturing (AIEDAM) 12(4), 357–372 (1998)
61. Subbarayan, S.: Integrating csp decomposition techniques and bdds for compiling configuration problems. In: Barták, R., Milano, M. (eds.) CPAIOR 2005. LNCS, vol. 3524, pp. 351–365. Springer, Heidelberg (2005)

62. Tiihonen, J., Soininen, T., Niemelä, I., Sulonen, R.: Empirical testing of a weight constraint rule based configurator. In: Proceedings of the ECAI Configuration Workshop (2002)
63. Trinidad, P., Benavides, D., Durán, A., Ruiz-Cortés, A., Toro, M.: Automated error analysis for the agilization of feature modeling. Journal of Systems and Software 81(6), 883–896 (2008)
64. Trinidad, P., Ruiz-Cortés, A.: Abductive reasoning and automated analysis of feature models: How are they connected? In: Proceedings of the Third International Workshop on Variability Modelling of Software-Intensive Systems, pp. 145–153 (2009)
65. White, J., Benavides, D., Schmidt, D.C., Trinidad, P., Dougherty, B., Ruiz-Cortés, A.: Automated diagnosis of feature model configurations. Journal of Systems and Software 83(7), 1094–1107 (2010)
66. White, J., Schmidt, D., Benavides, D., Trinidad, P., Ruiz-Cortés, A.: Automated diagnosis of product-line configuration errors in feature models. In: Proceedings of the Sofware Product Line Conference (2008)
67. Yi, L., Zhang, W., Zhao, H., Jin, Z., Mei, H.: Mining binary constraints in the construction of feature models. In: 2012 20th IEEE International Requirements Engineering Conference (RE), pp. 141–150 (September 2012)

Configurable Software Product Lines – Supporting Heterogeneous Configuration Knowledge

Elder Cirilo[1], Uirá Kulesza[2], Alessandro Garcia[1], Don Cowan[3],
Paulo Alencar[3], and Carlos Lucena[1]

[1] Pontifical Catholic University of Rio de Janeiro, Informatics Department,
Rio de Janeiro, Brazil
[2] Federal University of Rio Grande do Norte, Computer Science Department,
Natal, Brazil
[3] University of Waterloo, David R. Cheriton School of Computer Science ,
Waterloo, Canada
{ecirilo,afgarcia,lucena}@inf.puc-rio.br, uira@dimap.ufrn.br,
dcowan@csg.uwaterloo.ca, palencar@cs.uwaterloo.ca

Abstract. Although different types of enterprise information systems have been built as configurable software product lines, the growing heterogeneity and diversity in system development approaches makes it difficult to specify the configuration knowledge. In this paper we examine the deficiencies of current approaches to the specification of configuration knowledge, and as a solution propose the notion of Domain Knowledge Modeling Languages (DKMLs). We also present GenArch+, an extensible tool that supports the creation and composition of DKMLs. We illustrate and evaluate the use of DKMLs in four different product lines. Our quantitative and qualitative assessment suggests that the use of DMKLs brings improvements for heterogeneous configuration knowledge specification.

Keywords: Software Product Lines, Object-Oriented Frameworks, Configuration Knowledge, Product Derivation

1 Introduction

A variety of enterprise information systems are increasingly being built as configurable software product lines. A software product line (SPL) [18] aims at constructing (*deriving*) customer-specific products from a set of reusable features. Configurable software product lines [19] are a subclass of software product lines that are customized as a single product without programming new completion code. Systematic reuse of features through a configuration approach can potentially lead to significant productivity gains but requires explicit configuration knowledge. This knowledge states the configuration combinations that do not violate the valid relations between product line artifacts such as features and

J. Favaro and M. Morisio (Eds.): ICSR 2013, LNCS 7925, pp. 176–191, 2013.
© Springer-Verlag Berlin Heidelberg 2013

source code. Consequently, specifying configuration knowledge is as essential as specifying the base code artifacts.

Therefore the motivation behind this work is the need to improve the specification of configuration knowledge for enterprise software product lines. The mainstream development of modern enterprise software requires the convergence of multiple views and expertise. To deal with each one, participants in the development process use language specific to their domain knowledge [12]. Thus, the implementation of enterprise software product lines reuses a number of different technologies to address a series of concerns such as business process, state persistency, service orchestration and graphical user interface [7,6]. Framework is an example of a development technology where software systems are made using domain-specific constructions.

The main advantage of frameworks is that they offer the opportunity of writing code by performing smooth implementation steps such as writing XML code or completing a pre-defined interface. Even though frameworks are often convenient, they can be hard to learn and use. Indeed, one recent study [9] showed that developers in most cases complained about the difficulty with programming interface role diffusion, subtle precondition or dependency, unclear programming interface semantics, and undocumented rules. These issues lead to situations where it is difficult to specify and comprehend the configuration knowledge without proper guidance. We will refer to the existing challenges as the heterogeneous configuration knowledge problem.

Several different research approaches have been used to produce configurable product lines [5,3,14]. While they use annotative and model-supported techniques, current approaches suffer from the same problem: they do not support the specification of configuration knowledge that involves domain-specific constructions and programming interfaces that span heterogeneous languages and file types such as XML and Java. Model-supported techniques [5,3] tend to force the use of a pre-determined set of general abstractions and mechanisms. Thus, they do not provide any guidance in specifying the valid set of configurations that can be applied based on the framework's programming interfaces. Annotative techniques [14] are limited to the source code level. These techniques are so restrictive that to reveal the configuration knowledge the developer needs to investigate both the framework source code and documentation, which is often incomplete.

In this paper, we identify the shortcomings related to the development of configurable product lines based on frameworks (Section 3) and show how the use of DKMLs improves the specification of the configuration knowledge (Section 4). We also present GenArch+, an Eclipse-based plugin that supports the flexible construction and composition of DKMLs (Section 5). Finally, we evaluate the use of DKMLs in four different product lines (Section 6). The quantitative and qualitative indicators show that the use of DKMLs in conjunction with GenArch+ is promising. The results provide evidence that framework-based software product lines can be built and modeled in a more concise and comprehensible fashion than existing approaches. The evaluation also shows that GenArch+ reduces the effort of building and composing new DKMLs, which motivates their use in mainstream development of enterprise information systems. A motivating example is examined in Section 2. Section 7 presents related work and discussions. Finally, Section 8 concludes this paper.

2 Motivating Example: Product Line Implementation with Diverse Frameworks

In order to motivate our research into the heterogeneous configuration knowledge problem, we consider a category of web-based enterprise systems which are implemented using diverse frameworks. The OLIS (Online Intelligent Services) system is a product line for deriving web-based information systems with several end-user features. Some of the features of OLIS are: (i) *User Management*; (ii) *Event Announcement*; (iii) *Calendar*; and (iv) *Weather Service*. We consider a feature as a unit of functionality that satisfies a requirement and provides a potential configuration option.

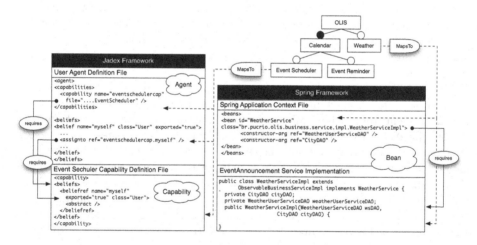

Fig. 1. Illustrative Cases of Configuration Knowledge in OLIS

The OLIS architecture is structured using the Layer architectural pattern. In this paper, we focus on the configuration knowledge related to the Agent and Business layers of the OLIS product line. The Agent layer is implemented on Jadex[1] a common goal-oriented framework. Jadex provides a set of abstractions such as agents, beliefs, goals, plans, capabilities, events and expressions. The Jadex programming interface relies on Java and an XML schema for specifying instances of its abstractions. The Business layer was implemented using the Spring[2] framework. Spring provides a service-oriented architecture based on the

---

[1] jadex.informatik.uni-hamburg.de

[2] http://www.springsource.org/

Bean abstraction, which is used to denote Spring-managed objects. The Spring container manages the object lifecycle by interpreting declarative data exposed in the form of XML documents defining the classes and properties of the injectable objects. These documents, called the Spring Application Context, express the Spring programming interface.

Figure 1 illustrates the usual form of instantiating Spring beans and Jadex agents and how the configuration knowledge occurs in this architectural style. Source code is represented using declarations of abstractions expressed in XML files and procedural code in Java classes. A distinguishing characteristic of feature-based product lines is the mapping from features to their implementation. These mappings represent the conditions (also called *presence conditions*) that control the inclusion or exclusion of the code assets or their parts. There exist several such mappings in the OLIS product line. A recurring characteristic is that they span a diversity of file types such as XML files and Java classes, and must conform to: (i) the framework's programming interfaces, and (ii) references that exist between file types. These requirements make the configuration knowledge of the OLIS product line sufficiently complex to represent the recurring challenges faced in the development of many configurable enterprise information systems [13]. Thus, the OLIS product line will be used in the next section to illustrate the difficulties in representing heterogeneous configuration knowledge.

3   Heterogeneous Configuration Knowledge Issues

The configuration knowledge of configurable product lines is supproted by many tools (Section 3.1). The limitations of these tools in adequately supporting the specification and understanding of this knowledge are discussed in Sections 3.2 and 3.3.

3.1   Feature-Based Product Derivation Tools

As discussed in the introduction, there are two main approaches for building configurable product lines: annotative and model-supported. Two tools representative of these different styles are pure::variants [3] and CIDE [14]. Both tools depart from the assumption that product lines are structured as a set of features. A feature model is used to represent both the hierarchical arrangement of the features and the set of constraints that restrict possible combinations of those features. The product line implementation uses source code configuration. Presence conditions are the pieces in the configuration knowledge used to evaluate whether specific parts of the source code must be present in a feature model configuration.

CIDE and pure::variants can be distinguished by the way presence conditions are specified. CIDE specifies the presence condition in the source code using an annotative approach similar to `#ifdef` and `#endif` statements. CIDE guides the developer when annotating the source code in that it avoids annotations that do not respect the language syntax and type system. In contrast, pure::variants is based on a modeling approach for structuring the product line. The product line architecture is represented by one or more object-oriented models, called Family models. The presence conditions attached to model elements define when an element must be included or excluded or when a transformation such as template transformation does not need to be evaluated. In pure::variants, developers are free to create requires and excludes constraints, which express the interaction between model elements.

3.2   Mismatch of Domain Knowledge Specification

Creating presence conditions is normally based on the source code [14]. For example, in CIDE the mappings illustrated in Figure 1 correspond to annotating the declaration tag of the WeatherService bean and the WeatherServiceImpl class with presence conditions in terms of the *Weather* feature. In pure::variants an instance of the Class concept can be created in the Family Model to represent the WeatherService bean where the presence of the concrete WeatherServiceImpl class is also defined. The configuration of the declaration tag needs to come from a template file owing to the lack of a proper connection with the source code.

These approaches often lead to a distorted view of the configuration knowledge. The developers are not able to reason locally about configurations. Even worse, their reasoning is not in terms of framework abstractions and programming interfaces which government the product line implementation. Therefore, when creating the presence conditions, the developers need to know the required and dependent source code artifacts. Unfortunately, the optional and required combination of mappings (given by programming interfaces semantics) is not specified explicitly in the existing tools. These combinations can only be discovered by investigating the source code or reading the framework documentation. For example, there is no mechanism that ensures the correspondence of the mapping from *Weather* feature to source code with the Spring programming interface semantics (see Figure 1). Consequently, understanding and guaranteeing the consistency of the configuration knowledge without domain-specific guidance is normally a tedious and error-prone activity.

3.3   Diffusion and Replication of Presence Conditions

In the example of Section 2, the feature *Weather* appears in two files (Spring Application Context and WeatherServiceImpl class) that realize the same framework abstraction. As a consequence a lack of mechanisms for representing the configuration knowledge through framework abstractions replicates presence conditions across the source code. Table 1 is an overview of the degree of feature crosscutting (diffusion) in four different framework-based product lines. This metric counts the number of features that crosscut more than one source code artifact. In the OLIS SPL, for example, there are 7 optional or alternative features, with 6 of them present in more than 135 of the 270 files that implement the product line. Thus, the features crosscut more than 50% of all source code. Similarly, a large percentage of crosscutting was found in other product lines, as also captured in Table 1.

As the size of product line code grows, it might become increasingly difficult to understand the overall purpose of the configuration knowledge. The number of artifacts makes it challenging to see how many and which artifacts are implementing a feature and how they interact. The previous example involves the exhaustive verification of multiple code snippets across heterogeneous artifacts with reasoning about non-trivial and implicit references.

Table 1. Crosscutting degree in four different product lines

Product Lines	Number of Features	Number of Files	Number of Files with Presence Conditions	Crosscutting Degree
OLIS	7	270	135	50%
eShop	8	93	49	52%
IPAgent	7	30	16	53%
eCommerce	31	173	47	28%

A workaround to reduce the impact of scattered presence conditions is to use querying mechanisms [16] that allow the inspection of features across code assets. Pure::variants provides some querying capabilities that facilitate the inspection of the product line source code while CIDE [14] supports reasoning about scattered features through a visualization mechanism that appears to amalgamate the separated concerns. However, these approaches still do not solve the fundamental problems discussed previously. The abstraction mismatch and feature diffusion remain, and require developers to spend additional time performing non-trivial queries on the product line source code. For these reasons, the problem should be re-formulated so that the programmers doing product line configuration only work with familiar abstractions. Thus, we argue that to address these challenges, product line developers need to apply domain-specific mechanisms to represent the configuration knowledge.

4 Modeling Heterogeneous Configuration Knowledge

In order to improve the specification of configuration knowledge for framework-based product lines we propose the notion of a domain knowledge modeling language (DKML). Rather than using general-purpose mechanisms, developers can rely on a specification that provides domain-specific syntax and guided development. The DKMLs explicitly indicate when the mappings from features to source code conform to a framework's programming interfaces and constraints.

Figure 2 shows an overview of our model-supported approach for engineering configurable product lines. The feature model distinguishes both the domains common characteristics and variability. The implementation model is a

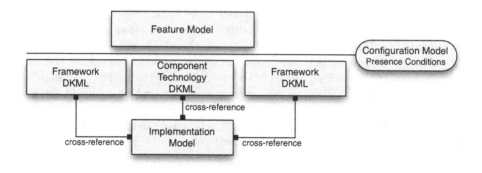

Fig. 2. Approach Overview

specification of the source code in terms of `Classes`, `Folders`, `Components`, `Files` and references to `Fragments` inside a code asset. The domain knowledge models are meant to avoid the replication and diffusion in the configuration knowledge specification. Finally, the configuration model contains the presence conditions, which indicate the existence or non-existence of domain knowledge model (DKM) elements or event parts in the source code. We use the terms DKML and DKM to denote the meta- and modeling levels, respectively.

4.1   DKML: Definition and Properties

A DKML is a language designed for specifying the configuration knowledge for a product line for a specific domain. A DKML consists of an abstract syntax with relations that must hold between language constructs. As an example, a DKML for Spring comprises the concept Bean, which contains an arbitrary number of Injection concepts, which in turn have a relationship with another Bean concept. A DKM conforming to this abstract syntax, for instance, defines a concrete Bean (e.g., `WeatherService`) comprising two Injection elements referring to the `WeatherUserServiceDAO` and `CityDAO` beans. Accordingly, the abstract syntax captures the abstractions as language concepts and encodes the framework's programming interface through relations.

Relations as references between the abstract syntax concepts and the implementation model define how the source code is configured according to the programming interface. For example, the concrete `WeatherService` bean from the previous example needs to refer to an XML tag that declares its dependencies on other beans via instances of the Injection concept. In addition, this bean refers to its implementation (`WeatherServiceImpl`). This type of reference is created for each abstraction, allowing fine-grained control over the source code configuration.

A DKML addresses the challenges presented in Section 3, as discussed in the following:

Taming Configuration Knowledge Mismatch. With DKMLs the configuration knowledge specification moves from generic or low-level languages to domain-specific languages. That is, the developers are able to create feature mappings in a more clean and concise form, such as the `WeatherService` bean implements the feature *Weather*. Feature mapping is controlled by the abstract syntax and relationships, thus guiding the developer in making correct mappings. References to implementation models identify the source code that implements the abstractions. Thus, the developers obtain an overview of the product line implementation in terms of the framework abstractions and programming interfaces with which they are familiar, such as Bean, Agents, Entities, and their relations.

Reducing and Modularizing Presence Conditions. The use of abstractions in the design of configuration knowledge also reduces the re-occurrence of the same presence condition along with the source code, thereby promoting a concise and modular representation. In the example of Section 2, the presence condition becomes a mapping relationship between the `WeatherService` bean and the feature *Weather*. References to implementation artifacts which are part of the Bean concept are used to propagate this condition during configuration of the source code.

4.2   Example: OLIS Product Line Implementation with DKMLs

We illustrate the use of DKMLs through the OLIS product line. This illustrative example consists of two DKMs (see Figure 3). The first DKM defines the implementation knowledge of the Agent layer using the dialect proposed by the Jadex framework. The second DKM represents the knowledge of the Business layer that was structured using Spring beans.

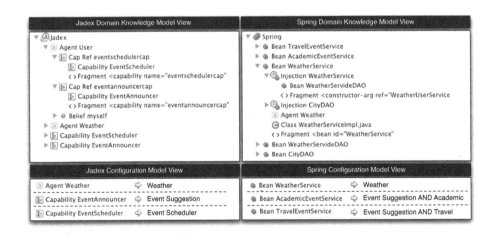

Fig. 3. OLIS Domain Knowledge and Configuration Models (partial view)

Figure 3 shows a partial view of the Jadex DKM for OLIS. There are two agents in this model. The User agent is a representation of each user in the system. Each User agent may have five different Capability elements, although Figure 3 illustrates only two: (i) Event Scheduler; and (ii) Event Announcer. The Weather agent, in turn, provides the weather information. The Spring DKM specifies the elements from the Business layer. It contains some Bean elements implementing OLIS services, which are the WeatherService, AcademicEvent-Service and TravelEventService. Other elements are integration Beans following the Data Access Object pattern used to link the Business with the Data layer. Spring Beans that implement the GUI Layer were represented in a separate model, omitted from this paper.

The configuration model contains the presence conditions. They are characterized as a constraint involving feature expressions and solution space elements. Figure 3 illustrates, for example, the Weather agent as an implementation of the *Weather* feature. In the same model, we can see a mapping between the expression *Event Suggestion AND Academic* and the AcademicEventServe bean. We represent presence conditions in separated views, one for each DKML.

Each DKM element is associated with its implementation through references. For example, the Bean concept expresses two references: (i) one to a Class element, which abstracts the element that implements its behavior; and (ii) another one to a Fragment element, which abstracts its structure declared in the Spring Application Context file. The WeatherService bean, for example, contains a reference to the WeatherServiceImpl class and another one to the Fragment <bean id="WeatherService"...>. References between different domain models are also supported. Note that the semantics of all illustrated relations, explicitly expressed via DKMLs, are not able to be specified using the general-purpose mechanisms of pure::variants and CIDE, as discussed in Section 3.

5   GenArch+: Product-Line Implementation with DKMLs

DKMLs must be easy to build and compose with each other without negating their domain-specific characteristics. Our solution for these two requirements is the concept of a product line implementation infrastructure based on a domain-independent schema and parametric polymorphism. The following subsections describe the key characteristics of GenArch+.

5.1   Domain Knowledge Schema

GenArch+ consists of two distinct layers (see Figure 4). The first layer, domain knowledge schema, is a defined minimal set of concepts that serves to give the second layer, DKMLs, a configuration foundation. This way, DKMLs are given unambiguous definitions, and can be interpreted by a tool. DKML is the only language to be manipulated directly by the developer. The domain knowledge schema is used by the meta-modelers. They can determine the universe of

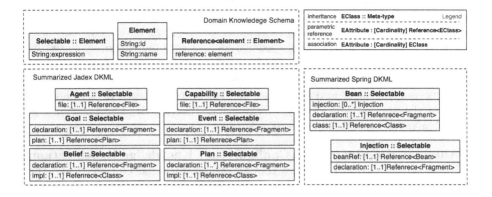

Fig. 4. Domain Knowledge Representation Schemas

DKMLs as composed of domain abstractions (*Element*), where some must have those instances present in every DKM, while others can have those instances optionally excluded (*Selectable*). Finally, model elements are also likely to be related to other elements (*Reference*).

DKMLs are constructed using inheritance (see Figure 4). Every DKML concept representing a framework abstraction must be a sub-type of *Element*. When a concept represents an optional abstraction, it needs to be a sub-type of *Selectable* (e.g., Agent). Hence, the tool enables the mapping between concept instances and feature expressions through an **expression** property. The *Reference* element is used to denote all types of relations between framework abstractions such as Injection and Bean. Typed references are captured via parametric polymorphism. For example, the **beanRef** property of the Inject concept only assumes a reference to model elements that are instances of the bean concept. It allows the infrastructure to interpret the DKML abstract syntax in domain-specific ways and guide the developer when creating the configuration knowledge. Therefore, in spite of its universality, the proposed schema is powerful enough to express domain-specific structural constraints. Parametric references tie together a DKML concept instance and a number of instances of other concepts. The infrastructure supports the design of metamodels that build models conforming to the ECore meta-metamodel semantics and the following reference rules:

- $\langle *, C_j, \{C_1 \cdots C_n\}\rangle$ (**ForAll**) - The concept C_j can incorporate zero or more references for each type of concept C_i in the set $\{C_1 \cdots C_n\}$.
- $\langle 1, C_j, \{C_1 \cdots C_n\}\rangle$ (**Mandatory**) - The concept C_j must incorporate one reference for each type of concept C_i in the set $\{C_1 \cdots C_n\}$.
- $\langle ?, C_j, \{C_1 \cdots C_n\}\rangle$ (**Optional**) - The concept C_j can incorporate at least one reference for each type of concept C_i in the set $\{C_1 \cdots C_n\}$.

5.2   The GenArch+ Tool

We extend our previous work [5] to support the aggregation of DKMLs. The abstract syntax of each DKML is specified as an Ecore model implemented by the Eclipse Modeling Framework (EMF). EMF is a plugin for defining domain-specific languages and supports standard cross-model reference mechanisms, diverse type relationships, and parameterized references. The EMF significantly facilitates the development of DKML extensions (Section 6). The functionality of the GenArch+ has two key characteristics:

- **Automated Guidance on Configuration Knowledge Specification:** Based on the well-formed rules (ForAll, Mandatory and Optional) and the ECore meta-metamodel semantics, GenArch+ guides the developers in the process of creating the references between model elements. GenArch+ is able to restrict which types of model elements can be part of a reference and forces the creation of missing elements or even references.
- **Automated Product Derivation:** GenArch+ achieves automatic product derivation using a constraint satisfaction problem representation of the product line. Model elements are represented as boolean variables that may assume the values 0 or 1 (selected or not selected). Presence conditions and references between model elements are expressed as propositional constraints. A constraint solver is used to evaluate the constraint satisfaction problem and infer valid configurations of all models, which is used further to configure the product line source code. The solver can also be used to verify the consistency of the configuration knowledge.

6   Evaluation

This section presents the evaluation of DKMLs built for a wide range of industrial-strength frameworks, which were used in turn to develop four product lines. The purpose of our evaluation is two-fold: (i) assess the usefulness of DKMLs in different scenarios, and (ii) quantify the benefits and drawbacks of mapping features to framework-provided abstractions, when compared to annotative (e.g., CIDE) and model-driven (e.g., pure::variants) approaches. Based on the results, we were able to observe how the use of DKMLs affected the conciseness and comprehensibility of the heterogeneous configuration knowledge representation (Section 6.1). We also gathered some insights on the effort required to create new DKMLs as the corresponding target product lines were built (Section 6.2).

6.1   Analyzing the Configuration Knowledge

We analyzed the use of DKMLs for product lines satisfying the following criteria: (i) their implementations were based on multiple frameworks, (ii) the frameworks were developed independently from each other, and (iii) each of them has more than 30 features. The code size of the product lines ranges from ~4000 LOC to ~14600 LOC. The configuration knowledge of the four target product lines were represented (and compared) using three approaches: CIDE, pure::variants, and GenArch+. The comparison was based on the analysis of structural properties of the configuration knowledge description.

Quantifying Configuration Knowledge Properties. We used a set of metrics to quantify properties of the configuration knowledge that have a direct or indirect effect on their comprehensibility. The most basic metric is the number of presence conditions (NPC), which captures the size of the configuration knowledge. This measure can also be used as an initial indicator of replication and verbosity in the configuration knowledge. Owing to the characteristics of each tool, we measure NPC in different ways in each of them: (i) in CIDE, we count the number of annotations in the source code; (ii) in pure::variants, the number of required constraints involving features in the Family Model plus the number of configuration statements in the source code; and (iii) in GenArch+, we count the number of presence conditions in the Configuration Model.

We have also analyzed the extent to which the presence conditions affect multiple product line artifacts. In order to support this analysis, we have applied the scattering degree measure [8]. The scattering degree (Scatt) is the number of the presence conditions in different locations. This metric quantifies the diffusion of the configuration knowledge. This measure can also be used to predict the effort required from the developers and maintainers of the configuration knowledge. Previous empirical evaluation of the crosscutting degree measure showed that it is a useful indicator of maintenance effort (and lack of fault tolerance) in a wide range of software engineering tasks [8,11]. The number of places that must be annotated with presence conditions indicates the effort that developers need to devote to comprehend and maintain the configuration knowledge. A large number of presence conditions spanning numerous code artifacts could make understanding the configuration knowledge difficult and as a consequence make change and evolution of the product line challenging.

Table 2. Metrics result – Tool x Product Line

Tools		Product Lines			
		OLIS	IPAgent	eShop	EasyC
CIDE	NPC	221	33	203	76
	Scatt	163	26	76	65
pure::variants	NPC	221	33	203	76
	Scatt	23	14	62	26
GenArch+	NPC	144	20	189	65
	Scatt	1	1	1	1

Results. Table 2 summarizes the results for GenArch+ using DKMLs as compared to those results obtained with pure::variants and CIDE. The model-supported and annotative approaches, respectively implemented by pure::variants and CIDE, have a higher number of presence conditions. As they are not able to isolate the framework-provided abstractions, they tend to lead to configuration knowledge with poorer modularity than GenArch+. In contrast, the use of DKMLs helps to reduce the number of presence conditions. The DKMLs require only one presence condition for all source code instantiating the framework abstraction. Of course what defines an abstraction is often open to interpretation and the granularity of the abstraction often depends on individual circumstances. For example, in both eShop and EasyC product lines, many features are related to properties of entity abstractions, which are a common characteristic of data-centric information systems (e.g., eBusiness). It leads to a high degree of fine-grained configurations scattered across different layers. As a consequence, the difference of the NPC metric from GenArch+ to other approaches moves from ~50% (OLIS and IPAgent) to ~15%, when we compare eShop and EasyC cases. Even though some presence conditions do not directly map to abstraction instantiations or crosscut different layers of the information systems, GenArch+ still avoids the intertwining of the presence conditions with the source code via the Configuration model. The opposite scenario prevails when using pure::variants and CIDE approaches, as we can observe by analyzing the results of the Scatt metric.

Table 2 summarizes the degree of diffusion observed in the configuration knowledge in all three cases. Better results were also found when using DKMLs. The better modularity achieved through the use of DKMLs might improve the management and traceability of features. They allow developers to focus on the configuration knowledge rather than having to care about implementation details. Therefore, it provides some evidence that model-supported approaches can simplify some of the recurring maintenance tasks, such as the change impact analysis. The use of DKMLs also encourages the design of tools to check whether refactoring activities [4] preserve the framework programming interface and constraints. Refactoring is often used when the adoption strategy involve bootstrapping existing products into a software product line.

6.2   Building Domain Knowledge Modeling Languages

Our experience has shown that, in practice, a single DKML will cover only a small portion of a product lines features. Thus, multiple DKMLs must be provided for a real-life software product line. However, developing a new domain-specific language for each domain can be costly and time-consuming [17]. In certain circumstances, this might impair the adoption of DKMLs for the development of configurable software product lines.

Our experience on using GenArch+ provided us with several insights regarding the costs of creating DKMLs. We observed that developing DKMLs on top of GenArch+ only involves the specification of their meta-models, namely the abstract syntax and the relations between concepts. The "hardest" part of creating new DKMLs is performed automatically by the EMF plug-in. EMF is responsible for automatically producing a large number of code elements required to classify the adapter classes, and persistency mechanisms. The Spring domain knowledge model required that only 2,97% (47) of the total number of lines of code must be developed manually. In the same way, the Jadex framework only required the manual specification of 1,89% (55) of the total lines of code to implement its respective DKML. The remaining, 2142 and 2869 lines of code could be automatically generated.

7   Related Work and Discussion

Recent research has been conducted on modeling languages that abstract framework-based code, product line configuration involving a diversity of file types and software analysis techniques that are variability-aware. This section highlights related work in two categories and also present some discussions.

Domain-Specific Modeling Languages and Frameworks. Research related to domain-specific modeling languages and frameworks is not new. For example, Antkiewicz et al. [1] proposed Framework-specific Modeling Languages (FSMLs) in order to help developers understand and verify framework usage. FSMLs are related to DKMLs in that both are modeling approaches for representing the knowledge about framework usage. Fortunately, the strategies provided by FSMLs to support automatic extraction and round-trip engineering can be used in our approach to improve DKM construction and maintenance. GenArch+ draws on this approach, but relies on the pure ECore model as its meta-metamodel rather than a customized meta-metamodel. This choice allows GenArch+ to leverage existing modeling languages by loading, editing, and saving different models conforming to the universal configuration schema. Another discussion of this subject is the GEMS project. This project emphasizes the creation of a graphical, guided editor that supports automatic configuration of models and full code generation. In contrast, our focus is on configurable product lines, where products are derived as source code configurations. In the case of multiple models, GEMS requires a composite meta-model to compose the models, while the GenArch+ approach relies on a generic editor which displays all models and their regular cross-references.

Code Configuration Involving Diversity of File Types. Hessellund et al. [12] present SmartEMF as a framework offering consistency checking and editing guidance of name-based references among multiple domain-specific languages specified in XML schemas. Besides being focused on the construction of product lines, one of the main advantages of our approach is that it is agnostic with respect to the frameworks being used. GenArch+ represents and guides the creation of mappings from feature to abstraction instances of arbitrary frameworks as long as there exists a DKML. Elsner et. al. [10] presented an approach and an infrastructure for constraint checking across configuration file types and multiple product lines. Similar to our approach, the source code and configuration files are converted to models, which facilitate the use of constraint languages (e.g., OCL, Constraint Programming). Our approach differs from [10] in that we focus on mainstream code-oriented product line engineering, while they consider the orchestration of configurations that crosscut multiple product-line assets.

Validation in the Presence of Variability. Recently, researchers have started to use software analysis techniques that are variability-aware [2,15]. The key idea is not to generate and analyze individual products, but to analyze the whole source code directly with the help of configuration knowledge. There are several proposals for variability-aware analyses in the literature, including parsing, type checking and dataflow analysis. Unfortunately, framework-based source code is not able to be processed directly by existing variability-aware analyses. There is a lack of information about the existence of concepts and their programming interface. The use of DKMLs therefore, can be seen as a step towards variability-aware analyses of framework-based configurable product lines. DKMLs encode the structure of framework programming interfaces, specifying which concepts may appear, and where and how they are related. They also define a clear mapping to code instantiating concepts. So now we are able to automate some analyses such as checking the consistency of the entire product lines without generating and analyzing individual products.

8   Conclusion

The heterogeneity of configuration knowledge in real-life product lines resembles the recurring challenges faced in the development of enterprise information systems. In this paper, we present a model-supported approach to specify framework-based product lines explicitly. The DKML addresses a number of challenges, such as: (i) concise and comprehensible specification of the configuration knowledge using framework-provided abstractions, (ii) modular reasoning about presence conditions; and (iii) guided creation of presence conditions. The approach is supported by an extensible infrastructure, called GenArch+, which enables agile implementation of new DKMLs, avoiding the overhead that could be caused when creating one or more DKMLs. In our evaluation, we have observed that the effort to reuse and create new DKMLs for a wide set of configurable information systems is worthwhile because of all the benefits. The use of DKMLs to specify the configuration knowledge relies on framework-provided abstractions that are already part of the developer mindset, while supporting improved modularity and brevity.

We expect that product lines based on other infrastructures could benefit equally well from DKML representation and guidance facilities. In future work, we intend to apply and evaluate our approach in complex product lines for other information systems. Extending GenArch+ to provide guidance for refactoring looks promising. In this case, the concept of refactoring product lines needs to be extended to consider changes that preserve the observable behavior related to framework programming interface. The current version of GenArch+, including illustrative examples, is available at "www.inf.puc-rio.br/~ecirilo/genarch".

References

1. Antkiewicz, M., Czarnecki, K.: Framework-specific modeling languages with round-trip engineering. In: Wang, J., Whittle, J., Harel, D., Reggio, G. (eds.) MoDELS 2006. LNCS, vol. 4199, pp. 692–706. Springer, Heidelberg (2006)

2. Apel, S., Kästner, C., Grölinger, A., Lengauer, C.: Type safety for feature-oriented product lines. In: 25th International Conference on Automated Software Engineering, pp. 251–300 (2010)
3. Beuche, D.: Modeling and building software product lines with pure::variants. In: 12th International Software Product Line Conference, p. 358 (2008)
4. Borba, P., Teixeira, L., Gheyi, R.: A theory of software product line refinement. In: Cavalcanti, A., Deharbe, D., Gaudel, M.-C., Woodcock, J. (eds.) ICTAC 2010. LNCS, vol. 6255, pp. 15–43. Springer, Heidelberg (2010)
5. Cirilo, E., Kulesza, U., Lucena, C.: A product derivation tool based on model-driven techniques and annotations. Journal of Universal Computer Science 14(8), 1344–1367 (2008)
6. Cirilo, E., Kulesza, U., Lucena, C.: Automatic derivation of spring–osgi based web enterprise applications. In: 11th International Conference on Enterprise Information Systems, pp. 228–233 (2009)
7. Cirilo, E., Nunes, I., Kulesza, U., Lucena, C.: Automating the product derivation process of multi-agent systems product lines. Journal of Systems and Software 85(2), 258–276 (2012)
8. Conejero, J., Figueiredo, E., Garcia, A., Hernndez, J., Jurado, E.: Early crosscutting metrics as predictors of software instability. In: 47th International Conference Objects, Models, Components, Patterns, pp. 136–156 (2009)
9. Daqing, H., Lin, L.: Obstacles in using frameworks and apis: An exploratory study of programmers' newsgroup discussions. In: 19th International Conference on Program Comprehension, pp. 91–100 (2011)
10. Elsner, C., Ulbrich, P., Lohmann, D., Schröder-Preikschat, W.: Consistent product line configuration across file type and product line boundaries. In: Bosch, J., Lee, J. (eds.) SPLC 2010. LNCS, vol. 6287, pp. 181–195. Springer, Heidelberg (2010)
11. Figueiredo, E., Silva, B., Sant'Anna, C., Garcia, A., Whittle, J., Nunes, D.: Crosscutting patterns and design stability: An exploratory analysis. In: 17th International Conference on Program Comprehension, pp. 138–147 (2009)
12. Hessellund, A., Czarnecki, K., Wąsowski, A.: Guided development with multiple domain-specific languages. In: Engels, G., Opdyke, B., Schmidt, D.C., Weil, F. (eds.) MODELS 2007. LNCS, vol. 4735, pp. 46–60. Springer, Heidelberg (2007)
13. Ishida, Y.: Challenge for the spl approach in enterprise software development. Technical report, NRI Information Technology (2007)
14. Kästner, C., Apel, S., Kuhlemann, M.: Granularity in software product lines. In: 30th International Conference on Software Engineering, pp. 311–320 (2008)
15. Kästner, C., Rhein, A., Erdweg, S., Pusch, J., Apel, S., Rendel, T., Ostermann, K.: Toward variability-aware testing. In: 4th International Workshop on Feature-Oriented Software Development, pp. 1–8 (2012)
16. Kimmig, M., Monperrus, M., Mezini, M.: Querying source code with natural language. In: 26th International Conference on Automated Software Engineering, pp. 376–379 (2011)
17. Mernik, M., Heering, J., Sloane, A.: When and how to develop domain-specific languages. ACM Computing Surveys 37(4), 316–344 (2005)
18. Pohl, K., Böckle, G., Linden, F.: Software Product Line Engineering: Foundations, Principles, and Techniques. Springer, Heidelberg (2005)
19. Raatikainen, M., Soininen, T., Männistö, T., Mattila, A.: Characterizing configurable software product families and their derivation. Software Process: Improvement and Practice 10(1), 41–60 (2005)

Extracting Models from ISO 26262 for Reusable Safety Assurance

Yaping Luo[1], Mark van den Brand[1], Luc Engelen[1], John Favaro[2],
Martijn Klabbers[1], and Giovanni Sartori[2]

[1] Eindhoven University of Technology
P.O. Box 513, 5600 MB, Eindhoven, The Netherlands
{y.luo2,m.g.j.v.d.brand,l.j.p.engelen,m.d.klabbers}@tue.nl
[2] Intecs S.p.A.
via Umberto Forti 5, 56121 Pisa, Italy
{john.favaro,giovanni.sartori}@intecs.it

Abstract. As more and more complex software is deployed in safety-critical embedded systems, the challenge of assessing the safety of those systems according to the relevant standards is becoming greater. Due to the extensive manual work required, validating compliance of these systems with safety standards is an expensive and time-consuming activity; furthermore, as products evolve, re-assessment may become necessary. Therefore, obtaining reusable assurance data for safety assessment or re-assessment is very desirable. In this paper, we propose a model-based approach for assuring compliance with safety standards to facilitate reuse in the assessment, qualification and certification processes, using the automotive safety standard ISO 26262 as a specific example. Three different modeling techniques are described: A structure model is introduced to describe the overall structure of the standard; a rule-based technique is used for extracting the conceptual model from it; and a mapping to the software and systems process engineering metamodel provides a description of its processes. Finally, validation in the context of a concrete use case in the FP7 project OPENCOSS shows that the resulting models of our approach resemble the industrial models, but that they, inevitably, require the fine-tuning of domain experts.

Keywords: Safety Assurance Reuse, Safety-Critical Systems, ISO 26262, Conceptual Model, SPEM.

1 Introduction

With the increasing complexity of software-intensive safety-critical embedded systems, more and more effort is necessary to ensure their safety. A number of international functional safety standards have been developed to provide development guidelines and keep the risk at an acceptable level [7]. Adherence to such standards is the basis for safety assurance and certification[1]. However, current

---

[1] In the remainder of this paper, we mention safety assessment only, because the ISO 26262 standard does not require certification by an assessment authority. Furthermore, for the definitions of the safety-related concepts in this paper, we refer to [4].

J. Favaro and M. Morisio (Eds.): ICSR 2013, LNCS 7925, pp. 192–207, 2013.
© Springer-Verlag Berlin Heidelberg 2013

safety assessment practices are among the most costly and time consuming tasks in development of safety-critical embedded systems [13]; moreover, re-assessment is often needed whenever such systems evolve. Therefore, it is crucial to find an efficient way to reduce the recurring safety assessment costs. This motivates the use of models that capture these safety standards and support the reuse of assurance artifacts. In some domains (such as the automotive domain), there is no authority providing an interpretation of the safety standard, and the modeling process is mainly performed by experts based on manufacturer requirements to ensure sufficient quality. Thus, the whole process of extracting the models from the safety standards becomes subjective. Furthermore, when a new version of the standard is released, the models need to be updated or modified by persons who may not yet have the competencies. Due to the invisible modeling process, most of the previous work needs to be redone. Hence, finding an objective way for creating the models is crucial.

The motivation for safety assurance reuse goes beyond re-assessment *within* product evolution. It can be even more valuable *across* product development efforts. Sometimes, different systems are developed with similar safety-related characteristics, and the assurance artifacts used for one system can be reused (with appropriate modification) in the assurance activities for the other, resulting in considerable savings. In addition, the assurance artifacts themselves become more reliable with repeated reuse. Just as systematic software reuse is facilitated by formal modeling of the software application domain (the "domain model"), *systematic assurance reuse* can benefit from formal modeling of the *standard* that governs the domain. It is the *model* of a safety standard that facilitates systematic reuse in safety assessment.

The idea of modeling standards is not new: modeling of safety standards is widely used for understanding and communication among engineers and software developers. Besides the aforementioned challenge concerning the subjectiveness of the modeling process, there are other significant challenges to confront. First, standards are invariably represented in natural language, with the resulting inevitable manual work of interpretation becoming more costly and less reliable. It also increases the difficulty of identifying the reusable information from the safety-related artifacts developed during the safety lifecycle. Second, standards themselves contain inconsistencies. There are a number of synonyms used in the standard, which makes it impossible to generate the models from the standards automatically. Sometimes, standards are even in contradiction with themselves. Finally, any formal model should support the demonstration of compliance with the safety standard, both for the development process and for the diverse artifacts created during product development. We advocate that standards need to be universally understandable and expressed in a language that is simple, well structured, but strict. For this goal, we believe that in the future it should be possible to transform standards into models automatically, and vice versa.

Work to date has generally involved conceptual modeling of standards for understanding. A conceptual model for the aeronautic standard DO 178B [2] is provided in [20] to improve communication and collaboration among safety engineers and software engineers. In [18], a conceptual model of the generic standard IEC 61508 [3] for electrical and electronic equipment is proposed for the development of compliant embedded software. Also, in [14], some research on process modeling has been done in the context of ISO 26262. All of these studies refer to compliance with the standards from a specific point of view; moreover, the modeling process is subjective, which may lead to inconsistencies of the models after future modifications. Furthermore, the *traceability* of the source of the models is not covered: no one knows where the concepts and relations in the models come from, except the expert who has identified or defined them. To the best of our knowledge, there does not yet exist a methodology to support extracting a conceptual model from the standard in an objective fashion, a crucial step along the way to systematic assurance reuse.

In view of these observations, we present a solution in this paper for creating models of safety standards in an objective manner, with the ultimate goal of using the models for demonstrating compliance and enabling reuse of assurance artifacts. As noted earlier, compliance demonstration requires two models: the conceptual model and the process model. We have developed the so-called "Snowball" approach for extracting the conceptual model from the standard. It is a rule based approach that reduces the amount of manual work and provides traceability between the model and the standard. For the process model, we use a mapping between the standard and the general process model, providing another way to reduce the subjectivity of the modeling process. ISO 26262, the recent standard for functional safety in the automotive domain, is used as a specific example in this paper; however, this work also forms the basis for facilitating a more general mapping between standards in different domains. Since the *Concept Phase*, described in Part 3 of the standard, is the starting point of the development process in ISO 26262, we illustrate our approaches by modeling this phase.

The rest of the paper is organized as follows: Section 2 reviews the ISO 26262 standard, and describes the proposed modeling approach for enabling safety assurance reuse in the context of OPENCOSS project. In Section 3, a rule-based approach is defined for extracting a conceptual model. Section 4 outlines a process model of the ISO 26262 *Concept Phase*. Section 5 discusses the validation of those models. Section 6 introduces the related work of safety assurance reuse. Finally, Section 7 summarizes our conclusions and future work.

2 Background

2.1 ISO26262

ISO 26262 is a goal-oriented standard for safety-critical systems within the domain of road vehicles. It is an adaptation of the generic IEC 61508 standard, which focuses on Electrical/Electronic (E/E) systems but provides a general design framework for safety-critical systems [15]. The ISO 26262 standard consists of ten parts. Part 1 provides the vocabulary; Part 2 introduces management of functional safety; Part 3 to part 7 are the main parts of standard described using

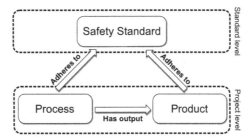

Fig. 1. Relation between standard and project

the classic V-model for the different phases of the development process; and part 8 to part 10 are the supporting parts for how to use the standard.

More and more manufacturers in the automotive domain are developing software-intensive systems in compliance with ISO 26262, but efficient deployment of this standard requires changes to the development process in specific projects. Two levels may be distinguished: the safety standard level and the project level. At the safety standard level, there are safety standards designed by safety organizations to ensure product safety. At the project level, there are work products as the outputs from each phase of the product development process. The relation between these two levels (Figure 1) is the compliance argument: it proves that the requirements of process and product at the project level adopt the recommendations of the ISO 26262 standard. The challenge here is that at the end of the project or at important milestones, evidence must be provided; consequently, a mapping between specific project files and work products in the standard must be made. In summary: there are process and product aspects at the project level, both of which must adhere to the standard.

ISO 26262 Models. Given its attention to both product and process, a safety standard effectively provides a reusable guideline for the development of safety-critical systems; thus, artifacts used in the demonstration of compliance with this reusable guideline can themselves become reusable. However, an enormous amount of manual work is normally involved for ensuring compliance with the standard. To overcome this drawback, a model-based approach is proposed to reduce costs. The purpose of modeling is a better understanding of a safety standard. Compare to the textual standards, the models of a safety standard are machine processable. It provides the predictable, deterministic, repeatable results for validating, which facilitates the reuse of safety assurance data.

In this paper, three kinds of models are proposed for the safety standards. The structure model and the conceptual model are introduced to support unambiguous understanding of the standard; the process model supports the demonstration of compliance of the process of the project with the process described in the standard. The overview of the resulting model is depicted in Figure 2.

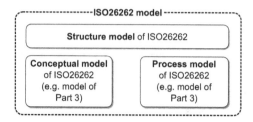

Fig. 2. Overview of ISO 26262 model

Since it is a challenge to describe the whole standard here, the ISO 26262 structure model (Figure 3) is built mainly according to the table of contents. The definitions of some main concepts in the structure model are listed as follows:

- Lifecycle: *"entirety of phases from concept through decommissioning of the item."* (ISO 26262 Part 1:1.72)
- Phase: *"stage in the safety lifecycle that is specified in a distinct part of ISO 26262."* (ISO 26262 Part 1:1.89)
- Requirements:*"a necessary attribute in a system; a statement that identifies a capability, characteristic, or quality factor of a system in order for it to have value and utility to a user."* [18]
- Work products: *"results of one or more associated requirements of ISO 26262."* (ISO 26262 Part 1:1.142)

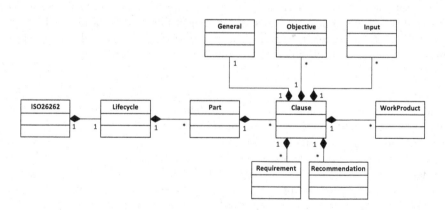

Fig. 3. Structure model of ISO 26262

A safety lifecycle is specified in ISO 26262. Each phase in the safety lifecycle includes a number of clauses. In each clause, there is an *Objective* and a *General* section to give a brief introduction of the purpose of each clause. In the *Requirements and Recommendations* section, requirements are discussed in detail. Additionally, the inputs to the clause are listed, while the work products are seen as the outputs.

Table 1. Methods and tools used for each model

Model	Extraction method	Description method	Tool
Structure Model	Manual modeling of the table of content	UML	Microsoft Visio 2010
Conceptual Model	Snowball approach	Ontology	Protege and OWLGrEd
Process Model	Mapping between standard and SPEM	SPEM	EPF

Due to the different characteristics and aims of these models, different methods are chosen to extract and describe these models. Most of the selected description methods in Table 1 are widely used in industry.

For the conceptual model, we defined the Snowball approach for extraction. The results are represented as an ontology; then OWLGrEd [8] is used for visualization. The Software & Systems Process Engineering Metamodel (SPEM) [16] is used for describing our process model, and SPEM supporting tool Eclipse Process Framework (EPF) [1] is used.

In section 3, the conceptual and process models are explained in detail.

2.2   OPENCOSS

OPENCOSS project [11] is a FP7 large-scale integrated project, which started since October 2011 with a consortium of seventeen companies from nine countries. It aims 1) to devise a common certification framework which spans different vertical markets in the transport sector, such as railway, avionics and automotive industries, and facilitates the reuse of assurance assets within, across, and between domains, and 2) to establish an open-source platform for safety certification infrastructure. The ultimate goal of the project is to bring about substantial reductions in recurring costs of safety (re-)certification, and at the same time to increase product safety through the introduction of more systematic certification practices. Both will boost innovation and system upgrades considerably.

In particular, the core challenge of the OPENCOSS project is to define a common conceptual and notational framework for specifying certification assets [5]. Using a common conceptual framework for different certification standards allows patterns of certification assessment to be shared, and supports cost-effective re-certification between different standards. The purpose is to get mutual recognition of and to discuss abstract notions from different domains. This paper contributes to this purpose by presenting an objective solution for modeling and analyzing the safety standards.

3   Extracting the Conceptual Model from ISO 26262

This section introduces a rule-based approach for extracting the conceptual model of the ISO 26262 standard. Since work products are the results of relevant requirements, the conceptual model extracted from the requirements plays a role of a guideline for complying to the standard. To obtain this kind of model, most current work is based on expert experience; consequently, traceability of the modeling process is ignored in manually creating and maintaining relationships. We have developed the Snowball approach to address this issue.

3.1   The Snowball Approach

The safety standard contains both high-level requirements, such as those described in *Objective* sections, and low-level requirements, represented in *Requirements and Recommendation* sections. The Snowball approach aims to assist users of the standard in generating a conceptual model of the standard.

Just like creating the snowman, it involves four steps as follows: First, a basic model with a number of concepts is created from the high-level requirements. Second, like rolling a snowball in the snow, the size of basic model becomes bigger and bigger when processing the low-level requirements according to the rules. Third, the big snowball is shaped into a "snowman" frame, which is the conceptual model of the standard and preliminary model for practical use. Finally, the snowman frame turns to a real snowman after being validated by domain experts.

Therefore, for reducing the subjectiveness of the process of extracting conceptual model from ISO 26262, some rules and steps are prerequisites.

Rules in the Snowball Approach. The conceptual model of the standard consists of a number of concepts and relations. Therefore, as part of the Snowball approach, some rules are defined for selecting those concepts and relations. This not only ensures consistency with the standard, but also supports traceability.

The rules for selecting concepts are as follows:

1. Most concepts arising from the terminology in the standard are originally assumed to be safety related. We then define several categories for grouping the concepts according to their (safety-related) purpose, such as process, product, error, etc. Those concepts that do not belong to any category are classified as non-safety related. The remaining concepts are selected as safety related, and are then used in the Snowball approach.
2. Clause titles are not classified as concepts in the conceptual model. Rather, they represent activities in the safety lifecycle, which will be included in the process model.
3. Safety related nouns in the high-level requirements are selected as concepts, such as *Item, Functional Safety Requirement*, etc.
4. Safety and non-safety related nouns in low-level requirements that have a clear relationship with the existing concepts are selected as concepts, such as *Functional Requirement, Non-Functional Requirement*, etc.

The rules for selecting relations are as follows:

1. Verbs between concepts are selected as relations, such as "has", "is determined by", "is resulted in", "is based on", etc.
2. If there is no specific verb between concepts, the relations are defined according to the prepositions; for instance, in "the boundary of item", the relation will be treated as "Item has boundary".

The rules for refinement and optimization are as follows:

1. All concepts that are instances of more general concepts need to be grouped. Some concepts can be seen as examples of more general concepts. For instance, *Functional Requirement, Non-Functional Requirement, Functional Safety Requirement* can be grouped into a single concept named *Requirement*.
2. Synonyms should be merged. In ISO 26262, seemingly different concepts sometimes represent a similar idea. For instance, *Item* and *System, Software Component* and *Software Unit, Safety Lifecycle Activity* and *Safety Activity*. Based on their respective definitions in the standard glossary, those concepts are treated as synonyms.
3. Relations must be precisely defined. Every relation in the ontology must have a unique name, and each relation must be clearly defined. For instance, when defining the relation as "has" between *Hazard* and *ASIL*, a following word is given, like "hasASIL". It could be used to specify what this relation is.

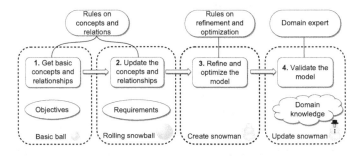

Fig. 4. Steps in Snowball approach

Steps in the Snowball Approach. In a concrete application of the approach, ISO 26262 Part 3 (the Concept Phase) was carefully analyzed manually, which involved both the high level and low level requirements. As discussed earlier, there are four main steps in the Snowball approach (Figure 4). In each step, rules for selecting concepts and relations are implemented. The following illustration focuses on the *Item Definition* clause in Part 3.

– Get the basic ball

We start from the objectives in ISO 26262 Part 3 to identify the basic concepts and relations. In this step, rules on concepts and relations are used. The result of this step is seen as the basic ball in the Snowball approach. A fragment is shown in Figure 5, where the rectangles represent concepts and the thick lines represent the inheritance relation between concepts.

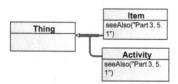

Fig. 5. Basic ball of *Item Definition* visualized with OWLGrEd

The original basic ball for the Concept Phase of Part 3 consists of 13 concepts directly descendant from *Thing*, which is the superclass of all other classes. The "seeAlso" attribute of each concept records the section number of its location in standard. In this way, the traceability of the modeling process is ensured; it also provides support to the user for modification.

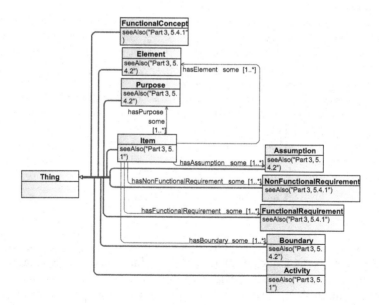

Fig. 6. Big ball of *Item Definition* visualized with OWLGrEd

– Rolling the ball
  A careful analysis of the detailed requirements in ISO 26262 Part 3 led us to
  add more concepts and relations to the basic ball. As in the first step, rules
  on concepts and relations are used. For example, from "the functional and
  non-functional requirements of the item", we could obtain two new concepts
  related with the existing concept *Item: Functional Requirement* and *Non-
  functional Requirement.* The result of this step is seen as the big ball in the
  Snowball approach. A fragment is shown in Figure 6, where the thin lines
  represent relationships between the concepts. The original big ball for Part
  3 consists of 51 concepts directly descendant from *Thing.*
– Shaping the snow ball
  Then, a refinement of the big ball is performed according to the rules on
  refinement and optimization. The result of this step becomes the conceptual
  model of the standard. Figure 7 shows a fragment of the conceptual model
  of ISO 26262 Part 3. The original conceptual model for Part 3 consists of 22
  concepts directly descendant from *Thing.* Many concepts of the big ball are
  grouped according to the refinement and optimization rule.

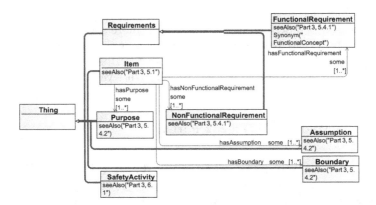

Fig. 7. Conceptual model of *Item Definition* visualized with OWLGrEd

– Creating the snowman
  Finally, domain knowledge is a prerequisite to transform the rough basis of
  the snowman into the real snowman. In other words, the conceptual model
  needs to be validated by domain experts before being used in practice. The
  details of this step will be explained in Section 5.

4 Extracting Process Model from ISO 26262

4.1 ISO 26262 Process Model and SPEM

As mentioned in Section 2, ISO 26262 is based upon a V-Model as a reference
process model for the different phases of product development. Therefore, as

Table 2. Mapping between concepts of ISO 26262 and SPEM

Concepts in ISO 26262	Concepts in SPEM
Development process	Process
Part	Phase
Clause	Activity
Objective	Purpose
Requirement and Recommendation	Task
General/Content of requirement	Description
Work Product	Work Product
Note	Guideline

mentioned earlier, it is effectively a reusable guideline for practical domain applications. For describing the process, SPEM has been selected, which is defined as a meta-model as well as a UML profile by Object Management Group (OMG) for process modeling.

Since the process described in the standard is more specific, a mapping from the standard to SPEM is needed. The concept mapping is defined in Table 2. Compared with the mapping in [6], our aim is to describe a more general process model; therefore, the mapping only focuses on high-level concepts.

4.2   Process Model of ISO26262 Part 3

In the following, the process model of ISO 26262 Part 3 is created. From the work breakdown structure view (shown in Figure 8), we can see that Part 3 is defined as a phase, whereby each clause in Part 3 is defined as an activity. After an analysis of the requirements, the tasks and their steps as well as the work products are defined for activities.

For the *Item Definition* clause in ISO 26262, there are two main requirements. The definition of tasks in this clause depends on the content of those requirements. In Figure 8, there are two tasks defined for this clause. For other clauses, the requirements are represented in groups, such as in the *Initiation of Safety Lifecycle* clause, where there are two requirement groups. In the activity diagram (Figure 9(a)) we can see that two tasks are defined. Further analysis revealed that those detailed requirements could be categorized into two groups. Based on this, two steps have been defined for the *Impact analysis and possible safety lifecycle tailoring* task. Therefore, the activities, tasks, and steps in the process model are defined according to the requirements in different levels. Finally, the work products are allocated to the relevant activities, tasks, or steps. They are all assigned to specific roles, such as safety project manager. In Figure 9(b), the detailed activity diagram shows this relation.

ISO26262 Part3

Presentation Name	Index	P...	M	Type
ISO26262	0			Delivery Process
Part3 concept phase	1			Phase
Item definition	2			Activity
Functional and non-functional requirements identification	3			Task Descriptor
Item boundary definition	4	3		Task Descriptor
Safety lifecycle initiation	5	2		Activity
Development category determination	6			Task Descriptor
Impact analysis and possible safety lifecycle tailoring	7			Task Descriptor
Hazard analysis and risk assessment	8	5		Activity
Hazard analysis and risk assessment initiation	9			Task Descriptor
Situation Analysis and Hazard Identification	10	9		Task Descriptor
Classification of hazardous events	11	10		Task Descriptor
Determination of ASIL and safety goals	12	11		Task Descriptor
Verification Task	13	12		Task Descriptor
Functional safety concept definition	14	8		Activity
Derivation of functional safety requirements	15			Task Descriptor
Allocation of functional safety requirements	16	15		Task Descriptor
Validation criteria	17	16		Task Descriptor

Description | Work Breakdown Structure | Team Allocation | Work Product Usage | Consolidated View

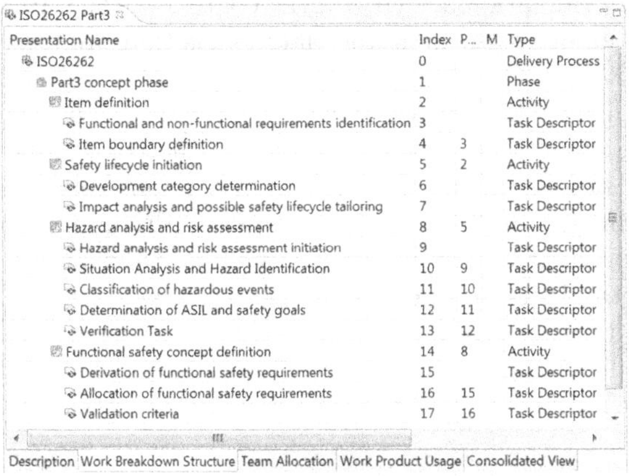

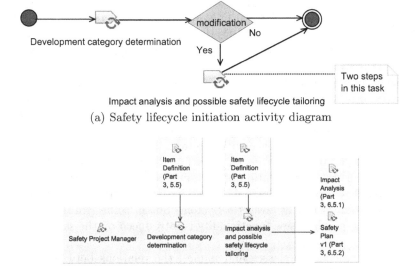

Fig. 8. Work Breakdown Structure view of the ISO 26262 Part 3 process model

(a) Safety lifecycle initiation activity diagram

(b) Safety lifecycle initiation activity detail diagram

Fig. 9. Activity diagrams for safety lifecycle initiation task

5 Model Validation

Validation focuses on the conceptual and process models. The last step of Figure 4 depicts the validation of the conceptual model. As noted earlier, an important goal of the Snowball approach is to achieve objectivity and cost-effectiveness in the production of the conceptual model, by automating as much as possible. But to be usable, the model must be valid: in other words, it must become "a real snowman."

In a preliminary validation activity, in the context of the OPENCOSS project, we compared our model with the industrial models that are used for compliance with ISO 26262 Part 3. Over 90% of the concepts in those models are covered by our conceptual model. Due to their specific focus, some concepts in industrial models have often been renamed; however, the corresponding concepts in the standard can still be identified. For example, in one case "Malfunction" was changed to "Malfunctioning behavior"; in another, "Preliminary architectural assumption" was changed to "Preliminary functional and architectural assumptions"; and so forth. Thus, we see that in the implementation of a model, some concepts are modified according to the specific project context; importantly, however, traceability is maintained by recording the section number of the concepts' locations in standard, so that the source of the concepts and relations can be traced.

The process model is almost identical, except for the special case of the Safety Element Out Of Context (SEooC). "A Safety Element out of Context (SEooC) is a safety element for which an item does not exist at the time of the development. A SEooC can either be a subsystem, a software component, or a hardware component." (ISO 26262 Part 10:10.1) Note that, *Item* in the ISO 26262 is for example the car itself. For the SEooC, the initiation of safety lifecycle activity is skipped and assumptions are made about the *Concept Phase*, resulting in a truncated process.

As encouraging as this result was, it is also necessary for the conceptual model to be validated by domain experts, because semantic alterations might have been introduced in the conceptual model due to the semi-automated nature of the techniques used. For this purpose, we had the conceptual model examined by two experts who have deep experience with the teaching and application of the ISO 26262 standard in industrial projects. They found some cases of subtle misinterpretation, such as the identification of Item and System as strictly synonymous in the preliminary conceptual model. In real-world industrial application of the standard, an Item is nearly always a System, but in some (rare) cases it can be a Function (e.g. when new functionality is introduced on the same hardware platform).

In addition to concept classes and names, the relations between them are examined and validated by the domain experts. Their explicit representation makes possible inconsistencies emerge quickly. For example, the cardinality of a relationship between the Safety Goal and Safe State was not clear to the domain experts: was it 1:1? This would be wrong, because in practice there may be *no* safe state in automotive scenarios. In another example, both the Hazardous Event and Safety Goal concepts had a relationship with an ASIL concept. In practice, however, it must be ensured that it is always the *same* ASIL, and this must be reflected in the model.

Such subtleties can be difficult or impossible for the semi-automated, rule based techniques of the Snowball approach to identify, partly because they often do not even emerge out of the standard itself but rather its real-world application. For this reason, validation by domain experts is likely to remain a necessary final step even after significant improvement in the techniques employed in the Snowball approach. Nevertheless, experience with domain experts confirmed that a formal representation of the conceptual model is an excellent basis for validation and the eventual elimination of inconsistencies. Furthermore, the availability of a semi-automatically generated model reduced by as much as 80% the amount of time to validate the final model by the domain experts, a significant savings.

Once the general model is validated, it is suitable for practical use in the context of compliance demonstration: Recalling that compliance is demonstrated through the relationship between the standard's model and the project's model, and that traceability is provided at both standard and project level, the effects of modifications at project level can now be traced to the standard level and the impact on the assurance argument determined and those assurance artifacts reused that are not affected by the modifications.

6 Related Work

Other work has advocated model based approaches to enabling assurance reuse. In [10], an approach was proposed for evolutionary chains of evidence to support evidence reuse. With a specific focus on evidence, they describe the benefits of using model-driven engineering (MDE) to support compliance with safety standards. They further argue that MDE could support the interpretation of standards; specialization of standards to industrial contexts; alignment of standards to organizational practices; planning for certification, etc. Besides these benefits, they argue that MDE could also be used for supporting safety assurance reuse management, such as evidence reuse, safety case reuse etc. Safety-case based approaches are provided in [19] and [17] for safety compliance and assurance reuse.

7 Conclusions and Future Work

In this paper, we presented a model-based approach to enabling safety assurance reuse through objective and cost-efficient modeling of the relevant standards. The Snowball methodology provides rules for extracting the conceptual model from a safety standard, thereby reducing the amount of manual work involved. Over 90% of the concepts in the industrial models are covered by our conceptual model. A better result will be obtained if the domain experts are involved in all the steps of Snowball approach, but it will be more costly. Besides, the availability of a semi-automatically generated model reduced by as much as 80% the amount of time to validate the final model by the domain experts. The process in the standard is modeled with the OMG SPEM. Although the approach currently operates only at a very high level, it provides a basis for describing a process model in the context of the safety standards.

In future work, we will focus on four directions. The first direction is to extend our methodology so that we can extract models from a collection of interrelated safety standards. The second direction is a comparative study of those safety standards through those models. For example, in some domains (such as automotive and avionics) similar systems have been developed according to different safety standards. This fact could be exploited to reuse safety assurance arguments from one system to the other, which necessarily involves a comparative study of the two respective standards. A high-level comparison between two safety standards (ISO 26262 and DO 178B) is outlined in [12]; but the challenge here is to compare the standards at the lower level in order to support safety assurance reuse. This could be achieved through conceptual mapping and process mapping. Another future direction is to define a domain specific meta-model for the processes found in safety standards, since SPEM is too general to describe the process model of the safety standards at the lower level. In [6], an extension for ISO 26262 is described. Still, in the OPENCOSS project, we deal with more than one standard, and an extension of SPEM is not sufficient. The last future direction is to use existing Natural Language Processing (NLP) techniques [9] and ontology learning methodologies to improve and further reduce the amount of manual work involved in a semi-automatic implementation of the Snowball approach.

Acknowledgements. The research leading to these results has received funding from the FP7 programme under grant agreement n° 289011 (OPENCOSS). We would like to thank Centro Ricerche Fiat (CRF) and Eric Verhulst for providing information and feedback on our work.

References

1. Eclipse Process Framework Project, http://www.eclipse.org/epf/
2. DO 178B: Software Considerations in Airborne Systems and Equipment Certification (1992)
3. IEC 61508: Functional Safety of Electrical/Electronic/Programmable Electronic Safety-Related Systems (2010)
4. OPENCOSS: Deliverable D2.2 - High-level requirements, report (2012), http://www.opencoss-project.eu/node/7
5. OPENCOSS: Deliverable D4.1 - Baseline for the common certification language (2012), http://www.opencoss-project.eu/node/7
6. Adedjouma, M.: Requirements Engineering Process According to Automotive Standards in a Model-Driven Framework. Ph.D. thesis, University of Paris-Sud (2012)
7. Armengaud, E., Bourrouilh, Q., Griessnig, G., Martin, H., Reichenpfader, P.: Using the CESAR Safety Framework for Functional Safety Management in the Context of ISO 26262, Embedded Real Time Software and Systems (2012)
8. Bārzdiņš, J., Bārzdiņš, G., Čerāns, K., Liepiņš, R., Sprogis, A.: UML style graphical notation and editor for OWL 2. In: Forbrig, P., Günther, H. (eds.) BIR 2010. LNBIP, vol. 64, pp. 102–114. Springer, Heidelberg (2010)
9. Chowdhury, G.G.: Natural Language Processing. Annual Review of Information Science and Technology 37(1), 51–89 (2003)
10. de la Vara, J.L., Nair, S., Verhulst, E., Studzizba, J., Pepek, P., Lambourg, J., Sabetzadeh, M.: Towards a Model-Based Evolutionary Chain of Evidence for Compliance with Safety Standards. In: Ortmeier, F., Daniel, P. (eds.) SAFECOMP Workshops 2012. LNCS, vol. 7613, pp. 64–78. Springer, Heidelberg (2012)

11. Espinoza, H., Ruiz, A., Sabetzadeh, M., Panaroni, P.: Challenges for an Open and Evolutionary Approach to Safety Assurance and Certification of Safety-Critical Systems. In: 2011 First International Workshop on Software Certification (WoSoCER), Hiroshima, Japan (2011)
12. Gerlach, M., Hilbrich, R., Weißleder, S.: Can Cars Fly? From Avionics to Automotive: Comparability of Domain Specifc Safety Standards. In: Proceedings of the Embedded World Conference (March 2011)
13. Jackson, D., Thomas, M., Millet, L.: Software for Dependable Systems: Sufficient Evidence? The National Academies Press, Washington, D.C. (2007)
14. Krammer, M., Armengaud, E., Bourrouilh, Q.: Method Library Framework for Safety Standard Compliant Process Tailoring. In: 37th EUROMICRO Conference on Software Engineering and Advanced Applications, pp. 302–305 (2011)
15. Langheim, J., Guegan, B., Maillet-Contoz, L., Maaziz, K., Zeppa, G., Phillipot, F., Boutin, S., Aboutaleb, I., David, P.: System Architecture, Tools and Modelling for Safety Critical Automotive Applications - The R&D Project SASHA. In: ERTS2 2010, Embedded Real Time Software & Systems, Toulouse, France, pp. 1–8 (2010)
16. OMG: Software and Systems Process Engineering Metamodel Specification (April 2008), http://www.omg.org/spec/SPEM/2.0/
17. Palin, R., Ward, D., Habli, I., Rivett, R.: ISO 26262 Safety Cases: Compliance and Assurance. In: Proceedings of the 6th IET International Conference on System Safety (2011)
18. Panesar-Walawege, R.K., Sabetzadeh, M., Briand, L.: Using UML Profiles for Sector-Specific Tailoring of Safety Evidence Information. In: Jeusfeld, M., Delcambre, L., Ling, T.-W. (eds.) ER 2011. LNCS, vol. 6998, pp. 362–378. Springer, Heidelberg (2011)
19. Ruiz, A., Habli, I., Espinoza, H.: Towards a Case-Based Reasoning Approach for Safety Assurance Reuse. In: Ortmeier, F., Daniel, P. (eds.) SAFECOMP Workshops 2012. LNCS, vol. 7613, pp. 22–35. Springer, Heidelberg (2012)
20. Zoughbi, G., Briand, L., Labiche, Y.: Modeling Safety and Airworthiness (RTCA DO-178B) Information: Conceptual Model and UML Profile. Softw. Syst. Model. 10(3), 337–367 (2011)

Assessing Software Quality through Web Comment Search and Analysis

Yanzhen Zou[1,2], Changsheng Liu[2], Yong Jin[1,2], and Bing Xie[1,2,*]

[1] Software Institute, School of Electronics Engineering and Computer Science,
Peking University, Beijing 100871, China
[2] Key Laboratory of High Confidence Software Technologies, Ministry of Education,
Beijing 100871, China
{zouyz,liucs09,jinyong11,xiebing}@sei.pku.edu.cn

Abstract. When reusing software resources appearing on the Internet, developers often encounter the problem that it is hard to know the quality of candidate software. In this case, developers usually want to search and find referable user comment on the Internet. To assist this process, we proposed a textual comment based software quality assessment approach in this paper. It could search and collect the user comments of the software resource on the Internet automatically. Furthermore, the sentiment polarity (positive or negative) of a comment is identified and all the comments are classified into positive or negative collection. Then the quality aspects which the comment talks about are extracted so as to draw out the merits and drawbacks of software resources. With these information, developers can do candidate software selection easier and quicker in the software repository. To evaluate our approach, we apply our approach on a group of open source software. The results show that our approach could achieve satisfying precision in software quality assessment.

1   Introduction

With the development of the Internet and software reuse, more and more reusable software resources are available on the Internet, such as Web Services, JAR packages and so on. To reuse these software resources appearing on the Internet, users often encounter the problem that it is hard to know the quality of candidate software resource since limited quality information are provided [1,2].

To deal with this issue, former works about software's quality mainly focus on code analysis [3-6] and architectural analysis [7-9]. For example, Akito Monden et al. [10] evaluated software reliability and maintainability by detecting code clones. Swapna Gokhale Michael et al. [11] used regression tree models to predict the number of faults in a software module based on the software complexity metrics. Nevertheless, the cost of using these methods to get quality information might be very expensive. It required developers understand its function correctly and input the right parameters. Besides, a bunch of numerical values returned by these methods are difficult for a novice to understand. On the other hand, some quality aspects are difficult to be measured by these methods, e.g., the flexibility of software resource.

---

* Corresponding author.

J. Favaro and M. Morisio (Eds.): ICSR 2013, LNCS 7925, pp. 208–223, 2013.

In this scenario, we find that former developers' feedbacks or reviews (collectively called comment in this paper) are useful references for new developers to understand the quality of software resources. With the development of Web 2.0, increasing number of developers submit their feedbacks on the Internet. It is partly because some developers may post their comments on the Internet through *blogs* and *forums*. Meanwhile, there are plenty of Open Source Communities, such as *SourceForge* and *Seekda*, providing feedbacks mechanism on the web. Therefore, more and more developers are used to utilizing web comments for software resource selection.

However, developers usually spend a lot of time to find a referable comment on the Internet. Firstly, though a large number of web comments provide a good reference base, there are so many comments that are useless to developers since they just give a simple overall evaluation. For example, the comments "it's an excellent project" or "it's too bad" provide less useful information if the developer want to know whether the API of the component is flexible. Secondly, since only looking through a small quantity of comments may lead to aberration, developer usually expect to skim comments as many as possible to get overall evaluation of the quality aspect. For example, if a developer wants to know whether *Log4j* is lightweight and easy to integrate into a specific project, he would concern not only who talked about *Log4j's* usability and flexibility but also how many people have talked about these two quality aspects.

To deal with these issues, we propose a textual comment based software quality assessment approach in this paper. Comparing with the various existing works, our approach provides the following benefits:

- It implement an Internet based software comments searching tool;
- It proposes a SVM based approach to identify the sentiment polarity of a comment, which is used to classify the comments into positive and negative ones;
- It extracts the quality aspects which the comments talk about so as to find the merits and drawbacks of software resource;
- We apply our work to 25 open source software in experiments. The comments collection and analysis results could be served as a good reference to help developers to select proper software resources.

This paper proceeds as follow. Section 2 describes the details of our approach. Section 3 carries some experiments to evaluate our approach. In section 4, we describe some related works. Then we conclude this paper in Section 5.

2   Our Approach

As shown in Fig. 1, there are two main phases in our approach: Comments Collection and Comments Analysis. In Comments Collection, our target is to collect relevant user comments about the software resource from the Internet. We implement Google based search tool and extract the comment segments from related web pages. Then these comments are input the next phase—Comments Analysis. It identifies the sentiment polarities of these comments and digs out what aspects these comments talk about. As a result, developer could find the merits and drawbacks of the candidate software resource. It could serve as a good reference for developers in reusable software resource search.

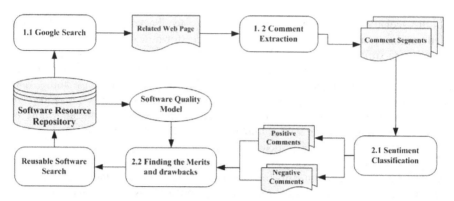

Fig. 1. Overview of Our Approach

2.1   Comments Collection

General web search engine is a useful tool to get information from the Internet, with its help people can seek out the resources using some simple keywords. We use Google to get the related raw information from the Internet.

Google Search

The relativity between the results and the software is a big problem if we only use the name of the software as the key word. To construct a better query, we take the software name and development context into account, such as programming language, brief description, the author and so on. The context information can be described as a 5-tuple <*name, version, language, description, author*>. The name is indispensable for the query and the other elements in the vector could be added to the query. The more elements we add, the more relevant are the obtained results.

How to use Hibernate?

If you want to create a perfect data modelling or associate objects with the befitting database in a trouble-free and straight forward style, Hibernate is the best choice for you. It is an immensely popular object relational mapping skeleton for Java enthusiasts. Along with power-packed performance concerning object/ relational persistence, it also makes its presence felt for Java query services. Hibernate applications delineate persistent groups that are charted to database tables.

Features that make Hibernate Demanding

• A clear spotlight on domain object modelling

• A superior presentation in object caching roped in with configurable personification tactics

Fig. 2. Target content in the corresponding page

The results returned from *Google* are composed by related web page items. Each item consists of title, snippet and the corresponding URL etc. The snippet is assembled of short sentences extracted from the corresponding page of the URL. For example, we search "hibernate java" and one snippet of results is "*... forward style, Hibernate is the best choice for you. It is an immensely popular object relational* *mapping skeleton for Java enthusiasts. ...*". It indicates that using the snippet alone as the software's comment is obviously not enough. The whole correct part of the corresponding page is what we need. For example, the actual part of software comment on *Hibernate* in the corresponding page is shown in Fig. 2. Therefore, we need open the corresponding web page and extract the textual comment segment.

Since the page's structure is unknown, it's impossible to use html parser tools to get the specific content we need directly. The information we need lay among the html tag like <p>, <span>, <div> and <td>, all these information is potentially relevant content. We use *VSM*-based similarity Computation [17] to find which part of the page is the most similar to the snippet that *Google* returned. In *VSM*, a text is represented as a vector $<W_1, W_2\ W_3\ ..., W_k>$. Each dimension indicates a term occurring in all the texts. Then *TF-IDF* weight is chosen to be the value of each dimension. As a term t_i, its TF metric in text d_j is computed as follows:

$$TF_{i,j} = \frac{n_{i,j}}{L_j} \tag{1}$$

In formula (1), $n_{i,j}$ is the number of times t_i occures in d_j, L_j is the total number of terms in d_j. IDF metric of t_i is computed as follows:

$$IDF_i = \log \frac{N}{df_i} \tag{2}$$

In formula (2), N is the total number of texts, df_i is the number of texts which contain term t_i. The TF-IDF weight of term t_i in text t_j is computed as follows:

$$W_{i,j} = TF_{i,j} * IDF_i \tag{3}$$

The similarity of two vectors $V_i=<W_{i,1}, W_{i,2},....W_{i,k}>$ and $V_j=<W_{j,1}, W_{j,2},....W_{j,k}>$ is computed as follows:

$$Similarity(V_i, V_j) = \frac{\sum_{t=1}^{k}(W_{i,t}*W_{j,t})}{\sqrt{\sum_{t=1}^{k} W_{i,t}^2 * \sum_{t=1}^{k} W_{j,t}^2}} \tag{4}$$

We use *HtmlParser* [42] to parse the corresponding page into a DOM tree, then the nodes of decorative HTML tags such as <a>, <image>, and <b> are removed. The text nodes, such as <table>, <tr>, <td>, <p>, <div> in the tree, and the snippet itself will be represented as a vector mentioned above. The specific method of finding the correct part of the page is to compute the similarity between the vector of snippet and the text node and then select the most similar one as the text needed.

There are some famous websites which publish and maintain software, such as *Apache, Maven Repository, SourceForge, Seekda* and so forth, from where we can find some comment information directly. The information is well organized and, to some extent, strictly checked comparing to the other websites. Therefore, we also design a crawler for each specific website. It searches the software within the website and then extracts the comments using *HtmlParser* [42]. Our search engine is extensible, new Crawler could be added to our approach.

Comment Extraction

The text segments returned from *Google* search engine consist of software description text and software comment text. In general, software description tends to describe what the software resource is and how to use it. These software descriptions are propagandas from their publishers. They rarely cover the software's limitations and reflect its real quality objectively. Hence, we try to extract comments from the search results returned by *Google* search engine further.

Relatively, descriptions are objective text information while comments are subjective text. Identifying whether a text is objective or subjective is a classification problem, so extracting comments from information returned *Google* Search Engine could use techniques of text classification.

Currently, machine learning is a mainstream technology to solve this issue. In this paper, we try to use Support Vector Machine (*SVM*) [18, 19] to classify the search results into objective text (description information) and subjective text (comment information). *SVM* have been shown to be highly effective at traditional text categorization, generally outperforming *Naive Bayes* [18]. Selection of feature is the key point of *SVM*, we choose the following four features according to our dataset:

- Length of the text (LEN). The comments we get are generally terse and concise, the descriptions are relatively longer and comprehensive.
- Number of first person pronouns (NFPP). The first person pronouns, I, my, etc, exist widely in comments, but they seldom appear in descriptions. So we make a first person pronouns list and count the number of words that hit the list of the need-to-classify text.
- Number of subjective sentiment words (NSWW). Some word or phrases, such as awesome, good, bad, cool, etc are colloquial, which exist mostly in comments. So we also make a subjective sentiment words list and count the number of words and phrase that hit the list of the need-to-classify text.
- Number of sentiment symbol (NSS).There are some symbols like "^-^", ":-)", ":)" and so forth, which are more likely to appear in comments.

Before extracting comments, three kinds of preprocessing have been completed in our paper which will help to improve the accuracy of analysis, they are Stop Words remove, Case-folded and Stemming. Stop words is the name given to words which are filtered out prior to, or after, processing of natural language data (text), they reduce the efficiency of natural language processing, so in our system we make a stop word list contain 42 words. Case-folded means that transferring all the words to capital. Stemming is a process to reduce inflected (or sometimes derived) words to their stem, base or root form .For example, the stemming result of "depressed", "depressive" is "depression".

2.2   Comments Analysis

Since only looking through a small quantity of comments may lead to aberration, developer usually expect to skim comments as many as possible to get overall evaluation of the quality aspect. To achieve this target, we analyze the collected software comment by which not only give the sentiment polarity of the comment, but also provide the aspects the comment talks about.

Sentiment Analysis of the Comment

After surveying the comments, we found some interesting characteristics: 1) The comment is pithy and terse. Programmers tend to directly show their attitudes in comments. The comment's polarity is always shown from the emotion words, such as some adjective like "excellent", "good", "bad", etc., or some verbs like "fail to", "return NaN ", "like", etc. The majority of comments are short, a length distribution is provided in our experiment. 2）Complex expressions seldom appear in comments. Double negation, too-to structure, and rhetorical questions are rarely used in comments which are similar to spoken expressions. 3）Domain-relative. The comment indicates what aspect or property the user cares about, such as whether the software is easy to use, the documentation is well-organized and in great detail, whether it's stable and so on. Some phrases and words frequently appear in comments.

Based on these experiences, we also want to use machine learning to distinguish positive and negative comments. Firstly, we construct an emotion expression dictionary (EED). It consists of positive words and phrases, negative words and phrases, function words and privative. The dictionary is extensible. Secondly, four features are extracted from the comment, they are as follows:

- — Number of positive words and phrases(PNUM);
- — Number of negative words and phrases(NNUM);
- — Function words(FW);
- — Distance between positive and negative words or phrases (DIS);

The DIS features is also used based on the observation that if the distance between positive and negative words or phrases is too small, it often has a *"neutralization effect"* which means the comment shows no real attitude. Taking the comment *"I don't care about whether the jar is good or bad"* as an example, the distance of positive word *"good"* and negative word *"bad"* is only 2 character. Thus, the comment provides no evaluation about the software.

When calculating the PNUM and NNUM, the privative should be taken into consideration. When privative occur before positive (or negative) words and phrases, NNUM (or PNUM) will be added. This rule can also be applied to some special grammar structure, such as "Too-to" or "Far from" structure.

Finally, SVM is also chosen to be the classifier. Samples with obtained features are used to train the classifier. When a new comment comes, the same features extractor will be used to extract the features described above. Subsequently, the features are analyzed by the trained classifier to obtain the polarity.

Finding the Merits and Drawbacks of the Software
As described above, we want to present what aspects the comment talks about further. For example, in the comment *"Hibernate's documentation is particularly excellent, especially for an open source project"*, the word *"excellent"* is in EED, the noun *"documentation"* is what *"excellent"* describe, so *"documentation"* will be extracted from the sentence.

To understand and measure the quality of software, researchers often built models of how quality characteristics relate to one another [20]. McCall quality model [20] and ISO 9126 [20, 21] are two famous quality models which have been widely discussed. For software reuse, we construct a practical model based on ISO 9126.

Table 1. Aspects of our quality model

Aspect	Specification
Documentation (DOC)	Whether the software's documentation is well organized, detail enough, etc.
Lightweight (LW)	Whether the software is lightweight
Interface (INF)	The evaluation of the interface of the software
Usability (USE)	Whether the software is easy to use
Flexibility (FLX)	Whether the software is flexible
Reliability (REL)	Whether the software works stably
Effectiveness (EFF)	Whether the software has a good performance and works efficiently

The aspects of the model are shown in table 1. We also construct an aspect-related terms set (ATS) for each aspect. For example, "*configuration*" is closely related to how to use software, so the term configuration is in the ATS of Usability. "GUI" and "API" are two types of interface of software, so the terms "GUI" and "API" are in the ATS of "Interface (INF)".

In the experiments, most of the software comments can be divided into three types:

— **Noun-Adj**: the noun is described by the adjective, e.g., the comment "*The interface is flexible*".
— **Verb-Noun**: the noun is the objective of the verb, e.g., the comment "I *like the interface*" or "*I dislike the documentation*".
— **Verb-Adv**: the adverb is used to describe the verb, e.g., "*it works perfectly*".

Dependency relations exist in the three pairs. The notion dependency is based on the idea that the syntactic structure of a sentence consists of binary asymmetrical relations between the words of the sentence [24]. We use Stanford parser [25] to analyze every sentence in each comment to get dependencies and phrase structure tree. The parser is a Java implementation of probabilistic natural language parsers which works very well at lexicalized dependency analysis. It could provide a textual description of grammatical relationships in a sentence. The dependencies are triplets: name of the dependency, governor and dependent [25]. For example, the dependencies of the sentence "*The documentation of Hibernate is excellent*" are shown in Fig. 3.

In Fig. 3, there are five dependencies —det (documentation-2, the-1), nsubj (excellent-6, documentation-2), prep (documentation-2, of-3), pobj (of-3, Hibernate-4), cop (excellent-6, is-5)—in the sentence. The terms det, nsubj, prep, pobj and cop are names of the dependencies [26]. The current version of Stanford Parser contains 52 types of dependency. Five types of dependencies—pobj, dobj, nsubj, nsubjpass and amod [26] —are considered in our approach, since these dependencies exists in the Specific Comment more frequently.

In conclusion, the detailed quality information extraction processes from Specific Comment are: 1) Finding the dependency pairs in which contain the terms in EDD. 2) The paris belong to the five types --- pobj, dobj, nsubj, nsubjpass and amod--are selected. 3) The words in the selected pairs which are not in the EDD are extracted. Pay attention to the words included in any ATS of the 7 aspects will be extracted and their corresponding aspects will be counted. For example, in the comment "*The configuration of Jboss is too complicated*", we get a dependency triplet: nsubjpass (complicated-7, configuration-2). The word "configuration" is in the ATS of Usability, so "configuration" will be extracted and the aspect Usability will be accounted. While in the comment "*Spring is a great J2EE framework*", although framework will be extracted, it will be ignored since it is not in any ATS of the 7 aspects.

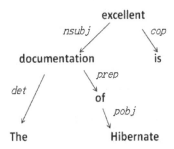

Fig. 3. Dependencies for sentence: The documentation of Hibernate is excellent

3   Evaluation and Results

In order to validate our approach, we search and collect comments for 25 popular open source projects with our approach. These open source software are chosen because we are familiar with them, such as Tomcat, Struts and so on. They vary in domains and only the latest versions are considered in comments collection.

After *Google* search and comment extraction, 2664 comments are collected for these open source software. In average, there are 106.6 comments for each software resource. In table 2, we illustrate the number of positive comments and negative comments for each project. The "Posi-Num" indicates the number of positive comments and the "Nega-Num" indicates the number of negative comments. For example, 139 positive comments and 13 negative comments are collected for "Jboss".

There are some threats to validity of our approach and our evaluation. Firstly, the richness of software comments is significant to the effectiveness of our approach. In our work, we could also find that some software resources' software comments are limited although they are excellent. On the other hand, it is difficult to validate the recall of software comments search on the Internet. However, we believe that software comments will abound on the Internet in the future, which provide enough raw data for our approach. Secondly, we try to validate whether our approach could assess the quality of the candidate software automatically using exist comments. It means that our approach could do comment extraction and comment analysis effectively, then the right quality terms are found and right quality aspects are mined. Therefore, we carried the following experiments.

Table 2. Results of web comment search (examples)

	Glassfish	Resin	Jboss	Xstream	JDom	Dom4j	HtmlParser	NekoHtml	Struts	JSF	Tapestry	Hibernate	JPA	Ibatis	Tomcat	Jetty	Quartz	Cron4j	Jcrontab	Htmlunit	Htppunit	Junit	Easymock	Log4j	Htpclient
Pos -Num	67	92	139	97	32	111	76	36	136	67	59	143	42	81	146	112	91	53	47	108	89	54	86	144	77
Nega - Num	12	15	13	5	8	13	18	7	14	19	29	12	9	12	15	11	12	8	6	11	8	19	12	21	14
Total - Num	79	107	152	102	40	124	94	43	150	86	88	155	51	93	161	123	103	61	53	119	97	73	98	165	91

3.1 Comments Extraction

In our approach, a *SVM* based classifier is proposed to identify whether a piece of text is software comment or software description. At the same time, four features, such as Length of the text (LEN), Number of first person pronouns (NFPP), etc., are used to train software comment samples. Thus, we called our comment extraction approach as *SVM4CE*. Then in the above dataset, 150 software comments are artificially selected as study samples and 150 related software descriptions are added as noises.

In our evaluation, we applied 3-fold cross-validation. We divide all the texts into 3 parts, 2 parts are used as training data set while 1 part left is used as the validation data. The process is then repeated 3 times, with each of the 3 parts used exactly once as the validation data. The three results are averaged as a single result.

Here precision, recall rate and F-Score are used to evaluate the effectiveness of our approach. The formulas are shown below. Given a specific class, A is the number of instance that correctly classified to this class, B is the number of instance that incorrectly classified to this class, C is the number of instance that belongs to this class but incorrectly classified to the other class.

$$\text{Recall} = A/(A + C) * 100\% \tag{5}$$

$$\text{Precision} = A/(A + B) * 100\% \tag{6}$$

$$F - \text{Score} = \frac{(\beta^2+1)*P*R}{(\beta^2*P+R)} * 100\% \tag{7}$$

As shown in table 3, our approach (*SVM4CE*) achieved the precision of 90.71% and the recall of 90.50% in comment extraction. It indicates that the four features we chosen are effective to identify whether a piece of information is description or comment.

Table 3. Results of Comments Extraction($\beta = 1$)

Method	precision	recall	F-score
SVM4CE	90.71%	90.50%	90.43%
Naïve Bayes	81.2%	83.4%	82.3%
LingPipe	78.1%	79.3%	78.7%

We also compare *SVM4CE* with Naïve Bayes and LingPipe [40]. Lingpipe is a famous tool kit for processing text using computational linguistics. Note that LingPipe uses positive and negative reviews of movie as the training data set; we replace it with software comments to compare them fairly. We can also learn that our approach is better than Naïve Bayes and LingPipe from Table 3. Note that Naïve Bayes is a probabilistic classifier which rests on the fact that the features are irrelevant. But in text classification, few features are irrelevant [36]. LingPipe is more suitable for long text classification but software comments are relatively short.

3.2   Sentiment Analysis

In our approach, we use another *SVM* based classifier with four different features (Number of positive words and phrases (PNUM), Function words (FW), etc.) to identify the polarity of comment. We called it *SVM4SA*. Then for 3-fold cross-validation, we select 300 positive comments and 150 negative comments randomly from the comments collected to evaluate the effectiveness of *SVM4SA*. This number difference is set because it shows that users are more likely to submit positive feedback. For example, there are 144 positive comments but 21 negative comments for "*log4j*".

Table 4 shows that the result of sentiment analysis. *SVM4SA* achieves 92% on both precision and recall, which is more efficient than the Naïve Bayes and *LingPipe*. As discussed above, the four features are interrelated with each other so Naïve Bayes is not as efficient as *SVM4SA*. While *LingPipe* is more suitable for long reviews but the comments of software comparatively short.

Table 4. Results of Sentiment Analysis ($\beta = 1$)

Method	precision	recall	F-score
SVM4SA	92%	92%	92%
Naïve Bayes	84.7%	85.1%	84.9%
LingPipe	82.1%	83.3%	82.7%

Table 5 gives some examples in sentiment classification and software quality summarization. For example, the comment text "*Dom4j is a very, very good Java XML API, high-performance, powerful*" is set to "positive". At the same time, "powerful" and "high-performance" are extracted as aspect-related terms. While the comment text "*Dom4j is briefly described as a more complex fork of JDOM. Because of this characterization, we dismissed dom4j without examining it closely.*" is set to "negative". And the term "complex fork" is extracted. It indicates that the process of sentiment classification and software quality summarization is interdependent.

Table 5. Some examples of sentiment analysis

Feedback Text of Dom4j	Sentiment analysis	EED Terms
Dom4j has saved me lots of time and effort over the last years. It is an easy, convenient and comfortable way to deal with DOM in Java.	Positive	Easy, convenient, comfortable
it's an easy to use, open source library for working with XML, XPath and XSLT on the Java platform using the Java Collections Framework	Positive	easy to use
DOM4J is a very, very good Java XML API, high-performance, powerful	Positive	powerful, high-performance
Dom4j is briefly described as a more complex fork of JDOM . Because of this characterization, we dismissed dom4j without examining it closely.	Negative	Complex fork

3.3   Quality Assessment

As described in section 3, a practical software quality model containing 7 aspects is constructed to measure the software in our approach. We apply our approach to the comments to find out what aspects these comments talk about and the results are shown in table 6. Here "*N/M*" indicates it mined from N positive comments and N negative comments indicates the corresponding quality aspect, blank indicates no comments talk about the aspect or the number of positive comments equals with negative ones.

We conduct sampling inspection on these software quality assessment results. Firstly, 5 students read the related software comments and tell us whether the quality aspect our approach provided is right. It indicates that the result could accurately reflect the actual condition of these software projects. For example, *GlassFish* Server provides online searches within a document, online searches in a document set, and deep cross-document links. *GlassFish* Server is consistently rated highly by developers for its ease of use and administration features [27].

Meanwhile, we still found some conflicting results such as 11 comments praised the efficiency of *GlassFish* but 3 negative comments also refer to this quality aspect. Though the main reason is there are conflict comments, we will improve the performance of our approach further in the future. For example, the construction of Emotion Expression Dictionary (EED) and aspect-related terms set (ATS) are constructed based on the samples study. We expect improve the work through collect more comment samples and integrate the technology of natural language process.

An interesting finding in our work is that most developers concern about software aspects such as documentation, usability and so on. However, they seldom submit software comments about maintainability or portability of software resources. Our quality model is pre-defined in software resource repository. Compared with giving the original aspect term and phrases in the sentence, we think focusing on some quality aspect that users are interested will be more helpful.

Our approach is applied to a sub-system of Trustier software resource repository (tsr.trustie.net), whose task is to enrich the software resources' quality information in the repository. With its help, users could retrieve the comments of candidate software, how many comments are positive or negative, which quality aspects the software have and what comments provide this quality assessment.

Table 6. Results of software quality assessment

	Document	Lightweight	Interface	Usability	Flexibility	Reliability	Efficiency
Glassfish	8/1			11/3			12/2
Resin						13/2	7/3
Jboss	5/2				17/0	15/1	
Xstream		11/0		13/0		9/0	7/0
JDom		9/0		7/1			
Dom4j				5/1	12/1		14/0
HtmlParser	0/4		13/0		7/1		4/0
NekoHtml				9/2			
Struts		6/2	3/0	15/2			16/1
JSF					0/5		8/2
Tapestry	0/5			2/7			7/1
Hibernate	11/0		12/1	3/7	15/1		
JPA		7/1		5/0			7/1
Ibatis		8/3			9/1		5/0
Tomcat	8/2			12/1		9/2	8/1
Jetty		15/2					16/0
Quartz	5/0	4/1	4/0	6/1	13/1		
Cron4j		6/0		5/0	3/1	4/0	
Jcrontab	1/3			4/0			
Htmlunit			9/0	5/2	7/2		4/1
Httpunit			6/1	2/8			
Junit		6/0					7/1
Easymock	0/2			5/1			5/0
Log4j		0/9			4/1	5/0	7/2
Httpclient				13/1			9/3

4   Discussion and Related Work

Our work aims to automatically analyze software comments from Internet to provide a comprehensive view of software resource. It is closely related to the following works:

4.1   Internet-Based Software Resource Collection

There are some existing methods trying to get related information of components from the Internet to help developers understand and reuse the components efficiently. For example, Wang et al. [12] collected information from the Internet to enrich descriptions of Web services. Besides, the reputation of component is also been concerned in component selection [13-15]. Li et al. [16] proposed a web services search engine named CoWS, which used the information captured from the Internet to provide quality-aware Web services search. However, these methods heavily relied on the structures and forms of specific types of components, such as QoS [16] and WSDL [12] of web services. For reusing the software resource on the Internet, Seacord et al. [28] in CMU designed Agora to get different forms of software resources on the Internet; Hummel et al. [29] proposed a test-driven technique ExtremeHarvest to obtain the software components on the Internet; Dong et al. [30] developed a search engine *Woogle* dedicated to web services search. Woogle collected the Web Service's WSDL file and its associated information from specific websites. However, these works did not provide quality guarantee for software resources, which could also be effort consuming for developers in acquiring needed resources.

4.2   Sentiment Analysis

In order to perform automated analysis of numerous comments from Internet to save users' time and energy, it is worthwhile to apply natural language processing methods to comments and extract the most valuable information. Sentiment analysis seeks to identify the view point(s) underlying a text span [31]. Pang et al. [18] applied machine learning techniques to detect the polarity (positive and negative) of movie reviews which out-perform human-produced baselines. Turney [32] presented a simple unsupervised learning algorithm for classifying reviews as recommended (thumbs up) or not recommended (thumbs down). The accuracy ranges from 84% for automobile reviews to 66% for movie reviews. Godbole et al.[33] presented a system that assigned scores indicating positive or negative opinion to each distinct entity over large corpus of news and blogs. A more fine-grained of sentimental analysis model is called aspect-based sentiment analysis. It aims to mine the features of entities in the comment, e.g., usability of a component, GUI of a software resource or reliability of a web application server. Topic model is an approach to address this issue. It identifies the abstract topics that occur in a collection of documents. Thomas Hofmann [34] created an early topic model called probabilistic latent semantic indexing (PLSI). Blei et al. [21] presented Latent Dirichlet allocation (LDA) based on the generalization of PLSI. Topic model has advantages when applied to large size documentations. However, the comments we get from the Internet are short, terse and domain-relative, our approach is more fine-grained comparing with topic model.

4.3   Web Page Information Extraction

Structure of a web page varies site by site and there is lots of unrelated information in HTML document such as ads, navigation menus. It is necessary to find a universal information extraction method which could reach a high precision. In our paper, we use an easy yet efficient method based on VSM and similarity computing which could meet our demand well. Finn et al. [40] used the Body Text Extraction (BTE) method which extracted content by identifying the single, continuous region which contained the least amount of HTML tags and the most words. Pasternack et al. [38] use maximum subsequence segmentation which based on optimization over token-level local classifiers and apply it to news websites. Weninger et al. [39] present a method to extract content text from diverse Web pages by using the HTML document's tag ratios and then cluster the resulting histogram into content and non-content areas. Reis et al. [37] introduced how to learn template-dependent wrapper based on Tree Edit Distance and DOM tree similarity for news page extraction. These methods either need large size samples for different types of HTML documents or require expert knowledge [38].

5   Conclusion

With the development of Web 2.0, increasing numbers of developers submit their software comment through Blogs, Forums and Open Source Communities. It provides useful reference for developers to assess the quality of these software resources. In this paper, we proposed a textual comment based software quality assessment approach, searching and analyzing user comments of software resources on the Internet automatically. Compared with Previous works, our approach could support more types of software resource, users needn't configure testing environment. With its help, developers can do candidate software selection easier and quicker in the software repository.

Acknowledgment. This research is sponsored by the National Natural Science Foundation of China under Grant No.61121063, 61103024, the High-Tech Research and Development Program of China (Grant No. 2012AA011202), the National Basic Research Program of China (973) under Grant No. 2009CB320703.

References

1. Wang, L., Zou, Y., Fang, L., Xie, B., Yang, F.: An Exploratory Study of API Usage Examples on the Web. In: The 19th Asia-Pacific Software Engineering Conference (APSEC 2012), Hong Kong, December 4-7, pp. 296–405 (2012)
2. Li, M., Hua, Z., Zhao, J., Zou, Y., Xie, B.: Internet-Based Evaluation and Prediction of Web Services Trustworthiness. In: The IEEE Signature Conference on Computer Software & Applications (COMPSAC), pp. 571–576 (2012)
3. Moser, R., Pedrycz, W., Succi, G.: A comparative analysis of the efficiency of change metrics and static code attributes for detect prediction. In: Proceedings of the 30th International Conference on Software Engineering, ICSE 2008, pp. 181–190
4. Kessentini, M., Vaucher, S., Sahraoui, H.: Deviance from Perfection is a Better Criterion than Closeness to Evil when Identifying Risky Code. In: Proceedings of the IEEE/ACM International Conference on Automated Software Engineering, ASE 2010, pp. 113–122 (2010)
5. Briand, L.C., Wüst, J., Daly, J.W., Victor Porter, D.: Exploring the Relationships between Design Measures and Software Quality in Object-Oriented Systems. Journal of Systems and Software 51, 245–273
6. Li, W., Henry, S.: Object-oriented metrics that predict maintainability. Journal of Systems and Software 23(1), 111–122 (1993)
7. [7] Gokhale, S., Trivedi, K.S.: Reliability Prediction and Sensitivity Analysis Based on Software Architecture. In: Proceedings of the 13th International Symposium on Software Reliability Engineering, pp. 64–75 (2002)
8. Goseva-Popstojanova, K., Trivedi, K.S.: Architecture-Based Approaches to Software Reliability Prediction. Int'l J.Computer & Mathematics with Applications 46(7), 1023–1036 (2003)
9. Roshandel, R., Medvidovic, N., Golubchik, L.: A Bayesian Model for Predicting Reliability of Software Systems at the Architectural Level. In: Proceedings of 3rd QoSA, Boston, MA, pp. 108–126 (July 2007)

10. Monden, A., Nakae, D., Kamiya, T., Sato, S., Matsumoto, K.: Software Quality Analysis by Code Clones in Industrial Legacy Software. In: Eighth IEEE International Symposium on Software Metrics (METRICS 2002), pp. 87–94 (2002)
11. Michael, S.G., Lyu, M.R.: Regression Tree Modeling for the Prediction of Software Quality. In: Proceedings of the 3rd ISSAT International Conference on Reliability and Quality in Design, pp. 31–36 (1997)
12. Wang, L., Liu, F., Zhang, L., Li, G., Xie, B.: Enriching descriptions for public Web services using information captured from related web pages on the Internet. In: IEEE International Symposium on Service Oriented System Engineering, pp. 141–150 (2010)
13. Yu, T., Zhang, Y., Lin, K.-J.: Efficient algorithms for Web services selection with end-to-end QoS constraints. ACM Transactions on the Web (TWEB) 1(1), 6–31 (2007)
14. Maximilien, E.M., Singh, M.P.: Conceptual model of Web service reputation. ACM SIGMOD Record 31(4), 36–41 (2002)
15. Nguyen, H.T., Zhao, W., Yang, J.: A trust and reputation model based on bayesian network for Web services. In: IEEE International Conference on Web Services, pp. 251–258 (2010)
16. Li, M., Zhao, J., Wang, L., Cai, S., Xie, B.: CoWS: An Internet-Enriched and Quality-Aware Web Services Search Engine. In: The 9th IEEE International Conference on Web Services, pp.419–427 (2011)
17. Guo, Q., Li, Y., Tang, Q.: Similarity computing of documents based on VSM. Application Research of Computers 25(11) (2008)
18. Pang, B., Lee, L., Vaithyanathan, S.: Thumbs up? Sentiment Classification using Machine Learning Techniques. In: Proceedings of the Conference on Empirical Methods in Natural Language Processing (EMNLP), pp. 79–86 (2002)
19. Tong, S., Koller, D.: Support vector machine active learning with applications to text classification. The Journal of Machine Learning Research 2, 45–66 (2002)
20. Kitchenham, B.: Software quality: the elusive target. IEEE Software 13, 12–21 (1996)
21. Jung, H., Kim, S., Chung, C.: Measuring software product quality: a survey of ISO/IEC 9126. IEEE Software 21, 88–92 (2004)
22. Mesleh, A., Kanaan, G.: Support vector machine text classification system: Using Ant Colony Optimization based feature subset selection. Computer Engineering & Systems, 143–148 (2008)
23. Mesleh, A.: CHI Square Feature Extraction Based SVMs Arabic Language Text Categorization System. Journal of Computer Science 3(6), 430–435 (2007)
24. Nivre, J.: Dependency grammar and dependency parsing. Technical Report MSI report 05133 (2005)
25. de Marneffe, M., MacCartney, B., Manning, C.D.: Generating Typed Dependency Parses from Phrase Structure Parses. In: LREC 2006 (2006)
26. de Marneffe, M., Manning, C.D.: Stanford Dependencies manual (2008)
27. An Oracle White Paper, Comparing Oracle GlassFish Server and JBoss: Which Application Server Is Right for You? (May 2010)
28. Seacord, R.C., Hissam, S.A., Wallnau, K.C.: AGORA: a Search Engine for Software Components. IEEE Internet Computing 2(6), 62–70 (1998)
29. Hummel, O., Atkinson, C.: Extreme Harvesting, "Test Driven Discovery and Reuse". In: Proceedings of the International Conference on Information Reuse and Integration (IEEE-IRI), pp. 66–72 (2004)
30. Dong, X., Halevy, A., Madhavan, J., Nemes, E., Zhang, J.: Similarity Search for Web Services. In: Proceedings of the 30th Very Large Data Base Conference, pp. 372–383 (2004)

31. Pang, B., Lee, L.: A Sentimental Education: Sentiment Analysis Using Subjectivity Summarization Based on Minimun Cuts. In: Proceedings of the ACL, pp. 271–278 (2004)
32. Turney, P.D.: Thumbs up or thumbs down?: semantic orientation applied to unsupervised classification of reviews. In: Proceedings of the 40th Annual Meeting on Association for Computational Linguistics, pp. 417–424 (2002)
33. Godbole, N., Srinivasaiah, M., Skiena, S.: Large-scale sentiment analysis for news and blogs. In: Proceedings of the International Conference on Weblogs and Social Media (ICWSM) (2007)
34. Hofmann, T.: Probabilistic Latent Semantic Indexing. In: Proceedings of the Twenty-Second Annual International SIGIR Conference on Research and Development in Information Retrieval (1999)
35. Blei, D.M., Ng, A.Y., Jordan, M.I.: Latent dirichlet allocation. The Journal of Machine Learning Research 3, 993–1022 (2003)
36. Joachims, T.: Text categorization with support vector machines: Learning with many relevant features. In: Nédellec, C., Rouveirol, C. (eds.) ECML 1998. LNCS, vol. 1398, pp. 137–142. Springer, Heidelberg (1998)
37. Reis, D.C., Golgher, P.B., Silva, A.S., Laender, A.F.: Automatic web news extraction using tree edit distance. In: Proceedings of the 13th International Conference on World Wide Web (WWW 2004), pp. 502–511 (2004)
38. Pasternack, J., Roth, D.: Extracting article text from the web with maximum subsequence segmentation. In: Proceedings of the 18th International Conference on World Wide Web, pp. 971–980 (2009)
39. Weninger, T., Hsu, W.H., Han, J.: CETR - Content Extraction via Tag Ratios. In: Proceedings of the 19th International Conference on World Wide Web, pp. 971–980 (2010)
40. Finn, A., Kushmerick, N., Smyth, B.: Fact or fiction: Content classification for digital libraries. In: DELOS Workshop: Personalization and Recommender Systems in Digital Libraries (2001)
41. Pfleeger, S.L., Fenton, N., Page, S.: Evaluating Software Engineering Standards. Computer 27(9), 71–79 (1994)
42. Html Parser, http://htmlparser.sourceforge.net

Consistency among Domain Analysts in Selecting Domain Documents and Creating Vocabularies

Chaitanya Nemmallapudi, William B. Frakes, and Reghu Anguswamy[*]

Software Reuse Laboratory,
Department of Computer Science and Applications, Virginia Tech.,
7054 Haycock Road, Falls Church, VA - 22043
{vinnu,reghu}@vt.edu, frakes@cs.vt.edu

Abstract. A study is reported on the consistency of the domain vocabularies created and the source documents selected by domain analysts for domain analysis using DARE (Domain Analysis and Reuse Environment). Consistency was analyzed by measuring the pairwise overlap scores between the domain analysts. The overlap scores of the vocabularies and the source documents were both found to be significantly greater than zero. The effect sizes were large. A positive correlation was also observed between overlap scores of the vocabularies and overlap scores of the source documents. The variability of domain vocabularies created automatically was compared to the variability of domain vocabularies produced manually by domain engineers. The variability of automatic and manual vocabularies was found to be significantly different. The difference was of medium effect size.

Keywords: Software reuse, domain engineering, domain analysis, text analysis, vocabulary extraction.

1   Introduction

Significant research and progress on software reuse has been reported over the past several decades [1]. However, despite the progress there are many open research questions. One such type of question concerns the consistency among domain analysts in selecting vocabulary and source documents for domain analysis. Also, the degree to which domain engineering can be automated needs to be addressed. To answer this question it is important to understand the relative variabilities of automatic and manual methods. This paper presents a quantitative study of these questions.

Domain engineering is key to systematic software reuse. The process of domain engineering is divided into two phases: domain analysis and domain implementation [2]. In the domain analysis phase, the domain analyst analyzes various systems in a domain to find similarities and variabilities. In the domain implementation phase, the information gathered in the domain analysis phase is used to create reusable assets. There are several approaches to domain engineering [2-7].

---

[*] Corresponding author.

J. Favaro and M. Morisio (Eds.): ICSR 2013, LNCS 7925, pp. 224–238, 2013.

DARE: Domain Analysis and Reuse Environment [2, 8] is a method and tool that assists domain analysts with domain analysis. One of the major goals of DARE research was to achieve automation of domain analysis activities. DARE helps domain analysts capture domain information from documents related to a domain. This domain information may be in the form of architectural diagrams, feature tables, facet tables and domain vocabulary. This information is recorded in a domain book, the final output of DARE.

Vocabulary, then, is a required sub-section in the domain book. The raw vocabulary can be extracted from many sources like source code, subject matter experts, and domain documents. A sub-set of documents from the domain to be analyzed are chosen. These documents can be artifacts of the existing systems like design documents, requirement documents, user manuals etc. Vocabulary can be extracted either manually or automatically. In manual extraction, domain analysts read the domain documents and select the terms that best represent the domain. Automatic information retrieval techniques can help extract the terms for the domain. DARE does not try to replace the domain analysts, but it rather helps the domain analysts in the process.

Researchers are now focusing on developing and applying information retrieval techniques to automatically extract syntactic and semantic knowledge from domain corpuses [9]. Manually extracting domain vocabulary is an expensive, time-consuming process. It requires domain analysts to analyze large amount of domain information and extract domain-specific keywords from it. The third experiment was conducted on the vocabularies created by both manual and automatic extraction methods as part of domain analyses using DARE. Automatically extracted vocabulary contains many redundant and meaningless terms. It can, however, be cheaper and faster[10]. There has been insufficient empirical study on how the automatic and manual methods relate.

This paper presents 3 experiments. Experiment I was conducted on the vocabularies created by manual extraction and Experiment II was conducted on the source documents selected. Experiment III was conducted on the vocabularies created by both manual and automatic extraction methods as part of domain analyses using DARE. Section 2 presents the experiments and the hypotheses for the study. Section 3 discusses the method used for conducting the experiments. Section 4 discusses the results. Section 5 presents the conclusions.

2   Experiments

Experiment I was conducted on the vocabularies created by 29 domain analysts to study the consistency among them. Experiment II evaluated the consistency among the source documents selected by 29 domain analysts. Our study was restricted to one domain, namely conflation algorithms [11, 12]. The main dependent variable in the two experiments was *symmetrical overlap* [13]. Symmetrical overlap is used as the measure for consistency. In this study, "*symmetrical overlap*" will be referred to as "*overlap*." Overlap is defined as follows: Consider two sets A and B. Overlap is defined as the number of items common to the two sets A and B, divided by the number of all items in the two sets. Mathematically, *overlap* is represented as:

$$O = \frac{|A \cap B|}{|A \cup B|} \tag{1}$$

Overlap is scaled so that the highest possible score is 1, which indicates that all the items in the two sets match and the lowest possible score is 0 which indicates there are no common items between the two sets. As an example, consider the cardinalities of A and B are 10 and 15 respectively. If 5 elements are common to both the sets, and the total number of items is 20 (10+15-5), then the overlap of the sets would be 5/20 or 0.25.

For Experiment III, data from the Tilley's study [14] was used. In Tilley's study 14 word frequency metrics were used as automatic extraction methods and tested to evaluate their effectiveness in identifying vocabulary in a domain. The word frequency metrics were run on the same source documents as identified by the domain analysts. The effectiveness was then measured by comparing the overlap between the vocabulary produced by each word frequency metric and the vocabulary produced by the domain analyst. The results in the study showed that most of the methods were about the same with a few methods significantly worse. This study had vocabularies created in various domains. Our study compared the vocabularies created manually by the domain analysts with those produced using the 14 automatic methods. Our study was restricted to one domain, namely conflation algorithms [12, 15] and there were 7 such vocabularies.

2.1   Hypotheses

Experiment I: Null hypothesis (H_0): The overlap scores between vocabularies of different domain analysts will be equal to 0. Alternate Hypothesis (H_A): The overlap scores between vocabularies of different domain analysts will be significantly greater than 0.

Experiment II: Null Hypothesis (H_0): The overlap scores between the source documents selected by different domain analysts will be equal to 0. Alternate Hypothesis (H_A): The overlap scores between the source documents selected by domain analysts will be significantly greater than 0.

Experiment III: Null Hypothesis (H_0): The overlap scores between different domain analysts will not be greater than the overlap scores between domain analysts and automatic extraction methods. (There will be no significant difference between the means of manual-manual and automatic-manual overlap scores). Alternate Hypothesis (H_A): The overlap scores between different domain analysts will be greater than that of overlap scores between domain analysts and automatic extraction metrics. (There will be a significantly greater difference between the means of manual-manual and automatic-manual overlap scores).

3   Method

3.1   Data Collection

To test the above hypotheses, data from domain engineering course projects at Virginia Tech were used. The DARE methodology was used for domain analysis, and domain books were created by each domain analyst as a result of these exercises. Each domain analyst collected documents related to the conflation domain. For this study, we have used the projects from the "Conflation" domain [12, 15]. As a rule of thumb, a minimum of three documents were selected by each analyst with no restriction on the maximum number of documents. Various source documents on the conflation domain consisted of source code (109), online references (98), journals (87), text files (23), course notes (13), books (9) and manuals (9). This is represented in Figure 1.

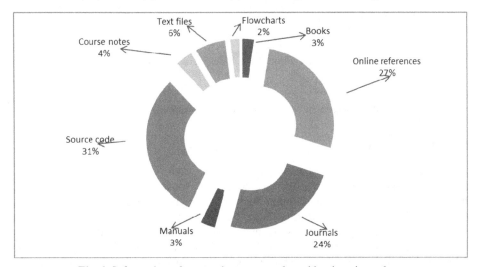

Fig. 1. Information of source documents selected by domain analysts

The tasks were to process domain documents and select the terms that best represented the domain. The analysts were allowed to use tools that automatically extracted index terms for the domain corpuses and then based on their domain knowledge, manually selected the terms that best represented the domain. The selected terms (vocabulary) were then used to create other artifacts of the domain book like the facet table, the feature table, and the domain architecture. The vocabularies created by the domain analysts and the source documents used for analysis were used as our test data.

The histogram in figure 2 shows the frequency of the vocabulary sizes created by the 29 domain analysts. The mean vocabulary size was 39.2 terms, and the median was 38.0. In terms of variability, the highest vocabulary size was 95 and the lowest vocabulary size was 15 yielding a range of 80. The standard deviation was 20.25. The general shape of the distribution is multi-modal and positively skewed. The boxplot shows that half the values were between 22 and 52.

Part of the data for Experiment III was obtained from the results of Tilley's study [14] in which "various information retrieval and filtering metrics were tested and evaluated to determine their effectiveness in identifying domain vocabulary". The vocabulary extracted using these metrics was compared with the manually selected vocabulary and the overlap scores were computed. There were 7 such vocabularies. In our study, these overlap scores are referred to as automated-manual overlap scores. We use them to compare with the overlap scores measured between various domain analysts (referred to as manual-manual overlap scores).

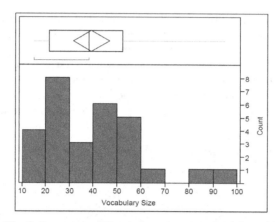

Fig. 2. Frequency of Vocabulary sizes (number of words)

3.2   Data Preparation

Experiment I: A java program was written that used vocabulary sets of various domain analysts to calculate the overlap scores. The vocabularies were obtained from the facet tables created by the domain analysts. We will call the facet names *"facet groups"* and the words that fall into the category of a facet group *"facet terms"*. We placed the facet group names and facet term names in two text files.   Since the vocabularies were manually created by the domain analysts, we had to take additional steps for data extraction. The vocabulary sets contained non-alphanumeric characters such as _, -, ( ). These characters had to be removed from the vocabularies since they might create noise. For e.g. the words "n gram" and "n-gram" might be considered as two different words although they represent the same term. This clean-up makes vocabulary sets more comparable. The vocabulary was then passed through a stemmer [16] to create a standardized vocabulary. We also found that some vocabulary sets contain phrases rather than single terms. For e.g. in some vocabulary sets, the phrase "domain engineer" was considered as a single term rather than two different words. For this reason, four variations of the vocabulary sets were identified for all the domain analysts. They are:

- Facet terms without phrases
- Facet terms with phrases.
- Facet groups without phrases
- Facet groups with phrases

For example, consider the following facet table for the conflation domain.

Table 1. Facet Table – an example

Conflation Methods	Performance	Algorithm
Automatic	Frequency	Table lookup
Manual	Precision	Successor variety
	Effectiveness	

- *Facet terms with phrases* will be the set: [Automatic, Manual, Compression, Precision, Effectiveness, Frequency, Table lookup, Successor variety] with 8 members.
- *Facet terms without phrases* will be the set: [Automatic, Manual, Compression, Precision, Effectiveness, Frequency, Table, Lookup, Successor, Variety] with 10 members.
- *Facet groups with phrases* will be the set: [Conflation Methods, Performance, Algorithm] with 3 members.
- *Facet groups without phrases* will be the set: [Conflation, Methods, Performance, Algorithm] with 4 members.

Counts of each variation are given in figures 3 and 4. Overlap scores were calculated for all of the four variations of the vocabulary sets of all domain analysts. The histogram in figure 3 shows the frequency of the facet groups created by the domain analysts. The mean number of facet groups was 6.2, and the median was 6.0. The general guideline for creating a facet classification is to have no more than 7 facet groups. However, 10 subjects, created more than 7 facet groups. In terms of variability, the highest number of facet groups created by a domain analyst was 10 and the lowest was 3. The standard deviation was 1.81. The general shape of the distribution is unimodal and positively skewed. The box plots show that 50% of the facet groups were between 5 and 7.

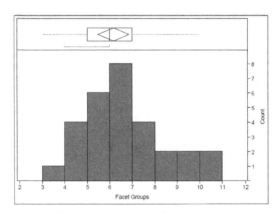

Fig. 3. Frequency of facet groups

The histogram in figure 4 shows the frequency of facet terms created by the domain analysts. The mean number of facet terms was 34.4, and the median was 31.0. In terms of variability, the highest number of facet terms created by a domain analyst was 89 and the lowest number of facet terms was 11. The standard deviation was 19.8. The general shape of the distribution is bimodal and positively skewed. The box plot shows that 50% of the cases fall between 18 and 45. The box plot also shows one outlier (90 terms).

Experiment II: A java program was written to compare the titles of the source documents and compute overlap scores between the source documents selected by the domain analysts. The titles of all the source documents were manually processed in

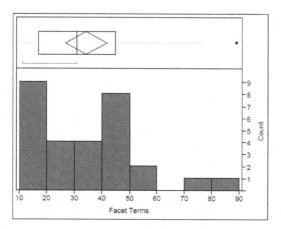

Fig. 4. Frequency of facet terms

order to maintain consistency. For references with no titles, a unique name was chosen and used consistently throughout the experiment.

3.3   Experiment I – Consistency of Vocabularies

The overlap scores of the vocabularies created by each domain analyst were compared on a pairwise basis with the other vocabularies. Facet groups and facet terms were compared separately. As mentioned before, the overlap score is the cardinality of the intersection of the pair wise vocabularies created by domain analysts over their union. It can be measured using the equation (2):

$$O(de_i, de_j) = \frac{|V_{de_i} \cap V_{de_j}|}{|V_{de_i} \cup V_{de_j}|} \tag{2}$$

V_{de_i} - Vocabulary created by Domain analyst i

V_{de_j} - Vocabulary created by Domain analyst j

3.4   Experiment II – Consistency of Source Documents

The domain analysts selected source documents to create domain vocabularies. Different analysts select different documents. The overlap score is measured as the cardinality of the intersection of source documents selected by the analysts over their union of the same. It can be measured using the equation (3):

$$D(de_i, de_j) = \frac{|Docs_{de_i} \cap Docs_{de_j}|}{|Docs_{de_i} \cup Docs_{de_j}|} \tag{3}$$

$Docs_{de_i}$ - Documents selected by Domain analyst i.

$Docs_{de_j}$ - Documents selected by Domain analyst j.

3.5   Experiment III – Automatic vs. Manual Extraction

Figure 5 shows how we compared the vocabularies of automatic and manual techniques. Figure 6 shows how we compared vocabularies of the manual techniques. The following notations were used:

$A_1 \dots A_{14}$ $\rightarrow$ Automatic extraction methods in Tilley's study [14]

$de_1 \dots de_{29}$ $\rightarrow$ 29 Domain analysts.

$O_{(dei, Aj)}$ $\rightarrow$ Overlap between vocabularies produced by domain analyst i and automatic extraction method j.

$\overline{O}_{(Automatic, Manual)}$ $\rightarrow$ Grand mean of the overlap score between vocabularies of domain analysts and automatic generators.

$O_{(den, dem)}$ $\rightarrow$ Overlap between vocabularies produced by domain analysts n and m.

$\overline{O}_{(Manual, Manual)}$ $\rightarrow$ Grand mean of the overlap score between vocabularies of domain analysts.

	A_1	$A2 \dots \dots$	$\dots \dots \dots \dots A_{14}$
de_1	$O_{(de_1, A_1)}$	$O_{(de_1, A_2)} \dots$	$\dots \dots O_{(de_1, A_{14})}$
de_2	$O_{(de_2, A_1)}$	$O_{(de_2, A_2)} \dots$	$\dots \dots O_{(de_2, A_{14})}$
.	.	.	.
.	.	.	.
de_7	$O_{(de29, A)}$	$O_{(de_{29}, A_{14})} \dots$	$\dots \dots O_{(de_7, A_{14})}$

$\overline{O}_{(Automatic, Manual)}$

Fig. 5. Comparison of overlap score means of Automatic-Manual

	de_1	$de_2 \dots \dots$	$\dots \dots de_{29}$
de_1	$O_{(de_1, de_1)}$	$O_{(de_1, de_2)} \dots$	$\dots O_{(de_1, de_{29})}$
de_2	$O_{(de_2, de_1)}$	$O_{(de_2, de_2)} \dots$	$\dots O_{(de_2, de_{29})}$
.	.	.	.
.	.	.	.
de_{29}	$O_{(de_{29}, de_1)}$	$O_{(de_{29}, de_2)} \dots$	$\dots O_{(de_{29}, de_{29})}$

$\overline{O}_{(Manual - Manual)}$

Fig. 6. Comparison of overlap score means of Manual-Manual

4   Results

In this section, we discuss the results of the experiments and how they support or contradict our hypotheses.

4.1   Experiment I – Results

Facet terms without Phrases: The facet terms (without phrases) of twenty nine different domain analysts' vocabularies were compared. The sample size was 406 or (29*28)/2 data points. The mean overlap score was 0.14, and the median was 0.13. In terms of variability, the highest overlap score was 0.54 and the lowest overlap score was 0 with a standard deviation of 0.08. The number of overlap scores that were zero was 13.

Figure 7 shows the boxplots of pairwise overlap scores of the domain analysts. For example the boxplot of domain analyst DE01shows the lowest overlaps score of 0 and highest of 0.32. Thirteen of the subjects have outliers or extreme outliers. Two pairs of extreme outliers observed in figure 7 are the pairs of domain analysts $O_{(15, 22)} = 0.54$ and $O_{(16, 23)} = 0.55$. By observing the vocabulary facet terms of these two domain analysts, it was found that, both of them used the names of different conflation algorithms as the vocabulary terms and this could be the reason for their high overlap scores.

The overlap scores of domain analyst DE08, are significantly different from others. It was observed that this domain analyst, unlike the others, worked on the conflation of storage systems, databases and directories that have similar data rather than the conflation of words and images. Hence the vocabulary or the facet terms selected by this domain analyst did not match with others' facet terms. Similarly, the overlap scores of the domain analyst DE14 are significantly different from others. This may be because most of the sources selected by this domain analyst are architectural diagrams in the form of flowcharts. Also, this domain analyst used an automatic indexing tool to extract the domain vocabulary. The most common words used in flow charts like 'Yes', 'No', etc., which do not represent the conflation domain, were selected as facet terms. Another pair of extreme outliers whose overlap scores are close to 0 is $O_{(26, 29)} = 0.03$. It was observed that the facet terms selected by domain analyst 26 represents the conflation algorithms domain in general whereas the facet terms selected by the domain analyst 29 represents suffix stripping algorithms, a part of the conflation algorithm domain.

T-test: A one-sample t-test using an alpha level of .05 tested if the mean was significantly different from zero. The sample mean of 0.07 (SD = 0.05) was found to be statistically different from this value, t (405) = 28.11, "p< .0005", suggesting that the mean overlap score of various domain analysts is significantly greater than 0. The effect size, Cohen's *d* value [12], was 2.79. This is a large effect size.

Facet terms with Phrases: The facet terms with phrases of vocabularies created by 29 different domain analysts were compared. The sample size is 406 data points. The mean score was 0.07, and the median was 0.07. In terms of variability, the highest overlap score was 0.29 and the lowest overlap score was 0 with a standard deviation of 0.05. Number of overlap scores that were zero was 41.

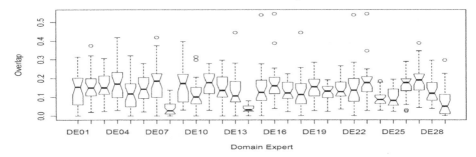

Fig. 7. Comparison of facet terms without phrases

The median overlap score of facet terms without phrases for domain analyst 14 is greater than 0 (Figure 7), which fell down to 0 when facet terms with phrases were considered (Figure 8). The vocabularies of domain analyst 24 and 25, $O_{(24, 25)} = 0.22$, have a good overlap. While observing the domain books of these domain analysts, a close match in the source documents of these domain analysts was found. The overlap scores that are outliers in the above box plot $O_{(15, 22)} = 0.51$, $O_{(16, 23)} = 0.41$ and $O_{(13, 18)} = 0.44$ are consistent with the outliers of facet terms without phrases, as discussed previously, but resulted in a lower overlap.

T-test: A one-sample t-test using an alpha level of .05 tested if the mean was significantly different from zero. The sample mean of 0.07 (SD = 0.05) was found to be statistically different from this value, $t (405) = 28.11$, "p< .0005", suggesting that the mean overlap score of various domain analysts is significantly greater than 0. The effect size, Cohen's d value, was 2.79. This is a large effect size.

Facet groups without Phrases: The facet groups without phrases of vocabularies created by twenty nine different domain analysts were compared. The sample size was 406 data points. The mean score was 0.06, and the median was 0.05. In terms of variability, the highest overlap score was 0.67 and the lowest overlap score was 0 with a standard deviation of 0.08. The number of overlap scores that were zero was 141.

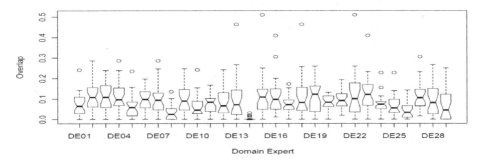

Fig. 8. Comparison of facet terms with phrases

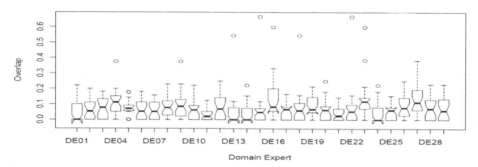

Fig. 9. Comparison of facet groups without phrases

The outlier pairs, as shown in figure 9, $O_{(15, 22)} = 0.33$ and $O_{(16, 23)} = 0.22$, are consistent with the outliers of facet terms. Domain Analyst 5 in the above box plot has an outlier whose value is 0. While observing the overlap scores, it was found that this domain analyst's choice of facet groups did not match with the few other domain analyst's facet groups. One possible reason could be that since the choice of facet groups should be made from a smaller set of words unlike the choice of facet terms which can be made from a wider set of terms, the probability of the domain analyst choosing a similar facet group name is low. Also, overlap score of domain analysts 24 and 25, $O_{(24, 25)} = 0.22$, was significant when comparing the facet terms, but in case of groups, none of them matched, even after the phrases were split into individual terms. This shows that the choice of grouping differs significantly among domain analysts. The source documents of domain analysts 24 and 25 had a significant overlap score of 0.59 which means that the sources selected were similar.

T-test: A one-sample t-test using an alpha level of .05 tested if the mean was significantly different from zero. The sample mean of 0.06 (SD = 0.08) was found to be statistically different from this value, t (405) = 14.61, "p < .0005", suggesting that the mean overlap score of various domain analysts is significantly greater than 0. The effect size, Cohen's *d* value, was 1.45. This is a large effect size.

Facet groups with Phrases: The facet groups with phrases of vocabularies created by twenty nine different domain analysts were compared; the sample size was 406 data points. The mean score was 0.02, and the median was 0. In terms of variability, the highest overlap score was 0.30 and the lowest overlap score was 0 with a standard deviation of 0.05. The number of overlap scores that were zero was 329.

In figure 10, it was observed that, most of the domain analysts have zero overlap scores when compared with others. The selection of facet groups with phrases yield lower overlap scores when compared to facet groups without phrases. One possible reason could be the choice of words i.e. for example one domain analyst may choose the name "Conflation techniques" to represent various conflation algorithms like n-gram, successor variety etc., but some other domain analyst may name it as "Conflation Methods." It might yield in higher overlap scores for facet terms but will result in low overlap scores for facet groups with phrases. Many outliers can be seen in figure 9. It was believed that since there is very low probability that the facet groups with phrases of two domain analysts will match, the median overlap score tends to zero and any partial match between the facet groups with phrases are considered as outliers. It was observed that median overlap for all the domain analysts is 0.

T-test: A one-sample t-test using an alpha level of .05 tested if the mean was significantly different from zero. The sample mean of 0.02, (SD = 0.05) was found to be statistically different from this value, t (405) = 8.40, "p< .0005", suggesting that the mean overlap score of various domain analysts is greater than 0. The effect size, Cohen's *d* value was 1.45. This is a large effect size.

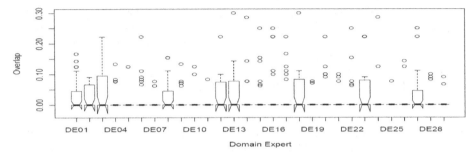

Fig. 10. Comparison of facet groups with phrases

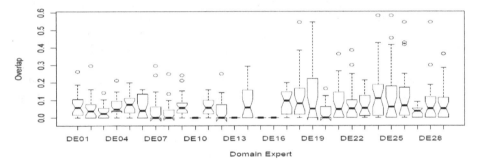

Fig. 11. Comparison of overlap scores of source documents

4.2   Experiment II – Results

357 source documents selected by the domain analysts were compared and studied for consistency by measuring the overlap. As a rule of thumb, a minimum of three documents were selected by each analyst with no restriction on the maximum number of documents.

Various source documents in the conflation domain consisted of source code (109), online references (98), journals (87), text files (23), course notes (13), books (9) and manuals (9). The overlap scores of the domain analysts' source documents are compared in Figure 11. The most extreme outlier pair in the box plot is the overlap score between de_{24} and de_{25}: D $_{(24, 25)}$. The source documents selected by these two domain experts are similar. One possible reason for the higher overlap could be the selection of source code. Both the domain experts have selected similar conflation algorithms (Lovins, Lancaster, Porter). They also chose these algorithms implemented in same the language (ANSI C).

The source documents selected by the different domain experts were not significantly different from each other. A few sources were common among the domain analysts. The source code, "Porter in C" was used by 16 domain experts. The next most frequently used source was the chapter, "Stemming Algorithms in Information Retrieval" by W. Frakes [16]. It was referred by 11 domain experts. The articles "An algorithm for suffix stripping [17]" and "Another Stemmer [18]" were used by 10 domain experts. The online reference, "Lancaster stemming algorithm (http://www.comp.lancs.ac.uk/computing/research/stemming/)" and the source codes, "Lovins in C (http://snowball.tartarus.org/algorithms/lovins/stemmer.html)" and "Implementation of the Paice algorithm in the programming language C (http://www.comp.lancs.ac.uk/computing/research/stemming/Links/implementations. htm) " were commonly used by 8 domain experts. It was also observed that there were 96 unique sources. The extreme outlier pair $D_{(24,\ 25)}$ has been discussed previously. The reason for most of the other outliers $D_{(26,\ 28)}$, $D_{(7,\ 9)}$ in the above box plot is due to the close match of source documents.

Correlation coefficients were computed to assess the relationship between the overlap scores of the source documents selected for the domain analysis and the overlap scores of the vocabularies created. The matrix in Table 2 shows the correlation coefficients. There is a weak positive correlation between overlap scores of source documents selected for domain analysis and their corresponding domain vocabularies. Overlap scores of facet terms without phrases had the highest correlation ($r = 0.34$) with overlaps scores of source documents; while facet groups without phrases had the lowest correlation ($r = 0.18$). A positive correlation between overlap scores of facet terms with phrases and facet terms without phrases, was observed with $r = 0.82$ and between facet groups with phrases and facet groups without phrases, with $r = 0.24$. Overall, a strong, positive correlation between overlap scores of facet group and facet term categories exists.

Table 2. Correlation matrix of overlap scores

	Source Documents	Terms without phrases	Terms with phrases	Groups without phrases	Groups with phrases
Source Documents	1	0.34	0.19	0.18	0.18
Terms without phrases	0.34	1	0.82	0.32	0.09
Terms with phrases	0.19	0.82	1	0.39	0.12
Groups without phrases	0.18	0.32	0.39	1	0.24
Groups with phrases	0.18	0.09	0.12	0.24	1

4.3   Experiment III – Results

Two sample T-tests were performed to evaluate the hypothesis for Experiment III. An alpha-level of 0.05 was used for the T-tests. The variability of domain vocabularies created automatically was compared to the variability of domain vocabularies produced manually by domain engineers. 841 manual-manual overlap scores were compared with 203 automatic-manual overlap scores. The T-tests compared the sample mean of *"facet terms with phrases"* created manually by domain analysts with *"facet terms with phrases"* created using automatic methods. The summary of results is as shown in Table 3. The results show that the mean overlap score of the vocabularies created manually by domain analysts are significantly higher than the vocabularies created using automatic extraction methods. The effect size (Cohen's d) is in the medium region [19].

Table 3. Summary of results for the T-tests

Std Err	Mean Difference	t-value ($p<0.05$)	Effect Size (Cohen's d) [14]
0.005	0.021	3.8	0.41

5   Conclusions

The overlap scores of vocabulary sets from domain analyses were computed and compared in terms of facet terms without phrases, facet terms with phrases, facet groups without phrases, and facet groups with phrases for different domain experts. It was observed that the facet terms and groups when selected without phrases yield higher overlap scores than facet terms and groups with phrases. The results also show that the mean value of the overlap scores of the vocabularies and the source documents was significantly greater than 0. However, in general the overlap scores of the vocabularies and the source documents were not significantly different between the domain experts.

Correlation coefficients were computed to determine whether there is any relationship between the vocabulary terms selected and source documents used to create them. A weak positive correlation between the sources documents selected for domain analysis and their corresponding domain vocabularies was observed. However, there was a stronger positive correlation between overlap scores of facet terms with phrases and facet terms without phrases ($r = 0.82$).

The variability of domain vocabularies created automatically was compared to the variability of domain vocabularies produced manually by domain engineers. 841 manual-manual overlap scores were compared with 203 automatic-manual overlap scores. The domain was conflation algorithms. The results show that the mean overlap score of the vocabularies created manually by domain analysts are significantly higher than the vocabularies created using automatic extraction methods. The effect size of the difference was medium (Cohen's $d = 0.41$).

The results from experiments I and II show that though there is consistency between domain experts in creating vocabularies and selecting documents, the overlap scores are low. The process needs further improvement to increase consistency which would be reflected by higher overlap scores. Results from experiment III show that if we consider manual extraction of domain vocabularies as the standard, then the automatic extraction methods are not up to these standards.

References

1. Frakes, W.B., Kang, K.C.: Software reuse research: status and future. IEEE Transactions on Software Engineering 31(7), 529–536 (2005)
2. Frakes, W., Prieto-Diaz, R., Fox, C.: DARE: Domain analysis and reuse environment. Ann. Softw. Eng. 5, 125–141 (1998)
3. Harsu, M.: FAST product-line architecture process. Tampere University of Technology (2002)
4. Kang, K., et al.: Feature-oriented domain analysis (FODA) feasibility study. Software Engineering Institute, Carnegie Mellon University, Pittsburgh (1990)
5. Simos, M.A.: Organization domain modeling (ODM): formalizing the core domain modeling life cycle. SIGSOFT Softw. Eng. Notes 20(SI), 196–205 (1995)
6. Kang, K., et al.: FORM: A feature-;oriented reuse method with domain-;specific reference architectures. Annals of Software Engineering 5(1), 143–168 (1998)
7. Tracz, W.: DSSA (Domain-Specific Software Architecture): pedagogical example. SIGSOFT Softw. Eng. Notes 20(3), 49–62 (1995)
8. Dos Santos, R.F., Frakes, W.B.: DAREonline: A Web-Based Domain Engineering Tool. In: Edwards, S.H., Kulczycki, G. (eds.) ICSR 2009. LNCS, vol. 5791, pp. 246–257. Springer, Heidelberg (2009)
9. Riloff, E.: From Manual Knowledge Engineering to Bootstrapping: Progress in Information Extraction and NLP. In: Ashley, K.D., Bridge, D.G. (eds.) ICCBR 2003. LNCS (LNAI), vol. 2689, p. 4. Springer, Heidelberg (2003)
10. Seljan, S., Gašpar, A.: First Steps in Term and Collocation Extraction from English-Croatian Corpus (2009)
11. Frakes, W.B., Baeza-Yates, R.: Information retrieval: Data structures & algorithms, vol. 152. Prentice Hall, Englewood Cliffs (1992)
12. Yilmaz, O., Frakes, W.B.: A Case Study of Using Domain Engineering for the Conflation Algorithms Domain. In: Edwards, S.H., Kulczycki, G. (eds.) ICSR 2009. LNCS, vol. 5791, pp. 86–94. Springer, Heidelberg (2009)
13. Das-Gupta, P., Katzer, J.: A study of the overlap among document representations. ACM, Bethesda (1983)
14. Tilley, J.: A Comparison of Statistical Filtering Methods for Automatic Term Extraction for Domain Analysis. In: Computer Science and Applications, p. 49. Virginia Polytechnic Institute and State University, Blacksburg (2008)
15. Frakes, W., Baeza-Yates, R.: Information retrieval: Data structures & algorithms, vol. 152. Prentice Hall, Englewood Cliffs (1992)
16. Frakes, W.B.: Stemming Algorithms. In: Frakes, W.B., Baeza-Yates, R. (eds.) Information Retrieval: Data Structures and Algorithms, pp. 131–160. Prentice-Hall, Englewood Cliffs (1998)
17. Porter, M.F.: An algorithm for suffix stripping. In: Karen Sparck, J., Peter, W. (eds.) Readings in Information Retrieval, pp. 313–316. Morgan Kaufmann Publishers Inc. (1997)
18. Paice, C.D.: Another stemmer. SIGIR Forum 24(3), 56–61 (1990)
19. Cohen, J.: Statistical power analysis for the behavioral sciences, 2nd edn. Lawrence Erlbaum Associates, Inc., Hillsdale (1988)

Mining Cohesive Domain Topics from Source Code

Bing Xie[1,2], Meng Li[1,2], Jing Jin[1,2], Junfeng Zhao[1,2,*], and Yanzhen Zou[1,2]

[1] Software Institute, School of Electronics Engineering and Computer Science,
Peking University, Beijing 100871, China
[2] Key Laboratory of High Confidence Software Technologies, Ministry of Education,
Beijing 100871, China
{xiebing,limeng09,jinjing10,zhaojf,zouyz}@sei.pku.edu.cn

Abstract. Using topic models to mine domain topics from source code has been a promising way for developers to comprehend the functional concerns implemented in the source code of a software system. However, not all the topics mined from source code are domain topics that represent functional concerns of the software. Besides domain topics, other topics may represent cross-cutting concerns or other concerns. These topics are noises in the context of helping developers to comprehend the functional concerns. In this paper, we propose an approach to filter out noises and mine Cohesive Domain Topics (CDTs) from source code. A topic is a CDT if its associated words represent certain functional concern and its associated source code elements collaboratively implement the functional concern. Firstly, we propose a series of Filtering Heuristics to filter out programming related information in source code which may bring in noises. Then, we mine raw topics from source code using Latent Dirichlet Allocation. Finally, based on the structural relationships among the source code elements associated to a topic, we propose a novel metric called Topic Cohesion to identify CDTs from the raw topics. Experimental results on a set of open source software show that our approach can effectively filter out noises and obtain CDTs from source code.

1 Introduction

Source code comprehension is an important activity during source code reuse [1–3]. Developers need to comprehend the functional concerns of a software system and the corresponding implementations in source code, before they perform any reuse task such as adding a new feature or modifying an existing feature.

For a small software system, developers can comprehend its functional concerns by manually browsing the source code or by using program analysis techniques (e.g. call graph, control or data flow, slicing, etc.). However, these techniques help little for developers to comprehend large software systems [4]. Because there is an overwhelmingly large amount of details at different levels of granularity, and the domain related information reflecting the system's functional concerns is mixed with programming related information [5].

---

* Corresponding author.

J. Favaro and M. Morisio (Eds.): ICSR 2013, LNCS 7925, pp. 239–254, 2013.
© Springer-Verlag Berlin Heidelberg 2013

Using topics models, such as Latent Dirichlet Allocation (LDA), to mine topics from the source code of a software system has been a new and promising way to help developers to comprehend the source code [2–7]. *A topic is a collection of semantically related words that represent certain concern in source code* [4]. Besides the words, for each topic, it is associated with a collection of source code elements. For example, a "user" topic, representing the *user management* concern, and its associated words as well as source code elements are shown in Fig. 1. The topics mined from source code can be classified into different categories according to the concerns they represent. Some topics, called *domain topics*, represent the functional concerns, while other topics may represent cross-cutting concerns or other concerns [8]. The "user" topic above is a domain topic. For more discussions of the semantics of the topics mined from source code, refer to Section 5.1. Domain topics are helpful for developers to comprehend the functional concerns implemented in source code, while other topics are noises in this context. However, most previous approaches do not distinguish domain topics from other noisy topics, which affects their effectiveness.

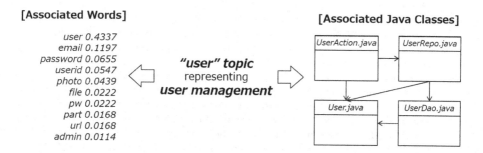

Fig. 1. Domain topic example: the "user" topic representing *user management* and its associated words and source code elements (i.e. Java classes)

In this paper, we propose an approach to filter out noises and mine Cohesive Domain Topics (CDTs) from source code. *A topic is a CDT if its associated words represent certain functional concern and its associated source code elements collaboratively implement the functional concern.* CDTs can effectively support the topic-based source code comprehension. Taking the "user" topic (Fig. 1) above for example, developers can easily comprehend the functional concern represented and the corresponding implementation in source code by exploring its associated words and source code elements correspondingly.

In particular, firstly we propose a series of Filtering Heuristics (FHs) to filter out programming related information in source code (e.g. programming language syntax and dependencies on external libraries) which may bring in noises. Then, we mine raw topics from source code using LDA. Finally, based on the structural relationships among the source code elements associated to a topic, we propose a novel metric called Topic Cohesion (TC) to identify CDTs from the raw topics.

We conduct several experiments on a set of open source software to evaluate the effectiveness of our approach. The empirical results show that our approach can effectively filter out noises and obtain CDTs from source code.

The contributions of this paper include:

- We propose a series of FHs to filter out programming related information in source code which may bring in noises. The FHs can filter out more noises than previous approach [4–6].
- We propose a novel metric called TC, which is based on the structural relationships among the source code elements associated to a topic, to identify CDTs from the topics mined from source code.
- We evaluate the effectiveness of our approach on a set of open source software. The empirical results are promising, and we open the data set on the Internet for further research[1].

The rest of this paper is organized as follows: In Section 2, we introduce some background knowledge and related work. Section 3 presents the details of our approach. Evaluation is covered in Section 4. Section 5 discusses several issues related to our approach. Section 6 lists our future work and concludes the paper.

2   Related Work

2.1   Topic Models

In Information Retrieval (IR), a *topic model* is a *generative model* for documents[2]: it specifies a probabilistic procedure by which documents can be generated [9]. Topic models include Latent Semantic Indexing (LSI), LDA, etc. [10].

LDA is perhaps the most common topic model currently in use [9]. It is adopted in this paper as well. For the sake of completeness, we briefly introduce LDA. The terms used in LDA are as follows:

- A *word* is the basic unit of discrete data, defined to be an item from a vocabulary $V = w_1, w_2, \ldots, w_v$.
- A *document* is a sequence of n words denoted by $d = (w_1, w_2, \ldots, w_n)$, where w_n is the nth word in the sequence.
- A *corpus* is a collection of m documents denoted by $D = \{d_1, d_2, \ldots, d_m\}$.

The basic idea of LDA is that documents are represented as random mixtures over latent topics, where each topic is characterized by a distribution over words. Given a *corpus* of m documents containing k topics expressed over v unique words, the distribution of ith topic t_i over v words can be represented by φ_i and the distribution of ith document d_i over k topics can be represented by θ_i. The

---

[1] For more details about the data set, visit http://mike.sei.pku.edu.cn/

[2] In this paper, the documents are the source code elements (e.g. Java classes). We use the terms "documents", "source code elements" and "Java classes" interchangeably.

goal is to estimate φ and θ. LDA assumes the following generative process for each document w in corpus D:

1. Choose $N \sim$ Poisson distribution(ξ).
2. Choose $\theta \sim$ Dirichlet distribution(α).
3. For each of the m words w_i:
   (a) Choose a topic $t_i \sim$ Multinomial(θ).
   (b) Choose a word w_i from $p(w_i|t_i, \beta)$, a multinomial probability conditioned on the topic t_i.

Several algorithms have been proposed to estimate the distributions above, and in this paper we use Gibbs sampling, which is widely adopted in approaches mining topics from source code [3, 4, 7]. For more details about LDA, we refer the readers to the original work of Blei et al. [10].

2.2 Applying Topic Models on Source Code

Applying topic models to examine source code has been an active research area recently. Many approaches have been proposed. For example, Maskeri et al. [4] tried to mine domain topics from source code for developers to comprehend the functional concerns of the software. Baldi et al. [8] proposed a theory of taking the topics mined from source code as aspects. Asuncion et al. [11] proposed an approach to recover software traceability links with topic models. Tian et al. [12] and Kawaguchi et al. [13] used LDA for automatic categorization of software in software repositories. Several tools [2, 3] have been proposed to visualize the topics mined from source code in IDE to assist source code comprehension. Moreover, topic models have also been used in researches on software evolution [14], bug localization [15], etc.

In this paper, we focus on mining domain topics from source code to help developers to comprehend the functional concerns implemented in source code. Our goal is similar to previous approaches [4] and [6]. However, not all the topics mined from source code are domain topics, which has been noted in [4, 6] as well. But they did not provide an effective mechanism to identify domain topics from other noisy topics. In this paper, we propose a series of FHs and a novel metric TC to filter out noises and mine domain topics from source code.

2.3 Classifying Topics Mined from Source Code

As mentioned above, the topics mined from source code can be classified into different categories. A mechanism is needed to classify the topics according to different application scenarios. Baldi et al. [8] propose an information entropy-based approach to identify topics representing cross-cutting concerns. Adams et al. [16] use historical code changes to identify cross-cutting concerns in source code. Although these approaches can effectively identify cross-cutting concerns, their effectiveness on identifying functional concerns has not been explored. Our goal is different from these approaches and we try to solve the problem from a different perspective. In particular, we try to use the concept of cohesion to identify domain topics from the topics mined from source code.

Cohesion can be defined as a measure of the degree to which source code elements of a module belong together [17]. Cohesion has been used to support different tasks, such as assessment of design quality [18] and reuse efforts [19], and identification of reusable components [20]. In this paper, we try to use cohesion to measure the degree to which the source code elements associated to a topic belong together, and use the results to identify domain topics.

There are different ways to calculate cohesion, which can be broadly classified into structural approaches [17, 21, 22], semantic or conceptual approaches [22, 23], information entropy-based approaches [7], slice-based approaches [24], etc. In this paper, we utilize the structural relationships among the source code elements associated to a topic to calculate the cohesion. For more details, refer to Section 3.3. To the best of our knowledge, we are the first to use the concept of cohesion to examine the topics mined from source code.

3   Approach

The overview of our approach is shown in Fig. 2. Generally, our approach consists of three steps organized in a pipeline form: source code preprocessing, mining raw topics using LDA, and identifying CDTs. In this paper, we focus on software written in Java and adopt the LDA topic model. The extensibility of our approach is discussion in Section 4.4.

Fig. 2. Approach Overview

3.1   Source Code Preprocessing

In order to apply LDA to source code, we need to extract domain-related words from source code. We use Java Development Tools[3] (JDT) to parse the source code and extract facts. The facts extracted include identifiers (e.g. class names, property names, variable names) and their types, method signatures, etc.

---

[3] http://www.eclipse.org/jdt/

Unlike plain text files written in natural languages, there are both domain related information and programming related information in the source code. The programming related information (e.g. programming language syntax and external libraries dependencies) is domain independent and conveys little functional information. Therefore, it is reasonable to filter out the programming related information in order to mine CDTs from source code.

In this step, we propose a series of Filtering Heuristics (FHs) to filter out programming related information. FHs can be grouped into three groups:*External Dependencies Filtering Heuristics* (EDFHs), *Identifiers Processing Heuristics* (IPHs), and *Stopwords Filtering Heuristics* (SFHs).

EDFHs. Besides the classes defined by the software, it depends on external libraries, e.g. JDK, JUnit, Log4j, etc. Most of the external libraries are programming related and domain independent, and should be filtered out. The EDFHs can filter out these external dependencies during source code parsing process. In particular, a *JDK Filtering Heuristic* filters JDK APIs; a *Common External Libraries Filtering Heuristic* filters APIs in common external libraries like JUnit, Log4j, etc.; and a *Local Dependencies Filtering Heuristic* filters APIs in the Java ARchive (JAR) packages imported in the local build path.

IPHs. Unlike words in plain text written in natural languages, words in source code are often embedded inside identifiers, e.g. "userName", "calculateBalance", etc. We propose three IPHs to process the identifiers to obtain words. The *Identifier Splitting Heuristic* (ISPH) splits identifiers according different naming conventions, e.g. *CamelCase* or *under_score* convention. The *Identifier Stemming Heuristic* (ISTH) (based on Snowball[4]) reduces the words extracted from identifiers to their *stems*. Moreover, we implement an *Identifier Expanding Heuristic* (IEH) to expand abbreviated identifiers. First, the IEH uses WordNet[5] API to test whether the identifier is a meaningful word. If so, the IEH assumes the word as a domain word and does not expand it. Otherwise, the IEH locates the position where the identifier is declared, and expands it according to the rules shown in Table 1. The expanded new identifiers are processed with the ISPH and ISTH as well. Examples are shown in Table 1.

SFHs. SFHs filter out different categories of stopwords in the words extracted from source code. The *General Stopwords Filtering Heuristic* filters general stopwords in English, e.g. "the", "and", "of", etc. The *Java Keywords Filtering Heuristic* filters Java keywords such as "for", "return", and "class". The *Programming Related Common Words Filtering Heuristic* filters programming related common words, such as "main", "arg", "util", etc. Usually, a complete list of stopwords is needed. But there is no need to provide such a complete list in our approach, because our approach can identify and filter out some topics composed

---

[4] http://snowball.tartarus.org/
[5] http://wordnet.princeton.edu/

Table 1. Examples of IPHs

Declaration	Raw	Expanded	IEH Rule	After ISPH & ISTH
User manager	manager	manager	not expanding	manag
User t	t	user	substitute	user
BrowseHistory bh	bh	browseHistory	acronym	brows, histori
Environment env	env	enviroment	prefix	environ
Message msg	msg	message	dropped letter	messag

of stopwords (discussed in Section 4.3). Nevertheless, filtering out stopwords can reduce noises and improve the understandability of the topics.

Finally, it is worth noticing that some of the heuristics are adopted in previous approaches [3, 4] as well, but we propose several new heuristics (e.g. EDFHs, IEH, etc.) which can filter out more noises than previous approaches.

3.2 Mining Raw Topics Using LDA

After the source code preprocessing step, we mine raw topics from source code using LDA. All the source code files of a software system are taken as the *corpus*, while each source code file (i.e. a Java class) is mapped to a *document* and the words extracted from source code are mapped to *words* in LDA.

We employed JGibbLDA[6] which is a Java implementation of LDA using Gibbs sampling for parameter estimation and inference. Several parameters need to be determined during the LDA process: The first two parameters α and β are hyperparameters of LDA [10]; k is the number of topics contained in the *document corpus* (i.e. the source code files); n is the number of Gibbs sampling iterations. In this paper, we use the *maximum likelihood* method in [25] to identify the optimal number of topics k, while α, β, and n are set to JGibbLDA default values $50/k$, 0.1, and 2000 according to [25].

Given the input and the parameters, the LDA attempts to: 1) identify a set of topics from the corpus; 2) identify the distribution of words for each topic (word-topic distributions); and 3) identify the distribution of topics for each document (topic-document distributions).

The outputs of LDA process include a set of topics, the word-topic distributions, and the topic-document distributions. Based on the word-topic distributions, the most likely words, commonly top 10, are associated to each topic. Users can figure out the semantics of the topic by exploring these associated words. In order to determine the documents associated to a topic, we can use either a threshold or a cut-off point to select the most likely documents [7]. Because we are going to recover the structural relationships among the documents associated to a topic and use the structural relationships to identify CDTs, a fixed threshold or a fixed cut-off point would be too arbitrary and not appropriate for different topics. In Section 3.3, we propose an incremental process to determine an appropriate number of documents for each topic.

---

[6] http://jgibblda.sourceforge.net/

3.3   Identifying CDTs

Referring to the concept of cohesion, we propose a novel metric called Topic Cohesion (TC) to identify CDTs from the raw topics mined in previous step. *TC is used to measure the degree to which source code elements associated to a topic belong together.* Our hypothesis is that if the source code elements collaboratively implement a functional concern, from the perspective of static analysis, they should be highly related to each other (i.e. high TC) through structural relationships (e.g. dependencies, inheritance, etc.). For example, the source code elements associated to the "user" topic (Fig. 1) are highly related to each other, and they collaboratively implement the functional concern represented by the topic, therefore, the topic is a CDT. On the contrary, if the source code elements are grouped together just because they share similar words, there should be few structural relationships among them (i.e. low TC). For example, source code elements associated to a "main" topic are grouped together just because they all have a *main* function, the relationships among these elements are occasional and usually few.

Calculating Topic Cohesion. TC is calculated using the structural relationships among the source code elements associated to a topic. All the relationships between two classes in Object-Oriented systems, such as associations, aggregation, composition, dependencies, inheritance, and realizations, are taken into consideration. The relationships can be classified into *internal relationships* and *external relationships*. If the two classes are associated to the same topic, the relationship is an *internal relationship*; otherwise, if the two classes are associated to different topics, the relationship is an *external relationship*. TC is calculated as the ratio of internal relationships and all relationships as follows:

$$tc = \frac{R_{int}}{R_{all}} = \frac{R_{int}}{R_{int} + R_{ext}} \tag{1}$$

where R_{int} is the number of *internal relationships*, R_{ext} is the number of *external relationships*, and R_{all} is the number of all relationships.

We use TC to identify CDTs from the raw topics mined from source code using LDA. Based on the assumption above, if TC is higher than a threshold (i.e. $tc > \lambda$, where λ is the threshold), which means the classes associated to a topic are highly related to each other, the topic is more likely to be a CDT; otherwise, the topic is more likely to be a noisy topic. The threshold λ may be different for different software, in this paper λ is assigned to 0.35 based on experience.

Identifying CDTs and Determining Documents. The collection of documents associated to a topic is a critical factor in calculating TC. As discussed in Section 3.2, it is not appropriate to use a fixed threshold or a fixed cut-off point to determine the number of documents associated to a topic. The reason is not difficult to understand. From the static analysis perspective, the numbers of source code elements implementing different functional concerns are not the same. In this paper, we propose an iterative process to determine the documents associated to a topic and whether the topic is a CDT. The pseudocode implementing the process is shown in Fig. 3.

```
D = {d₁, d₂, …, dₙ}; // D is all the documents associated to a topic
sort(D); // Sort D according to their possibilities p(tᵢ|dⱼ)
Dₛ = {d₁}, tc = calculateTC (Dₛ); // Initialize
/* Determine whether the topic is a CDT.
    If so, determine the initial set of selected documents */
while (p(tᵢ|dⱼ) >= δ and tc < λ)
    addDocument(Dₛ, dⱼ);
    tc = calculateTC (Dₛ);
/* If the topic is a CDT, expand the set of selected documents */
while (tc >= λ)
    addDocument(Dₛ, dⱼ);
    tc = calculateTC (Dₛ);
```

Fig. 3. Pseudocode implementing the process of determining the documents associated to a topic and whether the topic is a CDT

Firstly, we sort all the documents D associated to a topic according to their possibilities $p(t_i|d_j)$. Then, in the first loop, we try to add each document d_j to the selected document set D_s until the topic is identified as a CDT (i.e. $tc > \lambda$) or the document's possibility is little than the threshold (i.e. $p(t_i|d_j) < \delta$). Finally, if the topic is CDT, we further expand D_s until $tc < \lambda$ in the second loop, the maximum TC is taken as the final value. The threshold δ may be different for different software as well, in this paper δ is assigned to 0.1 based on experience. After the process, we can determine the documents associated to each topic and whether the topic is a CDT.

4   Evaluation

We conducted a case study on a set of open source software systems to investigate whether our approach can effectively filter out noises and identify CDTs from the topics mined from source code.

4.1   Data Set and Metrics

Data Set. As there is no widely accepted data set in the research area of mining domain topics from source code, we constructed a new data set and published this data set for further research. The data set consisted of five open source software systems written in Java. The first two open source software systems (TSR[7] and CoWS[8]) are developed by the Software Engineering Institute (SEI)

---

[7] http://tsr.sei.pku.edu.cn/
[8] http://www.cowebservices.com/

of Peking University. TSR is an open source software repository and CoWS is an open source Web services search engine. We choose these two systems because we can invite their own developers to evaluate the results returned by our approach. The other systems (Heritrix[9], Lucene[10], and Jena[11]) are all famous open source software systems that are widely used. Some statistics of these systems are summarized in Table 2, where NoC is the number of classes, NoM is the number of methods, LoC is the lines of code, and NoW is the number of words extracted from source code.

Table 2. Statistics of the results

Name	Description	NoC	NoM	LoC	NoW
TSR	Software repository	81	5,622	13,941	4,407
CoWS	Web Services search engine	154	7,038	18,855	6,410
Heritrix	Web crawler	615	32,658	56,413	31,236
Lucene	Text search engine library	805	55,950	132,506	52,037
Jena	Semantic Web framework	840	50,730	59,478	49,799

Metrics. The problem of identifying CDTs can be taken as a classification problem, namely classifying the raw topics into CDTs and noisy topics. The relationships between the classification results returned by our approach and the oracle results are shown in Table 3.

Table 3. Relationships between the results

	CDT	Noise
CDT-TC	True Positive (TP)	False Positive (FP)
Noise-TC	False Negative (FN)	True Negative (TN)

We choose the typical metrics, namely precision, recall, and accuracy, to evaluate the effectiveness of the classification. Based on the relationships shown in Table 3, the metrics are defined correspondingly as follows:

$$p = \frac{|TP|}{|TP| + |FP|} \tag{2}$$

$$r = \frac{|TP|}{|TP| + |FN|} \tag{3}$$

$$a = \frac{|TP| + |TN|}{|TP| + |FN| + |FP| + |TN|} \tag{4}$$

---

[9] http://crawler.archive.org/
[10] http://lucene.apache.org/
[11] http://jena.apache.org/

4.2 Case Study Process

For each software system, we run the approach proposed in this paper on its source code twice. For the first run ($R0$), we did not apply the FHs; For the second run ($R1$), we applied the FHs. We applied TC to automatically identify CDTs for both runs. The results were stored in database.

Then we invited 20 graduate students to examine the results. 14 of the participants are the developers of the TSR and CoWS. All of the participants have at least 3 years of experience in programming with Java, and have reused the above open source software systems previously.

We developed a website system for the participants to examine the topics. After logging into the system, the participants chose a project to start with. Then, the system randomly selected a topic from all the topics returned in both runs ($R0$ and $R1$). The random selection process was adopted to make sure that the participants did not know whether the topic was generated with or without the filtering heuristics. For each topic, details of a topic, including its name, its associated words and associated Java classes, were shown on the left side of the user interface. The participants were asked to examine the details of each topic and determine whether the topic is a CDT. The results were submitted to the database as well. And we took the majority results provided by the participants as the oracle to evaluate our approach. After exploring all the topics of a software system, the participants could switch to another software system.

4.3 Results Analysis

In this subsection, we first qualitatively analyze the case study results with examples, and then quantitatively analyze the results with statistics.

Qualitative Analysis with Examples. In this paper, we use TC to identify CDTs from the topics mined from source code. Our assumption is that if the TC value of a topic is higher that the threshold ($tc > \lambda$), the topic is more likely to be a CDT; otherwise, the topic is more likely to be a noisy topic. Several CDTs as well as noisy topics from the case study are shown in Table 4. From the results we can see that the TC values of CDTs are relatively higher than the values of noisy topis, which confirms our assumption and demonstrates that TC is an effective mechanism to distinguish CDTs from other noisy topics.

Another benefit of TC is that it can identify some topics composed of stopwords, e.g. "id uuid string" and "string log arg" topics in Table 4. This is because the source code elements associated to these topics are grouped together just because they share the same stopwords). Therefore, as mentioned in Section 3.1, there is no need to provide a complete list of stopwords in our approach.

Quantitative Analysis with Statistics. The statistics of the results for both runs ($R0$ and $R1$) are shown in Table 5, where W is the number of words, T is the number of all topics, C is the number of CDTs, P, R, A are the metrics precision, recall, and accuracy correspondingly.

Table 4. Examples of CDTs and noisy topics

Topic	Concern Represented	Cohesion	Type	Source
user email password	user management	0.68	CDT	TSR
feedback comment rate	user feedbacks processing	0.44	CDT	CoWS
robot agent polici	robots.txt processing	0.45	CDT	Heritrix
merg writer index	merging Lucene indexes	0.58	CDT	Lucene
ontolog spec maker	ontology model processing	0.38	CDT	Jena
id uuid string	# noises #	0	Noisy topic	TSR
integ map set	# noises #	0.003	Noisy topic	CoWS
string log arg	# noises #	0.05	Noisy topic	Heritrix

Table 5. Statistics of the results

Name	W-R0	W-R1	T-R0	T-R1	C-R0	C-R1	P-R0	P-R1	R-R0	R-R1	A-R0	A-R1
TSR	4,507	2,700	59	37	12	9	0.8	0.78	0.67	0.77	0.9	0.89
CoWS	6,410	3,901	55	26	11	9	0.7	0.85	0.64	0.67	0.87	0.85
Heritrix	31,236	21,905	71	55	16	13	0.63	0.71	0.75	0.77	0.85	0.87
Lucene	52,037	35,671	131	73	19	15	0.7	0.69	0.74	0.7	0.92	0.88
Jena	49,799	32,752	141	96	23	18	0.76	0.75	0.69	0.71	0.91	0.89

Firstly, we analyze the overall performance of our approach with the results of $R1$, in which both FHs and TC are applied. The average precision, recall, and accuracy for all software systems are 0.76, 0.72, and 0.88 correspondingly. From the results, we can see that our approach is very accurate, which means that our approach can precisely determine whether a topic is a CDT or a noisy topic. The precision and recall are acceptable considering the facts that our approach is purely automatic and the thresholds (λ and δ) may not be their best estimations.

Then we analyze the performance of FHs and TC separately by comparing the results of $R0$ and $R1$. Comparing the statistics in Table 5, we can see that the FHs can filter out lots of words (35% on average), and significantly reduce the number of topics mined from source code (37.8% on average). It is worth noticing that the reduction of words and topics almost does not affect the number of CDTs, which means most of the words and topics filtered out by FHs are noises. Moreover, the average precision for $R0$ and $R1$ is 0.74 (with standard deviation 0.02), the average recall is 0.71 (with standard deviation 0.01), and the average accuracy is 0.89 (with standard deviation 0.01), which means that the performance of TC is not only acceptable but also very stable (not affected by FHs).

From the analysis above, we can see that FHs and TC are complementary to each other in filtering out noises and identifying CDTs, which will save the developers a lot of efforts and help them use CDTs to comprehend the functional concerns implemented in source code.

4.4 Threats to Validity

Several issues may threat the validity of our approach.

Software Selection. In this paper, we only evaluated our approach on five open source software systems that we developed or reused. But it is worth noting that if we are not familiar with the source code of a software system, it is difficult for us to provide the oracle results to evaluate the effectiveness of our approach. From the preliminary results, we can see that our approach is promising, and developers can depend on approach to comprehend other software systems. In our future work, we will apply our approach to more open source software systems and invite the contributors of these systems to evaluate the results to further explore the effectiveness of our approach.

Human Factor. In the case study, we invited a group of graduate students to manually classify the topics mined from source code, and took the results as the oracle to evaluate the effectiveness of our approach. We designed several mechanisms to avoid bias. For example, the system randomly selected topics from both runs, and the majority opinions were taken as the final results. However, it is still possible that there are bias and noises in the results. Especially for the open source software systems that are not developed by the participants, although the participants are familiar with the software systems and have reused them in their own projects, they may not be familiar with every detail of the source code. Consequently, there may be false positive or false negative results, which may affect the internal validity of the case study.

Generalization. In this paper, we used several specific heuristics and methods, which seems to limit the generalization of our approach. In fact, our approach is very extensible. First, how to separate domain related information and pro- gramming related information in source code is still an open question. New filter heuristics can easily be added to the FHs proposed in our approach. For exam- ple, new heuristics can be added to further improve the quality of identifiers. Second, it is possible and easy to replace the LDA topic model used in our approach with other topic models, while the FHs and TC are still applicable. Third, the idea of our approach is also applicable for software systems written in other programming languages. For example, by replacing JDT with C/C++ Development Tooling, our approach is able to identify domain topics from open source software systems written in C/C++.

5 Discussion

5.1 Semantics of the Topics Mined from Source Code

In this subsection, we discuss the semantics of the topics mined from source code. Although many approaches have been proposed to mine topics from source code (see Section 2), it is difficult to explain the semantics of the topics. Some researches [4, 6] interpret the semantics as domain concepts similar to *functionalities* or *features*, while other researches [2, 8] interpret the semantics as cross-cutting concepts such as *aspects* or *architectural concepts*. In fact, the natures of the topics mined from source code are *linguistic clusters* [6] from the perspective of IR. The topics are identified just because of the linguistic relationships between the words and the documents.

The topics can be classified into different categories according to the concerns they represent, and there is no one-to-one mapping between the topics and external concepts (e.g. *functionalities*, *features*, *aspects*, etc.) used by human beings. Therefore, it is reasonable to classify the topics mined from source code according to different usage scenarios. In this paper, we focus on CDTs that reflect the functional concerns of the software, and propose an approach to identify CDTs from source code.

5.2   Limitations of IR Techniques on SE Data

IR techniques (e.g. search engines and topic models) have been widely adopted to solve Software Engineering (SE) problems, such as feature location, traceability recovery, etc. Although IR techniques can return or generate a lot of results when applied on SE data, there are also lots of noises in the results, which threats the effectiveness of these approaches [6, 26–28]. For example, from the results shown in Table 5, we can see that only a small percentage (about 22%) of the topics mined from source code are domain topics, while other topics are noises in this context. This phenomena has been noticed in [6] as well.

Most previous IR-based approaches are based on the assumption that source code is similar to plain text written in natural languages, but there is little empirical evidence to support this assumption. In fact, there are differences between the two [4]. For example, the information in source code includes both domain related information and programming related information. In addition, unlike plain text, source code is *structured document*. There are structural relationships (e.g. dependencies, inheritances, etc.) among the source code. When taking source code as plain text, these differences are neglected, which may bring in noises and affect the effectiveness of IR-based approaches.

In order to improve the effectiveness of IR-based approaches, it is reasonable to make use of the characteristics of source code (e.g. structural information) [27–29]. In this paper, we try to utilize the characteristics of source code to filter out noises and mine CDTs from source code. The empirical results show that our approach is promising.

6   Conclusion

Using topic models to mine domain topics from source code has been a new and promising way for developers to comprehend the functional concerns implemented in the source code of a software system. However, not all the topics mined from source code are domain topics which represent functional concerns of the software. In fact, there are a lot of noises. In this paper, we propose a series of FHs and a novel metric called TC to filter out noises and mine effective domain topics (called CDTs) from source code. Experimental results on a set of open source software show that our approach is promising.

In our future work, we plan to further explore the effectiveness and extensibility of our approach using more open source software systems, and try to apply our approach to software engineering tasks such as source code comprehension, traceability recover, feature location, etc.

Acknowledgement. This work is supported by the High-Tech Research and Development Program of China under Grant No. 2012AA011202; the National Basic Research Program of China (973) under Grant No. 2009CB320703; the National Natural Science Foundation of China under Grant No. 61121063, No. 61103024; and Quality Supervision & Inspection Quarantine Research Special Funds for Public Welfare Projects under Grant No. 201210256.

References

1. Abran, A., Moore, J., Bourque, P., Dupuis, R., Tripp, L.: Guide to the software engineering body of knowledge, 2004 version. IEEE Computer Society 1 (2004)
2. Gethers, M., Savage, T., Di Penta, M., Oliveto, R., Poshyvanyk, D., De Lucia, A.: Codetopics: Which topic am i coding now? In: 33rd International Conference on Software Engineering (ICSE), pp. 1034–1036. IEEE (2011)
3. Savage, T., Dit, B., Gethers, M., Poshyvanyk, D.: Topicxp: Exploring topics in source code using latent dirichlet allocation. In: IEEE International Conference on Software Maintenance (ICSM), pp. 1–6. IEEE (2010)
4. Maskeri, G., Sarkar, S., Heafield, K.: Mining business topics in source code using latent dirichlet allocation. In: Proceedings of the 1st India Software Engineering Conference, pp. 113–120. ACM (2008)
5. Abebe, S., Tonella, P.: Towards the extraction of domain concepts from the identifiers. In: 18th Working Conference on Reverse Engineering (WCRE), pp. 77–86. IEEE (2011)
6. Kuhn, A., Ducasse, S., Gírba, T.: Semantic clustering: Identifying topics in source code. Information and Software Technology 49(3), 230–243 (2007)
7. Liu, Y., Poshyvanyk, D., Ferenc, R., Gyimóthy, T., Chrisochoides, N.: Modeling class cohesion as mixtures of latent topics. In: IEEE International Conference on Software Maintenance (ICSM), pp. 233–242. IEEE (2009)
8. Baldi, P., Lopes, C., Linstead, E., Bajracharya, S.: A theory of aspects as latent topics. In: ACM Sigplan Notices, vol. 43, pp. 543–562. ACM (2008)
9. Steyvers, M., Griffiths, T.: Probabilistic topic models. Handbook of Latent Semantic Analysis 427(7), 424–440 (2007)
10. Blei, D., Ng, A., Jordan, M.: Latent dirichlet allocation. The Journal of Machine Learning Research 3, 993–1022 (2003)
11. Asuncion, H., Asuncion, A., Taylor, R.: Software traceability with topic modeling. In: 32nd ACM/IEEE International Conference on Software Engineering (ICSE), pp. 95–104. ACM (2010)

12. Tian, K., Revelle, M., Poshyvanyk, D.: Using latent dirichlet allocation for automatic categorization of software. In: 6th IEEE International Working Conference on Mining Software Repositories (MSR), pp. 163–166. IEEE (2009)
13. Kawaguchi, S., Garg, P., Matsushita, M., Inoue, K.: Mudablue: An automatic categorization system for open source repositories. Journal of Systems and Software 79(7), 939–953 (2006)
14. Thomas, S., Adams, B., Hassan, A., Blostein, D.: Modeling the evolution of topics in source code histories. In: 8th Working Conference on Mining Software Repositories, MSR (2011)
15. Lukins, S., Kraft, N., Etzkorn, L.: Bug localization using latent dirichlet allocation. Information and Software Technology 52(9), 972–990 (2010)
16. Adams, B., Jiang, Z., Hassan, A.: Identifying crosscutting concerns using historical code changes. In: 32nd ACM/IEEE International Conference on Software Engineering (ICSE), pp. 305–314. ACM (2010)
17. Bieman, J., Kang, B.: Cohesion and reuse in an object-oriented system. In: ACM SIGSOFT Software Engineering Notes, vol. 20, pp. 259–262. ACM (1995)
18. Briand, L., Wüst, J., Daly, J., Victor Porter, D.: Exploring the relationships between design measures and software quality in object-oriented systems. Journal of Systems and Software 51(3), 245–273 (2000)
19. Chidamber, S., Darcy, D., Kemerer, C.: Managerial use of metrics for object-oriented software: An exploratory analysis. IEEE Transactions on Software Engineering 24(8), 629–639 (1998)
20. Etzkorn, L., Davis, C.: Automatically identifying reusable oo legacy code. Computer 30(10), 66–71 (1997)
21. Briand, L., Daly, J., Wüst, J.: A unified framework for cohesion measurement in object-oriented systems. Empirical Software Engineering 3(1), 65–117 (1998)
22. De Lucia, A., Oliveto, R., Vorraro, L.: Using structural and semantic metrics to improve class cohesion. In: IEEE International Conference on Software Maintenance (ICSM), pp. 27–36. IEEE (2008)
23. Marcus, A., Poshyvanyk, D., Ferenc, R.: Using the conceptual cohesion of classes for fault prediction in object-oriented systems. IEEE Transactions on Software Engineering 34(2), 287–300 (2008)
24. Meyers, T., Binkley, D.: An empirical study of slice-based cohesion and coupling metrics. ACM Transactions on Software Engineering and Methodology (TOSEM) 17(1), 2 (2007)
25. Griffiths, T., Steyvers, M.: Finding scientific topics. Proceedings of the National Academy of Sciences of the United States of America 101, 5228–5235 (2004)
26. Oliveto, R., Gethers, M., Poshyvanyk, D., De Lucia, A.: On the equivalence of information retrieval methods for automated traceability link recovery. In: 18th International Conference on Program Comprehension (ICPC), pp. 68–71. IEEE (2010)
27. Dit, B., Revelle, M., Gethers, M., Poshyvanyk, D.: Feature location in source code: A taxonomy and survey. Journal of Software Maintenance and Evolution: Research and Practice (2011)
28. Ali, N., Guéhéneuc, Y., Antoniol, G.: Factors impacting the inputs of traceability recovery approaches. Software and Systems Traceability, 99–127 (2012)
29. McMillan, C., Poshyvanyk, D., Revelle, M.: Combining textual and structural analysis of software artifacts for traceability link recovery. In: ICSE Workshop on Traceability in Emerging Forms of Software Engineering, pp. 41–48. IEEE (2009)

Mining Instances of Structural Design Patterns from Class Diagrams Based on Sub-patterns

Dongjin Yu, Zhiqing Liu, and Jianlin Ge

School of Computer, Hangzhou Dianzi University, Hangzhou, China
yudj@hdu.edu.cn

Abstract. In order to improve the quality of a software system and reuse expert experience in software system design, design patterns have been extensively applied in the software industry. Mining design pattern instances from source codes can assist the understanding of the systems. In this paper, we propose eight sub-patterns based on common structural features of structural design patterns and their variants. We introduce two kinds of graph, of which one represents the system design and the other describes the sub-patterns. Our approach first selects the candidate classes in UML class diagrams to form the sub-graphs of the system graph, which are then checked isomorphic to the sub-pattern graph or not. These isomorphic sub-graphs are regarded as corresponding to instances of the sub-patterns. After that, we combine some relevant sub-patterns and compare the collectives with structural feature models. For these matched ones, we then apply behavioral analysis to obtain the final pattern instances. The results of the experiments demonstrate that our approach obtains better precision than the existing approaches.

Keywords: structural design patterns, pattern mining, sub-pattern, graph isomorphism, structural feature models, class diagrams, behavioral analysis.

1 Introduction

Along with expanding the scale of object-oriented software systems, the relationship between classes is becoming more and more complicated. Design patterns define a set of classes, and the relationship among them and their purpose in object-oriented software systems [1]. During the past decade, design patterns have been widely used by the software industry [2]. Meanwhile, with the increasing complexity and size of software systems, understanding and changing these systems is becoming a difficult task, particularly when the architecture and design documentation are incomplete or inconsistent with source codes. As the source codes of object-oriented software can be represented by a series of UML class diagrams, recovering the instances of design patterns from class diagrams helps developers to complete design documents, understand large systems and make changes more easily.

Each design pattern, whether it is creational, structural or behavioral, has its own unique structural features, or in other words a structural feature model. From a lower perspective, however, most design patterns have similar sub-components which make up of their feature models. Since structural design patterns describe how to combine

J. Favaro and M. Morisio (Eds.): ICSR 2013, LNCS 7925, pp. 255–266, 2013.

the classes into a larger structure, they have more similar sub-components than behavioral and creational design patterns.

The existing approaches to mining structural patterns generally identify patterns sequentially and few take advantage of the sub-components of design patterns to reduce the complexity of the patterns mining. If a certain feature is found not to be matched with that of the target design pattern, the intermediate results are usually abandoned before the mining process is restarted. But features identified beforehand could help find some other design patterns which have similar sub-components. In other words, mining these design patterns could start from the results obtained so far and does not need to re-scan class diagrams from scratch.

In order to further improve the precision, this paper proposes a novel approach to mine structural design pattern instances from class diagrams. It presents eight kinds of sub-patterns, which include a set of classes and the relations between them. It then introduces the structural feature model based on sub-patterns for each structural design pattern. The instances of structural design patterns are finally identified by comparing the code model with the structural feature model and by analyzing the behaviors of the classes.

The rest of the paper is organized as follows. After introducing the whole process of mining instances of GoF structural design patterns [3] from class diagrams in Section 2, we define eight kinds of sub-pattern and present corresponding structural feature models in Section 3. Section 4 then describes the process of mining sub-patterns and Section 5 shows how to combine sub-patterns and compare them with structural feature models to obtain the final pattern instances. Section 6 describes the behavioral analysis of different design patterns. The experimental results are given in Section 7, followed by the related works in Section 8. Finally, the last section concludes the paper.

2   Overview of the Approach

Structural design patterns are design patterns that ease the design by identifying a simple way to realize relationships between entities. The essence of mining structural design patterns is a process of matching patterns which can be further divided into the following four phases. As the source codes of object-oriented software can be represented by a series of UML class diagrams, our approach begins with the prepared class diagrams.

1) Generate the Class-Relationship Graph from class diagrams

In this phase, a series of prepared class diagrams are transformed into a *Class-Relationship Graph*, in which the vertices represent classes and the edges represent relationships between classes.

2) Extract sub-graphs from the Class-Relationship Graph that are isomorphic to the Class-Relationship Graph of the predefined sub-patterns

The candidate vertices in the *Class-Relationship Graph* for that of the predefined sub-patterns are identified first. These candidate vertices are then combined to form the sub-graphs, which are considered as instances of predefined sub-patterns if they are isomorphic to the *Class-Relationship Graph* of the predefined sub-patterns.

3) Combine extracted sub-graphs and match them with predefined structural feature models to obtain candidate patterns

An effort is made to combine relevant sub-patterns and match them with standard structural feature models. These matched ones are taken as the candidate patterns.

4) Analyze behavioral features to obtain final patterns instances

The behavioral features of candidate patterns are identified and matched with those of standard patterns. Pattern instances are finally obtained by filtering out false candidates with mismatched behavioral features.

3   Sub-patterns

Although structural design patterns have their own structural and behavioral features, most of them have similar sub-components which make them up at a lower level. We use the sub-patterns to represent common structural features of structural design patterns.

Definition 1. A *sub-pattern* represents a set of classes and the relationship between them, which is denoted as a 2-tuple: $Sub - pattern = (< C_1, ..., C_k >, R)$, where $C_1,...,C_k$ represent a set of classes, R represents a set of relationships among them, such as inheritance, association and aggregation.

$R = \{r(C_i, C_j) = \{inherit \mid agg \mid ass\}\}$, where

$r(C_i, C_j) = \{inherit\}$ represents that class C_j inherits class C_i .

$r(C_i, C_j) = \{agg\}$ represents that classes C_i and C_j have an aggregation relationship, where class C_i is the whole class, class C_j is the partial class.

$r(C_i, C_j) = \{ass\}$ represents that classes C_i and C_j have an association relationship, where class C_i has an attribute that is a type of class C_j .

Compared with design patterns, sub-patterns have fewer but clearer features. They can therefore be detected easily. Moreover, using sub-patterns to mine structural design patterns can significantly reduce the mining complexity, since some common sub-patterns can be extracted synchronously to avoid the detection of different design patterns from scratch. Last but not least, sub-patterns take the transformation between interfaces, abstract and concrete classes, and between inheritance and association relationships, into consideration. They can therefore be used to mine some design pattern variants.

Sub-pattern can be further divided into ordinary sub-patterns and variant sub-patterns.

3.1   Ordinary Sub-patterns

Unlike variant sub-patterns, ordinary sub-patterns describe a necessary feature of standard design patterns.

Definition 2. *ICA (Inheritance Child Association)* describes the inheritance and association relationship among three classes, where two classes have an inheritance relationship and the child class has an association relationship with another child class.

$ICA = (< C_1, C_2, C_3 >, R)$ where $R = \{(r(C_1, C_2) = \{inherit\}, r(C_2, C_3) = \{ass\})\}$.

Definition 3. *CI (Common Inheritance)* describes two classes that inherit the same single parent class.

$CI = (<C_1, C_2, C_3 >, R)$ where

$R = \{(r(C_1, C_2) = \{inherit\}, r(C_1, C_3) = \{inherit\})\}$.

Definition 4. *IAGG (Inheritance AGGregation)* describes two classes that have not only an inheritance relationship but also an aggregation relationship.

$IAGG = (<C_1, C_2 >, R)$ where $R = \{(r(C_1, C_2) = \{inherit\}, r(C_2, C_1) = \{agg\})\}$.

Definition 5. *IPA (Inheritance Parent Aggregation)* describes the inheritance and aggregation relationship between three classes, where two classes have an inheritance relationship and the parent class has an aggregation relationship with the third class.

$IPA = (<C_1, C_2, C_3 >, R)$ where $R = \{(r(C_1, C_3) = \{inherit\}, r(C_1, C_2) = \{agg\})\}$.

Definition 6. *MLI (Multi-Level Inheritance)* describes the inheritance relationship between three classes, where the first class is inherited from the second, which is further inherited from the third one.

$MLI = (<C_1, C_2, C_3 >, R)$ where

$R = \{(r(C_1, C_2) = \{inherit\}, r(C_2, C_3) = \{inherit\})\}$.

3.2   Variant Sub-patterns

The association relationship plays an important part when forming structural design patterns. Without an association relationship between the classes, a group of classes may not be considered as a given pattern. However, polymorphism often makes particular classes have an implied association relationship.

Similarly, the transformation between interfaces, abstract classes and concrete classes, the transitivity of the inheritance relationship, the association relationship, and roles merged are important factors for forming variants of standard design patterns. In order to identify more design pattern instances, three kinds of variant sub-pattern which consider these factors are defined as follows.

Definition 7. *IASS (Inheritance ASSociation)* describes two classes that have not only an inheritance relationship, but also an association relationship.

$IASS = (<C_1, C_2 >, R)$ where $R = \{(r(C_1, C_2) = \{inherit\}, r(C_2, C_1) = \{ass\})\}$.

Definition 8. *SAGG (Self-Aggregation)* describes one class that has an aggregation relationship with itself.

$SAGG = (<C_1 >, R)$ where $R = \{(r(C_1, C_1) = \{agg\})\}$.

Definition 9. *IIAGG (Indirect Inheritance AGGregation)* describes the inheritance relationship and aggregation relationship between three classes, where the first class is aggregated by the third one and inherited from the second one, which is further inherited from the third one.

$IIAGG = (<C_1, C_2, C_3 >, R)$ where

$R = \{(r(C_1, C_2) = \{inherit\}, r(C_2, C_3) = \{inherit\}, r(C_3, C_1) = \{agg\})\}$.

4   Mining Sub-patterns

This section first shows how to represent the system and sub-patterns using graphs, and then introduces the process of mining sub-patterns from class diagrams in detail.

4.1   Class-Relationship Graph

Definition 10. *Class-Relationship Graph*, or *GCR*, is a directed and weighted graph that represents a set of classes and the relationship between them, denoted as a 3-tuple $GCR = (V, E, v)$, where V is the set of vertices which represent classes, $E \subset V \times V$ is the set of edges which represent the relationship between classes, $v : E \to W_E$ is a function assigning weights to the edges, and $W_E = \{2, 3, 5, 6, 10, 15, 30\}$, as Table 1 describes.

Table 1. Weights of relationship

v (Items of W_E)	Relationship
2	Association
3	Inheritance
5	Aggregation
6=2*3	Association and inheritance
10=2*5	Association and aggregation
15=3*5	Inheritance and aggregation
30=2*3*5	Association, inheritance and aggregation

Definition 11. Let $GCR = (V_1, E_1, v_1)$, $GCR^{ksub} = (V_2, E_2, v_2)$, GCR^{ksub} is called the *k-Class-Relationship-SubGraph of* GCR, or *k-subGraph of* GCR, if $V_2 \subseteq V_1$, $|V_2| = k$, $E_2 = E_1 \cap (V_2 \times V_2)$, and $v_2(e) = v_1(e)$ *for all* $e \in E_2$.

Definition 12. Let $GCR = (V, E, v)$, $|V| = n$, $M = (m_{i,j})_{n \times n}$ is called the *Class-Relationship Matrix* of GCR, *or MCR*, where

$$m_{i,j} = \begin{cases} v(V_i, V_j) & (V_i, V_j) \in E \\ 1 & !(V_i, V_j) \in E \end{cases}$$

For simplicity, the *Class-Relationship Graph* corresponding to the *Class-Relationship Matrix* m *is denoted as* GCR_m.

Definition 13. Let $GCR = (V, E, v)$, $|V| = n$, $V_i \in V$, for the Class-Relationship Matrix of $M = (m_{i,j})_{n \times n}$, the *Composite Weight* of V_i is denoted as $F(V_i)$, where

$$F(V_i) = \prod_{j=1}^{n} m_{ij} .$$

Definition 14. Let $GCR^1 = (V_1, E_1, v_1)$, $GCR^2 = (V_2, E_2, v_2)$, if there exists a bijective function $f : V_1 \to V_2$ such that each $a, b \in V_1$, $(a, b) \in E_1$, if and only if $f(a), f(b) \in V_2$, $(f(a), f(b)) \in E_2$, $v_1((a, b)) = v_2((f(a), f(b)))$, then GCR^1 and GCR^2 are *Isomorphic Class-Relationship-Graphs*, donated as $GCR^1 \cong GCR^2$.

Definition 15. A $n \times n$ matrix $P = (p_{ij})$ is called a *Permutation Matrix* where $p_{ij} \in \{0,1\}$, $\sum_{i=1}^{n} p_{ij} = 1$ and $\sum_{j=1}^{n} p_{ij} = 1$ for $i = 1,...,n$, $j = 1,...,n$.

Let $GCR_{M'} = (V', E', v')$, $GCR_{M''} = (V'', E'', v'')$, $|V'| = |V''| = n$, $M' = (m_{i,j})_{n \times n}$ and $M'' = (m_{i,j})_{n \times n}$ are *Class-Relationship Matrixes* of $GCR_{M'}$ and $GCR_{M''}$ respectively. It can be proved that if there exists a Permutation Matrix P such that $M' = PM''P^T$, then $GCR_{M'} \cong GCR_{M''}$.

4.2 Mining Sub-patterns Based on Graph Isomorphism

Since both the system and predefined sub-patterns can be represented by *Class-Relationship Graphs*, the problem of mining sub-patterns is converted into searching for sub-graphs in *Class-Relationship Graphs* of the system which are isomorphic to those of the sub-patterns.

The algorithm for mining sub-patterns is illustrated in Table 2, and can be divided into the following 2 steps.

1) Search the candidate classes in GCR^s of the system (from line 2 to line 3)

For each class c_i in GCR^m, select the classes in GCR^s whose *composite weights* in GCR^s can be divided with no remainder by that of c_i in GCR^m. These selected classes for c_i constitute the *Candidate Class Set* of c_i.

2) Combine the candidate classes to generate *k-subGraphs* and determine if they are isomorphic to GCR^m of the sub-patterns (from line 4 to line 12)

The *k-subGraph* of GCR^s, or GCR^{s-ksub}, is generated by choosing each vertex in every *Candidate Class Set*, and then compared with GCR^m of sub-patterns. If GCR^{s-ksub} is isomorphic to GCR^m, then GCR^{s-ksub} is regarded as corresponding to the specific sub-pattern.

Table 2. Algorithm of Mining Sub-patterns

Input:
$GCR^m = < V_m, E_m, v_m >$ //*Class-Relationship Graph* of sub-pattern
$GCR^s = < V_s, E_s, v_s >$ // *Class-Relationship Graph* of system
Output:
MSet //Set of *Class-Relationship Graphs* of Identified sub-patterns

---

1   MSet $= \emptyset$;
2   for each c_i in V_m
3   CCS$(c_i) = \{c | c \in V_s \cap (F(c_i)|F(c))\}$ //generate Candidate Class Sets
4   for each m_1 in CCS(c_1), m_2 in CCS(c_k), ..., m_k in CCS(c_k) {
5   generate $GCR^{s-ksub} = < V_{s-ksub}, E_{s-ksub}, v_{s-ksb} >$, where
6            $V_{s-ksub} = \{m_1, m_2, ..., m_k\}$,   //pick one class from each Candidate
Class Set
7            $E_{s-ksub} = E_s \cap (V_{s-ksub} \times V_{s-ksub})$,
8            $v_{s-ksub}(e) = v_s(e)$, for all $e \in E_{s-ksub}$
9   //check if GCR^{s-ksub} and GCR^m are isomorphic or not

Table 2. (*Continued.*)

10	if IsIsomorphic(GCR^{s-ksub}, GCR^m)
11	MSet = MSet ∪ GCR^{s-ksub}
12	}
13	return Mset

5   Combine Sub-patterns to Obtain Candidate Pattern Instances by Structural Feature Models

A *Structural Feature Model* is a set of several relevant sub-patterns to represent the structural feature of certain structural design patterns. Table 3 describes five *structural feature models*, corresponding to five *GoF* structural design patterns. These models are made up of several relevant sub-patterns. For example, the structural feature model for the *Adapter* pattern consists of sub-pattern of *ICA*, but not *CI*, which means that class *Adapter* inherits class *Target*, and is associated with class *Adaptee,* but no inheritance relationship exists between class *Adaptee* and class *Target*. For simplicity, Table 3 only shows the class diagrams for the standard design patterns, but not their variants.

According to the method given in the previous section, all the sub-patterns are identified. We then combine the relevant ones and compare the collectives with the Structural Feature Model of specific patterns. Those that match are picked up as candidate patterns for further behavioral analysis, as described in the next section.

6   Behavioral Analysis

The candidates obtained by the structure analysis may contain false positive cases because structural analysis concentrates only on the structural aspect of design patterns. Most design patterns have their own unique behavioral features in addition to the structural ones. Analyzing the behavior of these candidates can filter out some false ones. For behavioral analysis, we employ the method given in [4]. This section takes the *Adapter* pattern as the example of behavioral analysis.

The *Adapter* pattern is a design pattern that translates one interface for a class into a compatible interface. An *Adapter* allows classes to work together that normally could not because of incompatible interfaces, by providing its interface to clients while using the original interface.

In the *Adapter* pattern, there shall be a common method, called *Request*, defined in the *Target* and *Adapter* classes. The *Request* method in the *Adapter* class shall call a method, called *SpecificRequest*, defined in the class *Adaptee*. The behavior characteristic model of the *Adapter* pattern is formally defined as follows, using the denotations given in Table 4:

$$\exists\, method_i\ \exists method_j\ \exists\, method_k$$

Table 3. Structural Feature Models of structural design patterns

Structural Design Patterns	Role of Class		Structural Feature Model	Class Diagram
Adapter	Target	C1	ICA&&(!CI)	
	Adapter	C2		
	Adaptee	C3		
Proxy	Subject	C1	(CI&&ICA)‖(CI&&IASS)	
	Proxy	C2		
	RealSubject	C3		
Decorator	Component	C1	(CI&&IAGG)‖(CI&&IAGG&&MLI)	
	Decorator	C2		
	ConcreteComponent	C3		
Composite	Component	C1	(CI&&IAGG)‖(CI&&SAGG)‖(CI&&IIAGG)	
	Composite	C2		
	Leaf	C3		
Bridge	Abstraction	C1	CI&&IPA	
	RefinedAbstraction	C2		
	Implementor	C3		

$(method_i \in methodList(T \arg et) \wedge$

$\quad method_j \in methodList(Adapter) \wedge$

$\quad method_k \in methodList(Adaptee) \wedge$

$\quad name(method_i) = name(method_j) \wedge$

$\quad parameter(method_i) = parameter(method_j) \wedge$

$\quad returnType(method_i) = returnType(method_j) \wedge$

$\quad call(method_j, method_k))$

Table 4. Denotations of Behavioral Features

Denotations	Meaning
$methodList(C)$	The set of methods in class C
$name(method_i)$	The name of method $method_i$
$parameter(method_i)$	The list of parameter types of method $method_i$
$returnType(method_i)$	The return type of method $method_i$
$call(method_i, method_j)$	$method_i$ invokes $method_j$

The behavior characteristic model of other patterns can be described in a similar way.

7   Experiments

We implemented a tool called DPDT based on the aforementioned approach, which produces the instances of design patterns discovered in the target system. We tested our approach with JHotDraw[5], JavaAWT[6], JUnit[7]. The results are evaluated by indexes of TP and FP. Here, TP, or True Positive, denotes the number of pattern instances that are identified and really exist in the system, while FP, or False Positive, denotes the number of pattern instances that are found, but not implemented in the system.

Tables 5, 6 and 7 present the results of the experiments.

Table 5. Number of Sub-patterns Detected

System	IASS	IAGG	ICA	IPA	IIAGG	CI	MLI	SAGG
JHotDraw6.0	6	1	271	329	1	5984	230	2
JUnit3.8	1	1	20	15	0	22	10	0
JavaAWT	12	4	216	270	0	1108	143	0

Table 6. Structural Feature Models and Final Instances Detected

Structural Design Pattern	Number of Candidates based on Structural Feature Models Mapping			Number of Final Instances based on Structural Feature Models Mapping and Behavioral Analysis		
	JHotDraw	JUnit	JavaAWT	JHotDraw	JUnit	JavaAWT
Adapter	271	20	216	7	0	17
Composite	4	1	4	2	1	3
Decorator	8	6	20	4	3	2
Bridge	146	13	120	67	8	62
Proxy	7	7	20	5	5	8

Table 7. Recovery Precisions

Structural Design Patterns	JHotDraw		JUnit		JavaAWT	
	TP	FP	TP	FP	TP	FP
Adapter	7(4)	0(0)	0	0	17	0
Composite	2(0)	0(0)	1	0	3	0
Decorator	4	0	3	0	2	0
Bridge	62(53)	5(5)	7	1	52	10
Proxy	5	0	5	0	8	0

Note: the numbers in brackets are the counts of recovered instances obtained in [8].

As can be observed from Table 7, we obtain good results except for the Bridge pattern. Comparing the results of our approach with that of paper [8], our approach obtains better precision. This is mainly because our approach employs the rigorous graph isomorphism technique and considers some variant factors, such as transformation between interfaces, abstract classes and concrete classes, and the transitivity of the inheritance and association relationships.

8   Related Works

Since the idea of design patterns was adapted for software engineering, many approaches have been applied to mine instances of design patterns from source codes. Although there are numerous kinds of design patterns, structural ones especially are receiving more attention. The approaches to mining structural design patterns can be divided into two categories: checking only structural aspects and checking both structural and behavioral aspects.

Most of the approaches which only focus on the structural aspects of patterns consider attributes, methods and the relationships between classes, such as generalization, association, aggregation, as the main properties that need to be checked. Antoniol et al. consider the number of public, private and protected attributes, and the number of operations when detecting design patterns [9], while Gueheneuc et al. consider inherited and overridden methods, the total number of methods, and the count of methods weighted with their number of method invocations as valuable metrics that characterize patterns [10]. Other approaches detect instances of design patterns based on subgraph isomorphism. For instance, Akshara Pande et al. decompose the system design graph and design pattern graph into a Generalization relationship graph and an Association relationship graph, from which a set of system relationship graphs that are isomorphic to the design pattern relationship graph are obtained as instances of the design patterns [11].

The behavioral aspect, typically described by method invocations, contains important knowledge to further judge those design patterns which have similar or the same structural features. Dong et al. check the number of attributes, operations and dependency links between classes for design pattern detection [4, 8]. Ming Qiu et al., however, focus on object creation and method invocations for design pattern detection

[12]. Francesca et al. decompose design patterns into traits which describe the structural features or behavioral features of the patterns [13]. Since each design pattern has its own features, mining instances of design patterns from source can be transformed into looking for a set of relevant traits. In order to reduce the complexity of the design pattern mining, Daryl Posnett et al. define three kinds of meta-patterns [14]. According to their definitions, a meta-pattern is part of a design pattern which contains structural and behavioral features of that design pattern.

The above approaches generally identify only one pre-specified pattern after startup. In other words, the intermediate results obtained during the process of mining one specified pattern cannot be reused for mining other patterns. Our approach, however, can mine multiple patterns synchronously which have similar sub-patterns, thus reducing running time. In other words, the recovered sub-patterns, or the intermediate results, can be assembled and compared with structural feature models of all kinds of structural patterns. Moreover, the sub-patterns defined in this paper are different from the micro-structures defined in [15] and [16], which contain both structural and behavioral features. Because behavioral features change frequently and are hard to detect, the sub-patterns presented in this paper contain only classes and the relationship among them, without any behavioral information. In addition, we also consider the structural variants when defining sub-patterns. Therefore, our approach can achieve greater precision. Finally, compared with approaches based on graph isomorphism like [11], our approach does not need to decompose the system graph and design pattern graph. Its complexity is thus reduced.

9   Conclusions

This paper proposes a novel approach to mining structural design pattern instances from class diagrams. It extracts structural information and identifies different sub-patterns based on graph isomorphism. It then combines relevant sub-patterns and compares them with structural feature models. For those that match, it does a behavioral analysis to obtain the final pattern instances. The results of our experiments demonstrate that this approach attains better precision than other existing approaches.

However, our approach cannot distinguish structural design patterns which are very similar to each other in their structural and behavioral aspects, such as Bridge and Strategy patterns. In the future, we will consider further the intents and motivations of design patterns in order to distinguish them. In addition, we will upgrade our approach to mine creational and behavioral design pattern instances as well.

Acknowledgments. The work is supported by the Natural Science Foundation of Zhejiang (No.LY12F02003), the Key Science and Technology Project of Zhejiang (No. 2012C11026-3, No. 2008C11099-1) and the open project foundation of Zhejiang Provincial Key Laboratory of Network Technology and Information Security. The authors would also like to thank anonymous reviewers who made valuable suggestions to improve the quality of the paper.

References

1. Gamma, E., Helm, R., Johnson, R., Vlissides, J.: Design Patterns: Elements of Reusable Object-Oriented Software. Addison-Wesley, Reading (1995)
2. Dong, J., Zhao, Y.J., Peng, T.: A Review of Design Pattern Mining Techniques. The International Journal of Software Engineering and Knowledge Engineering (IJSEKE) 19, 823–855 (2009)
3. Gamma, E., Helm, R., Johnson, R., Vlissides, J.: Design patterns, software engineering, object-oriented programming. Addison-Wesley (1994)
4. Dong, J., Zhao, Y.J., Sun, Y.T.: A Matrix-Based Approach to Recovering Design Patterns. IEEE Transactions on Systems, Man and Cybernetics – Part A: Systems and Humans 39(6), 1271–1282 (2009)
5. http://www.jhotdraw.org/
6. http://java.sun.com/j2se/1.5.0/docs/guide/awt/index.html
7. http://www.junit.org/
8. Dong, J., Lad, D.S., Zhao, Y.: DP-Miner: Design Pattern Discovery Using Matrix. In: Proceedings of the 14th Annual IEEE International Conference on Engineering of Computer Based Systems (ECBS), pp. 371–380. IEEE Press, Tucson (2007)
9. Antoniol, G., Fiutem, R., Cristoforetti, L.: Design pattern recovery in object-oriented software. In: Proceedings of the 6th IEEE International Workshop on Program Understanding, pp. 153–160. IEEE Press, Ischia (1998)
10. Gueheneuc, Y., Sahraoui, H., Zaidi, F.: Fingerprinting design patterns. In: Proceedings of the 11th Working Conference on Reverse Engineering (WCRE), pp. 172–180. IEEE Press (2004)
11. Pande, A., Gupta, M., Tripathi, A.K.: A New Approach for Detecting Design Patterns by Graph Decomposition and Graph Isomorphism. In: Ranka, S., Banerjee, A., Biswas, K.K., Dua, S., Mishra, P., Moona, R., Poon, S.-H., Wang, C.-L. (eds.) IC3 2010. CCIS, vol. 95, pp. 108–119. Springer, Heidelberg (2010)
12. Qiu, M., Jiang, Q., Gao, A., Chen, E., Qiu, D., Chai, S.: Detecting Design Pattern Using Sub-graph Discovery. In: Nguyen, N.T., Le, M.T., Świątek, J. (eds.) ACIIDS 2010. LNCS, vol. 5990, pp. 350–359. Springer, Heidelberg (2010)
13. Arcelli, F., Masiero, S., Raibulet, C.: Elemental design patterns recognition in Java. In: Proceedings of 13th Annual International Workshop on Software Technology and Engineering Practice, pp. 196–205. IEEE Press, Budapest (2006)
14. Posnett, D., Bird, C., Devanbu, P.T.: THEX: Mining meta-patterns from java. In: 7th IEEE Working Conference on Mining Software Repositories, pp. 122–125. IEEE Press, Cape Town (2010)
15. Fontana, F.A., Maggioni, S., Raibulet, C.: Understanding the relevance of micro-structures for design patterns detection. Journal of Systems and Software 84, 2334–2347 (2011)
16. Fontana, F.A., Maggioni, S., Raibulet, C.: Design patterns: a survey on their micro-structures. Journal of Software Maintenance and Evolution 33(8), 1–25 (2011)

Patterns for Use Case Context and Content

Marinos Georgiades and Andreas Andreou

Cyprus University of Technology, Limassol, Cyprus
{marinos.georgiades,andreas.andreou}@cut.ac.cy

Abstract. Patterns are well-proven solutions to common problems. They can increase the quality of a model, reduce the time to identify and specify requirements, and diminish redundancies, inconsistencies and omissions. Use case modeling is a very popular way of describing requirements. However, very limited work is done on uniting the concepts of patterns and use cases. This paper presents an attempt to provide a thorough set of use case patterns for both the context and the content of a use case. Furthermore, to ensure well-formedness and accuracy, the patterns are written in EBNF and tested in ANTLR.

1 Introduction

Use case modeling is a friendly and attractive way of describing the requirements of a software system. One reason for their popularity is that a well-written use case is relatively easy to read, since it is written in natural language following a scenario style. However, easy-to-read does not also mean easy-to-write. "It can be terribly hard to write easy-to-read use cases, because use cases are stories, prose essays, and so bring along all the associated difficulties of story writing in general" (p.2) [1].

Experience from long-time work on use case modeling shows that several kinds of use cases occur repeatedly [1-3]. The reoccurring good solutions can represent use case patterns, while reoccurring mistakes can help in building use case patterns by avoiding such mistakes. Patterns increase the quality of a model, reduce the time to identify and specify a system's requirements, and diminish redundancies, inconsistencies and omissions. Furthermore, because each pattern uses a specific and limited vocabulary, it is expected that redundancies, omissions and inconsistencies will be eliminated from the resulting use case model.

Use cases and patterns are two extensively used and influential concepts in system development during the last 15 years [4, 5]. Although people would expect much work done on uniting these concepts and providing several collections of use case patterns popular and extensively used, the fact is that work on use case patterns is limited to what is presented in two books [1,2] and a very few research articles. Some of these endeavors focus on general good practice use case patterns, some others focus only on the content (actions) of a use case, and the rest of them point to some issues related to the context (organization) of use cases. What is missing is a thorough set of use case patterns both for the context and the content of a use case.

J. Favaro and M. Morisio (Eds.): ICSR 2013, LNCS 7925, pp. 267–282, 2013.
© Springer-Verlag Berlin Heidelberg 2013

We do not claim that our work is complete and unmistakable, but our endeavor aims to provide use case patterns with more meticulousness regarding the organization of use cases as well as the content of each use case. Our approach provides a comprehensive set of use case patterns which include specific types of use cases and their interconnections at the context level, and specific types and sequence of actions for each use case type, at the content level. The use case patterns focus on the functionality of a software or information system. Additionally, we examine the types of primary and secondary actors involved in these patterns. Furthermore, to ensure well-formedness and accuracy, the patterns are written in EBNF and tested in ANTLR. Section 2 summarizes related work, while section 3 describes the proposed approach. Section 4 gives a comparative evaluation example, and section 5 presents our conclusions and ideas for future work.

2   Related Work

Adolph et al. provide patterns with general good practices for writing good use cases, such as how to define a clear boundary of the system, to identify actors based on the services they are involved in, etc. [1]. Therefore, their work is not about actual use-cases themselves. Contrarily, Overgaard & Palmkvist, in [2], talk about the actual use cases, but do not provide thorough interrelations between different use case patterns; they also undervalue CRUD by considering it as a unified use case pattern with each of the CRUD functions to be one or two internal actions. And they also stop at the "outside of the oval", by not providing specific types and sequence of actions for each use case pattern. Both books [1, 2] present examples of content – use-case actions – but these are not content patterns per se, something which is also noted in [4].

Langlands [4] provides well-organized patterns focusing on the internal structure of a use case, however his work does not stand on the organizational level of use cases, which in turn influences the specification (internal part) of each use case. Biddle and Noble, in [3], provide four use case patterns, with a general description. They also present a general description of only two use case content patterns which are generally applied on use cases. Additionally, they provide patterns of inclusion, extension and generalization, but in the form of general good practices; they do not show how their four use case patterns could be interrelated. In [5], Issa and Alali provide a list of patterns without showing any interconnections between them, and without presenting their content patterns. Additionally, there are missing patterns related to creating domain objects or modifying the state of a domain object. Diaz et al, in [6], focus on the linguistic analysis of the use case content, by studying the structure and composition of sentences. They provide a good guide for writing good use case content at a more general level - not patterns of system functionality.

3   The Proposed Patterns

We propose nine use case patterns, namely (a) *Create information object (IO)*, (b) *Correct IO*, (c) *Modify IO state*, which leads to the more specialized patterns *Cancel*

IO, Archive IO, and *Complete IO,* (d) *Erase IO,* which can also be considered as a specialized type of state modification, (e) *Read IO,* (f) *Read IO intra-report | inter-report,* (g) *Read supporting information,* (h) *Notify,* and (i) *Authorize | login.*

The following sections will explain each use case pattern with respect to the involved use case types and their interconnections, at the external level (context), as well as the actions and sequence of actions, at the internal level (content). Due to space limitations, the main emphasis will be given to the primary use case patterns *Create, Correct, Modify State,* and *Read,* and within the paragraphs discussing these primary patterns, we will also discuss the rest of the patterns.

3.1   Form

The patterns are written based on similar forms or templates provided by [1] and [2]. Each begins with a statement describing a problem, followed by a picture of the solution, a discussion of how the solution addresses the problems, and an example of its use.

3.2   Information Object

Before discussing the patterns, we need to explain the notion of the information object which plays a central role to the development and application of the proposed use case patterns. An information object (IO) is a digital representation of a tangible or intangible entity—described by a set of attributes—which the users need to manage through creating, modifying, reading, and erasing its instances, and be notified by the messages each instance (IOi) can trigger[1]. We distinguish information objects into the following categories: business role (as animate entity, e.g., doctor), inanimate entity (e.g., car), procedure (e.g., translation), document (e.g., book), event (e.g., appointment), site (e.g., country, hospital), and state (e.g., disease). By making this distinction, we will be able to better organize the elements of an information system (IS) (e.g., people-actors, functions-use cases), their relationships, and the identification of the attributes of an IO, which have to be processed by the use cases of each use case pattern.

3.3   Use Case Pattern Create Information Object

Problem. A new domain entity needs to be created (for the first time) in the information system[2].

---

[1] An IO is conceived and processed at an abstraction level, while an IOi is conceived and processed at a factual level; instances of the same IO differ only in the values of their attributes.

[2] The *Problem* definition should be understandable to everyone, and that is why we use the term "domain entity" (instead of "Information object"), which is a widely-used term.

Picture - Solution.

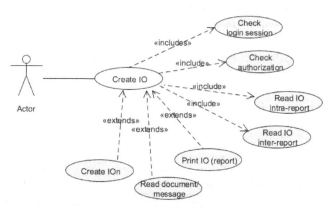

Fig. 1. UC pattern *Create IO*[3] - context level

Discussion. The use case pattern *Create IO* denotes that an information object instance's attributes are initiated for the first time, i.e. a new information object instance (IOi) is created. This occurs when the primary actor of the use case makes a request that initiates the creation of such an IOi. For example, the initiation of the use case *Create a vote* is triggered by the voter's request to vote; the initiation of the use case *Create a ticket* is triggered by the client's request to buy a ticket; the initiation of the use case *Create a client* is triggered by the client's request to register to the system; the initiation of the use case *Create prescription* is triggered by the patient's request to be examined. In each of these 'create' use cases, new instances of the information objects *vote, ticket, customer,* and *prescription* will be created and stored in the system. Subsequently, the other use case patterns (*correct prescription, cancel prescription,* etc.) will be applicable to the same IOi.

A common mistake of use case authors is the representation as a primary actor of the person/actor who inputs the data to create the new information, e.g. by considering as primary actor the actor that uses his/her keyboard to fill and submit a form, on his/her computer screen. Use case modeling main focus is on the requirement analysis level, that is, to help in gathering, organizing and specifying the requirements, without taking into account the implementation. For example, for the use case *Withdraw money*, if the primary actor will use the ATM or the cashier to take the money, the ATM or the cashier are merely the means to achieve the goal, not the primary actor. The primary actor, by definition, is the one who initiates the use case, and this role is most often called "requestor"; that is, the actor who requests the initiation of the use case so as to achieve the related goal. So, in both cases of the ATM example, the client is the requestor, viz. the person who initiates the withdrawal transaction. The ATM or the cashier are just the means for the client to achieve his/her goal. Hence, placing the cashier as the primary actor is flawed modeling because on the one hand

---

[3]   Use cases in yellow color are optional.

we enforce the implementation to include a cashier, and on the other hand we leave the customer outside the implementation (especially in the case that we will not consider it as secondary actor, either). In such a case of flawed use case modeling, if we wanted to have a cashier-free system, then we wouldn't be able to have it. We expand on Cockburn's concept on the role of requestor [7] and depict it as in figure 2, showing that different types of users act as "requestor". The position/specialty of the user that requests something may cause variation to the common functionality provided by the base use case. In the example below, a patient may initiate the use case *Cancel appointment* by requesting the cancellation of their appointment; however, cancellation could be requested by the doctor too – but not by the secretary who could just confirm or input into a form the information for the cancellation, being in this way a means to achieve the primary actor's goal. In the case where the cancellation by patient differs from the cancellation by doctor, then we can have use case inheritance as in figure 2b. Having said all these, the requestor for the primary actor is generally the role used for all the use case patterns. There could be other primary actor roles, such as the role of the specialist, however it is outside the scope of the present paper to expand on this matter.

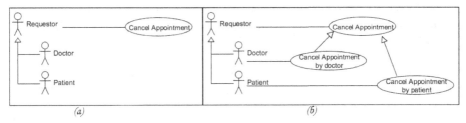

Fig. 2. (a) Different users can act as *requestor*; (b) Different requestors may cause variation in common functionality (use case inheritance)

Figure 1 shows the organization part of the *Create IO* pattern; to create an IOi, especially for systems with a higher level of security, a system needs to check if the user (s) involved is/are logged in the system and also authorized (have access rights) to perform the function provided by the particular use case. Therefore, the UC *Check login session* and the UC *Check authorization* should be included; they could also be defined as actions within the base use case, because they have small size. There are cases where users do not need to login, or the creation of information is performed by any user (authorized or not), therefore we denote this optionality with colour-filled, yellow use cases. *Check login session* and *Check authorization* could be also similarly applied for the other use case patterns. It's out of the scope of this paper to expand on this issue. We just note that a common mistake of use case authors is the use of "Login" as an included use case in another, basic use case; doing so means that every time a user needs to do something through the base use case, the user needs to re-login, which is a mistake in the majority of the cases. Such a behavior could stand for high security systems only. Also optionally included in *Create IO* are the use cases *Read report* or *Read document/message* about reading reports, documents or messages. This representation of optional inclusion means that the user will either always have to read a report or a document, in general, while creating an IO, or s/he will not at all. We repeat here that with optional use cases, we provide two mutually exclusive implementations – this is not like the case of an 'extending' use case which sometimes is executed and sometimes is not. More about the reading patterns is mentioned in the relevant subsequent section. Finally, a *Create* use case of another IO could extend the base use case. The full example of the *Create* pattern stresses this issue (figure 3).

Hitherto, we have shown the context of a *Create* use case pattern. Now, we will describe its content. The core of a *Create* use case is its main flow (i.e. the success scenario), followed by the alternative flow, both representing sequences of actions. Within the main flow, we also need to define the application of any "include", "extend" or "inherit" use cases, thus illustrating in a formal grammar the external relations of a *Create* use case. Specifically, the use case pattern descriptions are written in EBNF. Expressing the use case descriptions in EBNF allows us to formally prove key properties, such as well-formedness and closure, and hence, help validate the semantics. The proposed grammar has been developed with the Another Tool for Language Recognition (ANTLR) parser generator. ANTLR is a parser and translator generator tool that lets one define language grammars in EBNF like syntax. Due to space limitations we will show the most essential parts of the main flow only for the pattern UC *Create IO*.

Use case actions are of two types: (i) user actions which are performed by the users, and these are: choose, add, request, and confirm; (ii) system actions which are performed by the system, and these are: validate, save, prompt, notify, and calculate. Table 1 below shows the abstract syntax of the *Create* pattern.

Table 1. Abstract syntax of the Create pattern

mainFlow	
:	'Main Flow:' initialUA
	validateAuthorization?
	(presentCreateSA extended_by? Includes?)
	(enterChooseUA extended_by?)+
	submitUA
	checkSA
	saveSA
	(notifySA includes?)? ;

The parser rule *mainFlow* starts with an initial user action, that is, a request to create a new information object (table 2). Table 3 depicts a concrete syntax validated in ANTLR. Due to space limitations, not every parser rule will be explained (e.g. it's apparent that the *usecaseName* rule refers to the name of the use case, and in the case of the *Create* pattern, it starts with the verb *Create*).

Table 2. Abstract syntax of the initial parser rule of the *UC Create* main flow

initialUA :   'UA' *INTEGER* '.' primaryActor 'requests to' usecaseName '.';

Table 3. A concrete syntax of the initial parser rule of the *UC Create* main flow

UA 1. A doctor requests to create a prescription.

The parser rule *validateAuthorization* (in table 1) refers to a system action that will check if the actor is logged in and authorized to create this information object. In EBNF, the question mark symbol denotes optional behavior that may happen only once. Subsequently, the parser rule *presentCreateSA* involves another system action, that is, the system will prompt the user, with a form, to complete it and thus create an instance of the IO. The abstract syntax of this rule is depicted in table 4, while a concrete syntax is presented in table 5.

Table 4. Abstract syntax of the parser rule for prompting a user to fill a form and create an Ioi

presentCreateSA :	'SA' *INTEGER* '.' 'The system prompts' primaryActor 'to enter or choose the required and optional fields of the' io '.' ;

Table 5. Concrete syntax of the parser rule for presenting a form to create an Ioi

SA 2. The system prompts a doctor to enter or choose the required and optional fields of the prescription.

The parser rule *extended_by* (in tables 1 & 6) denotes that the *Create IO* use case can be extended by another use case. In such a case, the phrase "Extension point:" must be written on the right of the action that triggers the extension, followed by the ID and name of the extending use case. If an "include" use case needs to be invoked, then the relevant syntax in table 6 should be followed.

Table 6. Abstract syntax of the parser rules for invoking an extending or an included use case

extended_by :	'[' 'Extension point.' useCase ']';
includes :	'[' 'via' useCase ']' ;

Following, the parser rule *enterChooseUA* (in table 7) refers to the user's action of inputting data to the form for the creation of the IOi. Data should be entered or chosen (table 8). *enterChooseUA* is followed by the rule *extended?* in table 1, which denotes that entering or choosing data could be extended by another use case providing supporting information (reports, documents, etc.); such a supporting use case could trigger the involvement of a secondary actor. For example, for the UC *Create Prescription*, for the action *Choose medicine,* the doctor might need guidance by a medical guide or a medical counselor (see the example in figure 3).

Table 7. Abstract syntax of the parser rule for entering or choosing form data

enterChooseUA	
:	'UA' *INTEGER* '.' primaryActor userAction ioAttribute '.' (secondaryActor ('provides' | 'verifies') 'this information' '.')?
|	'iterate' enterChooseUA+ 'end iterate' ;

Table 8. Abstract syntax of the two methods of inputting data

userAction : *ENTER_DATA* | *CHOOSE_DATA*   ; //where *ENTER_DATA* : 'enter' | 'enters'; *CHOOSE_DATA* : 'choose' | 'chooses';

ioAttribute determines the value added into the form for an attribute of the IOi. If there are more than one attribute values to be added, then an iteration of this addition will take place as depicted in table 7 and in the example of table 11. The *submitUA* user action parser rule, which follows, denotes that the user submits the form, while the next rule *validateSA* defines a system action denoting that the system checks the values of the attributes, and if everything is correct, it saves the new information object through the parser rule *SaveSA* (tables 1, 9 and 11).

Table 9. Abstract syntax of the parser rules for submitting, validating and saving the form data

submitUA :	'UA' *INTEGER* '.' primaryActor 'submits the form of the' io '.' ;
validateSA :	'SA' *INTEGER* '.' 'The' 'System validates the attributes of the submitted form. ;
saveSA :	'SA' *INTEGER* '.' 'The System saves the form' '.' ;

Finally, the system, through the parser rule *notifySA* (table 10 and 1) notifies the primary actor and any interested secondary actors about the creation of the information object (between *validates* and *saveSA*, a confirmation action could take place).

Table 10. Abstract syntax of the par. rule for notifying other actors about the creation of the IO

notifySA :	'SA' *INTEGER* '.' 'The System' notify io 'to the following' actors '.';

Example. Figure 3 shows an example of the UC *Create Prescription*. As mentioned earlier in this section the UC *Create prescription* includes two use cases for checking if the user is logged-in and also authorized, and two "include" *Read inter-report* use cases, viz. one use case to read the examination details of the patient and one use case to read his/her treatment details. These need to be always executed in order for the *Create prescription* to be completed. There are also three "extend" relationships, implemented with one use case for printing the prescription, once it is created, one use case to read a councellor's message (opinion), which is invoked when the doctor needs some supporting information about a medicine, and the UC *Create examination*. Someone may assume that the latter is an "include" use case taking into account that for a prescription to be created an examination needs to be created first. However, there are cases where the doctor does not need to examine the patient in order to prescribe a new medicine.

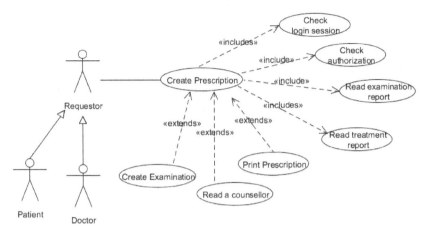

Fig. 3. UC *Create Prescription*: An example of the *Create* pattern at the external level

Table 11 shows a portion of the concrete syntax of the UC *Create Prescription*, validated in ANTLR.

Table 11. Concrete syntax of the UC *Create prescription*

UA 1. A doctor **requests to create** a prescription.
SA 2. **The system prompts** a doctor to **enter or choose the required and option al fields of** a prescription. [Extension point. **UC 12 read** Examination report]
UA 3. A doctor **enters** patientID **of** a prescription. A patient **verifies this infor mation.**
UA 4. A doctor **chooses** patientName **of** a prescription.
iterate
UA 5. A doctor **chooses** medicine **of** a prescription. [Extension point. **UC 22 read** a counselor /*message/*]
UA 6. A doctor **chooses** pharmacy **of** a prescription. [Extension point. **UC 23 read** pharmacy /*document/list*/]
end iterate
UA 7. A doctor **submits the form of** a prescription.
SA 8. **The System checks the attributes of the submitted form.**
SA 9. **The System saves the form.**
SA 10. **The System sends Notification about the creation of** a prescription to **the** following **Actors**: a doctor, a patient, a pharmacy. [**via UC 15 send Notifi cation of** a prescription]

3.4   Use Case Patterns Correct IO and Modify IO State

Problem
(i)	Some information of a domain entity needs to be corrected.
(ii)	The change of some information of a domain entity causes change in the functionality of the system.

Picture - Solution

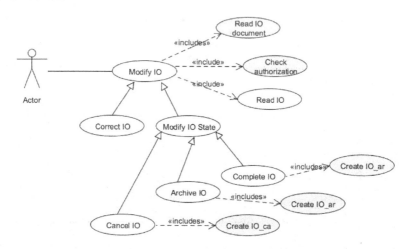

Fig. 4. UC pattern *Modify IO* decomposed to two patterns: *Correct IO*, *Modify IO state*

Discussion

The everyday activity of an information system causes information to change. This change may refer to simple correction of the attribute values of an IOi or it may be more complicated referring to modification of its state. In particular, correction of an IOi means that the IOi will retain the same state (postcondition) as the one before the correction. For example, for the UC *Correct Prescription*, changing the attribute value of *Medicine.dosage* from *2mg per day* to *3mg per day* will keep an IOi Prescription in *Pending state* and will not lead to the creation of new pre- or post- conditions (*Pending* is the state assigned to the IOi *Prescription* during its creation by the UC *Create Prescription*).

On the contrary, changing the attribute value of *Medicine.Provided* from *No* to *Yes* will put an IOi *Prescription* in the *Complete* state which corresponds to a new post-condition, that is, "Prescription is complete". Completing a prescription derives the precondition "Drug is handed to patient" compared to the UC *Correct Prescription* which has the precondition "Prescription is created". Additionally, this modification process is executed by another actor, that is, the pharmacy (or pharmacist), at a different place (pharmacy) contrary to the creation or correction of a prescription, which are executed by the doctor, at the clinic or hospital. Some frequent patterns of state modification use cases are the *Cancel IO, Archive IO*, and *Complete IO. Cancel IO* and *Archive IO* are usually initiated by a human actor (could be done automatically too, though) while *Archive IO* is usually initiated by a computerized actor (the system automatically archives an IOi based on a predetermined schedule). We may also conceive *Erase IO*, as a state modification use case, where its new postcondition might be "IOi is removed completely from the system's database". It is interesting to mention the importance of examining what the presuppositions or results are from the modification of a state; usually these presuppositions or results lead to the use of a new information object and a series of new use cases. Figure 7, of our detailed example, depicts this point followed by a relevant explanation.

Example. Figure 7 illustrates the decomposition of *Modify booking*, while the corresponding section explains how modification state use cases lead to the generation of new use cases.

3.5   Pattern *Read*: *IO*; *IO Report*; *Supporting info* (**Document, Message, etc.**)

Problem.

(i)   GUI forms need to be read when a user creates a new entity or changes the state of an existing one, in the IS.

(ii)   Reports need to be read about one or a combination of entities.

(iii)   Documents or messages need to be read to support a function.

Picture - Solution

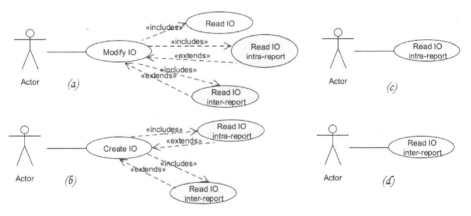

Fig. 5. UC pattern *Read* decomposed to 3 UC patterns: *Read IO, Read IO report (intra\inter)*, *Read supporting info* (the latter is not presented due to space limitations)

Discussion

GUI forms usually need to be read when a user creates a new IOi or changes the state of an existing IOi. The reading process should be represented as the included use case *Read IO* for the UC *Modify IO* (for both correction and state modification patterns), because it is composed of several actions, such as retrieving data from the database, checking, and presenting the existing attributes and values of an IOi. This behavior is depicted in figure 5a where the UC *Read IO* is included in the use case *Modify IO*. On the contrary, the reading procedure for the UC *Create IO* only concerns building a form of required and optional (empty) fields, and is thus represented as one or more simple action(s) in the *Create IO* use case specification. That's why it is not represented in figure 5b.

Apart from reading forms, reading reports is another type of the reading process, which leads to the establishment of relevant use cases. A read pattern use case receives search criteria usually from an actor, and uses the criteria to identify the correct information in the system. We distinguish two types of reports, those are, the intra-reports which are related directly to the IO under study, and the inter-reports which contain information about other IOs, and which are useful for the creation or modification of the IO under study. Examples of an intra-report are a report about appointments completed over a specific period (UC *Read January appointments* – figure 6a) or a report about the information of the current booked flight (UC *Read booking* – figure 7). An example of a use case with an inter-report is the use case *Read patient (record)* that may be implemented as an included or an extending use case of the use case *Create prescription* (figure 6b – latter implementation option). Figure 6b also illustrates through examples the two other Read patterns, i.e. *Read document* and *Read message*. The former is related to the reading of a document such as a guide, an essay, and generally any document that would be helpful for the implementation of the base use case. Similarly, the pattern *Read a message* refers to any supporting message to the implementation of the base use case; such a message could be textual, vocal or optical. Supporting use cases could usually involve supporting (secondary) actors, such as in the example of figure 6b.

For clarity, the figures do not include any authorization/login use cases or any use cases about printing information (e.g. the UC *Print IO* could extend the *UC Read IO intra-report*). We also need to note that the double relationships between use cases on reading reports and use cases on modifying or creating instances of IOs are optional, and also either an *extend* or an *include* relationship can take place, from each pair.

Example

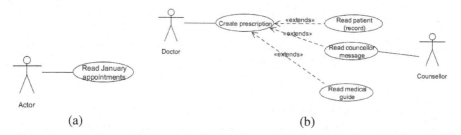

Fig. 6. Figure 6a and 6b depict use cases with an intra-report and inter-reports, respectively

4   Comparative Evaluation with a Best and a Real Case Example

In [1], the authors state that "it is usually easier to describe the individual routine transactions that a system may provide than it is to discover what the user really wants to do with the system. Doing it the easy way often leads to 'CRUD' (Create, Read, Update, and Delete) style use cases. It is not unusual to see use cases with names like Create Employee Record, Read Employee Record, or Delete Employee Record. While such use cases may be technically correct, they do not capture what is valuable to the user. Is creating an employee record important, or does the user really want to Hire Employee?" (p. 12). Firstly, we admit that using CRUD-style use cases may not always give the "perfect" verb to the name of the use case. For example, it's more valuable to the user to see *Register Customer* than *Create Customer*. We consider this an issue that can be easily tackled with the use of synonymous phrases to transform the CRUDdy verbs into more convenient ones. However, we believe that the expanded and in-depth CRUD-style set of use case patterns provided by our approach could promote completeness and correctness in terms of identifying, organizing and specifying use cases, since they correspond to a comprehensive list of functions that apply on electronic information, and additionally the use of a specific terminology could avoid problems of redundant or incorrect information.

We provide below two comparative examples, one at the external level and another one at the internal level, showing how the proposed approach could perform.

4.1   External Level Comparative Example

For airline reservations, the authors in [1] give the following indicative list of use cases: *Book Trip, Change Booking, Cancel Booking, Search for Flights, Promote Vacations.*

Based on our approach, we firstly identify the information objects and then apply the proposed use case patterns. The information objects are *booking, flight, trip, promotion* and *vacation* (because we need to store and process all these entities through time). For *booking*, we could have the use cases C*reate booking, Correct booking, Cancel booking, Archive booking, Complete booking, Read booking, Register client* (from its synonymous use case *Create client*) *Read flights*, and *Check login session*. It is interesting to mention the importance of examining what the presuppositions or results are from the modification of a state; usually these presuppositions or results lead to the use of a new information object and a series of new use cases. For example, cancelling of a booking, which denotes a modification of the state of booking, from pending to cancelled, presupposes a refund of money; therefore, we introduce the use case *Create Refund* included in the use case *Cancel booking*. Similarly, completing a booking presupposes issuing of a boarding pass (common policy of many airline companies). Figure 7 below shows the relevant use case diagram. Accordingly, we could have the use cases for each of the other identified information objects (*flight, trip*, etc.). It is apparent that based on the information objects and the proposed use case patterns, we can create a solid and reliable use case model of an information system.

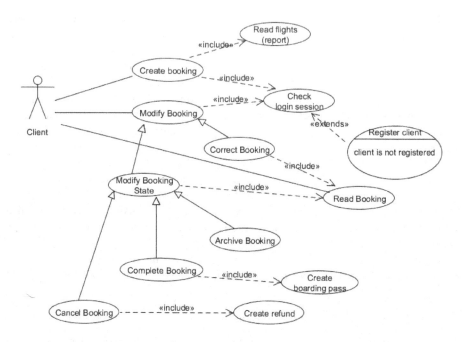

Fig. 7. The use case model derived from the IO booking and the proposed UC patterns[4,5]

4.2   Internal Level Comparative Example

The following is the main flow of the use case *Generate Prescription*, and it is taken from a real case [8]. We will compare it to the main flow of the UC *Create Prescription* defined by our approach, as depicted earlier in table 11 and also copied here below.

Actor action	System action
1. The nurse practitioner clicks "New prescription" button.	2. The system displays a form to fill out e-prescription information.
3. The nurse practitioner enters the e-prescription information (medication name, patient name, and a pharmacy location for patient).	4. The system displays the list of participating pharmacies.
5. The nurse practitioner selects one pharmacy from the list based on the patient's will.	6. The system displays message "The prescription was sent successfully".

Fig. 8. The basic flow of the use case *Generate prescription* taken from [8]

---

[4] For clarity reasons, the figure does not depict the extending use cases *Print booking* (extends *Create booking*), *Print flights* (extends *Read flights*), *Print boarding pass* (extends *Create boarding pass*).

[5] For some information objects, according to the context of the problem, the modification pattern may not be applicable. For example, in a voting system, due to specific policies, nobody can modify a vote after its creation.

Table 12. Concrete syntax of UC *Create prescription* validated in *ANTLR*

UA 1. A doctor **requests to create** a prescription.
SA 2. **The system prompts** a doctor to **enter or choose the required and optional fields**
    of a prescription. [Extension point. **UC 12 read** Examination report]
UA 3. A doctor **enters** patientID of a prescription. A patient **verifies this information.**
UA 4. A doctor **chooses** patientName of a prescription.
                          iterate
UA 5. A doctor **chooses** medicine of a prescription. [Extension point: **UC 22 read a**   coun
    sellor /*message*/]
UA 6. A doctor **chooses** pharmacy of a prescription. [Extension point: **UC 23 read** phar
    macy /*document/list*/]
                          end iterate
UA 7. A doctor **submits the form of** a prescription.
SA 8. **The System checks the attributes of the submitted form.**
SA 9. **The System saves the form.**
SA 10. **The System sends Notification about the creation of** a prescription to **the** follow
    ing **Actors:** a doctor, a patient, a pharmacy. [**via UC 15 send Notification of** a pre
    scription]

The first comment concerns action 1 where we avoid to define the means (interface objects) with which the actions will be performed, because this is usually done during design (e.g., the user may want to add information vocally, not by pressing a button).

Action 2 is similar in both descriptions in terms of the display of a form for the actor to complete it. However, our approach defines the actor (doctor) who is responsible (has the access rights) to complete the form, as well as the extending use case *Read Examination report.*

Action 3 is similar in both cases to some degree, with the difference that in our approach the secondary actor (patient) is asked from the primary actor (doctor) to verify the information added to the form.

The rest of the actions cover almost the same functionality, however it is apparent that our approach is much more precise and comprehensive. For example, through the 'iterate' tag, we know that the user is able to choose more than one medicines or pharmacies. Additionally, the concept of supporting use cases derives relevant use cases and supporting actors, as defined with the extending use cases in steps 5 and 6 of the use case specification example of table 12.

5   Conclusion

This paper presented a set of use case patterns for both the context and the content of a use case. The proposed patterns focus on the functionality of a software or an information system, and are related with creating information objects, correcting them, modifying their state by cancelling, archiving or completing them, reading intra- and inter- reports or supporting documents and messages related to information objects, just to mention the most significant of the proposed use case patterns. In each of these patterns, a number of use case types are involved and interrelated through *include, extend* and *inheritance* relationships. Furthermore, each pattern consists of a specific set and sequence of actions, such as *request, prompt, add, delete, choose, calculate, submit, validate, save, confirm,* and *notify.* The patterns were written in EBNF and tested in ANTLR. Expressing the use case descriptions in EBNF allowed us to formally prove key properties, such as well-formedness and closure, and hence, helped validate the semantics.

We will continue our work on the improvement of the patterns discussed in this paper, and also investigate other possible use case patterns. Their correctness and completion will be enhanced by a comprehensive testing of our proposition, which is currently being undertaken against real-world projects.

References

1. Adolph, S., Bramble, P., Cockburn, A., Pols, A.: Patterns for Effective Use Cases. Addison-Wesley (2003) ISBN: 0-201-72184-8
2. Overgaard, G., Palmkvist, K.: Use Cases: Patterns and Blueprints. Addison-Wesley (2004) ISBN 0-131-45134-0
3. Biddle, R., Noble, J., Tempero, E.: Patterns for essential use cases. In: Proceedings of Australasian Pattern Languages of Programming, KoalaPLoP (2001)
4. Langlands, M.: Inside the oval: use case content patterns (2010)
5. Issa, A., AlAli, A.: Automated Requirements Engineering: Use Case Patterns Driven Approach. IET-Software, IET 5(3), 287–303 (2011)
6. Diaz, I., Losavio, F., Matteo, A.L., Pastor, O.: Specification pattern for use cases. Information & Management 41(8), 961–975 (2008)
7. Cockburn, A.: Writing Effective Use Cases. Addison Wesley (2001) ISBN 0-201-70225-8
8. Nalluru, S., Shetty, A., Wei, F.: SRS for Health record system at Drexel convenient care center (2010), http://www.pages.drexel.edu/fw48/eport/documents/INFO627Project.pdf

A Common Representation for Reuse Assistants

Fábio P. Basso, Cláudia Maria Lima Werner, Raquel Mainardi Pillat,
and Toacy Cavalcante Oliveira

COPPE – PESC - Universidade Federal do Rio de Janeiro (UFRJ), Rio de Janeiro, Brasil
{fabiopbasso,werner,rmpillat,toacy}@cos.ufrj.br

Abstract. Software reuse practices and tools have been proposed over the last decades. From the reuser's perspective, it is necessary to provide facilitators in order to execute reuse tasks among tools. Accordingly, we propose the use of a common representation for Reuse Assistants (RA), which are computer executable reuse tasks specified in a model. This model is extensible since it extends Reusable Asset Specification metamodel, an OMG standard to define software assets such as artifacts and documents with structured information for reuse such as activities and guidelines. Besides, the metamodel is specified in Eclipse Modeling Framework (EMF), a widely used environment for metamodeling. The proposed extensions allow one to provide information to guide reusers through the execution of reuse tasks among tools, with structured information that can be used to generate deployment descriptors and scripts mapped for task execution languages. Thus, this paper presents this proposal by exemplifying developer's tasks that can be assisted by RAs.

Keywords: Reusable Asset Specification – RAS, Software reuse, Reuse assistant, Reuse facilitator.

1 Introduction

This work proposes a common representation for reuse tasks, called Reuse Assistants (RAs). RAs correspond to any kind of computer executable task that promotes reuse of some set of assets, such as programming APIs or software domain designs. Since a reuse process orchestrates the execution of reuse tasks inside a reuse tool [10], our challenge is to provide a common representation for tasks to allow tools chain [6], when users must use more than one tool in sequence to execute a complete reuse task.

Integrated Development Environments (IDEs) such as Eclipse[1] allow the specification of some sort of reuse assistants (i.e., wizards) as compiled plug-ins. Wizards are codified in Java and guide a reuser through a predefined sequence of tasks. Despite providing a framework that facilitates the development of plug-ins, once compiled, such wizards cannot be modified. Accordingly, we tested wizards as ANT[2] tasks [1], a task execution language, allowing chaining tools outside IDEs. However, these languages have limitations in regards to user interaction and are used to execute automated tasks related to application builder. Other proposals to support reuse

---

[1] Eclipse IDE. Av. at <http://www.eclipse.org>. At 15/12/2012.
[2] Project Apache ANT. Av. at <http:// ant.apache.org/>. At 15/12/2012.

J. Favaro and M. Morisio (Eds.): ICSR 2013, LNCS 7925, pp. 283–288, 2013.
© Springer-Verlag Berlin Heidelberg 2013

processes allow more interactivity features with users, with alternate flows, questions and loop also allowing processes execution [10]. On the other hand, they lack to provide detailed information about the artifacts that are changed by tasks, as well as guidance information about reuse activities that are common in wizards. In contrast, the Reusable Asset Specification (RAS) [9] allows detailing reuse assets with documentation, guidelines and context, but lacks to support execution. Therefore, these works lack to support a package to thoroughly assist reuse that is composed by: a) documentation; b) execution; c) specification; and d) modification and customization.

In this sense, this paper presents a proposal to specify RAs with an EMF[3] based metamodel. We have extended RAS to represent reuse assistants because it supports software reuse activities with descriptions and guidelines, helping reusers in performing tasks independently from a tool support. Accordingly, by combining our RAS extension with reuse processes in a common EMF representation, one can chain executions with a task execution tool such as ReuseTool [10], by previously validating and binding IO parameters used among tools. Thus, to illustrate the applicability of our proposal, we exemplify a RAs model that helps developers in programming activities related to Java libraries API reuse.

Next sections are organized as follows. Section 2 provides an illustrative example of RAs using our proposal. Section 3 presents an extension of the RAS metamodel to support reuse assistants. Section 4 discusses the related works and Section 5 presents our conclusion remarks.

2   Illustrative Example

A reuse assistant organizes a set of tasks that can be executed by reusers with the help of some provided documentation. Assistants are enacted by programs specifically developed to support the reuse of some particular set of artifacts and require strong formalization to hold on the bindings and validations between task's IO parameters, as shown in Figure 1 (A). This example of RA tasks highlights the following reuse scenario: assume that a software developer, using Java language, aims to reuse an artifact "*A1*", where *A1* is the *JExcel Java Library (a jxsl.jar library file)*. This library provides functionalities that enable developers to import Excel spreadsheets data by mapping them to domain classes' properties. To assist the developer´s activities, many tools can be used. We exemplified two tools in Figure 1 (A): 1) A tool to apply reverse engineering from domain classes' source-code to a UML model [3]. Thus, using the domain classes, one generates a table structure analogous to Excel spreadsheets. 2) A tool to generate source-code that contains logic to import Excel spreadsheets into classes' properties [2].

The first challenge to help developers is to provide documentation about how to use JExcel library (Artifact A1). Accordingly, RAS is used to define activities that developers must execute and it is also helpful to define dependencies from other Java libraries. Since the metamodel is designed in EMF to support RAS metaclasses, we have generated an Eclipse plug-in to support the design of reusable assets as shown in Figure 1 (B). The configured *Asset 1* supports guidelines to reuse a specific API named *jxsl.jar*. Note that many artifacts compose assets: the selected one is named

---

[3] Eclipse EMF. Av. at < http://www.eclipse.org/modeling/emf/>.
  At 15/12/2012

JExcel – jxsl.jar. This example shows all information required by programmers to know how to develop JExcel source-code provided by the information bellow the "Usage" element. Besides, it is possible to classify and contextualize artifact *A1* as well as specify dependencies between artifacts. Moreover, the activities below the "Artifact Activity" element provide guidelines for those tasks shown in Figure 1 (A). However, despite providing a rich set of metaclasses used to detail reuse activities, the standard RAS profile lacks structures to specify computer executable tasks related to the guidelines. Thus, we have extended RAS with new structures for execution.

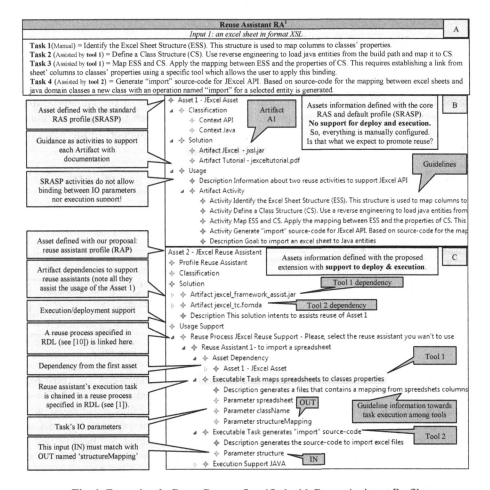

Fig. 1. Example of a Reuse Process Specified with Reuse Assistant Profile

In order to facilitate the reuse of *A1*, one could develop one assistant by implementing a model transformer that takes as input a UML model (a class), uses "Tool 1" and "Tool 2" and generates source-code mapped to Java JExcel, as shown in Figure 1 (C). It allows detailing those RAs exemplified in Figure 1 (A). Accordingly, we have used the proposed RAS extension to specify *Asset 2* shown in

Figure 1 (C). *Asset 2* provides reuse support for *Asset 1 - JExcel API,* using Asset Dependency information in each Reuse Assistant element. The Reuse Process element groups the two assistants exemplified in Figure 1 (A) and it is actually linked to a program named ReuseTool, specified with Reuse Description Language (RDL) [10]. Accordingly, *Reuse Assistant 1* element contains two executable tasks: 1) task *maps spreadsheets to classes' properties* is intended to assist the execution of activities 1, 2 and 3, depicted in Figure 1 (A); 2) the second executable task is mapped to *"Generate import source-code for JExcel API".* The remainder of this example supporting deployment and execution of these tasks is available in [1].

3   The Proposed RAS Extension

Reusable asset deployment requires information about execution. Thus, the following information should be provided: a) the programming language used to develop the executable task; b) class loader information such as the name of the class/program that owns the main operation (the program method used to start the task execution). Since existing RAS solutions shown in Figure 1 (A) have no support to this level of detail, we provide the *ExecutionSupport* metaclass (Figure 2).

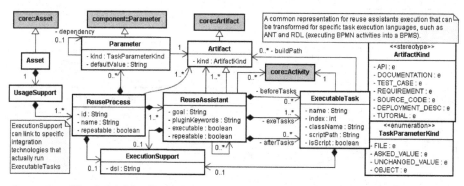

Fig. 2. RAS Profile Extension to Support Reuse Assistant Execution

With *ReuseProcess, ReuseAssistant* and *ExecutableTask* metaclasses, it is possible to specify how the tasks shown in Figure 1 (C) can be deployed and executed. These metaclasses aim to orchestrate tools chaining that actually executes reuse assistant's tasks. The RAS *core* metaclass named *Context* can be used to express keywords to link to specific tasks execution languages, such as ANT. However, we believe that a specific metaclass provides more adequate information as *ExecutableTask* and *ExecutionSupport.* With this information, a RAS client deployer for an Eclipse ecosystem can chain appropriate tools.

The input and output parameters must be formalized to validate if the chaining among tasks is possible [8]. The RAS *"ActivityParameter"* and *"Parameter"* metaclasses can be used to handle such information. However, such classes do not provide properties that allow a validation between parameters (parameter matching). To allow this, parameters must express a classification for their possible values (e.g., a native object, a file url, a prompted value) using the RAS *component's Parameter* metaclass. Thus, this kind of matching is based on parameter data types.

However, parameters matching must consider also the context of each task to validate a composition. In this sense, each metaclass we have modeled in EMF extends the *Element* class from a UML metamodel[4]. By enhancing UML, it is possible to specify annotations (Stereotypes and Tags) in each RA model element, e.g., to constraint IO parameters, as shown in Figure 1(C) through OUT and IN comments. Accordingly, constraints can be expressed as: **OUT)** *XMIVersion={1.2}*; **IN)** *ReqXMIVersion{1.1,1.3,2.1}*. In this example, these parameters do not match because the IN parameter does not support XMI version 1.2. Besides, by enhancing RAS, it is possible to constraint each task with a context (e.g., model-based tasks).

The activity type is also important, as shown in Figure 3. The task can be manually executed or supported by a tool. In this case, it is important to generate deployment descriptors, such as those of POM.xml used by Maven tool[5], as we did in [1] by configuring an Eclipse ecosystem to support the execution of automated and assisted tasks. Thus, with a common representation for deployment, we designed the metaclasses shown in Figure 3 as *DownloadInfo*, *DeployInfo*, *Repository* and *Path*.

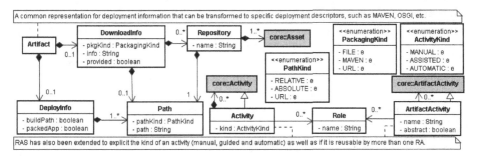

Fig. 3. RAS Profile Extension to Support Reuse Assistant Deployment

4   Related Work

RAS related works exemplify scenarios where assets are only documented. It is the case for Elgedawy et al. [5] who propose a RAS extension to describe Service Oriented Architecture (SOA) components. These components are interoperable by definition and do not relate to our proposal since different information is required other than those for chain reuse tools [4], which mostly are not interoperable and are manually adapted [7]. In this direction, this paper presented some RAS extensions allowing the representation of a chain among two reuse tools with guidelines in assistance. These specifications are EMF based and are transformed to specific tasks execution languages, such as ANT. Finally, they are managed by existing systems as Mylyn and MAVEN inside an Eclipse IDE ecosystem (see [1] for a complete study).

Biehl et al. proposed TIL, a domain specific language to specify integration among tools [4], and Polgár et al. proposed a framework to chain executions by interoperating tools as process activities [8]. Despite being interesting proposals, they lack in detailing software assets interchanged among chained tools, not allowing to

---

[4] Reduced UML Metamodel –
http://prisma.cos.ufrj.br/wct/projects/index.html
[5] Apache Maven - Av. at <http://maven.apache.org/> At 15/03/2013.

validate the binding between IO parameters such as different XMI versions [6]. Besides, the deployment of chained tools into execution environments is manually specified. On the other hand, RAS supports rich details, as context, classification, reuse activities, and artifact kinds, but it does not support details to chain tools. Thus, as a complementary contribution, we have extended RAS to solve some shortcomings: a) the traceability among IO parameters, allowing context validation; b) the source-code generation for ANT and RDL tasks (reuse processes); c) the generation of deployment descriptors in MAVEN; d) the automatic configuration of an Eclipse ecosystem.

5   Conclusion Remarks

Our work presented an overview of a RAS-based approach and an extension to support a common representation for Reuse Assistants. It includes a set of metaclass extensions allowing one to deploy reuse assistants as executable tasks to promote artifact reuse from the developer's point of view. We agree that reusable assets, e.g., reuse practices documentation, reuse assistants and software artifacts, exist in many reuse techniques. Accordingly, our proposal is to aggregate these techniques as reuse assistants in a chained execution. Thus, we presented an EMF based tool support for Reusable Asset Specification (RAS) to detail reuse assistants.

Acknowledgments. This work was partially supported by the Brazilian agencies CAPES and CNPq.

References

[1]   Basso, F.P., et al.: A Common Representation for Reuse Assistants - Applicability and Examples (February 06, 2013),
        http://www.adapit.com.br/files/irawp01.pdf
[2]   Basso, F.P., et al.: Using the FOMDA Approach to Support Object-Oriented Real-Time Systems Development. In: ISORC, pp. 374–381 (2006)
[3]   Basso, F.P., et al.: Towards a Web Modeling Environment for a Model Driven Engineering Approach. In: III BW-MDD, Natal – RN, Brazil (2012)
[4]   Biehl, M., et al.: Domain Specific Language for Generating Tool Integration Solutions. In: 4th Workshop on Model-Driven Tool & Process Integration, MDTPI (2011)
[5]   Elgedawy, I., et al.: Reusable SOA Assets Identication Using E-Business Patterns. In: World Conference on Services - II, pp. 33–40 (2009)
[6]   Kern, H., et al.: Integration of Microsoft Visio and Eclipse Modeling Framework Using M3-Level-Based Bridges. In: 2nd MDTPI, pp. 13–24 (2009)
[7]   Könemann, P., et al.: Difference-based Model Synchronization in an Industrial MDD Process. In: 2nd MDTPI, pp. 1–12 (2009)
[8]   Polgár, B., et al.: Model-based Integration, Execution and Certification of Development Tool-chains. In: 2nd MDTPI, pp. 35–46 (2009)
[9]   Reusable Asset Specification (September 2012),
        http://www.omg.org/spec/RAS/
[10]   Oliveira, T.C., et al.: ReuseTool - An extensible tool support for object-oriented framework reuse. Journal of Systems and Software 84(12), 2234–2252 (2011)

A Knowware Based Infrastructure
for Rule Based Control Systems in Smart Spaces

Yangyang Lu[1,2], Ge Li[1,2,*], Zhi Jin[1,2], Xueyuan Xing[1,2], and Yiyang Hao[1,2]

[1] Software Institute, School of Electronic Engineering and Computer Science,
Peking University, Beijing 100871, P.R. China
[2] Key Laboratory of High Confidence Software Technologies, Ministry of Education,
Beijing 100871, China
{luyy11,lige,zhijin,xingxy11,haoyy12}@sei.pku.edu.cn

Abstract. Many software systems are designed for realising some business logics which can be captured and represented as a set of logic rules, such as the logic rules for controlling devices in smart spaces. These logic rules in traditional software systems are usually coded in procedural style and interweaved with other elements of software such as the interface implementation etc. As we know, the logic rules are usually needed to be changed or updated frequently according to changing environment conditions and software requirements. However, mix of the logic rules and other elements makes it difficult to change and update the logic rules. Therefore, we propose a new infrastructure to separate the logic rules from the interweaved elements. In our infrastructure, the logic rules can be encapsulated as a knowware. The knowware is deployed in a reasoner as an independent component, which can interact with other parts of the system. By this way, the logic rules can be easily changed or updated as an independent component of the software system according to changing environment conditions and software requirements.

1 Introduction

Many software systems are designed for realising some business logics which can be captured and represented as a set of logic rules, such as the logic rules for controlling devices in smart spaces (e.g. smart house, smart building, and smart cities[1]). Nowadays, implementation of these logic rules are always interweaved with other elements in the final software systems. For example, according to traditional object-oriented methodologies, the logic rules would be implemented as logic program codes interspersed among different methods in different classes. Thus, the logic rules are interweaved with other elements, such as elements of processing on interaction, database, networking connecting, multi-threads, services, and so on.

As we know, logic rules are usually needed to be changed and updated according to changing environment conditions and software requirements. However,

---

* Corresponding author.
[1] http://www.icta.ufl.edu/gt.htm

J. Favaro and M. Morisio (Eds.): ICSR 2013, LNCS 7925, pp. 289–294, 2013.

according to the traditional software implementing method, the logic rules are usually coded in procedural style and interweaved with other elements of software. Mix of the logic rules and other elements makes it difficult to locate these logic rules in the software system, and makes it difficult to change and update some logic rules when necessary. Also, these logic rules cannot be reused easily as an independent part by different applications. If the logic rules could be represented as an independent set of rules in some rule languages (e.g. SWRL [9]), they would be easier changed or updated by system maintainers. Furthermore, as an independent component, it would be easier to reuse the logic rules in the software system.

At present, some researchers explore multi-paradigm programming to separate the logic rules from other elements in software systems [5]. For example, they propose to integrate Prolog and Java [2,12,3,1]. They express the logic rules in logic programming language (Prolog), and program other elements of the system in object programming language (Java). However, in their final programs, the codes of the logic rules still interweave with the programs of other elements. The problem of locating and reusing the logic rules has not been resolved.

Also, some researchers in aspect-oriented software development propose to explicit rules in software applications [7,4,6]. They take rules (especially business rules) as cross-cutting concerns, which represent the common behaviors of multiple classes [8]. The cross-cutting concerns are encapsulated as an aspect. However, the logic rules that we focus on cannot be treated as cross-cutting concerns, as they do not represent the common behaviors of multiple classes. Actually, they represents what requirements the software needs to satisfy and what constraints the software needs to follow.

In this paper, we propose a new infrastructure, by which the logic rules can be implemented as an independent knowware [11]. This knowware is deployed in a reasoner (e.g. Pellet [13]), which can be accessed through some interfaces by other elements in the software system. By this infrastructure, the logic rules are separated from other elements in the software system, and encapsulated in a knowware as an independent component of the software system. As the logic rules are represented explicitly in some rule languages (e.g. SWRL) as an independent knowware, they can be easily changed or updated. Furthermore, as an independent component, the knowware can be easily reused by other systems in similar domains.

2   Knowware Based Infrastructure for Smart Spaces

Knowware is proposed by Ruqian Lu in 2005 to separate the development of software and the development of knowledge [10]. The knowware refers to a knowledge module that is independent, commercialized, and embeddable in software or hardware for use [11]. Based on this idea of knowware, we propose a knowware based infrastructure for rule based control systems in smart spaces. By this infrastructure, the logic rules are separated from other elements in the system, and packaged in a knowware as an independent component of the software system.

The infrastructure consists of three part: a Knowledge Reasoning Part, an Interaction Processing Part and External Elements (as shown in Fig. 1).

- The Knowledge Reasoning Part contains a *knowware* and a *reasoner* to held the knowware. The knowware is composed of an *ontology* and some logic rules (detailed later in this section). When a knowware is deployed on the reasoner, the reasoner can run the inference according to the logic rules in the knowware.
- The External Elements in our infrastructure always include sensors and devices. According to our hypothesis, the sensors can provide the status of the environment, and the status of devices can be get by services or API.
- The Interaction Processing Part can be seen as interfaces between the Knowledge Reasoning Part and the External Elements. It gets the status of the environment and devices to the Knowledge Reasoning Part, and sets back the right status of the devices.

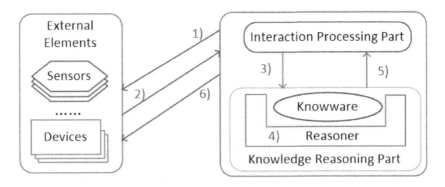

Fig. 1. Knowware based Infrastructure for Rule based Control Systems in Smart Spaces

To illustrate the usability of our infrastructure, we take a smart meeting room as an example of the smart space. In this smart meeting room, besides the meeting room furniture, there are some kinds of devices in the meeting room, including air conditions, lights, a projector, a screen and so on. Furthermore, sensors are deployed in this smart meeting room, including light intensity sensors, air humidity sensors, room temperature sensors and so on. These sensors can response the status of the environment.

As mentioned above, the knowware is composed of an *ontology* and some logic rules. The ontology contains many *concepts* about the smart space. In this smart meeting room, each kind of devices can be represented as an ontology concepts, such as *Light* and *Air_Condition*. Some concepts are shown in Fig. 2. Some instances of the concepts are also shown in Fig. 2. Furthermore, each concept has some properties. The properties have two categories. One is the data type properties that represent numeric attributes of the concepts, such as *isOn* that represents whether the device is turned on or off. The other is the object properties to express relations between the concepts, such as *isIn* to represent that the device is located in the room. Some properties of the concepts is presented in Table 1. Here we use the concept *Room* to represent the room itself. The concept *Room* has some properties, of which the values are gotten from the sensors.

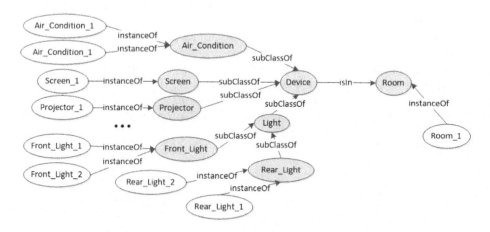

Fig. 2. Ontology of the Smart Meeting Room

Table 1. Some Properties of the Concepts in the Smart Meeting Room

Property Name	Type	Domain	Range
isOccupied	DatatypeProperty	Room	boolean
isIn	ObjectProperty	Device	Room
isOn	DatatypeProperty	Device	boolean
Air_Condition_Temperature	DatatypeProperty	Air_Condition	int

With the concepts and properties in the ontology, the logic rules can be expressed in the form of the predicate logic rules. The antecedent of the logic rules represents the constraints that should be satisfied. The consequent of the logic rules indicates the results that should be inferred if the antecedent is satisfied. For example, there are three logic rules in the smart meeting room as follows:

1. *If the room is occupied, and the air temperature is higher than 30 degrees centigrade, turn on the air conditioner to 26 degrees centigrade.*
2. *If the room is occupied, and the projector is turned off, then roll up the screen, and turn on all the lights.*
3. *If the room is occupied, and the projector is turned on, then put down the screen, turn off the front lights near to the screen and turn on the rear lights.*

The concepts in the ontology can be used as monadic predicates. The properties of the concepts are used as binary predicates. So, based on the concepts in Fig. 2 and the properties in Table 1, the three logic rules can be expressed in the form of predicate logic rules in Table 2.

Table 2. Some Logic Rules in the Smart Meeting Room

1. $Room(?r) \wedge isOccupied(?r, true) \wedge Room\_Temperature(?r, ?t)$ $\wedge swrlb : grearterThan(?t, 30) \wedge Air\_Condition(?x) \wedge isIn(?x, ?r)$ $\rightarrow isOn(?x, true) \wedge Air\_Condition\_Temperature(?x, 26)$
2. $Room(?r) \wedge isOccupied(?r, true) \wedge Projector(?p) \wedge isIn(?p, ?r)$ $\wedge isOn(?p, false) \wedge Screen(?s) \wedge isIn(?s, ?r) \wedge Light(?l) \wedge isIn(?l, ?r)$ $\rightarrow isOn(?s, false) \wedge isOn(?l, true)$
3. $Room(?r) \wedge isOccupied(?r, true) \wedge Projector(?p) \wedge isIn(?p, ?r) \wedge isOn(?p, true)$ $\wedge Screen(?s) \wedge isIn(?s, ?r) \wedge Front\_Light(?fl) \wedge Rear\_Light(?rl) \wedge isIn(?fl, ?r)$ $\wedge isIn(?rl, ?r) \rightarrow isOn(?s, true) \wedge isOn(?fl, false) \wedge isOn(?rl, true)$

With the logic rules packaged in the knowware, a control system in the smart meeting room can be constructed based on the infrastructure shown in Fig. 1. When the constructed control system runs, the life cycle of the control system contains the following six steps (as marked in Fig. 1):

1. The Interaction Processing Part requests actively and periodically to the External Elements to get the status of the environment and the devices.
2. The External Elements responses the status of the environment and the devices to the Interaction Processing Part.
3. The Interaction Processing Part sends the received status to the ontology in the knowware.
4. The reasoner in the Knowledge Reasoning Part takes the status as the initial values of properties of the ontology instances. Then the reasoner can run to infer the right status of the devices according to the logic rules.
5. Once the reasoning process is completed, the Knowledge Reasoning Part gets the inferred values of properties in the ontology, and then returns the right status of devices to the Interaction Processing Part.
6. According to the inference result, the Interaction Processing Part resets the right status to the devices.

By our infrastructure, the logic rules are separated and represented explicitly as an independent knowware. So, they can be easily changed or updated. For example, if the room is used for a party tonight, some logic rules may need to be changed to create the atmosphere of the party. The second and third logic rules in the smart meeting room can be updated to eliminate the projector's effects on front lights, while a new logic rule that leaves the lights on can be added. Furthermore, as an independent component, the knowware can be easily reused by other systems in similar domains. For example, the logic rules for the smart meeting room can be reused on a newly built room or an old room that need to be transformed to a new meeting room.

3   Conclusions

In this paper, we propose a knowware based infrastructure for control systems in smart spaces, which contains an independent knowware. The logic rules can be separated and encapsulated into this knowware. It is easy to change or update logic rules by our infrastructure. Also, as an independent component, the knowware can be reused by other systems in similar domains. In the future, we may try to consider more control situations and apply our infrastructure to more control systems in smart spaces.

Acknowledgment. This research is sponsored by the National Basic Research Program of China (973) No. 2011CB302704, the National Natural Science Foundation of China No. 61232015, the National 863 Program of China No. 2013AA01A605, and the Science Fund for Creative Research Groups of China No. 61121063.

References

1. Calejo, M.: InterProlog: Towards a declarative embedding of logic programming in Java. In: Alferes, J.J., Leite, J. (eds.) JELIA 2004. LNCS (LNAI), vol. 3229, pp. 714–717. Springer, Heidelberg (2004)
2. Castro, S., Mens, K., Moura, P.: Logicobjects: a linguistic symbiosis approach to bring the declarative power of prolog to java. In: Proceedings of the 9th ECOOP Workshop on Reflection, AOP, and Meta-Data for Software Evolution, pp. 11–16. ACM (2012)
3. Denti, E., Omicini, A., Ricci, A.: Multi-paradigm Java–Prolog integration in tuProlog. Science of Computer Programming 57(2), 217–250 (2005)
4. D'Hondt, M.: Explicit domain knowledge in software engineering (2002)
5. D'Hondt, M.: A survey of systems that integrate logic reasoning and object-oriented programming. Technical Report (2003)
6. D'Hondt, M.: Hybrid aspects for integrating rule-based knowledge and object-oriented functionality. Ph.D. thesis, Citeseer (2004)
7. D'Hondt, M., D'Hondt, T., et al.: Is domain knowledge an aspect? Lecture notes in Computer science pp. 293–293 (1999)
8. Elrad, T., Filman, R.E., Bader, A.: Aspect-oriented programming: Introduction. Communications of the ACM 44(10), 29–32 (2001)
9. Horrocks, I., Patel-Schneider, P.F., Boley, H., Tabet, S., Grosof, B., Dean, M., et al.: Swrl: A semantic web rule language combining owl and ruleml. W3C Member submission 21, 79 (2004)
10. Lu, R.: From hardware to software to knowware: It's third liberation? IEEE Intelligent Systems 20(2), 82–85 (2005)
11. Lu, R., Jin, Z.: From knowledge based software engineering to knowware based software engineering. Science in China Series F: Information Sciences 51(6), 638–660 (2008)
12. Majchrzak, T.A., Kuchen, H.: Logic java: combining object-oriented and logic programming. In: Kuchen, H. (ed.) WFLP 2011. LNCS, vol. 6816, pp. 122–137. Springer, Heidelberg (2011)
13. Parsia, B., Sirin, E.: Pellet: An owl dl reasoner. In: Third International Semantic Web Conference-Poster, p. 18 (2004)

An Action-Stack Based Selective-Undo Method in Feature Model Customization

Li Long, Zhao Haiyan, Zhang Wei, and Wang Weichao

[1] Key Laboratory of High Confidence Software Technology (Peking University),
Ministry of Education, China
[2] Institute of Software, School of EECS, Peking University, Beijing, 100871, China
{lilong11,zhhy,wangwc11}@sei.pku.edu.cn, zhangwei@pku.edu.cn

Abstract. Feature models are widely adopted in domain-oriented software reuse. The feature model customization is a process to determine which features are selected into or removed from an application. Auto-propagation is a practical strategy to assist customization but has a side-effect that may select or remove unintended features. To handle such a side-effect, a mechanism called selective-undo is needed that eliminates unintended selections and removals while preserving other selections and removals. This paper presents a selective-undo method based on action-stack by using the intrinsic relationships in a feature model, and investigates the implementation of the corresponding algorithms.

Keywords: Feature Model, Customization, Selective-Undo, Action-Stack.

1 Introduction

Feature model is widely adopted in domain-oriented software reuse [1]. The feature model customization is a process to determine which features in the domain feature model are selected into (called *bound* in this paper) or removed from an application [2]. Since there is constraints relationship between features, it is necessary to ensure that customizing results do not violate the constraints, and this is often supported by automated analysis of feature models. Auto-propagation is one of the automated analyses that automatically binds or removes certain features after a customizing action is performed to satisfy constraints [3]. However, the auto-propagation strategy has side-effect that may bind or remove unintended features [4].

This paper presents a mechanism called selective-undo algorithm based on action-stack to handle the side-effect of auto-propagation, and investigating the details of the algorithm. During the process of selective-undo, unintended *binding-states* (indicating a feature is *bound/removed/undecided*) can be switched from current value to another so that constraints are satisfied. Such switching of binding-states is called a *solution* to selective-undo. The method utilizes a data structure called action-stack and introduces an idea of mutating action-stacks to find solutions. Furthermore, since there may exist several solutions, this method will identify one solution at first, and present alternative solutions if the current solution is not accepted by the users.

J. Favaro and M. Morisio (Eds.): ICSR 2013, LNCS 7925, pp. 295–301, 2013.

2   Preliminaries

Feature models have been widely adopted to model and organize reusable requirements in a software domain [5].

Fig. 1 presents a part of the feature model in instant messaging software domain.

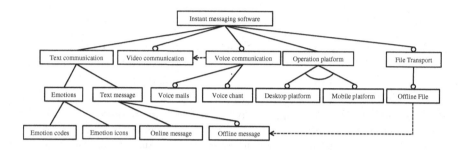

Fig. 1. An Example of Feature Model of Instant Messaging Software

Feature model is built as a tree structure by several features and its refinements. There are constraints between features. For example, *Voice mails -> Voice communications* is a constraint which means if feature '*Voice mails*' is bound, feature '*Voice communications*' must be bound.

A customization action in feature model either selects a feature or removes a feature by changing its binding-state to *bound* or *removed*. The process of feature model customization is labor-intensive and prone to err, and the result of customization may violate constraints imposed in the feature model. To address the potential conflicts introduced by the manually customization action, auto-propagation provides a mechanism to assist customization by automatically changing the binding-states of related features to satisfy constraints.

For example, there is a simple constraint *Video communications -> Voice communications* in Fig.1. If the feature *Video communications* is bound, the binding-state of feature *Voice communications* must be bound to satisfy the constraint.

However, there is one side-effect in auto-propagation in the sense that it may cause some features changed to the undesired binding-states. Hence, it is necessary to provide a mechanism to reset the binding-state of these features to undecided.

This paper proposes a method, called selective-undo, to automatically change the binding-states of related features to satisfy constraints whenever a feature's binding-state is changed from bound/removed to undecided.

If a feature is bound or removed, auto-propagation will be invoked to change the binding-states of other related features. If a feature is reset from bound or removed to undecided, then selective-undo will be enforced to ensure it will not violate the constraints in feature model.

3   An Action-Stack Based Selective-Undo Method

In this section, we introduce an action-stack based selective-undo method. We first give an overview of the method, and introduce the concept of action-stack and its support to one-step withdraw. Based on one-step withdraw, we present a mechanism to find an initial solution to selective-undo, and derive new solutions from known solutions. Fig.2 gives an overview of selective-undo method.

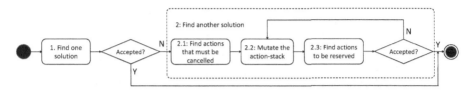

Fig. 2. Overview of the action-stack based method to selective-undo

3.1   Action-Stack and One-Step Withdraw Operation

The selective-undo method is based on a data structure called action-stack. The elements of action-stack are customization actions, including the operation and feature that be bound or removed by customizer (named key feature). After each customization action and its auto-propagation result, the action-stack records the action (which feature is bound or removed) and the set of related features (which feature is propagated). The customization action and related features is pushed into the stack as a pair. For example, if the feature *Video Communication* is bound, the feature *Voice Communication* is propagated bound. So (Bind *Video Communication*, {*Voice Communication*}) is pushed into action-stack. If feature A is removed, no features are propagated, then (Remove A, { }) is pushed into action-stack.

One-step withdraw operation can be done by action-stack. The purpose of one-step withdraw operation is cancelling the recent customization action. The method of one-step withdraw operation has two steps: first pop the top element of action-stack, then change the binding-states of key feature and related features to undecided.

3.2   Finding One Solution to Selective-Undo

The idea of finding one solution to selective-undo is based on the sequential of actions. Using action-stack and one-step withdraw operations can realize finding one solution. Since action-stack is a stack structure, each operation visits the top elements. For selective-undo, it needs to cancel the inside action. Just cancelling the inside action simply cannot realize selective-undo, because it may impact the auto-propagation of other customization action, and it may violate constraints.

A possible method is as follows when feature F is desired to reset to undecided. Firstly find which action related to F or the action is binding/removing F. Set the action is Action m. The m-1 actions before it can be reserved, and Action m must be cancelled. Whether the actions after Action m are reserved or not should be discussed by a tentative propagation. If the action is propagated and does not change F's binding-state, the action can be reserved. Otherwise, the action must be cancelled by doing one-step withdraw operation once.

Fig.3 is an example of a fragment in feature model for the method. The features in this fragment are expressed by letters. A expresses Single OS. B expresses Apple iOS. C expresses MS Windows. D expresses NTFS Support. E expresses CD Recorder. After customization actions: remove B, bind A, bind D and remove E, the feature model and action-stack is as Fig.3.

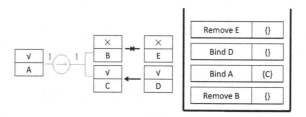

Fig. 3. Feature Model and Action-Stack (After Auto-Propagation)

Feature C is propagated bound after the customization action 'Bind A'. Now this method is used to find one-solution to selective-undo for feature C. First the action related to feature C is found ('Bind A'). One-step withdrawing three times makes C be undecided. Then discuss whether the actions after 'Bind A' can be reserved or not (Two actions: 'Bind D' and 'Remove E'). It can be found that C's binding-state will be changed if D is bound. So the action 'Bind D' must be cancelled. C's binding-state is not changed if E is removed. So the action 'Remove E' can be reserved.

3.3   Finding Another Solution from a Known Solution

The solution may be not accepted by user. For example, cancelling actions 'Bind B' and 'Bind D' is also a solution to the problem given in Fig.8. It inspires us that a new solution can be derived from a known one if that the known one is not accepted.

Before elaborating the method, we first introduce a theorem for customization.

Theorem.1 (Exchangeability). Exchanging the order of customization actions does not affect the results of auto-propagation.

Proof. Set customization actions are binding F1, F2, ..., Fn, and removing G1, G2, ..., Gn. They make binding-state of F be bound, G be removed: $(RDCEAC_\wedge F1_\wedge F2..._\wedge Fn_\wedge\neg G1_\wedge... _\wedge \neg Gn)\text{-}>F$, $(RDC_\wedge EAC_\wedge F1_\wedge F2..._\wedge Fn_\wedge\neg G1_\wedge... _\wedge \neg Gn)\text{-}>\neg G$. Such as: binding A firstly and removing B secondly makes C be bind, $(RDC_\wedge EAC_\wedge A_\wedge\neg B)\text{-}>C$ identically equals to true. According to commutative property, According to commutative property, $(RDC_\wedge EAC_\wedge\neg B_\wedge A)\text{-}>C$ identically equals to true. So, firstly removing B then binding A also makes C be bound.

The solution to selective-undo operation is expressed by two sets containing customization actions named Reserve-Set and Cancel-Set. All customization actions must be in either of the two sets. Reserve-Set is the set containing actions that be reserved. Cancel-Set is the set containing actions that be cancelled.

For preconditioning, the method finds actions that must be cancelled (named AMC). These actions can be ignored in later algorithm. Firstly, the method saves the action-stack. Then we reset all features' binding-states to undecided. AMC is found by doing auto-propagation for each action in action-stack separately. If the binding-state of the key feature is changed, the action is an AMC. For example, the feature model has now been customized as Fig.3. 'Bind D' is the only AMC in action-stack.

According to Theorem.1, changing the order of actions does not affect the result of customization. To find another solution from a known solution, changing the order of actions is a workable method. For finding another solution, we mutate the action-stack. The mutated action-stack is not a strict stack, which has character as follows: (1) the bottom item can be read and popped. (In strict stack, only top item can be read). (2) the order of items in the stack can be exchanged.

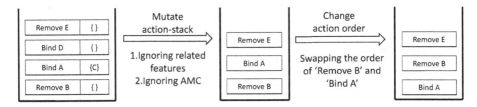

Fig. 4. Mutating the Action-Stack and Changing the Order (Because the action 'Bind A' is cancelled in last solution, the method put it first.)

After action-stack is mutated, judging which actions are reserved is the final step to find another solution to selective-undo. To selective-undo for feature F, firstly, all features' binding-states are reset to undecided. Then the method does auto-propagation for action-stack from button to top in order, and judges F's binding-state after each propagation operation. If binding-state of F is still undecided, reserve the action. Otherwise, the method cancels the action by doing one-step withdraw operation once to reset F to undecided.

Fig.4 shows the mutating procedure. After mutating, the method finds 'Bind A' and 'Remove E' can be reserved and 'Remove B' is cancelled. It gives another solution to selective-undo.

The method can satisfy two characters: Minimal Cancel-Set and Completeness.

Minimal. A solution found by the method: reserving action $\{a_{i1}, a_{i2}...a_{in}\}$, and cancelling action $\{a_{j1}, a_{j2},...a_{jm}\}$. Not any action cancelled can be reserved.

Proof. Suppose there exists a solution $\{a_{i1}, a_{i2}, ...a_{in}, a_j\}$, then set the order of the actions: $a_{i1}, a_{i2},....a_{ik}, a_j, a_{ik+1},...a_{in.}$ => When propagate a_j, the feature is changed to bound/removed. => Actions $\{a_{i1}, a_{i2}, ...a_{ik}\}$, a_j cannot make the feature undecided. => Actions $\{a_{i1}, a_{i2}, ...a_{in}, a_j\}$ cannot make the feature undecided. => $\{a_{i1}, a_{i2}, ...a_{in}, a_j\}$ is not a solution. So no action cancelled can be reserved.

Completeness. Each feasible solution to selective-undo can be generated by changing order of actions.

Proof. Set action-stack: $\{a1,a2,a3...an\}$, for a feasible solution: Reserve: $\{a_{r1},a_{r2},...a_{rm}\}$, Cancel: $\{a_{c1},a_{c2},..a_{cl}\}$ and m+l=n. Then change the order of action-stack to: $\{a_{r1},a_{r2}....a_{rm},a_{c1},a_{c2},...a_{cl}\}$ => This solution.

The method can give all solutions to selective-undo. However, it is an N-P Hard question to find all solutions once. To settle for second best, the method gives the solution one-by-one to let the customizer judge accepting it or not.

4   Related Work and Conclusion

The concept of feature model was first introduced by Kang[1] in domain analysis. For the problem of feature model customization, Mannion method [2] is a tree–based feature model customization method. This customization can guarantee satisfying the constraints between the child-feature of a change point, however, may not guarantee satisfying global constraints. Batory [3] also used the method based on propositional logic, referred to the idea of propagation of feature model customization. However, the above method does not provide selective-undo mechanism. The methods cannot freely switch the binding-states of features in feature model.

Wang et al. [6, 7] adopt priority to detect and mange the inconsistencies in feature models. In [6], Wang et al. generate fixes for the inconsistencies automatically. Each fix contains a set of low priority constraints. Executing the fix will delete these constrains and satisfy the high priority constraints in the feature model. In [7], the inconsistencies are tolerated through notifying the stakeholders the low priority constraints. These approaches focus on the feature model. However, our approach provides support for the inconsistencies in the feature model configurations.

In this paper, we introduce an action-stack based selective-undo method in feature model customization. On the basis of auto-propagation mechanism our selective-undo method solves the side effect of auto-propagation by resetting binding-states of feature to undecided without violating constraints in feature model. We not only present the method to find one solution for selective-undo, but also the way to derive other solutions from the first one when it is not accepted.

Our future work will focus on the efficiency of the method. In the experiment, the method gives good performance when the number of features is not large enough. However, when the number of feature increases, the cost of time is not satisfactory. How to find all solutions more quickly is also an important future work. A more accurate mutating algorithm may be a key point for it.

References

1. Kyo, C., Kang, S., Cohen, J., Hess, W.: Novak, and A. Peterson, Feature-Oriented Domain Analysis Feasibility Study, Technical Report CMU/SEI-90-TR-21, Software Engineering Institute, Carnegie Mellon University (November 1990)
2. Mannion, M.: Using First-Order Logic for Product Line Model Validation. In: Chastek, G.J. (ed.) SPLC 2002. LNCS, vol. 2379, pp. 176–187. Springer, Heidelberg (2002)
3. Batory, D.: Feature Models, Grammars, and Propositional Formulas. In: Obbink, H., Pohl, K. (eds.) SPLC 2005. LNCS, vol. 3714, pp. 7–20. Springer, Heidelberg (2005)

4. Long, L., Haiyan, Z., Wei, Z.: MbFM: A matrix-based tool for modeling and configuring feature models. In: 2012 20th IEEE International Requirements Engineering Conference (RE), Chicago, IL, pp. 325–326 (2012)
5. Zhang, W., Zhao, H., Mei, H.: A Feature-Oriented Approach to Modeling Requirements Dependencies. In: The 13th IEEE International Requirements Conference (RE 2005), Minnesota, USA, pp. 273–284 (2005)
6. Wang, B., Xiong, Y., Hu, Z., Zhao, H., Zhang, W., Mei, H.: A Dynamic-Priority based Approach to Fixing Inconsistent Feature Models. In: Petriu, D.C., Rouquette, N., Haugen, Ø. (eds.) MODELS 2010, Part I. LNCS, vol. 6394, pp. 181–195. Springer, Heidelberg (2010)
7. Wang, B., Hu, Z., Xiong, Y., Zhao, H., Zhang, W., Mei, H.: Tolerating Inconsistency in Feature Models. In: 3rd Workshop on Living With Inconsistency in Software Development, held with 25th IEEE/ACM International Conference on Automated Software Engineering (2010)

Feature Location in a Collection of Software Product Variants Using Formal Concept Analysis

Ra'Fat AL-Msie'deen[1,*], Abdelhak Seriai[1], Marianne Huchard[1],
Christelle Urtado[2], Sylvain Vauttier[2], and Hamzeh Eyal Salman[1]

[1] LIRMM / CNRS & Montpellier 2 University, France
{Al-msiedee,Seriai,huchard,eyalsalman}@lirmm.fr
[2] LGI2P / Ecole des Mines d'Alès, Nîmes, France
{Christelle.Urtado,Sylvain.Vauttier}@mines-ales.fr

Abstract. Formal Concept Analysis (FCA) is a theoretical framework which structures a set of objects described by properties. In order to migrate software product variants which are considered similar into a product line, it is essential to identify the common and the optional features between the software product variants. In this paper, we present an approach for feature location in a collection of software product variants based on FCA. In order to validate our approach we applied it on a case study based on ArgoUML. The results of this evaluation showed that all of the features were identified.

Keywords: Software Product Variants, Feature Location, FCA.

1 Introduction

Software product variants often evolve from an initial product developed for and successfully used by the first customer. These product variants usually share some common features but they are also different from one another due to subsequent customization to meet specific requirements of different customers [1]. As the number of features and the number of product variants grows, it is worth reengineering product variants into a Software Product Line (SPL) for systematic reuse. To switch to Software Product Line Engineering (SPLE) starting from a collection of existing variants, the first step is to mine a feature model that describes the SPL. This further implies to identify the software family's common and variable features. Manual reverse engineering of the feature model for the existing software variants is time-consuming, error-prone, and requires substantial effort [2]. Thus, we propose in this paper a new approach for feature location in a collection of software product variants. Our approach is based on the identification of the implementation of these features among object-oriented (OO) elements of the source code. These OO elements constitute the initial search space. We rely on Formal Concept Analysis (FCA) to reduce this search

---

* This work has been funded by grant ANR 2010 BLAN 021902.

J. Favaro and M. Morisio (Eds.): ICSR 2013, LNCS 7925, pp. 302–307, 2013.

space by identifying maximal subsets of features shared by maximal subsets of product variants and organizing these subsets by inclusion.

Our approach is detailed in the remainder of this paper as follows. Section 2 presents FCA, and Section 3 outlines our approach. Section 4 discusses our implementation and evaluation. Section 5 presents the related work. We conclude and draw perspectives for this work in Section 6.

2   Formal Concept Analysis (FCA)

Galois lattices and concept lattices [3] are core structures of a data analysis framework (FCA) for extracting an ordered set of concepts from a dataset, called a formal context, composed of objects described by attributes. A formal context is a triple $K = (O, A, R)$ where O and A are sets (objects and attributes, respectively) and R is a binary relation, i.e., $R \subseteq O \times A$. An example of formal context is provided in Figure 1 (left). A formal concept is a pair (E, I) composed of an object set $E \subseteq O$ and its shared attribute set $I \subseteq A$. $E = \{o \in O | \forall a \in I, (o, a) \in R\}$ is the extent of the concept, while $I = \{a \in A | \forall o \in E, (o, a) \in R\}$ is the intent of the concept. Given a formal context $K = (O, A, R)$, and two formal concepts $C_1 = (E_1, I_1)$ and $C_2 = (E_2, I_2)$ of K, the concept specialization order $\leq_s$ is defined by $C_1 \leq_s C_2$ if and only if $E_1 \subseteq E_2$ (and equivalently $I_2 \subseteq I_1$). C_1 is called a sub-concept of C_2. C_2 is called a super-concept of C_1. Let $\mathcal{C}_K$ be the set of all concepts of a formal context K. This set of concepts provided with the specialization order $(\mathcal{C}_K, \leq_s)$ has a lattice structure, and is called the concept lattice associated with K. In our approach, we will consider the AOC-poset (for Attribute-Object-Concept poset), which is the sub-order of $(\mathcal{C}_K, \leq_s)$ restricted to object-concepts and attribute-concepts. An object-concept (resp. attribute-concept) is the lowest concept (resp. a greatest concept) where an object (resp. an attribute) appears. In AOC-poset representations, objects are represented only in their introducer concept (and inherited by superconcepts), while attributes are represented only in their introducer concept (and inherited by their subconcepts), meaning that no concept should have empty object part and empty attribute part.

3   Our Approach to Feature Location

This section provides main concepts and hypotheses used in our approach.

3.1   Goal and Core Assumptions

The general objective of our work is to identify a feature model for a collection of software product variants based on the static analysis of their source code. We consider that "a feature is a prominent or distinctive and user visible aspect, quality, or characteristic of a software system or systems" [4]. We adhere to the classification given by [4] which distinguishes three categories of features: functional, operational and presentation features. Our work focuses on the identifying of functional features. In our approach we deal with software systems where the functional features are implemented at the programming language level (*i.e.*, source code). The functional features are implemented by object oriented building elements (OBEs) such as *packages, classes, attributes, methods* or *method body elements* (*local variable, attribute access, method invocation*). We consider that a feature corresponds to exactly one set of OBEs. This means that a feature always has the same implementation in all products where it is present. We also consider that feature implementations may overlap: a given OBE can be shared between several features' implementations. In this paper, we name such shared OBE as a *junction*.

3.2   Features versus Object-Oriented Building Elements

Feature location in a collection of software variants consists in identifying a group of OBEs that constitutes its implementation. This group of OBEs must either be present in all variants (case of a common feature) or in some but not all variants (case of an optional feature). Thus, the initial search space for the feature location process is composed of all the subsets of OBEs of existing product variants. As the number of OBEs is big, a strategy must be designed to reduce the search space.

Our proposal consists in dividing the OBE set in specific subsets: the *common feature set* – also called *common block* (CB) – and several *optional feature sets* (Block of Variations, denoted as BVs). Optional (*resp.* common) features appear in some but not all (*resp.* all) variants, they are implemented by OBEs that appear in some but not in all (*resp.* all) variants.

This is realized by building a formal context, which is composed of software variants (objects of the formal context) described by their OBEs (attributes of the formal context). The relation associates a software variant with the OBEs that appear in its source code. The corresponding AOC-poset is then calculated. A concept intent (containing the concept attributes) represents OBEs common to two or more variants (the objects included in the concept extent). As the concepts of the AOC-posets are ordered, the intent of the most general (i.e., top) concept gathers the OBEs that are common to all products. They constitute the CB. The intents of the remaining concepts are BVs. A concept intent corresponds to the implementation of one or more features. As an illustrative example, we consider four text editor software variants. *Editor_1* supports core text editing features: *open, close,* and *print* a file. *Editor_2* has the core text editing features and a new *select_all* feature. *Editor_3* supports *copy* and *paste* features, together with the core ones. *Editor_4* supports *select_all, copy* and *paste* features, together with the core ones. Figure 1 shows the formal context for the text editor variants and the AOC-poset for this formal context which shows the CB and BVs.

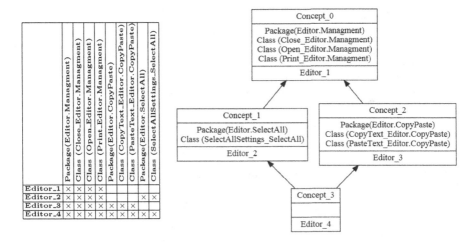

Fig. 1. The Formal Context and AOC-poset for Text Editor Variants

4   Experimentation

To validate our approach, we ran experiments on the Java open-source software ArgoUML [5]. We used 10 variants for ArgoUML. The advantage of ArgoUML variants is that they are well documented and their feature model is available for comparison with our results and validation of our proposal. ArgoUML variants are presented in Table 1: LOC (Lines of Code), NOP (Number of Packages), NOC (Number of Classes) and NOOBE (Number Of Object-oriented Building Elements).

Table 1. ArgoUML software product variants

Product #	Product Description	LOC	NOP	NOC	NOOBE
P1	All features disabled	82,924	55	1,243	74,444
P2	All features enabled	120,348	81	1,666	100,420
P3	Only Logging disabled	118,189	81	1,666	98,988
P4	Only Cognitive disabled	104,029	73	1,451	89,273
P5	Only Sequence diagram disabled	114,969	77	1,608	96,492
P6	Only Use case diagram disabled	117,636	78	1,625	98,468
P7	Only Deployment diagram disabled	117,201	79	1,633	98,323
P8	Only Collaboration diagram disabled	118,769	79	1,647	99,358
P9	Only State diagram disabled	116,431	81	1,631	97,760
P10	Only Activity diagram disabled	118,066	79	1,648	98,777

Table 2 summarizes the obtained results. For readability's sake, we manually associated feature names to CB and BVs, based on the study of the content of each block and on our knowledge of the software. Of course, this does not impact the quality of our results. In Table 2, CB represents a single common feature. For the given set of BVs [2 -10], each BV represents a single optional feature. For given set of BVs [11 - 22], each BV represents a junction between two or more features. The column (# OBEs) in Table 2 represents the number of OBEs that implement this feature.

Table 2. Feature Location in ArgoUML Software Variants

#	Feature Name	# OBEs	#	Feature Name	# OBEs
1	Class Diagram	74431	12	Junction cognitive/deployment	745
2	Diagram	1309	13	Junction cognitive/sequence	55
3	Use case Diagram	1928	14	Junction sequence/collaboration	111
4	Collaboration Diagram	935	15	Junction state/logging	6
5	Cognitive Diagram	10193	16	Junction deployment/logging	18
6	Activity Diagram	1583	17	Junction collaboration/logging	13
7	Deployment Diagram	1334	18	Junction use case/logging	22
8	Sequence Diagram	3708	19	Junction sequence/logging	51
9	State Diagram	2597	20	Junction activity/logging	3
10	Logging	1149	21	Junction cognitive/logging	169
11	Junction activity/state	57	22	Junction between features 14/17/19	18

In fact 22 features have been identified from ArgoUML software product variants. The 12 extra features (features 11-22) represent junctions between the other features [5]. The top concept (feature 1 called "Class Diagram" in Table 2) contains 74431 OBEs that are shared by all software product variants (*i.e.*, CB). In particular, it contains the *class diagram* feature, which is indeed a common feature, and is therefore present in every product. We compared the obtained CB with the common features of the original feature model [5]. CB corresponds exactly to one common feature (*i.e.*, class diagram). Concerning the obtained BVs, each BV from 2-10 corresponds exactly to one original optional feature. For BVs from 11-22, each block represents a junction.

5   Related Work

Loesch et al. [6] applied FCA to analyze the variability in a software product line based on product configurations (described by features), and construct a lattice that provides a classification of the usage of variable features in real products derived from the product line. An inclusive survey about approaches linking features and source code in a single software is proposed in [7]. Rubin *et al.* [8] present an approach to locate optional features from two product variants' source code. They do not consider common features and limit their proposal to two variants. Xue *et al.* [1] propose an automatic approach to identify the traceability links between a given collection of features and a given collection of source code variants. They thus consider feature descriptions as an input. Acher *et al.* [2] present automated techniques to extract variability descriptions in a software architecture and consider the architect's knowledge for reverse engineering architectural feature models. She *et al.* [9] propose an approach to define a feature model based on a set of already identified features. The main problem tackled is to identify the structure of the feature model. In particular, they present procedures to identify alternatives from an existing set of features. Their work is complementary to our work as it can take as input a feature set deduced from our approach and synthesize the feature model. Acher et al. [10] present an approach to synthesize a feature model based on the product descriptions. Their approach takes as input product description for a collection of product variants to build the FM. Products are described by characteristics (language, license, etc.) with different patterns on values (many-valued, one-valued, etc.).

Ryssel et al. [11] applied FCA to extract feature diagrams from an incidence matrix that contains matching relations as input. The matrix shows the parts of a set of function-block oriented models that describe different controllers of a DC motor. The approach proposed by Ziadi *et al.* [12] is the closest one. Authors propose a solution for feature identification from the source code of a set of product variants. They identify all common features as a single mandatory feature. However, they do not distinguish between optional features that appear together in a set of variants. Their approach doesn't consider the method body and do not use any classification technique to classify object oriented elements.

6 Conclusion and Perspectives

We present in this paper an approach for feature location in a collection of software product variants based on FCA. It has been applied on a collection of ArgoUML software products. The results of this evaluation showed that all of the features were identified. As future work, we will apply a clustering algorithm on the CB and BVs to determine more precisely each feature implementation based on both lexical similarity (*i.e.*, textual similarity between OBEs) and semantic similarity/dependency structure (*i.e.*, inheritance, attribute access, method invocation). We also plan to use the identified common and optional features to automate the building of the studied software family's feature model.

References

1. Xue, Y., Xing, Z., Jarzabek, S.: Feature location in a collection of product variants. In: IEEE 19th RE Conference, pp. 145–154 (2012)
2. Acher, M., Cleve, A., Collet, P., Merle, P., Duchien, L., Lahire, P.: Reverse engineering architectural feature models. In: Crnkovic, I., Gruhn, V., Book, M. (eds.) ECSA 2011. LNCS, vol. 6903, pp. 220–235. Springer, Heidelberg (2011)
3. Ganter, B., Wille, R.: Formal Concept Analysis, Mathematical Foundations. Springer (1999)
4. Kang, K., Cohen, S., Hess, J., Nowak, W., Peterson, S.: Feature-Oriented Domain Analysis (FODA) Feasibility Study (1990)
5. Couto, M., Valente, M., Figueiredo, E.: Extracting software product lines: A case study using conditional compilation. In: 15th CSMR Conference, pp. 191–200 (2011)
6. Loesch, F., Ploedereder, E.: Optimization of variability in software product lines. In: IEEE 11th ISPL Conference, pp. 151–162 (2007)
7. Dit, B., Revelle, M., Gethers, M., Poshyvanyk, D.: Feature location in source code: a taxonomy and survey. Journal of Software: Evolution and Process, 53–95 (2012)
8. Rubin, J., Chechik, M.: Locating distinguishing features using diff sets. In: 27th ASE Conference, ASE 2012, pp. 242–245. ACM (2012)
9. She, S., Lotufo, R., Berger, T., Wasowski, A., Czarnecki, K.: Reverse engineering feature models. In: ICSE, pp. 461–470 (2011)
10. Acher, M., Cleve, A., Perrouin, G., Heymans, P., Vanbeneden, C.: On extracting feature models from product descriptions. In: VaMoS, pp. 45–54. ACM (2012)
11. Ryssel, U., Ploennigs, J., Kabitzsch, K.: Extraction of feature models from formal contexts. In: 15th ISPL Conference, pp. 4:1–4:8. ACM (2011)
12. Ziadi, T., Frias, L., da Silva, M.A.A., Ziane, M.: Feature identification from the source code of product variants. In: CSMR 2012, pp. 417–422 (2012)

A Language for Building Verified Software Components

Gregory Kulczycki[1], Murali Sitaraman[2], Joan Krone[3], Joseph E. Hollingsworth[4],
William F. Ogden[5], Bruce W. Weide[5], Paolo Bucci[5], Charles T. Cook[2],
Svetlana V. Drachova-Strang[2], Blair Durkee[2], Heather Harton[6], Wayne Heym[5],
Dustin Hoffman[5], Hampton Smith[2], Yu-Shan Sun[2], Aditi Tagore[5],
Nighat Yasmin[7], and Diego Zaccai[5]

[1] Battelle Memorial Institute, Arlington, VA, USA
kulczyckig@battelle.org
[2] School of Computing, Clemson University, Clemson, SC 29634, USA
{murali,ctcook,sdracho,bdurkee,hamptos,yushans}@clemson.edu
[3] Mathematics and Computer Science, Denison University, Granville, OH 43023, USA
krone@denison.edu
[4] Computer Science, Indiana University Southeast, New Albany, IN 47150, USA
jholly@ius.edu
[5] Computer Science and Engineering, Ohio State University, Columbus, OH 43210, USA
{ogden,weide,bucci,heym,hoffmand,
tagore,zaccai}@cse.ohio-state.edu
[6] Integrated Support Systems, Seneca, SC 29672, USA
hkeown@g.clemson.edu
[7] Computer Science, University of Mississippi, Oxford, MS 38677, USA
yasmin@clemson.edu

Abstract. Safe and secure reuse is only achievable by deploying formally
verified software components. This paper presents essential design objectives
for languages for building such components and highlights key features in
RESOLVE—a prototype for such languages. It explains why the language
must include specifications as an integral constituent and must have clean and
rich semantics, which preclude unconstrained aliasing and other unwanted side-
effects. In order that arbitrarily complex components can be given concise and
verification amenable specifications, an adequate language must also include an
open-ended mechanism for incorporating additional mathematical theories.
Given these essential characteristics, safe and secure reuse cannot be attained
within popular languages, such as C++ or Java, either by constraining them or
by extending them. Better languages are necessary.

Keywords: assertions, clean semantics, components, reuse, specification.

1 Introduction

In order to achieve maturity as a field and to build safe and secure high assurance
systems, software engineering must move from its current "cut-and-try" approach to a
rigorous mathematically based system for engineering software. This engineering
requires a language carefully designed to facilitate construction of verifiable and

J. Favaro and M. Morisio (Eds.): ICSR 2013, LNCS 7925, pp. 308–314, 2013.

reusable software components and a verifying compiler—a compiler that checks that code is correct and generates executable code. This is unarguably a grand challenge for the computing community [1]. This paper motivates and delineates the essential features of a language or framework for building verified components. Understanding the features will help not just language designers, but also component developers in existing languages, informing them of potential pitfalls when features of their language are in conflict with the goal of verification.

While it is difficult to retrofit currently popular languages with features amenable for verification, the features themselves are not unrealizable. Automated verification efforts summarized in [2], for example, include one or more of these features. RESOLVE is a more comprehensive effort [3, 4, 5, 6]; its web IDE (available at www.cs.clemson.edu/group/resolve) allows reuse of existing components (ranging from ones for Arrays to Maps, Prioritizers, and Pointers) and construction of new ones [7]. A key question for every verification effort is one of scale. In answering this question, the important observation is that specifications for capturing human-understandable component behavior are necessarily simple in a language with clean semantics [8], given an extensible mathematical language [9] and that reasoning of correctness for any code that is straightforward for humans, is also straightforward for automated verifiers, given suitable annotations [10]; no deep thinking is necessary. The challenge is in investing the effort in devising suitable specifications and annotated implementations.

2   Essential Features of a Language for Verified Components

The essential features of a system for building verified software components must clearly include a language in which sophisticated, clean software can be written, and a specification system in which concise, precise intentions for the behavior of software components can be expressed. To insure the soundness of the verifying compiler, the specification and the programming mechanism must be fully coordinated in every detail, and about the only way to guarantee this is to integrate them into a single assertive language. The correctness objectives for the verification system and for the compiler can then be unified via a shared semantics for the language, and the all-too-common problem of incorrect behavior by seemingly verified software can be avoided. The need that specifications be an integral feature is the first of numerous indications that current languages are not adequate for meeting the grand challenge.

Another common problem occurs when verification is attempted in programming languages that lack clean semantics [8]. By clean semantics, we mean that all operations constructible in the language can only affect the objects to which they appear to have access. Without such semantics, seemingly "verified" constituents may not behave correctly when employed in a larger system. For a language to have clean semantics, its built-in data structures and composition mechanisms must be clean, and unconstrained aliasing must be avoided. Unfortunately, merely constraining an existing language to a clean subset will lead to an impractically weak language.

A major source of problems confronting verification is scale. From the specificational perspective, one such problem is that descriptions of the intended effects of programs might have to grow roughly in proportion to the size of the code. Given the limitation of human cognitive capacity, this is a serious concern.

The solution to the coding side of this scaling problem is to provide modularization mechanisms that support a divide and conquer approach via componentization of software, with large system construction taking place using progressively more powerful components. An analogous approach is required on the specificational side, with descriptions of more powerful components being formulated in terms of more sophisticated theories. The net effect is that the collection of mathematical theories used in specifying software must remain open ended in order to support the growth of software driven by the rapidly increasing power of hardware. So an immediate corollary is that machinery for developing mathematical theories must be a third constituent of the language for specifying software that we want to program.

Even with well-conceived program verification machinery, the cost of evolving poorly structured software into correct software is bound to remain prohibitively high. One of the primary strategies used by more mature engineering disciplines for achieving sound products at reasonable cost is to rely upon a comparatively small collection of highly reusable components, and this must surely be an approach that is strongly supported by a language for software verification.

There are several key features that the machinery provided for generating reusable components must have. Certainly it must exhibit the clean semantics mentioned above, since modular understanding is always essential to reuse. Second, it must provide the potential for a high degree of genericity, since keeping catalogues of reusable components to an intellectually manageable size is important. Third, it must provide an interfacing mechanism for presenting the object types and operations together with their abstract specifications, since information hiding is critical to keeping the specifications of higher-level code as simple as possible. Fourth, it must support the development of alternative implementations of an abstract interface, since different implementations of the same functionality are necessary to meet different performance goals, and if a component interface does achieve the desired degree of reusability, then it must be possible in a large system to deploy it in numerous places where varying performance requirements hold.

Reusable components are the setting in which the specificational simplification derived from changing to more sophisticated mathematical theories frequently occurs. So part of the machinery in a component implementation must provide the specification of a correspondence relation that properly matches the behavior of the entities at the implementation level with functionality prescribed for the more abstract entities presented by the component's external interface. Performance specification and verification capability is also essential, and so, component implementation machinery must provide for translating this information up to the external interface.

3   Clean Semantics

Correct reasoning about software, both formal and informal, is critically dependent on "separation of concerns." If a piece of code appears to be working on only a small portion of the overall state space, then any efficient verification system must be safe in restricting its attention exclusively to the code's effect on that subspace. Languages that restrict the effects of each programming construct to just the objects that are syntactically targeted by the construct are said to have clean semantics [8], so a language with clean semantics is a basic requirement if verification is to succeed.

The biggest impediment to clean semantics in a language is unconstrained and avoidable aliasing. As reference copying is the main cause of such aliasing, to support clean semantics without sacrificing efficiency, the language must support mechanisms to avoid reference copying (e.g., swapping or transfer) and parameter aliasing [8, 11]. However, this does not mean all pointers and aliasing can or should be avoided [12].

4   Language Support for Specifications

If languages or systems that do not share a common design are combined to specify, write, and verify software, the slightest of inconsistencies in their semantics could easily vitiate apparent correctness results. Consequently, we need one language that treats the development of software systems as an integrated whole. In particular, software's specifications should be viewed as an essential part of the software, and not as an add-on sideshow that might or might not describe the actual code.

A clean specification of List abstraction (devoid of complications due to pointers) is given in [3] and an updated, verification-friendly version of that specification, can be found in the RESOLVE Web IDE [7]. In the specification, a list is conceptualized as an ordered pair: a mathematical string of entries that precede the insertion point (denoted by *Prec*) and a string of entries that remain past the insertion point (denoted by *Rem*). A part of this specification is shown in the screen insert to the right in Figure 1. The screen insert at the bottom shows a formal specification of a list reversal operation, named Flip_Rem; this operation is an enhancement (or extension) to the list component. In this specification, Reverse is a mathematical function that reverses a string; its formal definition is given in the next section. It is specified to take a list, such as (<>, <1,2,3,4>) and produce (<4,3,2,1>,<>).

The meaning of correctness of an implementation of Flip_Rem (in Figure 1) depends on its specification and the specifications of operations it uses; i.e., the same code may be correct or wrong, underscoring that specifications should be an integral part. Stated more formally, pre and post conditions can produce effects involving two special semantic states: a vacuously correct state, VC, and a manifestly wrong state, MW. If, for example, some code attempts to invoke an operation in a state that does not meet the operation's precondition, then the resulting state is MW. Similarly if the code for an operation does not meet its post condition, then the outcome is also MW. The VC state is introduced when the code for an operation is started in a state that does not meet its pre condition. A program is semantically correct only if under no circumstances can it produce the MW state. In such an integrated approach, the potential for a verification system to be unsound is vastly reduced.

A compiler is only going to be capable of verifying the correctness of assertive code if that code includes sufficient hints in the form of justificational specifications, provided by the software engineer, to make intermediate deductions "obvious." Besides operation specifications, the language must support invariants and termination progress metrics for its looping constructs, representation invariants and abstraction relations for data abstraction implementations, among others [2].

5   Reusable Mathematical Theory Constituent

It is unlikely that the most appropriate theories for specifying the full compass of software applications will inevitably lie within the well-worked parts of mathematics, so the reliability of the general software verification process becomes quite suspect [13], unless it rests on a firmer foundation than citations into the mathematical literature. In short, the mathematics used in software specification and verification must be industrial strength rather than craftsman formulated. A system for developing, checking, and cataloguing mathematical theories then becomes an essential component of a software verification system [9]. For example, while a theory of mathematical strings could be codified in a specification language and employed for effective verification [5], in general, the language should make it possible to define and use new theories without modifying the verifier.

Several ideas from reusable component engineering are also appropriate for structuring mathematical theories. The first is separation of concerns. A client using a theory to formulate specifications only needs a summary or précis of the definitions and results (theorems) for that theory, but not anything about proofs for the results, so the précis should be in a separate syntactic unit from the proofs. This is analogous to separating interfaces and implementations of components. A second such idea is reuse itself. Well-considered and well-developed mathematical theories are appropriate for a variety of specifications, and the cost of their formulation and proof can be amortized over all these uses.

Making the verification of production software routine depends on a taxonomic thesis about how software engineers create software that they "know" is correct. The thesis is that most of such code is straightforward and it is plain to see that it is correct [10]. The remaining not-so-obvious parts are separable from the rest, and certainty of the correctness of each such part is developed through a serious individual process of abstract reasoning. If this thesis is correct, then a software verification system can achieve its objectives using two qualitatively different subsystems. The first addresses the not-so-obvious and is the general mathematics subsystem that handles theory and proof modules. The second is a code justification checker that examines the specifications embedded in code to determine whether they are "obviously" correct, given the specifications and annotations in the code and the definitions and theorems developed in the supporting theories.

6   Verified Reusable Components

When reusable components are fully specified and verified, the cost can be amortized over a large base of usage. This is possible if verification supportive component interfacing machinery cleanly decouples the implementations of components from their deployments. This decoupling is the motivation for the abstract specification of List component. Using that specification, it becomes possible to cleanly verify the realization (code) in Figure 1 is correct with respect to the specification of the enhancement operation Flip_Rem, also shown in the figure.

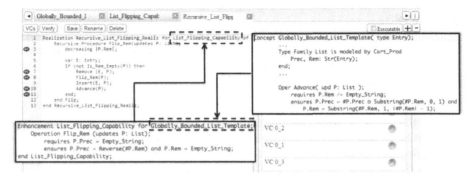

Fig. 1. Example Reusable Component Verification

The code in Figure 1 is the same as the one presented in [1], except that this one has now been mechanically verified. The syntactic slot for the decreasing clause in this recursive procedure enables a software engineer to annotate the code and facilitate automatic proof of termination. Here, in the blue ovals down the left hand side, the term VC stands for verification condition. The RESOLVE verifier has analyzed "Flip_Rem" code using its specification and specifications of operations it reuses, generated the VCs for total correctness (detailed in [3]), and proved them. Though not all components at the RESOLVE web IDE are verified or even verification amenable because this is still ongoing research, it is a useful prototype.

7   Conclusions

To meet the challenge of building verified software components, a verification-driven language design is necessary. Characteristics of such a language do not match those of currently popular languages. Recognizing this means that neither constraining an existing language nor adding on is a viable strategy. In particular, the overarching soundness requirement means that mechanisms for both specification and mathematical development of the theories used in these specifications must be an integral part of the language.

Succeeding in the goal of building verified software components still will not mean that all the software the compiler processes is absolutely correct because that software may not have been properly specified to meet the objectives of the real world system in which it is to be embedded. Regardless, developing a verifying compiler and building verified components would certainly represent a major advance for our field, but the challenge will only be met when the realities of what is involved are squarely faced. Among these realities is the need to educate the next generation of software engineering workforce on the principles of verified software construction [14].

Acknowledgments. We wish to thank our research groups for their contributions to the ideas discussed here. We also acknowledge United States National Science Foundation grants CCF-0811748, CCF-1161916, DUE-1022191, and DUE-1022941.

References

1. Hoare, C.A.R.: The Verifying Compiler. A Grand Challenge for Computing Research. JACM 50(1), 63–69 (2003)
2. Klebanov, V., et al.: The 1st Verified Software Competition: Experience Report. In: Butler, M., Schulte, W. (eds.) FM 2011. LNCS, vol. 6664, pp. 154–168. Springer, Heidelberg (2011)
3. Sitaraman, M., et al.: Reasoning About Software-Component Behavior. In: Frakes, W.B. (ed.) ICSR 2000. LNCS, vol. 1844, pp. 266–283. Springer, Heidelberg (2000)
4. Sitaraman, M., Adcock, B., Avigad, J., Bronish, D., Bucci, B., Frazier, D., Friedman, H.M., Harton, H.K., Heym, W., Kirschenbaum, J., Krone, J., Smith, H., Weide, B.W.: Building a Push-Button RESOLVE Verifier: Progress and Challenges. Formal Aspects of Computing 23(5), 607–626 (2011)
5. Adcock, B.: Working Towards the Verified Software Process. Ph. D. thesis, Computer Science and Engineering, The Ohio State University (2010)
6. Harton, H.K.: Mechanical and Modular Verification Condition Generation for Object-Based Software. Ph. D. Dissertation, Clemson University, 305 pages (2011).
7. Cook, C.T., Harton, H.K., Smith, H., Sitaraman, M.: Specification engineering and modular verification using a web-integrated verifying compiler. In: Proceedings of the International Conference on Software Engineering (ICSE), pp. 1379–1382 (2012)
8. Kulczycki, G.: Direct Reasoning. Ph. D. Dissertation, Clemson University, 183 pages (2004)
9. Smith, H.: Engineering Specifications and Mathematics for Verified Software. Ph. D. Dissertation, Clemson University, (to appear, 2013)
10. Kirschenbaum, J., Adcock, B., Bronish, D., Smith, H., Harton, H., Sitaraman, M., Weide, B.W.: Verifying Component-Based Software: Deep Mathematics or Simple Bookkeeping? In: Edwards, S.H., Kulczycki, G. (eds.) ICSR 2009. LNCS, vol. 5791, pp. 31–40. Springer, Heidelberg (2009)
11. Harms, D.E., Weide, B.W.: Copying and Swapping: Influences on the Design of Reusable Software Components. IEEE Transactions on Software Engineering 17(5), 424–435 (1991)
12. Kulczycki, G., Smith, H., Harton, H., Sitaraman, M., Ogden, W.F., Hollingsworth, J.E.: The Location Linking Concept: A Basis for Verification of Code Using Pointers. In: Joshi, R., Müller, P., Podelski, A. (eds.) VSTTE 2012. LNCS, vol. 7152, pp. 34–49. Springer, Heidelberg (2012)
13. DeMillo, R.A., Lipton, R.J., Perlis, A.J.: Social Processes and Proofs of Theorems and Programs. Comm. ACM 22(5), 271–280 (1979)
14. Cook, C.T., Drachova, S., Sun, Y.-S., Sitaraman, M., Carver, J., Hollingsworth, J.E.: Specification and reasoning in SE Projects Using a Web IDE. In: Proceedings Conference on Software Engineering Education & Technology, CSEE&T (2013)

Estimating the Economic Value of Reusable Green ICT Practices

Qing Gu and Patricia Lago

Department of Computer Science
VU University Amsterdam
The Netherlands

Abstract. Despite environmental concerns becoming increasingly urgent as a global issue, cost reduction is still the most important economic goal for many companies. Explicitly showing economic gains would be one of the most effective ways to motivate companies to optimize their use of ICT resources by means of sustainable software systems or green ICT practices. In this paper we propose using the e^3value technique (originally meant to model enterprises and end-users exchanging things of economic value) to estimate and quantify the business value of sustainable software and green ICT practices. We report the experiment we carried out to challenge the e^3value technique. In this experiment, we modeled a green ICT practice (*investing a desktop virtualization software to improve energy efficiency*) in a simplified yet realistic context. The results show that the applied practice would lead to an overall 47% reduction of expenses and 20% reduction of electricity consumption. Such quantification facilitates the comparison among alternative green practices and ICT-based decision making. In addition, we show that the use of e^3value technique not only supports communication of green practices among different types of stakeholders, but also facilitates reuse of the same green practice in different organizations having different ways of implementing them.

1 Introduction

Information and Communication Technology (ICT) and software systems are essential to maintain our modern way of life. The rapidly growing computation needs contribute significantly to environmental concerns due to ever increasing energy demands and greenhouse gas emissions [1, 2]. Decreasing ICT operation expenses become more and more crucial. How to make ICT greener (i.e. environmentally sustainable) and how to develop greener software has been gaining significant attention [3–5].

ICT can contribute to addressing environmental concerns in two ways, (1) by optimizing the implementation of ICT or migrating to sustainable software and thus minimizing its own environmental impact, and (2) by optimizing the business processes via more environmental sustainable software and thus minimizing the use of ICT resources [6, 7]. Currently, many green ICT practices

J. Favaro and M. Morisio (Eds.): ICSR 2013, LNCS 7925, pp. 315–325, 2013.
© Springer-Verlag Berlin Heidelberg 2013

already exist to improve the energy efficiency of both IT and its supported processes. Examples include reducing the energy consumption of PCs by enabling power management features [8], enforcing double-sided printing to save both paper and energy [9], applying cloud computing technology to significantly reduce hardware and software resources needed for individuals [10], and using a fleet management system and dynamic routing of vehicles to avoid traffic congestion and thus minimize energy consumption and transportation costs [11].

From the examples above we can see that greening ICT may save energy consumption (hence reducing cost) but it often requires additional investments, business process changes, and extra efforts from both companies and individuals. According to the analysis by Corbett [12], the most commonly cited driver for reusing green IT practices is cost saving. Especially in times of economic crisis, cost reduction becomes the most important economic objective [13] of many companies. If green practices do not lead to an explicit (and significant) reduction of costs, environmental goals are often regarded as a nice optional bonus rather than a must-have target.

There is no one-size-fits-all green solution due to the diversity of requirements and characteristics of companies. Executives need to assess the effectiveness of green ICT practices not only from a technical perspective but more importantly from an economic point of view, and not only look into short-term return on investments (ROIs) but also have a vision on long-term ones.

In addition, when green ICT practices involve software, calculating costs and ROIs is more difficult. The impact of software cannot be estimated in isolation, as it depends on many indirect factors including operation costs, hardware usage, human involvement, and system configuration. Often there is an intuition of some advantage gained when investing in such practices. This intuition is sufficient only if the company and decision makes are already fully committed to re-greening their software and ICT portfolio. In most cases evidence and quantification is the only way to handle the complexity of the practices mentioned above, and hence to create such commitment.

In our previous work [14] we proposed a green practice model which enforces linking together the economic impact and environmental effects of green practices. This model, however, does not support the quantification of economic value of green practices. Rather, the model encourages the description of financial consequences associated to each environmental effect of green practices.

The Going Green Impact Tool[1] is a software tool that compares the economic value among multiple green practices specifically for data centers. This tool provides a very comprehensive analysis on the key environmental and economic consequences of the application of certain green practices, which aids executives to determine the most effective practice. The major limitation of this tool lies in the fact that it works only for pre-defined practices, including: server optimization, power management, virtualization, free cooling and the re-use of waste heat. End-users are not able to add other solutions for analysis and comparison.

---

[1] http://ercim-news.ercim.eu/en79/special/the-going-green-impact-tool

Currently, to our knowledge there is no single tool that is able to aid decision makers to run a holistic assessment and make informed decisions. In this paper, we propose to use the e^3value, which is a management software tool to model business networks and has been successfully applied in several real life business case studies [15], to estimate and quantify the economic consequences of the application of green practices. To this end, we carried out an experiment of modeling a green ICT practice called "desktop virtualization". The results show that by applying this practice a company would reduce overall expenses with 47% and reduce electricity consumption with 20%. This research combines formalized descriptions of green ICT practices with economic models estimating the business values of ICT solutions. By modeling the application of a green practice, we can customize the value exchanges to real scenarios and estimate the expected ROIs.

The estimations above showed that while intuition was promising, the actual figures were delivering amazingly higher ROIs. We argue that such quantifications would convince organizations more easily to adopt green ICT practices, and motivate them to reuse green ICT solutions even if requiring significant investments. The remainder of the paper is structured as follows. Section 2 reports the experiment we carried out and Section 3 discusses the lessons we learned from the experiment. Section 4 concludes the paper.

2   An Experiment on Quantifying Economic Value of Green ICT Practices

2.1   Background on e3value

The e^3value technique models enterprises and end-users exchanging things of economic value, such as goods, services, and money, in return for other things of economic value. In the following, we introduce the main concepts or constructs supported by the e^3value modeling tool and their associated notations [16,17].

- **Actor.** An economically, and often legally, independent entity. Examples of an actor include a customer, an organization and a company. In the notation, an actor is represented by a plain rectangle.
- **Value object.** Something that actors exchange which is of economic value for at least one actor. A value object is a service, a good, money, or an experience. Examples of value objects are products, delivery service and tuition fee. In the notation, a value object is represented as a label on a value exchanging.
- **Market segment.** A set of actors that share a set of properties. Actors in a market segment assign economic value to value object equally. In the notation, a market segment is represented by a set of stacked rectangles.
- **Value interface.** Something that group value ports together and show economic reciprocity. Economic reciprocity means that actors/market segment will only offer value objects if they will receive value objects in return. In the notation, the value interfaces are drawn at the sides of actor/market segments as a thin rectangle with rounded corners, with value interfaces within.

– **Value port.** Something that is used by an actor/market segment to provide or request a value object. In the notation, a value port is shown as a small arrow inside a value interface.
– **Value exchange.** Connect two value interfaces and represent a potential trade of value objects. In the notation, value exchanges are drawn as lines connecting the port of actors/market segment to each other.
– **Dependency path.** The path where value exchanges, which is used to count the number of exchanges. In the notation, dependency path starts with a start stimulus and ends with a stop stimulus.

Many e^3value constructs can be associated with numbers or parameters, such money transfers as well the number of consumer needs (here the need for concurrent computing). If done correctly, the e^3value modeling tool generates net value flow sheets, which show for each actor in the model the amount flowing into and out from an actor.

2.2 Our Experiment

Aiming at assessing the feasibility of quantifying economic values of green ICT practices, we carried out an experiment by modeling the application of a practice called *desktop virtualization*, which has been selected from the list of green solutions provided by MJA (Meerjarenafspraken meaning long-term agreements)[2]. This practice is described as:

A desktop virtualization software facilitates the use of thin clients (i.e. workstations with minimal hardware configurations). These thin clients are far more energy efficient than regular fat client computers. There is however an increase in server side computing due to the extra load of providing the desktops, which leads to an increase in energy consumption of servers.

From this description, we elicited the following expected effects and associated economic impact:.

– *Decrease energy consumption of client workstations, which decreases energy consumption costs of client workstations.*
– *Increase energy consumption of servers, which increase energy consumption costs of servers.*
– *Acquisition of thin clients, which may rise IT equipment acquisition costs.*
– *Need to implement or purchase virtualization software, which requires short term investment.*

Using the e^3value modeling tool, we modeled an AS-IS situation (i.e. usage of fat-client without virtualization) and TO-BE situation (i.e. usage of thin clients with virtualization) with the period of *three years*. Figure 1 shows the AS-IS situation, where company X purchases a number of fat-clients and servers from

---

[2] The MJA is a voluntary agreement between the Dutch government and the largest energy consumers in the Netherlands, these being both large industries (e.g. banks and telecom providers) and higher education institutes (e.g. universities).

hardware suppliers in order to meet its computation needs, pays money to electricity suppliers for the electricity consumed by these fat clients and servers, and hosts an IT department (within the company or outsourced) to maintain the hardware devices ensuring they perform as expected. Figure 2 illustrates the TO-BE situation, where company X purchase thin clients rather than fat clients and the IT department has an additional task of providing and maintaining a virtualization software to deliver desktop virtualization service.

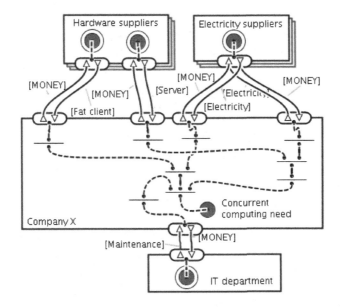

Fig. 1. Usage of fat clients, without virtualization

Value exchanges can be calculated along multiple dependence paths presented in the models. The paths start with the start stimulus 'Concurrent computing need' of Company X. Such need can be fulfilled by a combination of three components: thin clients, a server, and maintenance service (see the AND fork in Figure 2 labeled with (1)). To give an example of the dependent paths, consider the value exchanges related to the thin clients (2), which consists of acquisition of thin clients (3) and energy consumption of these thin clients (4). The acquisition of thin clients requires value exchange with the hardware suppliers (5) and the use of these thin clients requires electricity, which requires another value exchange with the electricity suppliers (7). Since the electricity is charged per month whereas the computing need is charged for three years, the fork (6) automatically normalizes costs in 1-month fractions.

After modeling the actors and value exchanges between them, we assigned parameters (with assumptions) to each value exchange in order to estimate the costs. The parameters we assigned for the two situations are listed in Table 1.

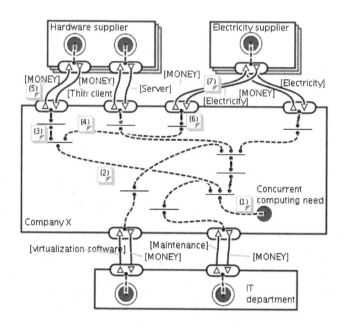

Fig. 2. Usage of thin clients, with virtualization

Table 1. The parameters assigned to As-Is and To-Be situations

Attribute	As-Is situation	To-Be situation
Number and type of clients	50 fat clients	50 thin clients
Price for each clients	600 euro	400 euro
Number of servers	1	1
Energy consumption of a client per month	180W*10h*22d= 39.6kW	20W*10h*22d = 4.4 KW
Energy consumption of a server per month	250W*24h*30d=180kW	400W*24h*30d = 288KW
Price of energy per kWh	0.5 euro	0.5 euro
Maintenance cost per client per year	50 euro	25 euro
Maintenance cost per server per year	400 euro	400 euro
Desktop virtualization software license per year	NA	400 euro

With the provided parameters, the $e^3 value$ modeling tool generated a spreadsheet that calculates the costs spent and revenue gained by each actor after three years. From the report, we could quantify the economic benefits that we should expect by reusing the green ICT practice:

- Energy consumption costs of client workstations is decreased: from 35,640 euro to 3,960 euro.

- Energy consumption costs of servers is increased: from 3,240 euro to 5,184 euro.
- Acquisition of thin clients requires an investment of 20,000 euro.
- Desktop virtualization software license requires an investment of 1,200 euro.

In this example estimation results show that the applied practice would lead to an overall 47% reduction of expenses and 20% reduction of electricity consumption.

3   Discussion

3.1   Assumptions Made in the Experiment

For the sake of space and readability, the green practice in our experiment has been modeled in a simplified yet realistic context.

First of all, we limited the number of actors, including only the ones that are essential and highly relevant to the green practice. In real life, thin clients and fat clients can be purchased from multiple vendors in multiple times and with potentially different prices. To simplify the models, we assumed that all the equipment is purchased from a set of vendors concurrently with a fixed price.

Second, we simplified the calculation of electricity tariff. Electricity prices may vary depending on regions, countries, distribution network of the same country, type of customers, and type of contracts. In this experiment, we assumed that electricity is provided by a set of providers of the same type and with a fixed rate. However, rates are all taken from real providers.

Third, we constructed the relation between IT maintenance and the company in a simplified manner. In reality, the way in which IT services are arranged can be quite complex and the cost for IT maintenance can be charged differently. In this experiment, we assumed an average maintenance cost per hardware per year. In addition, often a company already has a number of computers in use; when deciding to apply desktop virtualization, the disposal cost of legacy hardware equipment should also be considered. Customization is needed when modeling the value exchanges and estimating the expected ROIs in real scenarios.

3.2   Advantages of Visualizing Value Exchanges

The results show that the models in our experiment well simulate the value exchanges under the simplified context and make the economic value of the green practice explicit. The e^3value technique provides a graphical overview of a resource exchanging network of a company. The visualization of participants and their relations in terms of value exchanges aids the analysis of the economic viability of the network. During our experiment, we noticed that the model helps us think thoroughly about the business model where the desktop virtualization practice would be applied. We need to decide, for instance, which actor(s) is (are) responsible for paying the electricity bills. In many companies, electricity bills are paid by their financial departments. However, some companies break down the energy consumption of the ICT services to each internal department and consequently each department has to pay its energy bill from its own budget. In that case, we need to model all the departments where desktop virtualization would be used as well as the resource exchanges occurred at the departments (e.g. with the electricity suppliers and the company). From this example we can see that when applying the same green practice under different business models, it may lead to different economic value for different participants. Since the e^3value technique helps to consider a green practice in the context of the business model of a company, it encourages the alignment between business strategies and environmental ICT solutions.

Explicitly modeling the resource exchanges related to green practices within the business model of a company also urges ICT technicians to be aware of economic value of certain ICT solutions. Technicians often consider only quality attributes (e.g. performance, security) when proposing ICT solutions to meet business needs of a company. The short- and long- term economic impact of the ICT solutions, however, often get little attention, as long as the solutions meet the budget planned. Using the e^3value technique, ICT technicians are able to compare alternative ICT solutions, especially from the economic perspective, and decide the one that suits best the company's needs. For instance, desktop virtualization can be implemented in many different ways: by using thin clients and storing the "virtualized desktop images" on a central server (as we modeled in our experiment); or by running multiple virtual machines on local hardware such as laptops without a server. While the former requires a central image management software, the latter requires the realization of desktop virtual machines. These two solutions may require different actors and different value exchanges. With the help of the e^3value technique, technicians are able to compare the economic influence of different solutions and thus make informed decisions.

3.3 The e^3value Technique vs Spreadsheet Applications

One could argue that without using the e^3value technique, a spreadsheet application, such as excel sheet, recoding and calculating the cost would also be sufficient. We agree that using excel (or similar software tools) would be computationally equivalent to the e^3value modeling tool in terms of the calculation of costs. In fact, the report generated by the e^3value modeling tool is in the form of excel spreadsheets. However, e^3value models are different from spreadsheet applications, which focus only on numbers and calculations. The e^3value modeling tool, instead, provides a graphical interface both for illustrating the inter-related financial dependencies between actors for filling parameters by end-users. The e^3value model cannot be replaced by any spreadsheet applications specifically because it helps to achieve the following two goals.

A first goal is to support communication of green practices among different types of stakeholders. While technical stakeholders would be comfortable in working directly with formulas and textual calculation (like in Excel), there is the need to communicate about a practice with business people and strategic decision makers. For instance, communication is needed when justifying among alternative practices, or comparing the pros and cons of different ways of implementing the same practice within a company. Such communication must be supported by a visual (i.e. more readable) notation.

A second goal we want to achieve is to facilitate reuse of the same green practice in different organizations having different ways of implementing them (e.g. because of different departments involved, or different factors that are variable in one company and constant in another). Whenever a practice should be reused, its contextualization changes. While applying the changes in a visual model is straightforward (assuming one knows the modeling notation), applying the same changes in a textual calculation (like in Excel) is error prone and hinders reuse.

3.4   Reuse Green ICT Practices

Reusing green ICT practices in different organizations requires customizing the e3value model to estimate their organization-specific business impact in terms of the economic value. The level of customization depends on how green practices are reused.

If a green practice is implemented in the same way but in different organizations, the e^3value model associated to the practice can be reused as-is but the value of the factors need to be customized. More specifically, supposing the green practice in our experiment will be reused by another organization, the value filled in Table 1 needs to be customized to adapt to the organizational settings, e.g. the *number of clients* will be changed according to the number of employees of the specific organization, the *Price of energy per kWh* will be changed according to the offer of the specific energy supplier. It is clear that in this scenario customizations are limited to "standard variables" whose values change per organization.

If a green practice is implemented in a different way, the complete e^3value model associated to the practice (and not just the variable values) changes too. For example, supposing the green practice in our experiment will be reused by another organization that decides to outsource IT maintenance to another company, the changes to the e^3value model will be limited. In this case, *IT department* in Figure 2 will be replaced by an IT company and the maintenance fee in Table 1 might be changed according to the agreement between the IT company and the organization. However, supposing the green practice will be reused by another organization that decides to move desktop virtualization to the cloud, the changes to the e^3value model will be significant. In that case, a cloud provider will be added as an additional actor in Figure 2, value exchanges between the organization and the cloud provider will be added, servers will be (most likely) removed, and value exchanges between IT department and the organization should also be customized. It is clear that in these scenarios customizations regard the overall context where the practice should be applied, and the context changes can be more or less extensible.

In summary, when reusing green ICT practices there are different types of context changes that are likely to be encountered, and the possible business impacts also differ in their level and significance. Reusing and customizing the e^3value model help highlighting issues relevant to reusing practices in different contexts. Being green IT an area still in progress, green practices are likely to belong to the second type of customization (for the near future at least). The first type of customization (limited to standard variables) will be possible when more standard and well experimented practices will become available.

3.5   Future Improvements

For demonstration purposes, we show in Section 2 that it is feasible to use the e^3value technique to estimate the economic impact of green practices. The models, however, can be improved in the future in multiple ways. First of all, the models can be further customized to a real case scenario with actual actors and pricing, and most importantly, a real life business model. Second, the energy consumption of hardware devices can be measured instead of estimated to improve the accuracy of the cost estimation. Third, the short-term investments (e.g. acquisition of hardware devices) and long-term costs (e.g. energy consumption) can be distinguished and analyzed in order to provide a thorough estimation of economic impact of green practices.

4   Conclusions

In this paper we applied the e^3value technique to estimate the economic value of green ICT practices. Such economic value can be influenced by various aspects including investment cost, size of companies, pricing and duration. The application of e^3value technique allows to perform trade-off analysis to select among different green practices, particularly from an economic perspective. When cost of green is quantified and ROI is estimated, informed decisions can be made before actual investments.

Most green ICT practices do not yet particularly address software-specific aspects. Our approach allows to clearly separate the role of software (e.g. virtualization software in the experiment here presented) from the role of other factors, and calculate its direct and indirect economic impact. This is the first step towards calculating how much green software costs, and motivating organizations to reuse green ICT solutions based on informed decisions.

We are launching a nationwide project among the companies that are active in re-greening their IT portfolio. We plan to carry out industrial studies that will both demonstrate the value of the method for decision making, and allow them (and us) to uncover and reuse best practices, or new opportunities, by directly addressing investments in software applications.

Acknowledgment. The authors would like to thank Jaap Gordijn for his assistance in constructing the e^3value models here presented. We would also like to thank Frank Hartkamp (program advisor Agentschap NL) for providing us access to the MJA green ICT practices, and Jaak Vlasveld (program me manager Consortium Green IT Amsterdam Region) for interesting discussions on the role of business value estimations of green ICT practices.

References

1. Omer, A.M.: Energy, environment and sustainable development. Renewable and Sustainable Energy Reviews 12(9), 2265–2300 (2008)
2. Asif, M., Muneer, T.: Energy supply, its demand and security issues for developed and emerging economies. Renewable and Sustainable Energy Reviews 11(7), 1388–1413 (2007)
3. Mingay, S.: Green ICT: A new industry shockwave (2007)
4. Mattern, F., Staake, T., Weiss, M.: ICT for green: how computers can help us to conserve energy. In: Proceedings of the 1st International Conference on Energy-Efficient Computing and Networking. e-Energy 2010, pp. 1–10. ACM, New York (2010)
5. Vereecken, W., Van Heddeghem, W., Colle, D., Pickavet, M., Demeester, P.: Overall ICT footprint and green communication technologies. In: Proceedings of the 4th International Symposium on Communications, Control and Signal (ISCCSP), pp. 1–6. IEEE (2010)
6. Park, J.K., Cho, J.Y., Shim, Y.H., Kim, S.J., Lee, B.G.: A proposed framework for improving IT utilization in the energy industry. World Academy of Science, Engineering and Technology 58 (2009)
7. Davidson, E., Vaast, E., Wang, P.: The greening of IT: How discourse informs IT sustainability innovation. In: Proceedings of Conference on Commerce and Enterprise Computing, pp. 421–427. IEEE (2011)
8. Murugesan, S.: Harnessing green IT: Principles and practices. IT Professional 10, 24–33 (2008)
9. Mitchell, R.L.: Get up to speed on green IT. Technical report, Computerworld (2008)
10. Liu, L., Wang, H., Liu, X., Jin, X., He, W., Wang, Q., Chen, Y.: GreenCloud: a new architecture for green data center. In: Proceedings of the 6th International Conference Industry Session on Autonomic Computing and Communications Industry Session, pp. 29–38. ACM (2009)
11. Boudreau, M., Chen, A., Huber, M.: Green IS: Building sustainable business practices. Information Systems: A Global Text (2008)
12. Corbett, J.: Unearthing the value of green IT. In: ICIS, p. 198. Association for Information Systems (2010)
13. Sarkar, P., Young, L.: Managerial attitudes towards green IT: An explorative study of policy drivers. In: Proceedings of PACIS, pp. 1–14 (2009)
14. Gu, Q., Lago, P., Potenza, S.: Aligning economic impact with environmental benefits: A green strategy model. In: Proceedings of First International Workshop on Green and Sustainable Software (GREENS), pp. 62–68 (June 2012)
15. Gordijn, J., Yu, E., van der Raadt, B.: E-service design using i* and e³ value modeling. IEEE Software 23(3), 26–33 (2006)
16. Henkel, M., Perjons, E.: Ways to create better value models. In: Proceedings of the 3rd Workshop on Value Modeling and Business Ontologies (VMBO 2009), Stockholm, Sweden (2009)
17. Gordijn, J., Akkermans, H.: E3-value: Design and evaluation of e-business models. IEEE Intelligent Systems 16(4), 11–17 (2001)

Composition and Self-Adaptation of Service-Based Systems with Feature Models

Javier Cubo, Nadia Gamez, Lidia Fuentes, and Ernesto Pimentel

Dpto de Lenguajes y Ciencias de la Computación, Universidad de Málaga
{cubo,nadia,lff,ernesto}@lcc.uma.es

Abstract. The adoption of mechanisms for reusing software in pervasive systems has not yet become standard practice. This is because the use of pre-existing software requires the selection, composition and adaptation of prefabricated software parts, as well as the management of some complex problems such as guaranteeing high levels of efficiency and safety in critical domains. In addition to the wide variety of services, pervasive systems are composed of many networked heterogeneous devices with embedded software. In this work, we promote the safe reuse of services in service-based systems using two complementary technologies, Service-Oriented Architecture and Software Product Lines. In order to do this, we extend both the service discovery and composition processes defined in the DAMASCo framework, which currently does not deal with the service variability that constitutes pervasive systems. We use feature models to represent the variability and to self-adapt the services during the composition in a safe way taking context changes into consideration. We illustrate our proposal with a case study related to the driving domain of an Intelligent Transportation System, handling the context information of the environment.

Keywords: Service Composition, Self-Adaptation, Feature Models.

1 Introduction

Current pervasive systems are composed by a wide variety of services and devices. To reduce effort and costs, these systems may be developed using existing *Commercial-Off-The-Shelf* (COTS) components or (Web) services implemented by different vendors. Technologies such as Service-Oriented Architecture (SOA) [1] enable the building of fully working systems, as efficient as possible to improve the software reusability. The adoption of mechanisms for reusing software in pervasive systems has not yet become standard practice. This is because the use of pre-existing software requires the selection, composition and adaptation of prefabricated software parts. The discovery process aims to discover the most suitable services for a client request. The adaptation process solves, as automatically as possible, mismatch cases which may be given at the different interoperability levels among interfaces, while services are composed. Moreover, reusing software in critical domains (medical, automotive, aeronautics or security) is a difficult task, due to real complex problems such as guaranteeing high levels of efficiency and safety. For instance, in particular,

J. Favaro and M. Morisio (Eds.): ICSR 2013, LNCS 7925, pp. 326–342, 2013.

the driving domain within the Intelligent Transportation Systems[1] (ITS) is a complex and safety critical environment. ITS are comprised of autonomous vehicles that can operate with minimum input from the driver. One of the critical aspects in this domain is the driver's interaction with the traffic environment. Therefore, these systems need to be developed taking into account the variability of the complex driving domain, which involves a dynamic adaptation to changing situations in the traffic environment, in order to fit the driver's safety and needs.

In addition to the wide variety of services (with different behaviours, components, elements, etc.), pervasive systems are composed of many networked heterogeneous devices (sensor nodes, smartphones, tablets, vehicles' on-board computers, or devices with RFIDs or cameras) with embedded software. Therefore, the heterogeneity can be present at any level. This can be addressed by using Software Product Line (SPL) engineering [2], which specifically focuses on variability management. SPLs aim to provide techniques for creating infrastructures that allow the rapid and systematic production of similar software systems, promoting the reuse of common core assets.

SOA and SPL approaches to software development share a common goal. They both encourage an organization to reuse existing assets and capabilities, rather than repeatedly redevelop them for new systems [3]. Then, we use these two complementary technologies to promote the safe composition in service-based systems. These systems have to be capable of handling changing situations during the composition, called *context changes*. Context information plays an important role in pervasive systems, to control their reaction depending on certain situations or to fit the user's needs. So, it is essential to manage contexts while composing services.

For this reason, as an initial attempt to solve these issues, we have developed and validated with several examples, the DAMASCo framework [4] based on SOA, which focuses on reusing services in pervasive systems accessed via their public interfaces, by means of context-aware service discovery, composition and adaptation.

However, DAMASCo still has some limitations as regards the service composition, since it does not take into account the variability of the services during the composition, which may also be changing depending on the contexts. We therefore need to address this new challenge of managing the variability of both services and contexts during the service composition process at runtime.

Feature Models (FM) [5] have been widely adopted by the SPL community to specify which elements, or *features*, of a family of products are common and which are variable. Then, a feature model permits the specification of where the variability is, independently of the core asset, and enables reasoning about all the different possible configurations of a family (corresponding to a service family in our case).

Therefore, in order to overcome the current restrictions of DAMASCo, in this work, as the main contribution, we propose to extend the DAMASCo framework with feature models to handle the runtime composition by means of service family discovery and self-adaptation when required. Thus, we use feature models to represent the variability of the services and to enable the service composition to dynamically reconfigure them when needed taking the context changes into account. To this end, we make use of Dynamic Software Product Lines (DSPLs) [6, 7], an emerging field that produces families of software products capable of adapting to

---

[1] http://www.ewh.ieee.org/tc/its/ Accessed on 4 February 2013.

requirements that change at runtime. Following this paradigm, the service composition will be performed by selecting, at runtime, a specific configuration of the service family adapted to the context requirements. To illustrate our proposal, we use a case study related to the driving domain of an ITS, in which we compose pre-existing services and adapt them to satisfy a client request.

The remainder of the paper is organized as follows. In Section 2, we show the motivation behind our proposal, comparing it with related work. Section 3 presents the DAMASCo framework as the background to our approach and explains how it is extended with feature models. In Section 4, we define a mapping between the intermediate interface model used by DAMASCo and the feature models, and we apply our approach to a case study in the ITS domain. Section 5 presents a discussion of how our proposal overcomes some limitations of DAMASCo related to the variability of service-based systems. Finally, in Section 6 we outline some conclusions and plans for future work.

2   Related Work

In the last times there have been several approaches [8,11,12,13,14,15,16,17,18] that take advantage of using Dynamic Software Product Lines applied to Service Oriented Architectures. The rationale behind this is twofold: (i) the loosing coupling in SOAs can provide DSPLs with the technical underpinnings of flexible feature management; (ii) DSPLs can provide the modeling framework to undersign a self-adaptative SOA-based system by highlighting the relationships among its parts [8].

Following this convergence, in [8], with the purpose of reconfiguring service-oriented systems at runtime, the authors use the Common Variability Language[2] (CVL) to augment processes defined in the Business Process Execution Language (BPEL) [9] with variability, which makes it possible to easily generate a DSPL and they use a dynamic version of BPEL to manage and run it. Although this approach is very focused on two particular languages (CVL and DyBPEL), the feasibility of combining these two technologies is demonstrated. In our case, we exploit this combination for managing not only the dynamic reconfiguration, but also the safe composition and self-adaptation of services described using different business process languages without the need for any knowledge of variability languages. This is an important advantage because we define a mapping to automatically create the feature model representing a family of services from a business process specification. Our framework uses an intermediate interface model that can be generated from different platforms such as BPEL or Windows Workflow Foundation, WF [10].

With a similar motivation as our approach with regard to the necessity of SOA-based systems manage their inherent variability, in [11], SPL concepts to model SOA systems as service families are used. As we propose, the modeling of the SOA variability is performed by means of feature modeling and commonality/variability analysis technique. Particularly, SoaML[3] is extended with variability modeling notation. The main benefit of this approach is that different service variants can be

---

[2] http://www.omgwiki.org/variability/doku.php Accessed on 4 February 2013.
[3] http://www.omg.org/spec/SoaML/ Accessed on 4 February 2013.

explicitly modeled, thus maximizing their reusability. However, this is not used to help the adaptation of the SOA systems at runtime. The authors study this task in [12], in which a member of the architecture can be dynamically adapted to a different member of the family at runtime. However, unlike our proposal, they do not deal with the service composition nor provide an automatic mapping to avoid SPL non-specialists have to handle with variability languages.

Montero et al. [13, 14] define a mapping between Feature Models and Business Process Model Notation[4] (BPMN) They provide a new semantic for feature models [13] in order to automate the family engineering process, obtaining the structure of a business process by means of model driven transformations. In [14], they propose the product evolution model for modeling runtime variability in business-driven systems to represent in which trigger events a business process evolves and how this evolution is managed. We also define a mapping, but with a different goal. Thus, we focus on representing the services, variability with feature models and using the DSPL paradigm to reconfigure them in order to make the service composition possible, by supporting the context changes.

Another approach that captures the variability in Business Process Modes is Provop [15], a framework for modeling and managing large collections of business process variants. In comparison to our proposal, they only mention allowing the dynamic reconfiguration of process variants at runtime as a future challenge, while we directly tackle this issue in this work.

In [16], the problem context-aware Dynamic Service-Oriented SPLs is tackled. The goal of this work is to simultaneously define at the same time a service-oriented and context-aware product derivation that monitors the context evolution in order to dynamically integrate the appropriate assets inside a running system where, as we propose, their target platforms follow the service-oriented approach. The authors address the self-adaptation problem, but they do not consider the service composition. In addition, as we have previously argued, our approach avoids forcing the definition of the services using feature models, since we propose an automatic mapping for this.

Finally, there are several approaches that use feature models to deal with the service composition [17, 18]. In [17] the matching between services during the composition is performed with feature models. The authors use feature modeling techniques to specify the variability of provided and required services, thus increasing the flexibility of the matching process. They define a mapping, but unlike us they do not provide any explanation of how the service self-adaptation process is performed. White et al. [18] use feature models to derive a new and correct service composition when a failure occurs. They demonstrate that leveraging feature models to automatically derive new service compositions, when a dependent service fails, the complexity of needing to model each individual error is eliminated. We also take advantage of this benefit, not only for composing the services when an error occurs but also for composing and self-adapting services that must work together correctly.

In summary, we take the demonstrated advantages of combining SOA and DSPL technologies by extending the DAMASCo framework with feature models, in order to manage the service variability during the discovery and composition of a service and to self-adapt the services when the context changing situations require it.

---

[4] http://www.omg.org/spec/BPMN/ Accessed on 4 February 2013.

3   Our Approach

In this section, we first present the DAMASCo framework as the foundation of our approach which will then be described. It consists of extending this framework with feature models to support service composition whilst managing the variability safely.

3.1   Background: Service Reuse with DAMASCo

DAMASCo focuses on discovery, composition, adaptation and monitoring related to context-aware pervasive systems, where devices and applications dynamically find and use components and services from their environment.

It is based on SOA, the foal of which is to achieve loose coupling among interacting services, which is necessary and beneficial to the industry. However, SOA needs to be more agile and easier to model and reuse service applications. Modeling techniques, designing architectures, and implementing tools to support adaptation of the dynamic aspects in these systems represent new challenges in this research field. To address this, DAMASCo uses a model-based service-oriented architecture approach that makes the design, development and deployment of processes more agile. We focus on pervasive systems, such as ITS domain systems, composed of a service repository, users (clients requesting services), and a shared domain ontology.

DAMASCo adopts an expressive and user-friendly graphical notation based on transition systems, which reduces the complexity of modeling services. In addition, to discovering services, in DAMASCo, operation profiles of a signature refer to OWL-S concepts with their arguments and associated semantics. Once services have been discovered, in the case there are mismatch problems, an adaptor to solve problems is automatically generated using software adaptation. An adaptor is a third-party service in charge of coordinating services involved in the system. The whole process consists of a set of processes constituting the DAMASCo architecture, as shown in Fig. 1. The elements of DAMASCo have been implemented in Python as a set of tools which generate a framework integrated in the toolbox ITACA[5].

Service Interfaces. Each interface in DAMASCo is made up of a context profile, a signature, and a protocol specified as a transition system. At the user level, client and service interfaces can be specified by using: (i) context information in XML files for context profiles; we assume context information is inferred by means of the client's requests, in such a way that as a change occurs the new value of the context attribute is automatically sent to the corresponding service; (ii) WSDL[6] descriptions are used for describing the signatures in service-oriented platforms; and (iii) business processes defined in industrial platforms, as BPEL processes or WF workflows, for protocols that define service behavior. We consider clients and services implemented as business processes which provide the WSDL and protocol descriptions.

---

[5] Accessible at http://itaca.gisum.uma.es
[6] http://www.w3.org/TR/wsdl Accessed on 4 February 2013.

Model Transformation. First, interface specifications, which have not been previously transformed by the framework, are abstracted (Fig. 1, tag A). Context-Aware Symbolic Transition Systems (CA-STSs) are extracted from the BPEL services or WF workflows, which implement the client(s) and services, through our model transformation process [19]. We have defined CA-STS as an extension of Labelled Transition Systems (LTS) [20]. These intermediate models are graphical user-friendly, and CA-STS permits capturing contexts and their changes at runtime.

Semantic-Based Service Discovery. Then, a service discovery process (Fig. 1, tag B) finds out services satisfying the client's request, i.e., with compatible capabilities to the client requirements based on similar contexts, semantic matching of signature, and behavioural compatibility. Our process identifies mismatch situations using ontologies and synchronous product [20] to determine if adaptation is required or not.

Composition and Adaptation. If adaptation is not required, then the services of the systems are already deployed without having to adapt them, only performing the composition of them. Otherwise, a full service composition and adaptation process is executed (Fig. 1, tag C). Thus, an adaptation contract to solve mismatch problems is automatically obtained, and a CA-STS adaptor specification is generated [19]. Next, the corresponding BPEL or WF adaptor service is obtained from the CA-STS adaptor specification using our model transformation process (Fig. 1, tag D). Finally, the whole system is deployed, allowing the client and services to interact via the adaptor.

However, DAMASCo does not take into account the possible variability of the services when the matching is performed, nor the variability in the context changes. Therefore, to make our approach more useful, we propose extending DAMASCo by managing the service variability with feature models to safely handle the variability in the composition and self-adaptation of the services at runtime.

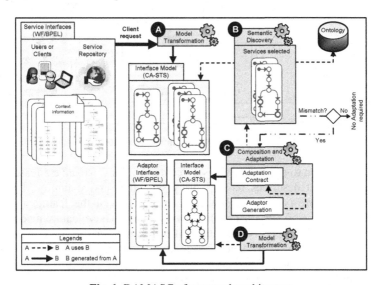

Fig. 1. DAMASCo framework architecture

3.2   Adding Feature Models to Support Safe Composition

Here, we explain how we integrate the feature models into DAMASCo, as shown in Fig. 2, in order to deal with the variability of the services during the composition. First though we briefly describe some necessary concepts of feature models.

Formally, a Feature Model [5] is a hierarchical decomposition of features to specify which elements of a family of products are common, which are variable and the reasons why they are variable, i.e., whether they are alternative or optional elements. Furthermore, apart from the relationship between the features in the diagram (called *tree constraints*), a feature dependency analysis can identify dependencies between features (called *cross-tree constraints*). Examples of such dependencies are the mutual dependency and mutual exclusion relationships. A feature model configuration is the selection of a set of features belonging to the feature model. A configuration is valid if all the features are contained in the configuration, and the non-selection of all other specific features is allowed by the feature model [21]. Thus, a valid configuration must satisfy the tree and cross-tree constraints. In our case, every valid configuration represents a potential service, but only a subset of all these possibilities are already deployed in the service repository.

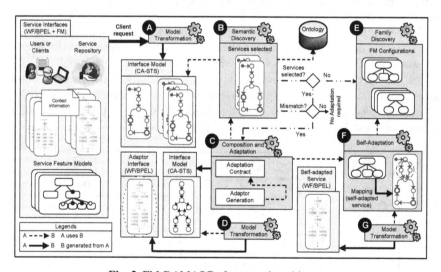

Fig. 2. FM-DAMASCo framework architecture

Firstly, in addition to the BPEL/WF service descriptions, we have a feature model for each service that describes its variability, i.e., the service family. Then, each business process corresponds with a valid configuration of the feature model that represents it, i.e., a specific product of the service family. These feature models can be designed by a user developer. Nevertheless, if we do not want to force them to have all the services represented by feature models, we can automatically generate the feature model that contains the variability corresponding to a specific service instance using the mapping that we will describe in Section 4. We focus on the representation of the service variability with respect to the context, for instance, a navigation service family may have traffic management as an optional feature, and so, this feature can be selected in a configuration where road traffic information at real time has to be considered as part of the context.

After a client executes a request, both the DAMASCo model transformation and the semantic-based service discovery process (Fig. 2, tags A and B) are activated. The semantic discovery, as previously described, tries to find the proper services for the client's request. However, due to the high variability of the services, it is possible that although a service instance of the repository matches the request, a small variation of a service could be enough to match exactly. For example, let us imagine there is no deployed navigation service with a traffic monitoring component, but there is a traffic feature in the navigation service family. In this case we need to incorporate a new process to the DAMASCo framework, that we call service family discovery (Fig. 2, tag E). We use the feature models to find a new matching, regarding the features that may suit a certain context. If the family discovery process finds the service family with the adequate feature for the context, a new valid configuration of that family containing this feature is automatically created by our feature modeling tool, Hydra[7]. We want to highlight the new configuration is valid, so, both tree and cross-tree constraints specifying restrictions between the components and context are satisfied. Hydra cannot create a configuration that does not satisfy the restrictions, so the reconfiguration is done safely, as invalid configurations are not possible.

Once the configuration representing the particular services is automatically generated by Hydra, the new service self-adaptation process added to DAMASCo (Fig. 2, tag F) is executed. Then, the CA-STS (intermediate interface model) corresponding with this feature model configuration is automatically created using the mapping defined in Section 4. Finally, this new CA-STS interface is transformed into a WF/BPEL process, following the procedure explained in Section 3.1, which is composed with the other services to satisfy the request.

4   Self-Adaptation Using Feature Models

To illustrate our proposal, we firstly present a driving domain scenario of an ITS. We assume some services have been implemented, and we manage the service composition handling the changing situations of the environment. Secondly, we define a mapping to generate the correspondences between the CA-STS model representing a service interface and the feature model of a service family. Lastly, we apply the mapping and the self-adaptation process to our case study.

4.1   Case Study: A Driving Domain

Our example consists of a driver and a service repository, whose services may be composed to get a specific purpose. The driver can perform a navigation request, and depending on context and service variations, the system must be adapted to work correctly in any situation. Services such as message console, on-board entertainment, navigation, maps, traffic management, weather information, or POI notifications, are

---

[7] Accessible at `http://caosd.lcc.uma.es/spl/hydra`

some of the applications in vehicles [22]. In our driving scenario, we have implemented (in BPEL and WF) the following services: message console, navigation, maps and traffic services. Figure 3 shows the transition systems (represented with our CA-STS interface model) corresponding to the implemented services, obtained through the model transformation process (see Figure 1), in which we have abstracted parameters to simplify the interfaces.

The driver uses the message console to request the navigation to a specific destination, which in turn interacts with the navigation service that is in charge, using the maps service, of calculating the route to the destination. The context information detailed in the context profile of each service means the service requires such contexts, and they have to be considered during the composition of the system at runtime. For example, the message console service automatically obtains both the location and the language of the driver (*loc* and *lang* contexts) from the GPS and on-board computer settings, respectively. On the other side, the driver will indicate the context info related to the route type (*route* context), as well as whether he/she wants to avoid the toll road or not (*toll* context) and with traffic monitoring or not (*traffic* context). These driver preferences may change at runtime. Default values for these contexts are used if the driver does not specify them. DAMASCo performs the composition process of this scenario, in which CA-STS service interfaces are synchronised through an adaptation process that solve any mismatch problems during the composition. As explained in Section 3, we use a semantic-based discovery that uses an ontology to search services that match with the client's request. We have generated a driving domain ontology for our example using Protégé 4.0.2.

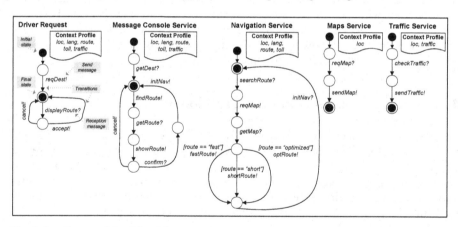

Fig. 3. Interface models of the driver request and the services for the driving domain scenario

Once DAMASCo performs the composition, it can control dynamic context changes, by capturing and handling such changes, and it simulates the dynamic update of the environment according to the context changes at runtime. Now, let us imagine the driver decides that the route be calculated avoiding any possible traffic problems at runtime. Therefore, in this case the traffic context needs to be considered in the services participating in the composition. In addition, the semantic discovery process cannot find a navigation service which checks the traffic management. Therefore, the FM-DAMASCo uses the discovery family process, which finds a feature traffic, among the navigation service family, and the self-adaptation of the navigation service for adding this feature to it. This will be explained in Section 4.3, but first, we present the mapping between CA-STS models and feature models.

4.2   Mapping between Interface Models and Feature Models

In order to avoid new feature models having to be defined for services already deployed in a specific pervasive system, we define a mapping between the CA-STS interface model and the feature model (Table 1). This mapping allows the automatic generation of the feature model that corresponds with a service defined in BPEL or WF. Then, we also use the model transformation between WF/BPEL and CA-STS. As shown in Table 1, for each service we create a new feature model with the service name as the root feature. This root feature has two mandatory children: protocol and context. The context feature has all the context items defined in the context profile as optional children. They will be the contexts that may be considered during the service execution. The protocol will contain as children, the features with the ordered message names according to the message sequence defined in the corresponding CA-STS. Then, for every message, which implies a transition in the CA-STS model, a new mandatory feature message must be added as a child of the protocol feature.

Table 1. Mapping between CA-STS Model and the Feature Model of the service family

Finally, we map the alternative sequences (such as *ifelse* or *pick* activities in BPEL or WF) represented in the CA-STS interface as different branches or transitions. Since these alternatives will send or receive several messages depending on different values of data, we add a mandatory child of the protocol feature that will contain alternative XOR features for every message. Furthermore, we must add a cross-tree constraint with a mutual dependency of the value that implies a message (e.g., *Value₁ implies Message₁*). In addition, if this data coincides with a context item, then we add the values as alternative XOR features of the data context.

Apart from the purpose of using the mapping to represent the services without a previous correspondence with a feature model, this mapping is also used to help the self-adaptation of services when required during the composition. Following the DSPL paradigm, the runtime self-adaptation can be defined in terms of replacing the current feature model configuration for a new configuration adapted to the current requirements. As described in Section 3.2, in the case that the semantic discovery process does not find the service instance that matches with the client request, the service family discovery will try to find, from among the family, a variation of the existent services that better fits the request. Then, in our approach, applying the DSPL paradigm for self-adaptation during composition also means having to replace a feature model configuration with another one. In this case, we replace the configuration representing the service which better matches with the request with another configuration with a small variation to exactly match the request.

Therefore, our process uses both configurations (the previous and the new one [23, 24]), the feature model, the CA-STS interface of the service that fits better, and the mapping to automatically create the new CA-STS which represents the adapted service. In the next section, we detail this process and the mapping over our example.

4.3   Applying our Approach in ITS

Figure 4 shows the feature model of the navigation service. As defined in the mapping it is composed of the protocol and context features. The protocol contains the mandatory features that have to be in all the navigation services (the ones that appear in the navigation service of Figure 3) and several optional features, such as the traffic management or the point of interest (POI) alerts. Furthermore, some features have several XOR alternative children, like the type of route to be calculated (fast, short or optimized route). The context contains all the possible (optional features) context items that the navigation system may consider, such as location, traffic, weather, and so on. For the sake of simplicity, we have only represented (in Figure 4) the possible context values for the type of route context to calculate the route according to the driver preferences, and for the traffic context to indicate whether the driver requires traffic monitoring (traffic true) or not (traffic false).

As explained in the mapping definition, there are also dependencies between the context values and the alternative features in the protocol. For instance, *Fast implies FastRoute* means that if the context feature *Fast* is selected in a valid feature model configuration, then the protocol message feature *FastRoute* must also be selected. In this way, we avoid creating invalid configurations where the context variations are not satisfied by the protocol. This is verified every time we create a new configuration during the self-adaptation process in order to carry out a safe reconfiguration.

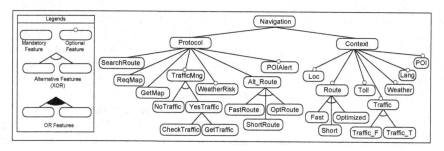

Fig. 4. Feature Model for the navigation service

The self-adaptation of the navigation service to include the traffic management is depicted in Figure 5. Firstly, the navigation feature model configuration represents the corresponding navigation service shown in Figure 3. This configuration does not consider the traffic monitoring in its context, so the protocol calculates the route without taking traffic incidences into account. Furthermore, other contexts (such as the notification of nearing points of interest and the calculation of the route taking into account weather warnings) are not considered in this configuration, so their correspondent optional features are removed. In the case that the driver wants to incorporate the traffic context into the navigation service, this service can be adapted as that context and feature are contemplated in the navigation family (Figure 4). At feature model level, this adaptation consists of adding the optional features (and its children) related to the traffic not selected in the previous configuration, in a new configuration, as observed in the navigation feature model adapted configuration (shown in green in Figure 5). Then, our self-adaptation process uses the CA-STS interface of the previous navigation service, the navigation FM configuration, the navigation FM adapted configuration, and the mapping to automatically generate the CA-STS interface model of the navigation service adapted, which already consider the traffic management (corresponding to the part of the CA-STS interface in green, surrounded by a dashed blue circle in Figure 5). The adapted navigation service will be composed with the rest of the services of our driving scenario, including the traffic service in the composition, in the same way as explained in Section 4.1. With this application, we illustrate how by using our approach we obtain a safe reuse based on a self-adaptation of the navigation service, with the purpose of fulfilling a request that a priori would have not been satisfied by any other existing service of the repository.

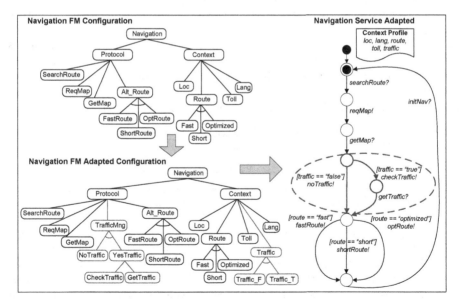

Fig. 5. Self-Adaptation of the navigation service

5   Discussion

In this section, we discuss (i) the benefits and drawbacks, (ii) the main contributions for the ITS domain, and (iii) other possible applications of our approach.

Benefits and Drawbacks. The main benefit of our proposal is that, using the SPL approach, we can significantly increase the number of client requests satisfied in a repository with a relatively small number of services deployed. For instance, in our navigation service family we have three optional features (Figure 3) in the protocol. This means that these features can be present or not in a service valid configuration. Selecting or unselecting these three optional features we have a total of $2^3=8$ valid configurations, i.e., 8 different services for this family. So, although there will be deployed, e.g., 2-3 different navigation service instances in the repository, with our approach we can carry out 8 different kinds of requests for this service. These numbers are only considering the optional features of a family. But if we consider the variable (OR and XOR) features, the number of configurations increases greatly. Table 2 shows the number of possible valid configurations with respect to the number of family services for a specific domain and considering the average of the variable parts per service. Thus, 10 services working together could satisfy $(2^{10}-1)=1023$ different potential client requests. Nevertheless, if as we propose in this work, instead of 10 single services we have 10 service families with an average of $2^3=8$ possible configurations per service, then we can satisfy 8*1023=8184 requests. Then, using our approach, in this small service repository with a few members per family, we will increase the number of possible requests satisfied by more than 7000. Furthermore, a real repository for a specific domain (e.g., the driving domain) can have 20 services with an average of 6 variations (optional and alternative features) per service. In this case, we have a total number of 1280 possible valid configurations and the number of possible client requests satisfied by these configurations increases exponentially.

Table 2. Number of possible valid services configuration

Service Families	Variations per Service	Valid Configurations
10	3	80
10	6	640
20	6	1280
30	10	30270

Obviously, this entails an aggregate cost, as to set up a SPL infrastructure may require great effort and the designing of 20 service families is a non-trivial task. Although the defined mapping can be used to automatically create a feature model from an interface model, this will represent a single service and not a whole family. Then, the variability must be added to the feature model by hand. However, though the definition of the service families may have an initial cost, as soon as individual services start to be automatically adapted in order to satisfy different client requests, which would otherwise require the implementation of new services, this initial effort becomes cost-effective. Therefore, the adoption of the SPL approach is justified in repositories where the number of services and possible variants per service is not very small. For instance, for 10 services with 3 variations per service, we can satisfy more than 7000 requests more than in the case of 10 single services. However, if we have a repository with 3 services and 2 variations per service, we only satisfy 5 requests more using our approach. In this case, the effort to build the family is not rewarded. Another example which involves a greater cost that provided benefits is in static environments where not many client requests are made during the system execution. In this case, it is pointless to have big service families with configurations that will never be used. We must therefore look for a compromise between the repository size and the necessity of defining the service families considering the benefits obtained.

Finally, we wish to stress that the service family discovery process is performed at family level not at configuration level. Therefore, in order to search for matches, the process does not have to look for the thousands of .xml files representing all the configurations (30270 in the case of 30 services), but only in the 30 .xml files representing the families, which is a fast task for current computers.

Contributions in the ITS Domain. Traditionally, when a vehicle is designed and manufactured, it is given a specific set of hardware and software components. This is a disadvantage in case new applications have to be incorporated to the vehicle, reducing the cost-effectiveness of the implementation and maintenance of vehicular software. For this reason, AUTOSAR[8] (AUTomotive Open System ARchitecture) is a worldwide development cooperation of car manufacturers, suppliers and other companies such as software industry. The main purpose is to provide a basic infrastructure to help develop vehicular software. Nevertheless, AUTOSAR currently only delivers the standard specifications not an implementation of the basic software.

Aspects such as electronic tolling, road safety, the user interface, and the provision of information to the driver, are crucial in the vehicular environment. In order to achieve these objectives, it is essential to develop a correct architecture for the definition of services. Some work [25] has already been worked on the creation of a service-oriented architecture for an on-board computer, by using the composition as OSGi technology and the development of system management information through web and distributed environments. In addition, techniques to address the variability of the complex driving domain have to be considered, allowing the adaptation to changing situations in traffic environments and to meet the drivers' safety and needs.

The generation of an architecture and the implementation of the services is beyond of scope of this work. Our proposal is complementary to these two different efforts (work in [25] and the AUTOSAR initiative), since we tackle the reuse and maintenance of previously implemented services with the main goal of facilitating the handling the variability, in this case, of the driving domain. And we do this by means of self-adaptation mechanisms based on SOA and SPL paradigms.

Other Applications. In this work, we have focused on applying the DSPL approach to self-adapt the services when is required during the context-aware composition. But, as we have mentioned, other applications can be also tackled with our approach, such

---

[8] http://www.autosar.org/ Accessed on 4 February 2013.

as service dynamic reconfiguration or evolution. On the one hand, ITS domain is an example of systems that should be able to adapt their devices to some context changes with minimum human intervention, and so a given kind of dynamic self-adaptation is necessary to adapt them to context changes, such as network degradation or sudden events. In this sense, DAMASCo uses the DSPL approach by replacing the current FM configuration for a new one adapted to the context change, as explained in [26]. On the other hand, ITS is also an outstanding example of a modern system that is in permanent evolution, as new devices, technologies or facilities continuously appear. This means it is desirable to have a mechanism that helps with the propagation of evolution changes in deployed systems. For this task, DAMASCo will use the results of our previous work for managing the evolution of product families [23, 24] and together with the mapping it will be able to evolve with new components of services already deployed. With these two applications, apart from the context-aware composition, we demonstrate the wide range of applicability of our approach based on SOA and SPL technologies working together.

6   Conclusions

In this paper, we have illustrated the need to handle the variability during the service composition in pervasive systems. Our proposal to address this challenge is based on both SOA and DSPL paradigms. Thus, we extend our DAMASCo framework with feature models to represent the variability and to dynamically reconfigure services in a safe way according to context change situations. Specifically, we have developed two new processes in DAMASCo: a service family discovery and a self-adaptation mechanism, which have been described throughout the paper. We have implemented our approach in a scenario of the ITS domain, and we have discussed the benefits, drawbacks, contributions, and other possible applications it could have.

As regards future work, we are currently working on the other two applications we discussed in the previous section. We plan to define a model-driven process to switch from one running service configuration to another by executing a plan in DAMASCo in order to self-adapt the services to context changes at runtime. In addition, to perform evolution we need to define how modifying or aggregating new behaviour (not previously contemplated for the family) into already existing services.

Acknowledgements. Work partially supported by the projects TIN2008-05932, TIN2008-01942, TIN2012-35669, TIN2012-34840 and CSD2007-0004 funded by Spanish Ministry of Economy and Competitiveness and FEDER; P09-TIC-05231 and P11-TIC-7659 funded by Andalusian Government; and FP7-317731 funded by EU.

References

1. Erl, T.: Service-Oriented Architecture (SOA): Concepts, Technology, and Design. Prentice-Hall, Englewood Cliffs (2005)
2. Pohl, K., Böckle, G., Linden, F.: Software Product Line Engineering – Foundations, Principles, and Technique. Springer, Heidelberg (2005)

3. Krut, R., Cohen, S.: Service-Oriented Architectures and Software Product Lines - Putting Both Together. In: Proc. of SPLC 2008, p. 383. IEEE Computer Soc., Los Alamitos (2008)
4. Cubo, J., Pimentel, E.: DAMASCo: A Framework for the Automatic Composition of Component-Based and Service-Oriented Architectures. In: Crnkovic, I., Gruhn, V., Book, M. (eds.) ECSA 2011. LNCS, vol. 6903, pp. 388–404. Springer, Heidelberg (2011)
5. Lee, K., Kang, K.C., Lee, J.: Concepts and Guidelines of Feature Modeling for Product Line Software Engineering. In: Gacek, C. (ed.) ICSR 2002. LNCS, vol. 2319, pp. 62–77. Springer, Heidelberg (2002)
6. Hallsteinsen, et al.: Dynamic Software Product Lines. Computer 41(4), 93–95 (2008)
7. Shen, L., Peng, X., Liu, J., Zhao, W.: Towards Feature-Oriented Variability Reconfiguration in Dynamic Software Product Lines. In: Schmid, K. (ed.) ICSR 2011. LNCS, vol. 6727, pp. 52–68. Springer, Heidelberg (2011)
8. Baresi, L., Guinea, S., Pasquale, L.: Service-Oriented Dynamic Software Product Lines. Computer 45(10), 42–48 (2012)
9. Andrews, T., et al.: Business Process Execution Language for Web Services (WSBPEL). Systems, IBM, Microsoft, SAP AG, and Siebel Systems (2005)
10. Scribner, K.: Microsoft Windows Workflow Foundation: Step by Step. Microsoft (2007)
11. Abu-Matar, M., Gomaa, H.: Variability Modeling for Service Oriented Product Line Architectures. In: Proc. of SPLC 2011, pp. 110–119. IEEE Computer Soc., Los Alamitos (2008)
12. Gomaa, H., Hashimoto, K.: Dynamic Software Adaptation for Service-Oriented Product Lines. In: Proc. of SPLC Workshops 2011. ACM (2011)
13. Montero, I., Pena, J., Ruiz-Cortes, A.: From Feature Models to Business Processes. In: Proc. of SCC 2008, pp. 605–608. IEEE Computer Soc., Los Alamitos (2008)
14. Montero, I., Peña, J., Ruiz-Cortes, A.: Representing Runtime Variability in Business-Driven Development Systems. In: Proc. of ICCBSS 2008, February 25-29, p. 241. IEEE Computer Soc., Los Alamitos (2008)
15. Hallerbach, A., Bauer, T., Reichert, M.: Capturing Variability in Business Process Models: The Provop Approach. Journal of Software Maintenance and Evolution: Research and Practice 22(6-7), 519–546 (2010)
16. Parra, C., Blanc, X., Duchien, L.: Context Awareness for Dynamic Service-Oriented Product Lines. In: Proc. of SPLC 2009, pp. 131–140 (2009)
17. Naeem, M., Heckel, R.: Towards Matching of Service Feature Models based on Linear Logic. In: Proc. of the 1st Workshop on Services, Clouds, and Alternative Design Strategies for Variant-Rich Software Systems (SCArVeS) Co-Located with SPLC 2011 (2011)
18. White, J., Strowd, H.D., Schmidt, D.C.: Creating Self-Healing Service Compositions with Feature Models and Microrebooting. Int. Journal of Business Process Integration and Management 4(1), 35–46 (2008)
19. Cubo, J., Canal, C., Pimentel, E.: Context-Aware Composition and Adaptation Based on Model Transformation. Journal of Universal Computer Science 17(15), 777–806 (2011)
20. Arnold, A.: Finite Transition Systems. International Series in Computer Science. Prentice-Hall, Englewood Cliffs (1994)
21. Batory, D.: Feature Models, Grammars, and Propositional Formulas. In: Obbink, H., Pohl, K. (eds.) SPLC 2005. LNCS, vol. 3714, pp. 7–20. Springer, Heidelberg (2005)
22. Lee, J., Kotonya, G., Robinson, D.: A Negotiation Framework for Service-Oriented Product Line Development. In: Edwards, S.H., Kulczycki, G. (eds.) ICSR 2009. LNCS, vol. 5791, pp. 269–277. Springer, Heidelberg (2009)

23. Gamez, N., Fuentes, L.: Software Product Line Evolution with Cardinality-Based Feature Models. In: Schmid, K. (ed.) ICSR 2011. LNCS, vol. 6727, pp. 102–118. Springer, Heidelberg (2011)

24. Gamez, N., Fuente, L.: Architectural Evolution of FamiWare using Cardinality-Based Feature Models. Journal of Information and Software Technology 55(3), 563–580 (2013)

25. Santa, J., Úbeda, B., Gómez-Skarmeta, A.F.: A Multiplatform OSGi Based Architecture for Developing Road Vehicle Services. In: Proc. of CCNC 2007, pp. 706–710. IEEE Computer Soc., Los Alamitos (2007)

26. Gamez, N., Fuentes, L., Aragüez, M.A.: Autonomic Computing Driven by Feature Models and Architecture in FamiWare. In: Crnkovic, I., Gruhn, V., Book, M. (eds.) ECSA 2011. LNCS, vol. 6903, pp. 164–179. Springer, Heidelberg (2011)

Leveraging Reuse-Related Maturity Issues for Achieving Higher Maturity and Capability Levels

Luigi Buglione[1,2], Giuseppe Lami[3], Christiane Gresse von Wangenheim[4],
Fergal Mc Caffery[5], and Jean Carlo Rossa Hauck[4]

[1] Engineering.IT SpA - Via R. Morandi 32, 00148 Rome, Italy
[2] Ecole de Technologie Superieure (ETS) – Montréal, Canada
[3] ISTI-CNR (Italian National Research Council) – Pisa, Italy
[4] Federal University of Santa Catarina (UFSC), Brazil
[5] Regulated Software Research Group & Lero - Dundalk Institute of Technology, Ireland
luigi.buglione@eng.it, giuseppe.lami@isti.cnr.it,
{gresse,jeanhauck}@gmail.com, fergal.mccaffery@dkit.ie

Abstract. During the past 20 years *Maturity & Capability Models* (MCMs) become a *buzzword* in the ICT world. Since the initial Crosby's idea in 1979, plenty of models have been created in the Software & Systems Engineering domains, addressing various perspectives. By analyzing the content of the Process Reference Models (PRM) in many of them, it can be noticed that reuse-related issues have unfortunately often little importance in the appraisals of the capabilities of software organizations while in practice they are considered as significant contributors in traditional process and organizational performance appraisals. While MCMs represent a good mean for assessing the status of a set of processes, integrating two or more models with a common area of focus can offer more information and value for an organization. The aim of this paper is to present some information about Reuse best practices and models, keep the best components from each model and – using the **LEGO** (Living **EnG**ineering pr**O**cess) approach to process improvement - merge those best practices from several types of maturity models into an organizational Business Process Model (BPM) in order to achieve in an easier and faster way higher organizational maturity and capability levels.

Keywords: Maturity & Capability Models (MCM), CMMI, SPICE (ISO/IEC 15504), Reuse-related issues, Improvement, LEGO approach.

1 Introduction

Recently somebody said that the 'copy & paste' computer function was one of the greatest inventions of last forty years[1]. It seems just something for kidding, but for instance from a human-computer interaction (HCI) viewpoint it was a very common-sense metaphor from every day reuses practice: copy-paste-edit, moving what yet

---

[1] http://goo.gl/d3hEo

J. Favaro and M. Morisio (Eds.): ICSR 2013, LNCS 7925, pp. 343–355, 2013.

exists. In terms of estimation practices, it'd lead to analogous estimation. But differently from other practices, reuse was not elevated in the Software Engineering studies and guides to the 'management' level, as it was something 'minor', while it's a fundamental practice and way to manage and plan e.g. product lines. Moreover, from a software measurement perspective, for measurers applying a functional size measurement (FSM) method such as IFPUG Function Point Analysis (FPA), originally reuse was included into one of the so-called GSC (General System Characteristics) in the VAF (Value Adjustment Factor), classified within Non-Functional Requirements (NFRs) and rated with a lower value than the so-called FURs (Functional User Requirement), simply contributing to 'adjusting' the unadjusted FP value (UFP). And being something within the NFR side, it was (and still is) more difficult to evaluate and rate it, also from the process side.

Observing the plenty of 'maturity models' appearing on the ICT arena during last 30 years, there were several ones in well-defined domains such as Project Management (e.g. PM3O or PMMM) or Test Management (such as TMMI or TPI), but few ones about Reuse[2]. This just because 'reuse' is a keyword for a very wide area of action, including – just to name a few – product lines, the organization of software factories for thinking and creating 'objects' to be shared and continuously improved and much more.

Thus, there is a huge need for any organization to first reinforce the knowledge and subsequent application of proper reuse practices and processes (in a broader sense, not strictly in the development terms), starting from a 'functional' reuse (reusing complete chunks of logical data and functionalities for creating new functionalities) towards a 'technical reuse' (reusing physical parts of existing logical data and functionalities for creating new functionalities) within ICT organizations [32]. Unfortunately, little efforts have been made to face such a need.

Right now few studies [21][24][25][28][31] analyzed the way for an evolutionary path to reuse, proposing or discussing the idea for 'reuse maturity models', often compliant with the well-known horizontal models such as SPICE (ISO/IEC 15504) [6][7] or CMMI [3][16][17]. But there was no 'breakouts' as well as done in other specific domains such as Project or Test Management, as previously stated. The aim of this paper is to propose a LEGO (**L**iving **E**n**G**ineering pr**O**cess)[3] application for the Reuse management area, matching together different reuse-specific processes using a four-step process, in order to obtain a comprehensive process to be applied in an organization, which could further enable to have on the technical side better estimates (the more and better reused, the lowest the effort to produce a new software solution) and for the economic side higher ROIs.

The paper is organized as follows: Section 2 discusses a possible taxonomy of MCMs by *orthogonality*, in order to better understand the possible intersections among them. Section 3 proposes a series of specific reuse maturity models and frameworks, for extracting any possible element of interest (EoI) for reinforcing a typical reuse engineering (horizontal) process. Section 4 summarizes the LEGO

---

[2] To be meant as ISO says as the "use of an asset in the solution of different problems" (ISO/IEC 24765:2010 – Systems and Software Engineering Vocabulary).

[3] **LEGO** is a new approach proposed for helping organizations in building and reinforcing their own process models moving from the combination of single items from multiple maturity & capability models (MCM). More details on Section 4.1.

approach, with its main elements and four-step process and shows the deployment of LEGO to the Reuse Management process, joining the ISO/IEC 15504 REU process area with the EoI from the previously examined reuse models/frameworks. Finally, Section 5 provides some conclusions and the next steps for this work.

2   Maturity and Capability Models (MCMs): Representations and Dimensions

Maturity & Capability Models (MCMs) represent a simple, common-sense mechanism for benchmarking entities of interest (EoI) according to established criteria. Typically most of those models are structured using five maturity levels, as well as in a Likert scale (or by the fingers of a hand). The more mature (or capable) a certain organization (or process), the higher the level. The quality of a MCM can be perceived from users if the practices for a model are properly distributed in a way to do not create any step of the 'maturity stairway' too much challenging, but having a regular progression and evolution towards higher levels. The further evolution in MCM was distinguishing 'maturity' and 'capability'. Maturity is referred to an organization, capability to single processes to be run within an organization[4]. A consolidated capability evaluation can be converted to a maturity evaluation (e.g. in CMMI there is the so-called 'equivalent staging' mechanism [1].

2.1   Why Do We Need Choosing a MCM?

This is why from the release of the Sw-CMM in the early '90s, moving from the Crosby's experience [2], plenty of MCM with the same architecture has been proposed over the years, with more than 40 models yet in 2003 when the term "MM-mania" was coined [8]. Since then, new MCM continue to be proposed joining several issues (e.g. Agile Methodologies, Architecture, Reuse, Testing, etc.)[5]. When more MCM are available within a certain application domain of interest, some suggested criteria for choosing the proper MCM to use for process assessment and improvement activities could be to choose the one that has:

- higher number of missing/improvable elements that we would want to include in our Business Process Model (BPM)[6];
- deeper granularity in the definition of processes.

2.2   Coverage and Classification of MCMs

In order to make comparisons and mapping among different MCM, a series of classifications and taxonomies are needed. For instance, MCM are typically classified by their application domains: Software-System Engineering, Security Engineering,

---

[4] Definitions of organizational maturity and process capability can be found in the ISO/IEC 15504-7 and ISO/IEC 15504-1 respectively.

[5] An updated list of such models is available at: http://www.semq.eu.

[6] For BPM it must be intended the whole process management system of an organization, wider than the solely summation of several PRM from distinct maturity models as CMMI.

Usability, etc. Few years ago, we proposed another possible criterion, looking at them in terms of *orthogonality* of the content of their PRM along the project lifecycle [19][20]:

- **Horizontal** - some of the MCM have processes that go through the whole supply chain, from requirements till their delivery: they could be classified as *'horizontal'* models. Examples of horizontal models in the ICT world are CMMI, ISO 12207/15504 or the FAA i-CMM [11].
- **Vertical** - other MCM focus on a single perspective or process category: they could be classified as *'vertical'* models [9], because going into a deeper detail on a specific viewpoint. Examples for the second group includes e.g. TMM [12] or TPI [13] in the Test Management domain, and P3M3 [14] and OPM3 [15] in the Project Management domain.
- **Diagonal** - the third categorization refers to those models whose content is in a middle way between Organizational and Supporting processes, and this is referred here as *diagonal* models. People CMM (P-CMM) [4] is an example for such category.

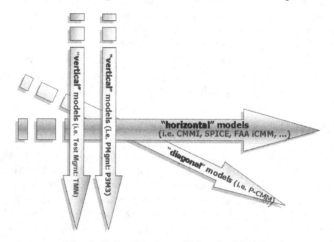

Fig. 1. A classification of Maturity Models

But the final purpose of an organization is to globally improve its BPM, results and performances by higher maturity & capability levels in its practices. And the usage of a single MCM, no matter if quite comprehensive, cannot be the final solution by a mean to achieve the desired outcomes: more MCM should be selected and joined, according to the organization's needs, maturity and capability levels at a certain moment in time. Nonetheless it would be shared thought[7], no practical ways to put it into practice have been suggested right now.

3   Reuse-Related Issues in Typical Horizontal MCMs

A question to pose is: are reuse-related issues adequately considered and evaluated in the overall context of a process improvement initiative with the current MCMs for

---

[7] E.g. SEI's PRIME (http://www.sei.cmu.edu/prime/) initiative or this 2008 SEI's study.

Software & Systems Engineering? Now it's time to take into account two of the most popular MCMs for Software & System Engineering in order to discuss the extent they address reuse-related issues: CMMI-DEV and ISO/IEC 15504 standard. We are moving from the two more known horizontal MCMs (H-MCM) because in such way it's possible to have a value-chain view, using 'reuse' as part of the whole picture and not as a detail to be analyzed separately. While CMMI includes a specific Process Reference Model (PRM), the ISO/IEC 15504 standard does not. In fact, ISO/IEC 15504 gives (in its Part 2) just a set of requirements to define a compliant PRM (i.e. a PRM having the needed characteristics to be applied in the assessment and improvement mechanism the standard itself provides). However, the ISO/IEC 12207 standard [10] provides a PRM for software that has been defined in a compliant way as respect the requirements defined in ISO/IEC 15504. Thus, it is not surprising that in the practice the ISO/IEC 12207 PRM is widely used in the application of the ISO/IEC 15504 standard. For these reasons, in the following of this paper we will use the term ISO15504-12207 to refer to the ISO/IEC 15504 standard for Process Capability Determination and Improvement + the compliant PRM defined in the ISO/IEC 12207 standard. Table 1 presents a summary of some of the reuse-related issues included in those two maturity models. The first evidence is that reuse is not addressed by these two PRM in the same way. In fact, the CMMI does not include any Process Areas directly addressing reuse issues but only a couple of practices in Technical Solution (TS) process area; on the contrary the ISO/IEC12207/15504 provides a process group on reuse composed of three processes (REU processes). Moreover it is possible to observe that reuse-related issues are mostly present as appraisal criteria rather than in terms of single processes capability/maturity indicators in the respective PRM.

Table 1. Reuse-related issues in CMMI-DEV and ISO models

Model	CMMI-DEV	ISO 15504/12207
Domain	Sw-SE	Sw-SE
PRM (source)	CMMI-DEV v1.3	ISO/IEC 12207
PRM (no. processes)	22	47
Process Categories	4 (Engineering, Process, Project, Support)	9 (Primary: Acquisition, Supply, Operation, Engineering; Organizational: Management, Reuse, Resource & Infrastructure, Process Improvement Management; Support: Supporting)
PRM reuse-related processes	None (Reuse practices are partly dealt with)	3 (REU.1 Domain Engineering; REU.2 Reuse Assets Management; REU.3 Reuse Program Management)
PAM ext. appraisals	SCAMPI v1.3 [5]	ISO/IEC 15504-2 [6] ISO/IEC 15504-5 [7]
PAM reuse-related issues	TS-SP-2.1 (Develop Alternative Solutions and Selection Criteria) TS-SP-2.4 (Perform Make, Buy or Reuse Analyses)	26 REU.1, REU.2, REU.3 related BPs

Starting from the information provided in Table 1, we can discuss in more detail the way CMMI and ISO15504-12207 address reuse-related issues both form the process definition and the appraisal/evaluation side.

While the CMMI, on the process side, does not include any direct reference to reuse-related issues, the ISO15504-12207, because it includes three processes directly addressing reuse, covers the principal aspects reuse implies both from a technical and managerial viewpoint. In particular, the processes included into the Software Reuse Group are: Domain Engineering process (aimed at developing and maintaining domain models, domain architectures and assets for the domain), Reuse Assets Management process (aiming at managing the life of reusable assets from their conception to retirement), and Reuse Program Management (aiming at planning, establishing, managing, controlling, and monitoring the organization's reuse program and systematically exploiting reuse opportunities).

On the appraisal side, CMMI presents the Specific Practice 2.4-3 "Perform Make, Buy, or Reuse Analyses" associated to the Specific Goal SG3 "Implement the Product Design" of the Technical Solutions (TS) Process Area. Also the Specific Practice 2.1-1 "Design the Product or Product Component" associated to the Specific Goal SG1 "Select Product-component Solutions"" of the same Process Area, addresses, but only in an indirect way, reuse.

The 26 Base Practices (i.e. process performance indicators) associated to the three reuse-specific processes represent the way reuse is referred by ISO15504-12207 from the appraisal viewpoint. Nevertheless, because according to the ISO/IEC 15504 scheme the Base Practices cannot be used as Capability Indicators, from a Capability/Maturity perspective such a standards doesn't take into account reuse as an indicator of Process Maturity for the overall software process (to be intended as composed of a sub-set of the processes provided by the PRM).

On the basis of the previous considerations, reuse-related issues aren't adequately considered and evaluated in the overall context of a process improvement initiative according to the two principal MCMs for Software & Systems Engineering considered. Therefore two main possibilities arise for improving the reuse-side of the organization:

- Setting up and managing distinct appraisal initiatives for the different domains of interests (with their related PRM) and after coordinating results for a common, improvement plan within the organizational BPM scope;
- Managing a single appraisal initiative, merging before the process elements into a single PRM.

Thus, we started to explore what was produced during last past 20 years in terms of MCMs on Reuse, summarizing the most relevant information in Table 2.

Table 2. Some Reuse Models/Frameworks

Model/ Framework	Repr. Type	ML (#)	Architect-Type	Comments/Notes
[21] RCMM (Reuse CMM)	Staged	5 [1-5]	Level-based	---
[22] Management tool	Staged	6 [0-5]	Level-based	Series of typical agile reqs verified + 14 BTOPP elements for reusing factors
[23] REBOOT approach (and Reuse Maturity Model)	Continuous	---	---	23 Key process areas in 5 process categories
[26] RMM (Reuse Maturity Model)	Staged	5 [1-5]	Matrix-based	5 MLs, 10 key reuse drivers
[27] 3RMM	Staged	5 [1-5]	Level-based	Several scalability factors and reuse variables
[29] RCM (Reuse Capability Model)	Staged	4 [1-4]	Level-based	4 Critical Success Factor Classes for reuse capability improvement provided
[30] RMM (Reuse Maturity Model)	Staged	6 [1-6]	Level-based	Suggestions for integrating reuse practices within the (old) Sw-CMM
[35] Lim's model	Staged	5 [1-5]	Matrix - based	10 factors of influence (drivers)
[18] RiSE Maturity Model	Staged	5 [1-5]	Matrix-based	Macro-goals for each level; 10 Factors of influence (organizational; business, technological; process)

4   Experiencing LEGO to Reuse Management

4.1   The LEGO Approach

Recently a common-sense approach, called **LEGO** (Living **EnG**ineering pr**O**cess) [33] was proposed for stimulating organizations to improve their own processes, taking pieces (such as the real LEGO bricks) from multiple, potential information sources to be integrated to form a unique, reinforced picture for a particular process or set of processes. The starting point – for this paper – is that any model/framework can represent only a part of the observed reality, not all of its possible views, simply because it needs to represent one single viewpoint at a time. Thus, through handling similar elements from different sources, we can hopefully find more 'fresh blood' for improving the organizational processes. LEGO has four main elements, as shown in Figure 2:

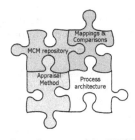

Fig. 2. The four elements of the LEGO approach

1. a 'Maturity & Capability Models' (MCM) repository (www.gqs.ufsc.br/mcm), from relevant processes or MCMs (meaning also the other dimensions – not yet the process dimension) can be identified;
2. knowledge about the process architecture of each model, for understanding how to transform desired elements from a certain model into the target format, especially when considering that the source models may have different architectures that need to be integrated into a single model;
3. mapping(s) & comparisons between relevant models, in order to understand the real differences or the deeper level of detail from 'model A' to import into 'model B';
4. a process appraisal method (PAM) to be applied on the target BPM (Business Process Model).

LEGO has also a related four-step process:

1. **Identify your informative/business goals:** clearly identify your needs, moving from the current BPM version and content.
2. **Query the MCM repository:** browse the MCM repository, setting up the proper filters in order to obtain the desired elements (processes; practices; etc.) to be inserted in the target BPM.
3. **Include the selected element(s) into the target BPM:** include the new element(s) in the proper position in the target BPM (e.g. process group, maturity level, etc.).
4. **Adapt & Adopt the selected element(s):** according to the process architecture of both process models (the target and the source one), the selected elements may need to be adapted, tailoring such elements as needed.

4.2   Applying LEGO to Reuse

One of the main requirements for improving estimates saving time by building more consistent systems is to reinforce the management of reuse practices from an overall viewpoint, from their elicitation through to the day-to-day management, as shown from a long time e.g. by QIP [34].

The focus of this work is exclusively on external models as opposed to actual (living and active) organizational practices, so that any reader can easily access to the original sources and fully understand the LEGO process, that could (eventually, if interested) be replicated in his/her own organization through forward moving from their existing organizational Business Process Model (BPM). Our aim is to show how to hybridize ideas for obtaining a better and more comprehensive final result. Thus, we list the preconditions, process and main results from the application of the LEGO process to the Software Reuse domain, in order to propose a better process that may be applied in an organization:

1. Identify your informative/business goals: Improve the estimation capability and results by a refinement in the overall management of requirements (business, technical):
2. Query the MCM repository: In this paper we consider a sub-set of the ISO/IEC 12207 reuse-related processes (i.e. belonging to the REU process Group) as the baseline for working upon, adding eventual practices from the other Reuse-related

models/frameworks listed in Table 1. After a detailed analysis, we discarded some of the above presenting models, in particular [21], proposing only a high-level staged path with no detailed elements, focusing on the remaining ones. Table 3 proposes the list of potential elements of interest (EoI) to consider for improving ISO/IEC 12207 reuse-related processes.

Table 3. Reuse Maturity & Capability Models (MCM): Elements of Interest

Model/ Framework	Elements of Interest (EoI)
Management Tool	• The study considers a series of characteristics typical to the Agile Developmernt/Management domain • It considers also from a continuous perspective a Level 0 for 'no reuse' • It considers 15 reuse factors linked to the maturity levels by categories (business; domain; organizational; process; people; technology) • Appendix G presents a mapping between the 15 factors and CMMI-DEV process areas (w/strength) • Appendix H presents a summary of the 15 factors scaled by maturity level (suggestion)
REBOOT Reuse Maturity Model	• Deal with organizational and technical aspects of reuse • 23 Key process areas in 5 categories (organization; Project Management; Dev. Process; Library; Metrics)
RMM	• 10 key drivers considered, using a matrix-based representation/approach • Particularly stressed the people/organization drivers, as well as the legal/contractual issues • To be inserted into a level-based structure
3RMM	• Information on Environments (Repository, Software, Information) + Administrative Management
RCM	• 21 Critical Success Factors corresponding to issues most critical to improving reuse capability • Intended for self-assessment and planning purposes
Lim's model	• Particular attention to the following factors o Motivation/culture; planning for reuse; metrics; legal issues; reuse inventory (assets)

RiSE Maturity Model	• Representation of the influence factors using a matrix-based view, retrieving also from past experiences and models
	• Particular interest for the following factors:
	   o Organization (Software reuse education, Rewards and Incentives; Independent team)
	   o Business (Product family approach)
	   o Technology (Repository system usage)
	   o Processes (Quality Models, Measurement, Origin of the reused asset)

3. **Include the selected element(s) into the target BPM:** Looking at the analysis of potential EoI in Table 3. The main improvements/suggestions seem to be mainly associated with the REU processes. Table 4 shows how our suggestions were introduced in the current REU processes, describing a new possible improved process that may be mapped against your own QMS internal process(es) covering that subject. The solely REU.1 process was not taken into account because its purpose, having very few details to be improved observing the reuse models listed above in previous table.

4. **Adapt & Adopt the selected element(s):** After adapting the original REU processes, as shown in the previous table, it should be mapped against the related QMS internal process covering that subject. Since many organizations adopt an ISO management system (e.g. ISO 9001:2008), a cross-check for validating potential improvements from the design phase could be achieved through re-applying the related mapping document to their own internal process (e.g. using the N/P/L/F – Not/Partially/Largely/Fully achieved ordinal scale from CMMI or

Table 4. Two ISO/IEC 15504 reuse-related processes: suggestions for improvements

ISO/IEC 15504 REU processes	Suggested Improvements
REU.2	**Reuse Asset Management**
BP 01 - Define and document an asset management strategy	• People-related aspects, as necessary skills and experience, are to be addressed in the asset management strategy [Management Tool – Factor 2] • The asset management strategy should consider and differentiate the aspects related to the asset development for reuse respect to those related to asset development with reuse [REBOOT]
BP02 - Establish a classification scheme for assets	• The integration between the asset classification scheme and the Configuration Management rules is to be addressed [Management Tool – Factor 10]
BP 03 - Define criteria for assets	• Possible measurements, to be used as a basis for the definition of criteria for assessment, are to be identified and documented [RiSE MM – Process Factors; RCM] • The determination of asset value should be the basis for the criteria definition [RCM]
BP04 - Establish the asset storage and retrieval mechanisms	• The technology support for storage and retrieval is to be defined [RiSE MM - Technological Factors]
BP 05 - Identify reusable assets.	• The integration between the asset identification and the Configuration Management rules is to be defined [Management Tool – Factor 10]
BP06 - Accept reusable assets	• The technological support for classification and record of assets as well as for their provision to the intended users is to be addressed [Management Tool – Factor 13; RiSE MM -Technological Factors] • Assets integrability is an issues to be addressed [RCM]
BP 07 - Operate asset storage	• The technological support for storage of assets is to be addressed [Management Tool – Factor 13; RiSE MM -Technological Factors]
BP08 - Record use of assets	• -
BP 09 - Notify re-users of asset status	• The notification should rely on established communication channels and an adequate organizational support [Management Tool – Factor 4 and 15]
BP10 - Retire assets	• The technical aspects of the withdrawal from the repository are to be addressed [Management Tool – Factor 13]
REU.3	**Reuse Program Management**
BP 01 - Define organizational reuse strategy	• The top management support is to be explicitly given at organizational reuse strategy definition time [Management Tool – Factor 2] • People-related aspects, as necessary skills and experience, are to be addressed in the reuse strategy [Management Tool – Factor 2] • The organizational reuse strategy should consider and differentiate the aspects related to the asset development for reuse as respect to those related to asset development with reuse [REBOOT] • The reuse organizational reuse strategy should indicate whether and at what extent the product Families approach is adopted [RiSE MM – Business Factors] • The training and education initiatives and activities should be included within the reuse program items [RiSE MM – Business Factors]
BP 02 - Identify domains for potential reuse	• -
BP 03 - Assess reuse capability	• The assessment of the reuse capability of the organization should include cost benefits analysis [Management Tool – Factor 6]
BP 04 - Assess domains for potential reuse	• A measurement scheme should be provided to support of the evaluation of the level of similarities among products in a certain domain [Management Tool MM – Factor 1]
BP 05 - Evaluate reuse proposals	• A measurement scheme should be provided to support of the evaluation of suitability of reusable items [RiSE MM – Process Factors; RCM]
BP 06 - Implement the reuse program	• ---
BP 07 - Collect and manage learning	• Details on the way learning is stored in the repository are to be provided [Management Tool – Factor 13] • The integration between the learning storage and the communication channels for spreading such a knowledge is to be addressed [Management Tool – Factor 4]
BP 08 - Get feedback from reuse	• Communication tool support is to be addressed [Management Tool – Factor 15]
BP 09 - Monitor reuse	• Monitoring is to be included in the reuse planning [Management Tool – Factor 5; RiSE MM – Organizational Factors]

SPICE). In our case, moving from CMMI-DEV, it could be used the Mutafeljia & Stromberg's mapping [36] as a basis. In this paper, our focus was limited to only the design phase. However, a case study with the application of the hybrid-REU processes will be included in a future paper.

The EoI presented in Table 3 as well as the included elements respect the BPs of the REU.2 and REU.3 processes provided in Table 4 are not to be considered exhaustive. These two tables are on the contrary to be considered as a starting point for the application of the LEGO approach in practice.

5   Conclusions and Prospects

Software reuse is the process aimed at defining a set of systematic operating procedures to specify, produce, classify, retrieve, and adapt software artifacts for the purpose of creating software systems from them. Even if there are many existing reuse management models and frameworks, each one represents only one possible view of the inner reality that would be captured and reused: the *'one size doesn't fit all'* motto could be rephrased as *'one model doesn't fit all'*. Thus, at least 2 (or more) models/frameworks should be considered for improving your own processes (whatever they are), in the areas/issues needed.

   In order to cope with this need, we recently proposed **LEGO** (Living EnGineering prOcess) as an open approach for improving the processes of a business process model (BPM), based upon the comparative analysis of the process architecture and elements of several concurrent models within a certain domain. Since estimation is one of the key processes for determining the success of an organization, we applied LEGO to Reuse, practices with the aim to improving the current ISO/IEC 15504 REU processes by integrating it with other reuse-related maturity models. The final result was the design of a more encompassing hybrid-REU processes that could help organizations to improve their estimates from the beginning of the value chain as well as their construction practices, in order respectively to save time and create more consistent systems.

   In the future, we will   apply this hybrid-REU processes to real case studies, proposing it as the meta-model to be used for the performing the initial gap analysis against the organizations' BPM related processes as part of   an improvement initiative. Another action will be to refine the search of further reuse MMs, trying to catch information also related to ISO 15504 Process Attributes (PAs) and not only Base Practices (BPs), as initially done in this paper (e.g. some technological element supporting better performances).

> *'Creativity is allowing yourself to make mistakes.*
> *Art is knowing which ones to keep,*
> Scott Adams (1957-)

Acknowledgements. This work has been also supported by the CNPq (Conselho Nacional de Desenvolvimento Científico e Tecnológico – www.cnpq.br), an entity of the Brazilian government focused on scientific and technological development.

This research is supported in part by the Science Foundation Ireland (SFI) Stokes Lectureship Programme, grant number 07/SK/I1299, the SFI Principal Investigator Programme, grant number 08/IN.1/I2030 (the funding of this project was awarded by Science Foundation Ireland under a co-funding initiative by the Irish Government and European Regional Development Fund), and supported in part by Lero (http://www.lero.ie) grant 10/CE/I1855.

References

[1] Constant, D.: Re: CMMI Representations, which one is the better? Yahoo SPI Mailing List (February 10, 2004), http://goo.gl/5uhAP

[2] Crosby, P.B.: Quality is free. McGraw-Hill (1979) ISBN 0-451-62585-411

[3] CMMI Product Team, CMMI for Development, Version 1.3, CMMI-DEV v1.3, Continuous Representation, CMU/SEI-2010-TR-033. Technical Report, Software Engineering Institute (November 2010)

[4] Curtis, B., Hefley, W., Miller, S.: People Capability Maturity Model (P-CMM) Version 2.0. 2/ed, CMU/SEI-2009-TR-003, Maturity Model, Software Engineering Institute (July 2009), http://goo.gl/2p0M8

[5] SEI, Standard CMMI Appraisal Method for Process Improvement (SCAMPI), version 1.3: Method Definition Document, Software Engineering Institute, Handbook, CMU/SEI-2011-HB-001 (March 2011), http://goo.gl/18IAX

[6] ISO/IEC, IS 15504-2: Information technology – Process assessment – Part 2: Performing an assessment (October 2003)

[7] ISO/IEC, IS 15504-5: Information technology – Process Assessment – Part 5: An exemplar Process Assessment Model (March 2006)

[8] Copeland, L.: The Maturity Maturity Model (M3). Guidelines for Improving the Maturity Process, StickyMinds (September 2003), http://goo.gl/MgUS2

[9] Abran, A., Moore, J.W., Bourque, P., Dupuis, R., Tripp, L.T.: Guide to the Software Engineering Body of Knowledge (SWEBOK) 2004 Version. IEEE (2004), http://goo.gl/OhLDp

[10] ISO/IEC, IS 12207: Information technology – Software Life Cycle processes (2008)

[11] Ibrahim, L., Bradford, B., Cole, D., LaBruyere, L., Leinneweber, H., Piszczech, D., Reed, N., Rymond, M., Smith, D., Virga, M., Wells, C.: The Federal Aviation Administration Integrated Capability Maturity Model, (FAA-iCMM), Version 2.0. An Integrated Capability Maturity Model for Enterprise-wide Improvement, FAA (September 2001)

[12] Burnstein, I., Homyen, A., Grom, R., Carlson, C.R.: A Model to Assess Testing Process Maturity, Crosstalk. The Journal of Defense Software Engineering, 26–30 (November 1998), http://goo.gl/xg8zF

[13] Koomen, T., Pol, M.: Test Process Improvement: a Practical Step-by-Step Guide to Structured Testing. Addison-Wesley (1999) ISBN 0-201-59624-5

[14] OGC, P3M3: Portfolio, Programme & Project Management Maturity Model, Version 1.0, Office of Government Commerce (February 2006), http://goo.gl/tTbq9

[15] PMI, Organizational Project Management Maturity Model (OPM3), Knowledge Foundation, Project Management Institute, 2nd edn. (2008)

[16] CMMI Product Team, CMMI for Service, Version 1.3, CMMI-SVC v1.3, CMU/SEI-2010-TR-034. Technical Report, Software Engineering Institute (November 2010)

[17] CMMI Product Team, CMMI for Acquisition, Version 1.3, CMMI-ACQ v1.3, CMU/SEI-2010-TR-032, Technical Report, Software Engineering Institute (November 2010)

[18] Cardoso Garcia, V., Lucredio, D., Alvaro, A., Santana de Almeida, E.: Towards a Maturity Model for a Reuse Incremental Adoption. In: SBCARS 2007, Brazilian Symposium on Software Components, Architectures and Reuse, http://goo.gl/DVHP9

[19] Buglione, L.: Leveraging people-related maturity issues for achieving Higher Maturity & Capability Levels. In: Proceedings of IWSM/MENSURA 2009, Amsterdam, Netherlands, November 4-6, pp. 35–47 (2009)

[20] Buglione, L.: Maturity Models: modelli esclusivi o integrabili?, Qualità On-Line, Rivista dell'AICQ (Novembre 2007), http://goo.gl/5xvKQ

[21] Jasmine, K.S., Vasanth, R.: A New Capability Maturity Model For Reuse Based Software Development process. IACSIT International Journal of Engineering and Technology 2(1) (February 2010), http://goo.gl/1KE18

[22] Spoelstra, W.: Reusing software assets in agile development organizations - a management tool: a case at a medium sized software development organization. University of Twente, Netherlands. Thesis (2010), http://essay.utwente.nl/59917/

[23] Sindre, G., Conradi, R., Karlsson, E.A.: The REBOOT Approach to Software Reuse, Journal of Systems & Software (JSS). Special Issue on Software Reuse 30(3), 201–212 (1995), http://goo.gl/Sa2Eo

[24] Frakes, W., Terry, C.: Software Reuse: Metrics and Models. ACM Computing Surveys 28(2) (June 1996), http://goo.gl/6mBR4

[25] Reuse Research Center, Software Reuse Fundamentals, Presentation, http://goo.gl/OYWHt

[26] Koltun, P., Hudson, A.: A Reuse Maturity Model. In: WISR4 4th Workshop on Institutionalizing Software Reuse, Center for Innovative Technology, Reston, Virginia, USA (November 1991)

[27] Lloréns, J., Fuentes, J.M., Prieto-Diaz, R., Astudillo, H.: Incremental Software Reuse. In: Morisio, M. (ed.) ICSR 2006. LNCS, vol. 4039, pp. 386–389. Springer, Heidelberg (2006)

[28] Basset, P.G.: The Theory and Practice of Adaptive Reuse. In: Symposium on Software Reusability (SSR 1997). ACM, Boston (1997)

[29] Davis, T.: The reuse capability model: a basis for improving an organization's reuse capability. In: Proceedings of the Second International Workshop on Software Reusability, Herndon, VA (1993)

[30] Griss, M.L.: CMM as a Framework for Adopting Systematic Reuse. Object Magazine, 60–62, 69 (1998), http://goo.gl/k0iXI

[31] Mandava Kranthi, K., Konda, B.M., Thammi Reddy, K., Ravi Kiran, B., Vindhya, A.: A Systematic Mapping Study on Value of Reuse. International Journal of Computer Applications (0975 – 8887) 34(4), 37–44 (2011), http://goo.gl/3oEpm

[32] GUFPI-ISMA, Linee Guida per l'uso Contrattuale dei Function Point, Documento Tecnico 2006-01, Gruppo Utenti Function Point Italia – Italian Software Metrics Association (June 2006)

[33] Buglione, L., Gresse von Wangenheim, C., Hauck, J.C.R., McCaffery, F.: The LEGO Maturity & Capability Model Approach. In: Proceedings of the 5th World Congress on Software Quality, Shanghai, China (October 2011)

[34] Basili, V.R., Caldiera, G., Rombach, H.D.: The Experience Factory. In: Marciniak, J.J. (ed.) Encyclopedia of Software Engineering, vol. 1, pp. 469–476. John Wiley & Sons, Inc. (1994), http://goo.gl/DZIlU

[35] Lim, W.C.: Managing Software Reuse, 1st edn. Prentice-Hall, ISBN 9780135523735

[36] Mutafeljia, B., Stromberg, H.: Process Improvement with CMMI v1.2 and ISO Standards. Auerback Publications (2008), http://goo.gl/BFUqq

Appendix: ICSR 2013 Workshop Summaries

Davide Falessi[*]

Fraunhofer Center for Experimental Software Engineering, USA
dfalessi@fc-md.umd.edu

Abstract. ICSR 2013 hosted three co-located workshops, whose subject matter ranged from fundamental issues such as the measurement of component reusability to more specific issues within the scope of the conference theme of safe and secure reuse. This appendix summarizes the purpose and organization of the workshops and provides the interested reader with indications for further interaction with the organizers and participants.

International Workshop on Designing Reusable Components and Measuring Reusability

Chairs: Reghu Anguswamy and William B. Frakes

Software Reuse Laboratory, Department of Computer Science, Virginia Tech.
reghu@vt.edu, frakes@cs.vt.edu
http://www.nvc.cs.vt.edu/ICSRworkshop-DReMeR-13/index.html

Component-based software engineering (CBSE) has been a direct result of advances in software reuse over the past three decades. Designing software components for future reuse has been an important area in software engineering. The success of CBSE depends on how successfully a user integrates reusable components into a system. Practitioners and researchers need to address the problem of how to build reusable components. Non-reusability of found components is a major obstacle to the success of software reuse. Hence, design principles for building reusable components are necessary. There is no generally accepted list of reuse design principles that are independent of language and domain. In a previous workshop two decades ago [1], design principles for designing reusable components were identified. An objective of this workshop is to update the list with current design principles.

Reusability of a software component is the degree to it can be reused. It has been identified in the past that measuring reusability is a challenge [2]. According to Frakes and Kang [3], research is needed to identify and validate measures of reusability, including good ways to estimate the number of potential reuses. The reuse working group of NASA: NASA Earth Science Data Systems (ESDS) Software Reuse Working Group, has introduced and implemented the reuse readiness levels (RRLs) which looked into the

---

[*] ICSR 2013 Workshop Chair.

J. Favaro and M. Morisio (Eds.): ICSR 2013, LNCS 7925, pp. 356–359, 2013.

potential readiness of reusing software artifacts [4, 5]. However, they have also identified the need for further research in measuring and validating metrics for software reusability. Another objective of the workshop is to assess the current status and deliberate on the future roadmap for developing metrics to measure software reusability.

1. Frakes, W.B., Lea, D.: Design for Reuse and Object Oriented reuse Methods. In: Sixth Annual Workshop on Institutionalizing Software Reuse (WISR 1993), Owego, NY (1993)
2. Frakes, W., Terry, C.: Software reuse: metrics and models. ACM Computing Surveys 28(2), 415–435 (1996)
3. Frakes, W.B., Kang, K.C.: Software reuse research: status and future. IEEE Transactions on Software Engineering 31(7), 529–536 (2005)
4. Marshall, J.J., Downs, R.R.: Reuse Readiness Levels as a Measure of Software Reusability. In: IEEE International Geoscience and Remote Sensing Symposium, IGARSS 2008 (2008)
5. Mattmann, C.A., et al.: Reuse of software assets for the NASA Earth science decadal survey missions. In: 2010 IEEE International Geoscience and Remote Sensing Symposium, IGARSS (2010)

3rd International Workshop on Security and Dependability for Resource Constrained Embedded Systems

Chairs: Brahim Hamid and Carsten Rudolph

IRIT- University of Toulouse , Fraunhofer Institute for Secure Information Technology SIT
brahim.hamid@irit.fr, carsten.rudolph@sit.fraunhofer.de
www.irit.fr/SD4RCES/SD4RCES13/

Resource constrained embedded systems (RCES) refers to systems which have memory and/or computational processing power constraints. They can be found literally everywhere, in many application sectors such as automotive, aerospace, and home control. In addition, they have different form factors, e.g. standalone systems, peripheral subsystems, and main computing systems. Computing resources of RCES, e.g. memory, tasks, and buffers, are generally statically determined. The generation of RCES therefore involves specific software building processes. These processes are often error-prone because they are not fully automated, even if some level of automatic code generation or even model-driven engineering support is applied. Furthermore, many RCES also have assurance requirements, ranging from very strong levels involving certification (e.g. DO178 and IEC-61508 for safety-relevant embedded systems development) to lighter levels based on industry practices.

RCES are becoming increasingly complex and have various communication interfaces. Therefore, they have to be seen in the context of bigger systems or complete infrastructures. Consequently, their non functional requirements such as security and dependability (S&D) become more important as well as more difficult to achieve. The integration of S&D requires the availability of both application expertise and

S&D expertise at the same time. In fact, S&D could also require both specific security expertise and specific dependability expertise. Most organizations developing RCES have limited S&D expertise.

The objective of this workshop is to foster the exchange of ideas among practitioners, researchers and industry involved in the deployment of secure and dependable resource-constrained embedded systems. Special emphasis will be devoted to promote discussion and interaction between researchers and practitioners focused on the particularly challenging task of efficiently integrating security and dependability solutions within the restricted available design space for RCES. Furthermore, one important focus is on the potential benefits of the combination of model-driven engineering with pattern-based representation of security and dependability solutions. Of particular interest is the exchange of concepts, prototypes, research ideas, and other results which contribute to the academic area and also benefit business and industrial communities. Some of the topics that we seek to include in the workshop are related to the development of models and tools to support the inclusion of S&D issues into the RCES engineering process.

Critical Software Component Reusability and Certification across Domains

Chairs: Silvia Mazzini[1] and Tullio Vardanega[2]

[1]Intecs S.p.A. and [2]University of Padova
silvia.mazzini@intecs.it, tullio.vardanega@math.unipd.it
http://www.intecs.it/CSC2013/

1   Introduction and Workshop Goal

This workshop addressed the interaction between component-based software reuse and safety, together with its implications on certification. Safety concerns the prevention of accidents, and can be characterized as an "emergent property that arises at the system level when components are operating together". Systematic reuse of software components in critical environments would benefit from a solid and rich certification framework. Compositional certification is a challenging approach currently under study to standardize and promote software components reuse. When safety is at stake, cross domain reuse and certification become particularly complex and challenging issues: paving the way for a suitable certification framework requires a thorough discussion among all stakeholders.

The goal of the workshop was to determine which aspects of component reuse affect safety, and to what extent cross domain reuse can have an impact on safety issues and composition. Component certification and safety parameters must be considered from a cross-domain point of view in order to gain the maximum benefit from the definition of a suitable certification paradigm. The workshop aimed to bring together practitioners from software reuse and certification domains to exchange experience, discuss current and emerging problems, and construct an agenda for future work in this area.

2   Topics of Interest

- How can safety-related aspects of components be specified?
- How is reuse currently addressed in the safety international standards?
- What are the legal aspects of reuse and safety?
- To what extent can software reuse be based on already established (certified) properties?
- How can we enable composable qualification and certification of software across domains?
- What new processes could be defined to ensure components that are certifiable across domains?
- Reuse of proven software components may increase reliability, but has little or no effect on safety
- Specific hazards of new implementation may not have been considered.

3   Related Projects

These topics are important key-points for a number of projects that contributed to the definition of the workshop's subject and objectives and actively participated in the debate sharing their valuable know-how and posing challenging questions. To mention some of the main involved projects:

- OpenCoss (http://www.opencoss-project.eu)
- SafeCer (http://www.safecer.eu)
- Concerto (ARTEMIS Call 2012: Guaranteed Component Assembly with Round Trip Analysis for Energy Efficient High-integrity Multi-core Systems)
- TCrest (http://www.t-crest.org)
- SESAMO (http://www.sesamo-project.eu)

Acknowledgements. The workshop chairs thank the Program Committee members for their valuable input and participation: Sasikumar Punnekkat, MDH, Sweden; Michel Chaudron, Chalmers & Gothenborg University, Sweden; Ivica Crnkovic, MDH, Sweden; Tim Kelly, University of York, United Kingdom; Thomas Vergnaud, Thales Communications & Security, France; Huascar Espinoza, TECNALIA, Spain; Marc Born, ikv++ technologies ag, Germany; Alain Rossignol, ASTRIUM Satellites SAS, France; Jean-Loup Terraillon, ESA/ESTEC, The Netherlands; Paul Arberet, Centre National d'Etudes Spatiales, France.

Author Index